Mastering GitLab 12

Implement DevOps culture and repository management solutions

Joost Evertse

BIRMINGHAM - MUMBAI

Mastering GitLab 12

Commissioning Editor: Pavan Ramchandani
Acquisition Editor: Rohit Rajkumar
Content Development Editor: Drashti Panchal
Senior Editor: Rahul Dsouza
Technical Editor: Komal Karne
Copy Editor: Safis Editing
Project Coordinator: Jagdish Prabhu
Proofreader: Safis Editing
Indexer: Pratik Shirodkar
Production Designer: Aparna Bhagat

First published: August 2019

Production reference: 2201219

Published by Packt Publishing Ltd.
Livery Place
35 Livery Street
Birmingham
B3 2PB, UK.

ISBN 978-1-78953-128-2

www.packt.com

For my family, who supported me throughout the entire effort of writing this book.

Packt.com

Subscribe to our online digital library for full access to over 7,000 books and videos, as well as industry leading tools to help you plan your personal development and advance your career. For more information, please visit our website.

Why subscribe?

- Spend less time learning and more time coding with practical eBooks and Videos from over 4,000 industry professionals

- Improve your learning with Skill Plans built especially for you

- Get a free eBook or video every month

- Fully searchable for easy access to vital information

- Copy and paste, print, and bookmark content

Did you know that Packt offers eBook versions of every book published, with PDF and ePub files available? You can upgrade to the eBook version at www.packt.com and as a print book customer, you are entitled to a discount on the eBook copy. Get in touch with us at customercare@packtpub.com for more details.

At www.packt.com, you can also read a collection of free technical articles, sign up for a range of free newsletters, and receive exclusive discounts and offers on Packt books and eBooks.

Contributors

About the author

Joost Evertse is an all-round professional with over 20 years of experience in IT in the financial and telecom sectors. He has worked for big and small organizations and has lived in different worlds, including Unix, Oracle, Java, and Windows. Creating order from chaos has been a big focus during his system-engineering years. After 10 years of system administration, he moved into software development and started using CI/CD tools, including GitLab.

At the end of 2016, he started at a significant financial company in the GitLab team, shifting his focus more toward the entire CI/CD pipeline, with the mission of making the CI/CD platform more stable and highly available. His team eventually migrated GitLab to a private cloud and improved release cycles.

About the reviewer

Orlando Monreal is a software engineer with over 12 years of experience, currently working at HCL Technologies Mexico, as part of the Source Code Management team in his project account. He has worked with GitLab applications as an administrator and contact for application support queries, handling upgrade processes and troubleshooting performance and configuration-related issues with the application.

Packt is searching for authors like you

If you're interested in becoming an author for Packt, please visit authors.packtpub.com and apply today. We have worked with thousands of developers and tech professionals, just like you, to help them share their insight with the global tech community. You can make a general application, apply for a specific hot topic that we are recruiting an author for, or submit your own idea.

Table of Contents

Section 2: Migrating Data from Different Locations

Preface

GitLab is a tool to enhance the workflow of teams and enable parts of the DevOps life cycle. It started out as a tool only for source code management, but today, GitLab can offer help ranging from managing an initial idea to building and testing source code, all the way from development to production.

You'll learn ways to use all of the features available in GitLab to enhance your business via the integration of all phases of the development process. You'll benefit from lower friction by creating one platform on-premises or in the cloud, increase collaboration, and drive competitive advantage with more efficient operations.

Who this book is for

This book is for developers and DevOps professionals who want to master the software development workflow in GitLab and boost their productivity by putting their teams to work on GitLab via an on-premise installation or cloud-based infrastructure.

What this book covers

Chapter 1, *Introducing the GitLab Architecture*, provides a short introduction to the company and the people that created the product, along with a high-level overview of GitLab and its components.

Chapter 2, *Installing GitLab*, shows you how to install and configure GitLab via several different methods. This can be done from scratch, or via the Omnibus installer. Special attention is given to Docker and Kubernetes when outlining containerized solutions. Finally, a cloud installation via the DigitalOcean infrastructure is taken as an example.

Chapter 3, *Configuring GitLab Using the UI*, explains the options in the GitLab web UI that can be configured after installation. This chapter also covers the administration pages where these instance-level options are situated.

Chapter 4, *Configuring GitLab from the Terminal*, looks at the different ways of configuring GitLab. The first approach is by using the Omnibus package installer provided by GitLab, which automates most of the installation. The chapter continues with configuring a source installation. Configuring Docker containers and managing a Kubernetes installation are also covered.

Chapter 5, *Importing Your Project from GitHub to GitLab*, outlines the process of migration from GitHub via a hands-on lab. It starts by exploring settings that should be altered in your GitHub project. After this, the settings necessary in GitLab to prepare an import are shown, and finally, the procedure for running the import is addressed.

Chapter 6, *Migrating from CVS*, begins with a comparison of the fundamentally different systems of CVS and Git. It then provides directions on preparing for migration. Actual conversion is addressed, as is the cleaning up of artifacts not needed anymore.

Chapter 7, *Switching from SVN*, begins by explaining the subtle and not-so-subtle differences between SVN and Git. The reader is shown how to migrate using two different methods: mirroring with SubGit and using the svn2git tool.

Chapter 8, *Moving Repositories from TFS*, first deals with the differences between TFS and Git. Subsequently, the act of migrating information from a TFS project to Git is shown via the use of the git-tfs tool.

Chapter 9, *GitLab Vision - the Whole Toolchain in One Application*, explains GitLab's vision of providing the whole DevOps toolchain to the developer, looking at the origins of XP and the Agile manifesto. The emergence of the DevOps paradigm is also explored, and the toolchain that GitLab provides is summarized.

Chapter 10, *Create Your Product, Verify It, and Package It*, shows how the product vision for GitLab and its workflow is centered around the idea of providing a complete toolchain to create a product. This chapter focuses on the different phases and explains the relevant concepts with examples.

Chapter 11, *The Release and Configure Phase*, discusses one of the big features of GitLab: the ability to offer the complete journey to production with different, easy-to-design stages. This way, you can create different environments and, ultimately, automate the whole pipeline for a product.

Chapter 12, *Monitoring with Prometheus*, handles ways of monitoring your GitLab environment by using the built-in Prometheus feature and default scripting languages. The second part of this chapter explains the different security tests that are available.

Chapter 13, *Integrating GitLab with CI/CD Tools*, explains how, although GitLab aims to provide a complete toolchain in the real world, there will always be a need for integration. This chapter explains some of the bigger possible integrations that are configurable out of the box. It closes with a section on how webhooks provide a general way to consume information from GitLab.

Chapter 14, *Setting Up Your Project for GitLab Continuous Integration*, describes GitLab CI concepts that are present on the application server and can be fine-tuned and customized per project. The second part of the chapter mainly focuses on how to get your project ready to use these CI concepts and set up a runner for it to use.

Chapter 15, *Installing and Configuring GitLab Runners*, explains the way GitLab runners work, by installing them. The next step is creating an example project and building it with a shell executor.

Chapter 16, *Using GitLab Runners with Docker or Kubernetes*, examines the architecture of Docker-based runners and runners using the Kubernetes API, using the same examples as in earlier chapters.

Chapter 17, *Autoscaling GitLab CI Runners*, demonstrates the architecture of runners using autoscaling. The number of runners required will decrease and increase based on demand. The example shown uses VirtualBox and **Amazon Web Services (AWS)** to deploy instances.

Chapter 18, *Monitoring CI Metrics*, deals with monitoring specific GitLab runners. Using a lab, we demonstrate how to enable monitoring inside the runner. After this introduction, the specific functional and system metrics are explained.

Chapter 19, *Creating a Basic HA Architecture by Using Horizontal Scaling*, visualizes the way in which different components interact. Secondly, the preparation of databases is shown, as well as several all-in-one application servers. Finally, the shared filesystem for repositories and Redis caching in this **high availability (HA)** setup is explained. We will use Terraform and Ansible to create the demonstration environment.

Chapter 20, *Managing a Hybrid HA Environment*, builds on the earlier architecture of horizontal HA, but continues to grow in complexity. The main difference is that the application servers combined several components that are now split into new tiers.

Chapter 21, *Making Your Environment Fully Distributed*, builds on earlier chapters. A fully distributed architecture aims to create more fault tolerance by again splitting components into new tiers. There is now an SSH node and several sidekiq tiers.

Chapter 22, *Using Geo to Create Distributed Read-Only Copies of GitLab*, starts with an explanation of the GEO product, which is part of the Enterprise Edition license. Using the same tools as in earlier chapters from Section 5 of this book 'Scale the Server Infrastructure (High Availability Setup)', we will explain how to set up GEO to create replication between two different geographical locations.

To get the most out of this book

To get the most out of this book, you should have access to a Linux or macOS machine, have an internet connection, and have Amazon AWS, Google, and Microsoft Azure accounts. These are all necessary to run the examples.

Some basic IT knowledge is necessary to read this book. The subjects you need experience in are as follows:

- Linux
- Shell scripting
- Basic programming skills in Ruby and JavaScript
- A basic understanding of Docker containers
- A basic understanding of using Terraform to create infrastructure as code
- A basic understanding of Ansible

Download the example code files

You can download the example code files for this book from your account at www.packt.com. If you purchased this book elsewhere, you can visit www.packtpub.com/support and register to have the files emailed directly to you.

You can download the code files by following these steps:

1. Log in or register at www.packt.com.
2. Select the **Support** tab.
3. Click on **Code Downloads**.
4. Enter the name of the book in the **Search** box and follow the onscreen instructions.

Once the file is downloaded, please make sure that you unzip or extract the folder using the latest version of:

- WinRAR/7-Zip for Windows
- Zipeg/iZip/UnRarX for Mac
- 7-Zip/PeaZip for Linux

The code bundle for the book is also hosted on GitHub at https://github.com/PacktPublishing/Mastering-GitLab-12. In case there's an update to the code, it will be updated on the existing GitHub repository.

We also have other code bundles from our rich catalog of books and videos available at https://github.com/PacktPublishing/. Check them out!

Code in Action

Visit the following link to see the code being executed:

http://bit.ly/2KirIoO

Download the color images

We also provide a PDF file that has color images of the screenshots/diagrams used in this book. You can download it here: https://static.packt-cdn.com/downloads/9781789531282_ColorImages.pdf.

Conventions used

There are a number of text conventions used throughout this book.

CodeInText: Indicates code words in text, database table names, folder names, filenames, file extensions, pathnames, dummy URLs, user input, and Twitter handles. Here is an example: "Let's continue with installing web documents in /usr/local/www."

A block of code is set as follows:

```
server {
listen 8080;
server_name localhost;
```

When we wish to draw your attention to a particular part of a code block, the relevant lines or items are set in bold:

```
server {
listen 8080;
server_name localhost;
```

Any command-line input or output is written as follows:

```
$mkdir /usr/local/www
$chmod 755 /usr/local/www
$cd /usr/local/www
```

Bold: Indicates a new term, an important word, or words that you see onscreen. For example, words in menus or dialog boxes appear in the text like this. Here is an example: "You can do this by clicking the **Choose File** button near the **Logo** section."

 Warnings or important notes appear like this.

 Tips and tricks appear like this.

Get in touch

Feedback from our readers is always welcome.

General feedback: If you have questions about any aspect of this book, mention the book title in the subject of your message and email us at customercare@packtpub.com.

Errata: Although we have taken every care to ensure the accuracy of our content, mistakes do happen. If you have found a mistake in this book, we would be grateful if you would report this to us. Please visit www.packtpub.com/support/errata, selecting your book, clicking on the Errata Submission Form link, and entering the details.

Piracy: If you come across any illegal copies of our works in any form on the Internet, we would be grateful if you would provide us with the location address or website name. Please contact us at copyright@packt.com with a link to the material.

If you are interested in becoming an author: If there is a topic that you have expertise in and you are interested in either writing or contributing to a book, please visit authors.packtpub.com.

Reviews

Please leave a review. Once you have read and used this book, why not leave a review on the site that you purchased it from? Potential readers can then see and use your unbiased opinion to make purchase decisions, we at Packt can understand what you think about our products, and our authors can see your feedback on their book. Thank you!

For more information about Packt, please visit packt.com.

1
Section 1: Install and Set Up GitLab On-Premises or in the Cloud

This section will give you a solid understanding of GitLab deployment options and GitLab component architecture, leaving you able to install and configure GitLab on-premises and in the cloud.

This section comprises the following chapters:

- Chapter 1, *Introducing the GitLab Architecture*
- Chapter 2, *Installing GitLab*
- Chapter 3, *Configuring GitLab Using the Web UI*
- Chapter 4, *Configuring GitLab from the Terminal*

.

Introducing the GitLab Architecture

Understanding the context of the GitLab project will help us to appreciate the choices that were made with regard to the design of the GitLab workflow. The GitLab project started out as a small, open source project, and has grown to be an organization of 400 people and thousands of volunteers. It is currently available in two versions, a free **Community Edition (CE)** and an **Enterprise Edition (EE)** with a proprietary license. There are several tiers of support for the enterprise version. Although it is proprietary licensed, the source code for that version is publicly available from GitLab.

To master GitLab, it is necessary to have a solid understanding of its individual components. In this chapter, we will look at the basic components of a GitLab installation, paying special attention to GitLab **Continuous Integration (CI)** and the accompanying runners. As the different components can be distributed across servers or even cloud providers, we will also provide an overview of those providers and how GitLab views them.

In this chapter, we will be covering the following topics:

- The origins of GitLab
- GitLab CE or EE
- The core components of GitLab
- GitLab CI
- GitLab Runners
- Cloud native

Technical requirements

To follow along with the instructions in this chapter, please download the Git repository with examples, commands and instructions, available at GitHub: `https://github.com/PacktPublishing/Mastering-GitLab-12/tree/master/Chapter01`. Look in the `Readme.md` file for a general explanation of the content of the directory.

To run or install software used in this chapter you need one of the following platforms:

- Debian 10 Linux codename 'Buster'
- CentOS 7.x or RHEL (Red Hat Enterprise Linux) 7.x
- macOS Sierra or later

The origins of GitLab

The story began in 2011, when Dimitri Zaporozhets, a web programmer from Ukraine, was faced with a common problem. He wanted to switch to Git for version management and GitHub to collaborate, but that was not allowed in his company. He needed a tool that did not hinder him in developing code and was easy to use. Like many developers, he had issues with the collaboration tool that he was obliged to use. To get around those issues, he created his side project in Ruby on Rails: GitLab. Together with his colleague, Valery Sizov, he developed this project alongside his regular work.

After this initiative, the project grew enormously:

Date	Fact
2011	Sytze Sybrandij, the future CEO of GitLab, is impressed by the GitLab project and code, and offers Zaporozhets the opportunity to try to commercialize it via `https://about.gitlab.com/`.
2012	GitLab was announced to a broader audience via Hacker News (`https://news.ycombinator.com/item?id=4428278`).
2013	Dimitri Zaporozhets decides to work full-time on GitLab and joins the company.
2015	GitLab becomes part of the Y Combinator class and received VC funding that year.
2018	GitLab receives another $100 million of VC funding and is valued at $1 billion.
2019	The GitLab company employs over 600 employees.

The initial idea of GitLab was to earn money from open source technology by offering support services. However, what happened was that companies started to bring in consultants only to upgrade GitLab, and then they would stop the service contract. It became clear that going for a 100% open source was not going to be competitive. Instead of this, therefore, they chose **open core**. Under open core, a company releases a core software system under an open source license. A different version of the software is sold under a commercial license and contains more features.

So, GitLab was split up into two editions: an open source version, and an enterprise version.

Exploring GitLab editions – CE and EE

The core of the GitLab software is called the **CE**. It is distributed under the MIT license, which is a permissive free software license created at the Massachusetts Institute of Technology. You are allowed to modify the software and use it in your creations.

No feature that ever made it to CE will ever be removed, or moved to a closed source version. When GitLab EE was created in 2013, it was, at its core, GitLab CE, but it had additional enterprise features, such as **Lightweight Directory Access Protocol (LDAP)** groups. Those features are not open source, per se, but can be added to the core version if they are perceived by the company as a core feature. The idea was that companies should also contribute as much as possible to solving problems and creating new features.

In 2016, the GitLab EE product was divided into three tiers: Starter, Premium, and Ultimate. Each tier is about five times more expensive than the previous one and contains more features and support options, as mentioned in the following table:

Version	Features (short list)
Starter	Everything on core GitLab CE: • CI/CD • Project Issue Board • Mattermost integrations • Time tracking • GitLab pages
Premium	More enterprise features such as the following: • Maven and NPM repository functionality • Protected environments • Burndown charts • Multiple LDAP servers and Active Directory support

Ultimate	All options, including the following: • All security scanning tools • Epics • Free guest users • Web terminal for the web IDE

GitLab has a lot of features, but let's concentrate first on the basic building blocks.

The core system components of GitLab

GitLab is not a monolithic application. It tries to follow the Unix philosophy, which means that a software module should do only one particular thing, and do it well. The components that GitLab is made of are not as small and elegant as Unix's awk and sed, but each component has a single purpose. You can find a high-level overview of these components in the following diagram:

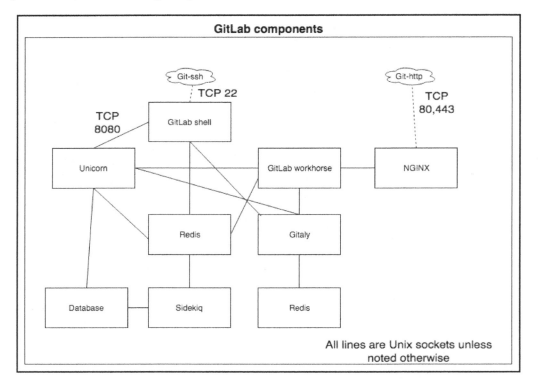

Gitlab started as a pure Ruby on Rails application, but some components were later redesigned using Go. Ruby on Rails is a development framework built on top of the Ruby programming language. It implements a model-view-controller pattern and offers methods to connect to different databases (for example, ActiveRecord). It values convention over configuration and **don't-repeat-yourself (DRY)** programming. It is very well suited to rapid development, and at the same time, it is highly performant and has many features.

Let's dive a little deeper into those components in order to understand their roles.

NGINX

The Unicorn web component cannot be used directly as it does not offer all the features for handling clients. The reverse proxy that is bundled by default is NGINX. It is also possible to use Apache as a frontend for GitLab, but it is preferable to use NGINX. There are many web servers available that could be installed in front of Unicorn, but in the end, there are basically two types, which are as follows:

- Process-based (forking or threaded)
- Asynchronous

NGINX and lighttpd are probably the two most-well known asynchronous servers. Apache is without a doubt the de facto standard process-based server. The biggest difference between the two types is how they handle scalability. For a process-based server, any new connections require a thread, while an event-driven, asynchronous server such as NGINX only needs a few threads (or, theoretically, only one). For lighter workloads, this does not matter much, but you will see a big difference when the number of connections grows, especially in terms of RAM. When serving tens of thousands of simultaneous connections, the amount of RAM used by NGINX would still hover around a couple of megabytes. Apache would either use hundreds, or it would not work at all. This is why NGINX is the better choice.

Debugging NGINX

The first thing you will want to look at are the log files which by default are called `error.log` and `access.log`. In a GitLab environment installed from source these log files will typically reside in `/var/log/nginx/` and in a GitLab omnibus install in `/var/log/gitlab/nginx`.

Following is an example of the error log:

```
2019/09/08 20:45:14 [crit] 2387#2387: *95 connect() to
unix:/var/www/gitlab-app/tmp/sockets/unicorn.sock failed (2: No such file
or directory) while connecting to upstream, client: 127.0.0.1, server:
localhost, request: "GET /-/metrics HTTP/1.1", upstream:
"http://unix:/var/www/gitlab-app/tmp/sockets/unicorn.sock:/-/metrics",
host: "127.0.0.1:8080"
```

Unicorn

Unicorn is an HTTP server for applications that deal with well-performing clients on connections that show low latency and have enough bandwidth. It takes advantage of features that are present in the core of Linux-like systems. It is called a **Rack HTTP server** because it implements HTTP for Rack applications. Rack, in turn, is actually a Ruby implementation of a minimal interface to deal with web requests, which you can use in your code.

 You can find the project at `https://rack.github.io`.

Unicorn runs as a daemon server in Unix and is programmed in Ruby and the C programming language. Using Ruby means that it can also run a Ruby on Rails application such as GitLab.

Debugging Unicorn

Maybe installing Unicorn produced errors, or you are experiencing bad performance that you suspect is caused by Unicorn not working properly.

There are several ways to find the cause. The log files can point you in the right direction.

Timeouts in Unicorn logs

The following output is what a Unicorn worker timeout looks like in `unicorn_stderr.log`. This is not necessarily bad; it just means that a new worker is spawned:

```
[2015-06-05T10:58:08.660325 #56227] ERROR -- : worker=10 PID:53009 timeout
(61s > 60s), killing
```

```
[2015-06-05T10:58:08.699360 #56227] ERROR -- : reaped #<Process::Status:
pid 53009 SIGKILL (signal 9)> worker=10
  [2015-06-05T10:58:08.708141 #62538] INFO -- : worker=10 spawned pid=62538
  [2015-06-05T10:58:08.708824 #62538] INFO -- : worker=10 ready
```

It could be that there are just not enough Unicorn workers available to respond to the requests at hand. NGINX buffers a lot of requests so we must check on the handover socket whether Unicorn can keep up. To do this, a little nifty script is available here: https://github.com/jahio/unicorn-status.

It can be called with the following command:

```
$ ruby unicorn_status.rb /var/opt/gitlab/gitlab-rails/sockets/gitlab.socket
10
Running infinite loop. Use CTRL+C to exit.
----------------------------------------
Active Requests Queued Requests
20 11
```

The first argument here is the unicorn_status.rb script, the second is the socket to connect to ../.socket, and the last argument is the poll interval (10).

Unicorn processes disappear

On Linux, there is a mechanism called **Out-of-Memory (OOM) Killer** that will free up memory if the system is running low on memory, and you don't have any swap memory left. It might kill Unicorn if it is using too much memory.

Use dmesg | egrep -i 'killed process' to search for OOM events:

```
[102335.3134488] Killed process 5567 (ruby) total-vm:13423004kB, anon-
rss:554088kB
```

Other kinds of errors or 100% CPU load

The ultimate way to debug Unicorn processes is to run strace on them:

1. Run sudo gdb -p (PID) to attach to the Unicorn process.
2. Run call (void) rb_backtrace() in the GDB console and find the generated Ruby backtrace in /var/log/gitlab/unicorn/unicorn_stderr.log:

```
from
/opt/gitlab/embedded/lib/ruby/gems/2.4.0/gems/bundler-1.16.2/lib/bu
ndler/cli/exec.rb:28:in `run'
  from
```

```
/opt/gitlab/embedded/lib/ruby/gems/2.4.0/gems/bundler-1.16.2/lib/bu
ndler/cli/exec.rb:74:in `kernel_load'
  from
/opt/gitlab/embedded/lib/ruby/gems/2.4.0/gems/bundler-1.16.2/lib/bu
ndler/cli/exec.rb:74:in `load'
  from /opt/gitlab/embedded/bin/unicorn:23:in `<top
(required)>'<br/> from /opt/gitlab/embedded/bin/unicorn:23:in `load
  from
/opt/gitlab/embedded/lib/ruby/gems/2.4.0/gems/unicorn-5.1.0/bin/uni
corn:126:in `<top (required)>'
  from
/opt/gitlab/embedded/lib/ruby/gems/2.4.0/gems/unicorn-5.1.0/lib/uni
corn/http_server.rb:132:in `start'
  from
/opt/gitlab/embedded/lib/ruby/gems/2.4.0/gems/unicorn-5.1.0/lib/uni
corn/http_server.rb:508:in `spawn_missing_workers'
  from
/opt/gitlab/embedded/lib/ruby/gems/2.4.0/gems/unicorn-5.1.0/lib/uni
corn/http_server.rb:678:in `worker_loop'
  from
/opt/gitlab/embedded/lib/ruby/gems/2.4.0/gems/unicorn-5.1.0/lib/uni
corn/http_server.rb:678:in `select'
```

3. When you are done, leave GDB with `detach` and `q`.

Sidekiq

Sidekiq is a framework for background job processing. It allows you to scale your application by performing work in the background. For more information on Sidekiq, consult the following website: `https://github.com/mperham/sidekiq/wiki`.

Each Sidekiq server process pulls jobs from the queue in Redis and processes them. Like your web processes, Sidekiq boots Rails so that your jobs and workers have the full Rails API available for use, including ActiveRecord. The server will instantiate the worker and call perform with the given arguments. Everything else is up to your code.

Debugging Sidekiq

As with Unicorn, there are several ways to debug Sidekiq processing. The easiest way is to log in to GitLab as an administrator and view the logs from there, and especially view the queues and jobs on the **Background Jobs** page, as shown in the following screenshot:

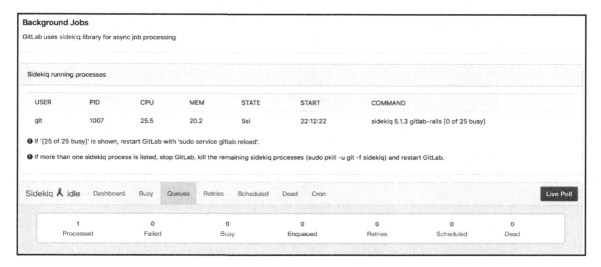

Sometimes, you experience troubles and find situations on your Linux server.

Sidekiq processes disappear

As mentioned before, in the Unicorn section, the OOM Killer might kill Sidekiq if it is using too much memory.

Use `dmesg | egrep -i 'killed process'` to search for OOM events:

```
[102335.3134488] Killed process 8887 (ruby) total-vm:13523004kB, anon-
rss:5540458kB
```

A Sidekiq process is seemingly doing nothing

If Sidekiq isn't doing any work and it seems stuck most of the time, this means that the program is waiting for something. A common wait situation is when you are doing remote network calls. If you think this could be the case, you could make Sidekiq processes dump a backtrace to the log by sending it a TTIN signal.

This is what a Sidekiq worker looks like in the log file in
`/var/log/gitlab/sidekiq/current`:

```
{"severity":"INFO","time":"2019-06
23T19:00:14.493Z","class":"RemoteMirrorNotificationWorker","retry":3,"queue
":"remote_mirror_notification","jid":"69eb806bfb66b82315bcb249","created_at
":"2019-06-23T19:00:14.461Z","correlation_id":"toX0HnYW0s9","enqueued_at":"
2019-06-23T19:00:14.461Z","pid":471,"message":"RemoteMirrorNotificationWork
er JID-69eb806bfb66b82315bcb249: done: 0.03
sec","job_status":"done","duration":0.03,"completed_at":"2019-06-23T19:00:1
4.493Z"}
```

Since GitLab 12.0, the default output log format for Sidekiq is JSON, this makes it easier to
read the log files into a tool like logstash because it is more structured.

Other kind of errors or 100% CPU load

The ultimate way to debug Sidekiq processes is to make it dump a backtrace via GDB:

1. Run `sudo gdb -p (PID)` to attach to the Sidekiq worker process.
2. Run `call (void) rb_backtrace()` in the GDB console and find the generated
   Ruby backtrace in `/var/log/gitlab/sidekiq/current`:

   ```
   2018-09-21_19:55:03.48430 from
   /opt/gitlab/embedded/lib/ruby/gems/2.4.0/gems/redis-3.3.5/lib/redis
   /connection/ruby.rb:83:in `_read_from_socket'
   2018-09-21_19:55:03.48431 from
   /opt/gitlab/embedded/lib/ruby/gems/2.4.0/gems/redis-3.3.5/lib/redis
   /connection/ruby.rb:87:in `rescue in _read_from_socket'
   2018-09-21_19:55:03.48432 from
   /opt/gitlab/embedded/lib/ruby/gems/2.4.0/gems/redis-3.3.5/lib/redis
   /connection/ruby.rb:87:in `select'
   ```

3. It is very hard to read backtraces, but this process was doing network operations
   while being traced, we can see a (`_read_from _socket`). You can read the
   source code to check what it is doing (there are line numbers mentioned).
4. When you are done, leave GDB with `detach` and quit.

You can also use other tracing tools to examine the behavior of the looping process. On
Linux, for instance, `strace -p <pid>` allows you to view the system calls that are being
made by the process.

GitLab Shell

This component is used to provide access to Git repositories through SSH. In fact, for pushes via the `git-http` protocol, it is also called instead of the Rails app. It's essentially a small Ruby wrapper around the Git client. Git, through SSH, uses predefined commands that can be executed on the GitLab server. For authorization, it makes calls to the GitLab API. Before GitLab 5.0, this functionality was delivered by Gitolite and powered by the Perl programming language.

The source code of this project can be found here: `https://gitlab.com/gitlab-org/ gitlab-shell`. You can see the following page:

You can install it locally, but it's really only useful when deployed together with other GitLab components. When you have that installed (see `Chapter 2`, *Installing GitLab*, for instructions on how), the next section describes a way to debug when you have problems.

Debugging GitLab Shell

In an omnibus installation, the log file for GitLab Shell can be found in the following location:

```
/var/log/gitlab/gitlab-shell/gitlab-shell.log
```

Alternatively, it may be found in the following location, for installations from source:

```
/home/git/gitlab-shell/gitlab-shell.log
```

What you will generally find are log lines that concern the basic operations of GitLab Shell:

- Git commands (such as `git push` and `git pull`).
- Authorization calls to the GitLab Rails API to check whether you are allowed to connect
- Execution of pre-receive hooks
- Actions requested
- Post-receive actions
- Any custom post-receive actions

Here, we have listed some lines from the log file:

```
bash-4.1$ tail gitlab-shell.log
time="2018-09-26T08:59:53+02:00" level=info msg="executing git command"
command="gitaly-upload-pack unix:/var/opt/gitlab/gitaly/gitaly.socket
{\"repository\":{\"storage_name\":\"default\",\"relative_path\":\"xxx/xxx.g
it\",\"git_object_directory\":\"\",\"git_alternate_object_directories\":[],
\"gl_repository\":\"xxx\"},\"gl_repository\":\"project-
xx\",\"gl_id\":\"key-xx\",\"gl_username\":\"xxxxxx\"}" pid=18855 user="user
with key key-xx"

time="2018-09-26T08:59:53+02:00" level=info msg="finished HTTP request"
duration=0.228132057
method=POST pid=18890 url="http://127.0.0.1:8080/api/v4/internal/allowed"

time="2018-09-26T08:59:54+02:00" level=info msg="finished HTTP request"
duration=0.030036933 method=POST pid=18890
url="http://127.0.0.1:8080/api/v4/internal/pre_receive"

time="2018-09-26T08:59:54+02:00" level=info msg="finished HTTP request"
duration=0.094035804 method=POST pid=18979
url="http://127.0.0.1:8080/api/v4/internal/post_receive"
```

One way to find errors is to look for certain patterns, such as `failed`, as follows. This particular error points to a 500 error from Unicorn while checking whether a user has the right authorization to make a call to the GitLab API.

This error should show up in the Unicorn logs (`production.log`) if you search for an HTTP 500 error:

```
bash-4.1$ grep -i failed gitlab-shell.log
time="2018-09-26T08:05:52+02:00" level=error msg="API call failed"
body="{\"message\":\"500 Internal Server Error\"}" code=500 method=POST
pid=1587 url="http://127.0.0.1:8080/api/v4/internal/allowed"
time="2018-09-26T08:45:13+02:00" level=error msg="API call failed"
body="{\"message\":\"500 Internal Server Error\"}" code=500 method=POST
pid=24813 url="http://127.0.0.1:8080/api/v4/internal/allowed"
```

Redis

Redis is a caching tool and HTTP session store that allows you to save cached data and session information from your website to an external location. This means that your website doesn't have to calculate everything every time; instead, it can retrieve the data from the cache and load the website much faster. The user sessions are in memory even if the application goes down. Redis is a fast caching tool because it uses memory first. It has several useful advantages:

- Everything is stored in one place, so you only have to flush one cache.
- It is faster than Memcache. This is noticeable when using the websites of large shops.
- Sessions are stored in memory and not in the database.
- The backend becomes faster.

Redis is not merely a cache, but is also a data structure store. It is basically a database and should be viewed conceptually as such. With regard to its operation and how it handles data, it has more in common with a NoSQL database.

Basic data operations in Redis

We can discover some of the basics of Redis by playing with the data structures. You can install Redis using instructions found at https://github.com/PacktPublishing/Mastering-GitLab-12/tree/master/Chapter01/InstallingRedis.md.

Start the `redis-cli` command-line utility, and it will connect to the local Redis server:

```
$redis-cli
127.0.0.1:6379>
```

It is not fair to view Redis as a simple hash database with key values. But still, the five data structures that are provided do actually consist of a key and a value. Let's sum up the five data structures:

- **String**: You can use the `set` command to write a value to Redis. In the case of a simple string, you can simply save the value in the datastore shown as follows. After setting the string value, you can retrieve the value again by issuing the `get` command:

```
$ redis-cli
127.0.0.1:6379> set mykind "Human"
OK
127.0.0.1:6379> get mykind
"Human"
127.0.0.1:6379>
```

- **Hash**: In the same way as the string, you can `set` an arbitrary number of values to a key. Generally speaking, Redis treats values as a byte array and doesn't care what they are. This make Redis very handy for representing objects. Again, with the `get` command, you can retrieve the values. GitLab uses this type to store web session information from users:

```
$ redis-cli
127.0.0.1:6379> set programs:tron '{"name": "tron","kind":
"program"}'
OK
127.0.0.1:6379> get programs:tron
"{\"name\": \"tron\",\"kind\": \"program\"}"
```

- **List**: The list type in Redis is implemented as a linked list. You can add items to the list quite quickly with `rpush` (right push, to the tail of the list) or `lpush` (left push, to the head of the list). On the other hand, accessing an item by index is not that fast because it has to search the linked list. Still, for a queue mechanism, this is a good solution.

```
$ redis-cli
127.0.0.1:6379> rpush specieslist human computer cyborg
(integer) 3
127.0.0.1:6379> rpop specieslist
"cyborg"
127.0.0.1:6379> rpop specieslist
"computer"
127.0.0.1:6379> rpop specieslist
"human"
127.0.0.1:6379> rpop specieslist
(nil)
```

- **Sets**: Another datatype is the set. You add members with the `sadd` command. Don't forget that these sets are unordered, so if you ask for the members with `smembers`, the order will mostly be different to how you entered it:

```
$ redis-cli
127.0.0.1:6379> sadd speciesset human computer cyborg
(integer) 3
127.0.0.1:6379> smembers speciesset
1) "computer"
2) "human"
3) "cyborg"
```

- **Sorted sets**: Fortunately, there is an ordered set as well. It is almost the same, but one difference is that you add a score to the entry, and that will automatically score the sort order, as you can see from the following:

```
127.0.0.1:6379> zadd speciessortedset 1 human
(integer) 1
127.0.0.1:6379> zadd speciessortedset 2 computer
(integer) 1
127.0.0.1:6379> zadd speciessortedset 3 cyborg
(integer) 1
127.0.0.1:6379> zrange speciessortedset 0 -1
1) "human"
2) "computer"
3) "cyborg"
```

Gitaly

In the first versions of GitLab, all Git operations relied on using a local disk or network share. Gitaly is a project that tries to eliminate reliance on the **Network File System (NFS)**. Instead of calls to a filesystem service, Gitaly provides GitLab with a system based on **Remote Procedure Calls (RPCs)** to access Git repositories. It is written in Go and uses **gRPC Remote Procedure Call (gRPC)**, a cross-platform RPC framework from Google. It has been steadily developing since the beginning of 2017, and since GitLab 11.4, it can replace the need for a shared NFS filesystem.

You can find an overview of Gitaly and its place in the GitLab architecture in the following screenshot:

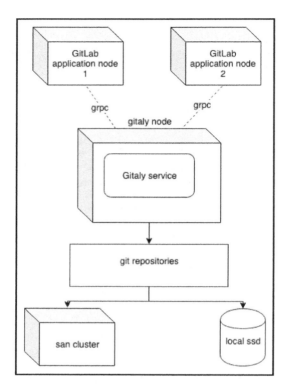

On a small installation, it runs in the same servers as all other components. In big clustered environments, you can set up dedicated Gitaly servers, which can be used by Gitaly clients such as the following:

- Unicorn
- Sidekiq
- `gitlab-workhorse`
- `gitlab-shell`
- Elasticsearch indexer
- Gitaly as a client

The source code of this project can be found here: `https://gitlab.com/gitlab-org/gitaly`.

Debugging Gitaly

You can use debugging tools that are available for Golang. But for starters, you can take a look at the log file.

For source installs, use this:

```
/home/git/gitaly/
```

For Omnibus installations, use this:

```
/var/log/gitlab/gitaly/current
```

The following is an example of a log line:

```
2018-09-26_13:23:40.57373 lrv162w2 gitaly: time="2018-09-26T13:23:40Z"
level=info msg="finished streaming call" grpc.code=OK
grpc.method=SSHUploadPack grpc.request.glRepository=project111111
grpc.request.repoPath=namespace/project-b1.git
grpc.request.repoStorage=default grpc.request.topLevelGroup=hb-backend
grpc.service=gitaly.SSHService grpc.time_ms=150 peer.address=@
span.kind=server system=grpc
```

You can see the log level is info and this is a log event that captures a Git SSH command (method=SSHUploadPack). It started a Git pack command on the server, which means it rearranged and compressed data in a repository.

To generate more verbose logging, you can set the log level to a debug in the configuration file. It is configured via a **Tom's Obvious Minimal Language** (**TOML**) configuration file. This file is documented in the Gitaly source code repository mentioned previously.

For source installations, look here:

```
/home/git/gitaly/config.toml
```

You can change the following section and change the level:

```
# # Optional: Set log level to only log entries with that severity or above
# # One of, in order: debug, info, warn, error, fatal, panic
# # Defaults to "info"
# level = "warn"
```

For Omnibus installs, the following directives can be added to gitlab.rb to influence the level of monitoring of Gitaly. Set it to debug to enable debug-level logging:

```
gitaly['log_directory'] = "/var/log/gitlab/gitaly"
gitaly['logging_level'] = "debug"
```

GitLab Workhorse

GitLab Workhorse is a sophisticated reverse proxy that is set up in front of GitLab. Initially conceived to solve the problem of handling `git-http` requests, it started as a weekend project with the name `gitlab-git-httpserver`. The functionality was previously delivered by `gitlab-grack` (`https://gitlab.com/gitlab-org/gitlab-grack`). The main web application server, Unicorn, was not especially suited to cater for these requests, which can take a long time to finish. Handling these directly in Unicorn actually reverses the advantages that Unicorn can provide fast and scalable HTTP requests.

Workhorse was created in Golang, and was conceived by Jacob Vosmaer, one of the GitLab developers. You can read all about the process of creating it at `https://about.gitlab.com/2016/04/12/a-brief-history-of-gitlab-workhorse/`.

Although it was first designed to handle the Git HTTP protocol, GitLab Workhorse increasingly gained functionalities, such as these:

- Certain static files, such as JavaScript and CSS files, are served directly.
- It can intercept requests from Rails about opening a file. Workhorse will open the file and send the content in the response body.
- It can intercept calls for Git **Large File Storage** (**LFS**) and insert a temporary path after preparing the file in the upload location. Git LFS is a feature where large files can be stored outside the project space in GitLab.
- It can control WebSocket connections for Rails, such as the terminal output.

Workhorse sits behind NGINX, which handles request routing and SSL termination.

Debugging GitLab Workhorse

As workhorse is a Golang written application, you can use methods for this language to debug programs.

It also supports remote error logging with Sentry. To activate this feature, set the `GITLAB_WORKHORSE_SENTRY_DSN` environment variable.

For Omnibus installations

The following is defined in the file (`/etc/gitlab/gitlab.rb`):

```
gitlab_workhorse['env'] = {'GITLAB_WORKHORSE_SENTRY_DSN' =>
'https://foobar'}
```

For Source installations

The following environment variable can be set in the file (`/etc/default/gitlab`):

```
export GITLAB_WORKHORSE_SENTRY_DSN='https://foobar'
```

Of course, the first thing to look at is the log files that are produced by this component. On an Omnibus-based GitLab installation, you can find them in `/var/log/gitlab/gitlab-workhorse`.

The following is an excerpt of the default log file (current):

```
"Mozilla/5.0 (Macintosh; Intel Mac OS X 10_13_5) AppleWebKit/605.1.15
(KHTML, like Gecko) Version/11.1.1 Safari/605.1.15" 0.478
 2018-08-16_20:26:43.42795 localhost:8080 @ - - [2018/08/16:20:26:43 +0000]
"GET /root/mastering-gitlab-12.git/info/refs?service=git-upload-pack
HTTP/1.1" 401 26 "" "git/2.15.2 (Apple Git-101.1)" 0.066
 2018-08-16_20:26:50.60861 localhost:8080 @ - - [2018/08/16:20:26:50 +0000]
"POST /root/mastering-gitlab-12.git/git-upload-pack HTTP/1.1" 200 329 ""
"git/2.15.2 (Apple Git-101.1)" 0.249
```

In the preceding log file, you see, for example, `git-http` operations such as `git-upload-pack`.

Database

There are two database varieties available for GitLab: PostgreSQL and MySQL/MariaDB. The use of the latter is not recommended because the fast development of iterations of GitLab, as a product, have focused primarily on PostgreSQL, meaning that a number of optimizations are not available on MySQL. Furthermore, the zero-downtime method is not available when using MySQL, and neither are features such as subgroups and GEO, which will be explained later in this book.

As explained earlier, Ruby on Rails uses a so-called MVC approach. MVC is a well known architectural pattern that was developed by Trygve Reenskaug in the Smalltalk language. It was later enhanced for web applications (Model 2). The model in MVC is implemented by the `ActiveRecord` library, which is part of Ruby on Rails.

The authoritative source for the data model can be found here: `https://gitlab.com/gitlab-org/gitlab-ee/blob/master/db/schema.rb`. It is auto generated and represents the current state of the database.

The default PostgreSQL database that is included in the Omnibus package can handle workloads for up to 10,000 users. Also, if you would like to create a **Disaster Recovery (DR)** plan using a cold standby setup, you can use specific failover mechanisms.

A frequently used technique is to create a cold standby database (PostgreSQL DB 2) at another site, as illustrated by the following diagram:

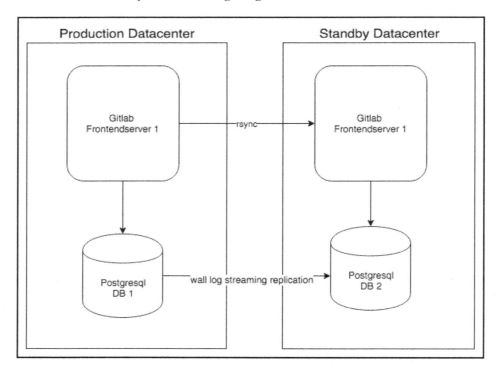

When you want to scale or increase the number of application servers, you need to scale the database too. There are three important aspects of database scaling. Firstly, you want to be able to scale database client connections as efficiently as possible. To do this, you can use PgBouncer, which is a lightweight connection pooler.

Secondly, you want to have several database instances, one being the master node, and replicate the data from the master to the slave. In the former, DR situation, this was done by the basic built-in replication mechanism of PostgreSQL. In the current situation, a specific tool, repmgr, is used, a tool for clustering PostgreSQL and handling the failover.

Finally, a service discovery tool such as **Consul** can be used to detect the PostgreSQL status of each node, and update the PgBouncer service setting that determines which Postgres instance to connect to.

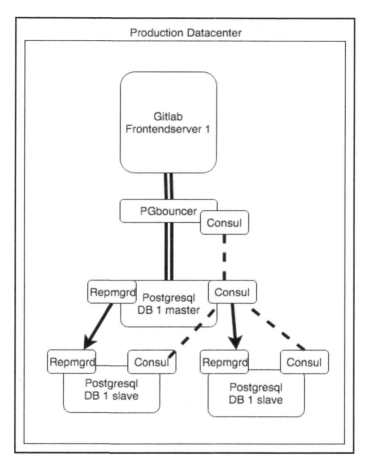

As you can see, there are different ways of setting up your database for GitLab. The architectures highlighted in the preceding diagram will be used in examples for building high-availability environments in *Scaling the Server Infrastructure (High- Availability Setup)* section of this book.

Debugging PostgreSQL

When you hit problems with PostgreSQL you can generally find the logs at `/var/lib/pgsql/data` but you can lookup the `log_directory` in `postgresql.conf`. On Omnibus installations, the log file is `var/log/gitlab/postgresql/current`.

An example of the log showing a shutdown and a startup of the database:
```
2019-09-09_23:02:58.04140 received TERM from runit, sending INT instead to
force quit connections
2019-09-09_23:02:58.04141 LOG:  received fast shutdown request
2019-09-09_23:02:58.07704 LOG:  aborting any active transactions
2019-09-09_23:02:58.08152 FATAL:  terminating connection due to
administrator command
2019-09-09_23:02:58.08163 LOG:  worker process: logical replication
launcher (PID 10480) exited with exit code 1
2019-09-09_23:02:58.08458 LOG:  shutting down
2019-09-09_23:02:58.12229 LOG:  database system is shut down
2019-09-09_23:05:53.07284 LOG:  listening on Unix socket
"/var/opt/gitlab/postgresql/.s.PGSQL.5432"
2019-09-09_23:05:53.13131 LOG:  database system was shut down at 2019-09-09
23:02:58 GMT2019-09-09_23:05:53.15987 LOG:  database system is ready to
accept connections
```

You can change the log settings of PostgreSQL to show more detail. For instance, you can redirect the log messages to a central server. More details on how to do this can be found here `https://www.postgresql.org/docs/9.5/runtime-config-logging.html`.

GitLab CI

GitLab CI is a feature that helps perform the **Continuous Integration** (**CI**) of software components. When several developers work together using a versioning system, problems can arise when changes made by one developer break the product as a whole. The best way to make sure this happens less often, or at least early in the process, is to use integration tests more frequently, hence the name continuous.

GitLab CI was launched as a standalone project in 2013, but was later integrated into the main GitLab package. Combined with the GitLab Runner software, this feature has been very popular with developers and is an important driver of the business. It also enabled GitLab to build their product into a solution that not only does CI, but even continuous delivery up to production environments. The current product vision for GitLab is to serve as a complete DevOps life cycle product, from idea to production.

Forrester classified GitLab as a leader in CI in *The Forrester Wave: Continuous Integration Tools, Q3 2017*. This is shown in the following diagram:

Feedback, one of the important aspects of the **Extreme Programming (XP)** movement, is an important element of GitLab CI. It also serves as a way to communicate between developers.

Pipelines and jobs

Pipelines and build jobs are basic building blocks for a **Continuous Integrations/Continuous Delivery (CI/CD)** system nowadays. In GitLab, it is very easy to start a pipeline. You only need to add a `.gitlab-ci.yml` file to your project and then, on every commit/push to your repository, a pipeline will start. Every project has a pipeline's overview; you can find it in the left-hand menu bar, under CI/CD:

Alternatively, you can view all jobs, by going to the Pipelines' **Jobs** page, as shown in the following screenshot:

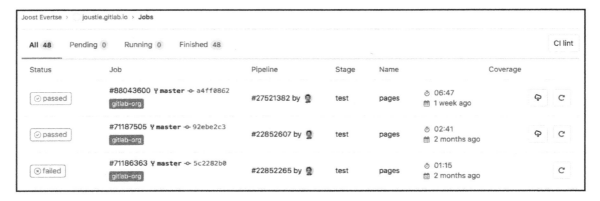

You can check the log of a job by clicking on the status of the job (for example, **failed** or **passed**). You can debug why some jobs fail and see exactly what happened:

The importance of using pipelines and jobs for CI/CD cannot be overstated. In this section, you've seen the basic interface to pipelines in GitLab, but in several chapters time, this will be discussed in more detail (*Utilizing GitLab CI and CI Runners* section).

GitLab Runners

GitLab Runners were originally developed by Kamil Trzciński in 2015. They're now one of the most popular features of GitLab.

The initial GitLab-CI-Runner was a very simple application written in Ruby, but worked well in quite basic setups. You can think of it as a reference implementation of what a bare runner could look like.

Issues with the old runner

The main problem with the old runner is that it could only run one concurrent job at a time. If you wanted to run more, you could either set up a new server or create an additional user to build jobs.

Secondly, it always ran projects on the server shell. This made it really hard to test projects using different versions of Ruby or any other dependencies. It was not stateless, meaning you had a contaminated build environment. Builds were therefore not very trustworthy. Nowadays, having a stateless and clean build environment every time is essential.

Another aspect of the old Runner that made it less favorable was that it only ran on Linux-based platforms. To make it work on macOS, a big GitLab user platform, you had to carry out additional hacking. Support for Microsoft Windows was out of the question.

Finally, there were some heavy administrative burdens. The server was hard to scale, because setting up a new server took a long time due to the dependencies you needed to take care of in order to build projects.

The newer runner is a binary that you can put on a machine of any kind. It is really easy to set up as a service and can work with multiple projects and multiple GitLab CI coordinators. It also provides support for Docker, making it really easy to set up a build environment with different versions.

Switching to Go

Go (or Golang) is a new language (less than 10 years old). It is already widely used by some impressive parties, such as Docker (`https://docker.com`), Google, Kubernetes (`https://kubernetes.io`), and Prometheus (`https://prometheus.io`). Go is a versatile tool that can help you to program at a low level, close to the operating system or at a high level in a language such as Java. It is perfectly suited to creating systems software. The language was created in 2009 by R. Griesemer, R. Pike, and K.Thompson while working for Google. The latter is very famous for co-creating the first Unix implementation and the B programming language. The most important feature of the Go language is that it can compile one binary without dependencies for multiple operating systems such as Linux, macOS, the BSDs, and Windows. This also means it runs on different processor architectures (i386, amd64, ARM, and PowerPC).

A short list of the benefits of Go follows:

- Very good standard libraries (with good optional ones available elsewhere).
- It is very fast to develop and test in Go.
- The culture/community chooses boring solutions over complex ones (which is good).
- Cool tools such as Gofmt, race detector, and `go vet`.
- Made for concurrency—for instance, you can use goroutines and channels.
- Type safety—will save you many times from run-time errors and wrongly defined data types.
- Garbage collection—while programmers who use C know how to clean up, this can still be helpful.
- Closures or anonymous functions—enable the use of functional principles (higher-order functions).

All these characteristics make Go the perfect choice for GitLab Runners. With Go, you can create a relatively small binary that runs on a lot of platforms. It contains all that is needed to run your projects.

In a GitLab environment, jobs are being executed by the Runners. They run them as they are defined in a `.gitlab-ci.yml` file. The Runner itself can be running on a **Virtual Machine (VM)** such as VmWare (VM), VPS, a laptop, a Docker container, or in a Kubernetes cluster. Communication is one way from runner to GitLab and is mostly via an HTTP API, so that path must be accessible by the Runner.

The `.yml` file defines what stages your CI/CD pipeline has and what to do in each stage. This typically consists of build, test, and deploy stages.

 GitLab mentions *boring* in its handbook as a valued way of reducing complexity; see `https://about.gitlab.com/handbook/values/#efficiency`.

The project can be found at `https://gitlab.com/gitlab-org/gitlab-runner`:

A runner can either be specific to a certain project or it can serve multiple projects in GitLab. If it serves all projects, it's known as a Shared Runner. GitLab Runners implement a number of **executors** that can be used for your builds in different scenarios:

- **Shell executor**: The runner simply executes a shell. The dependencies for the build have to be installed manually.
- **Docker-based executor**: The runner runs from a container. This makes it easier to create clean builds because dependency management is shifted to the container image. It is also easier to create a build environment with services that need each other, such as PostgreSQL.
- **Autoscaling Docker SSH**: A Docker machine creates instances with the Docker Engine to run Docker containers.
- **Kubernetes**: GitLab Runner can use Kubernetes to run builds on a Kubernetes cluster.

Runners have evolved enormously over the last couple of years. GitLab itself sees them as one of the most important components of their suite. This section has given more insight into the development of this popular tool.

Cloud native

Toward the end of 2016 and at the start of 2017, there was a public debate in the GitLab community about whether reverting back from the cloud to bare metal would be cost-effective for `GitLab.com`. At the time, the filesystem used for repositories was Ceph. The performance of that distributed filesystem was not good enough to handle `GitLab.com`. They asked the community for advice and received a lot of feedback from people who experienced similar moves firsthand. In the end, the decision was made to stay in the cloud (`https://about.gitlab.com/2017/03/02/why-we-are-not-leaving-the-cloud/`). Instead, GitLab would focus on creating a solution, not on the filesystem level, but making sure that Git input/output (I/O) behavior is better managed at the application level. This can be seen as the birth of the Gitaly component. Sid Sijbrandij emphasized the importance of being a software company, not an infrastructure company.

In August 2018, GitLab migrated their cloud-based offering, `GitLab.com`, from Azure to **Google Cloud Platform** (**GCP**). The main reason for switching to GCP according to CEO, Sid Sijbrandij was as follows:

> *"Google as a public cloud, they have more experience than the other public cloud providers because they basically made a cloud for themselves [...] you find that in things such as networking, where their network quality is ahead of everyone else. It's more reliable, it has less jitter, and it's just really, really impressive how they do that, and we're happy to start hosting GitLab.com on that."*

It seems the move paid off; users have reported that `GitLab.com` is noticeably faster. Another transformation that is likely to cause further acceleration soon is the move to using Kubernetes as a container orchestrator. This is an important part of their strategy to incorporate functionality in a lot of places in GitLab besides the autoscaling of GitLab runners. GitLab's own high-availability tool, GEO, was used to synchronize the data from one cloud to another. Running on Google's architecture also allows GitLab to utilize object-storage for particular features as well, such as Git LFS.

Summary

In this chapter, we have learned about the people and the organization behind GitLab. Starting from the beginning, we have shown you how the project has developed over the years. We went through the core components of GitLab and how to install them. For some components, we included ways to debug the installation.

We also gave a brief introduction to GitLab CI and the client programs that interact with it, such as GitLab Runner. We showed you why this feature is so important and how it is perceived by the IT industry.

In the next chapter, we will install and configure GitLab on different kinds of systems. If you're new to the product, prepare to be amazed!

Questions

1. When and by whom was GitLab initially developed?
2. How is GitLab funded?
3. Name all the programming languages that are used in the GitLab software.
4. Which licenses are used by GitLab?
5. Why are they using these licenses?
6. Name the core components of GitLab.
7. How many offices does GitLab have?
8. What is stored in Redis?
9. What has Gitaly replaced?
10. Which cloud service was chosen by GitLab to focus on in 2018?

Further reading

- Sidekiq—source and documentation: `https://github.com/mperham/sidekiq`
- Ruby on Rails: `https://rubyonrails.org`
- Unicorn: `https://thorstenball.com/blog/2014/11/20/unicorn-unix-magic-tricks/`
- *Cloud Native programming with Golang* by *Mina Andrawos, Martin Helmich*: `https://www.packtpub.com/in/application-development/cloud-native-programming-golang`
- *Nginx HTTP Server - Fourth Edition* by *Clement Nedelcu, Martin Fjordvald*: `https://www.packtpub.com/in/virtualization-and-cloud/nginx-http-server-fourth-edition`
- *Mastering Redis* by *Jeremy Nelson*: `https://www.packtpub.com/in/big-data-and-business-intelligence/mastering-redis`
- *PostgreSQL Administration Cookbook, 9.5/9.6 Edition* by *Simon Riggs, Gianni Ciolli, Gabriele Bartolini*: `https://www.packtpub.com/in/big-data-and-business-intelligence/postgresql-administration-cookbook-9596-edition`

2
Installing GitLab

In this chapter, we will discuss several ways of installing GitLab. We will start with the recommended way of installing GitLab on your own machine, using the omnibus installer. Secondly, we will show how to do a complete install from the GitLab source files. This will all take place on the Debian Linux platform. Then, we will move to a more modern way of running an application, by showing you how to use a Kubernetes orchestrator. Finally, we will demonstrate installation using a cloud platform, DigitalOcean. They have predefined GitLab images that are internally configured using the omnibus installer.

In this chapter, the following points will be covered:

- Installing using omnibus packages
- Running from source files
- Using GitLab from Docker
- Deploying GitLab using Kubernetes
- Creating droplets on DigitalOcean

Technical requirements

For managing omnibus installations, there is one central configuration file called `gitlab.rb`. You need to create it or copy an example. There is a template available that you can find at `https://gitlab.com/gitlab-org/omnibus-gitlab/blob/master/files/gitlab-config-template/gitlab.rb.template`. It is not updated after upgrades as we are using these files just for demonstration purpose. In large parts of this chapter, I will quote and discuss parts of this file.

To follow along with the instructions in this chapter, please download the Git repository available on GitHub: `https://github.com/PacktPublishing/Mastering-GitLab-12/tree/master/Chapter02`.

Although GitLab can be installed on a variety of platforms, in this chapter we choose Debian 10 (Buster) to show you how it's done. You can download Debian from `http://debian.org`.

We will require the following tools as well:

- **Docker**: `https://docker.com`
- **Helm**: `https://helm.sh`
- **kubectl**: `https://kubernetes.io/docs/tasks/tools/install-kubectl`

Installing GitLab using omnibus packages

There are several ways to install GitLab. The best way is to install it using the omnibus installer, a Chef-based configuration package. The installer software is actually a fork from a Chef project at `https://github.com/chef/omnibus`. The reason for this being the best way to install it is that it takes care of a lot of boilerplate for you. There are a lot of details surrounding a GitLab installation and it is easy to make mistakes. Automating this via Chef omnibus eliminates a lot of complexity and possible errors. The installer can be used to install GitLab on several platforms:

- Ubuntu
- Debian
- CentOS (any Red Hat derivative)
- OpenSUSE
- Raspbian

We will use Debian as an example in the section below 'Running the installer'.

Omnibus structure

Globally, the omnibus package consists of the following:

- A project definition
- Individual software definitions

- A GitLab configuration template
- Chef components such as cookbooks and attributes
- Runit recipes for managing services
- Tests
- Last but not least, the `gitlab-ctl` commands

Project definition

This file contains metadata and describes details of the project, as well as the dependencies contained in the project. You can find it in the omnibus source code at `config/projects/gitlab.rb`.

Individual software definitions

Found in the `config/software/` folder, it contains all of the software that is part of the omnibus install. For instance, if you want to use PostgreSQL (a relational database), you will find the configuration, the license, its dependencies, and instructions on how to build or get the software. Sometimes, a patch is needed and that will be incorporated too.

A GitLab configuration template

All configuration directives are read from a `/etc/gitlab/gitlab.rb` file, which should be placed on the destination system where omnibus is to be applied. There are a lot of settings you can manipulate using that file. The standard way to specify settings is by using the following:

```
component['settings'] = $value eg. gitlab_rails['webhook_timeout'] = 10
```

Chef components

There are several **Chef** cookbooks that are part of GitLab omnibus and they may or may not be executed depending on the configuration you specify.

Runit recipe

GitLab has chosen **runit** (`https://wiki.archlinux.org/index.php/Runit`) as the process supervisor that handles all of the services that are installed with the omnibus-gitlab package. On install, it determines which init system is used and it makes sure it is called appropriately during boot. It manages the stopping, starting, reloading, and enabling of services.

Tests

The omnibus-gitlab repository uses ChefSpec to test (behavior driven testing framework) its cookbooks. Tests may, for example, look for files that should be there and conditions after running a command. Normally, these tests only matter if you are changing the source code (`https://gitlab.com/gitlab-org/omnibus-gitlab/`) of the omnibus-gitlab installer. You will find these in the `spec` folder.

gitlab-ctl commands

This is the most import command when using the omnibus-gitlab package. It is available after running the installer. This tool can be used to manage general things such as the starting/stopping/reloading of all omnibus-gitlab provided services, but it also provides a vital function in applying changes in the `gitlab.rb` configuration file. Never forget to apply changes with the following command:

```
gitlab-ctl reconfigure
```

The main commands are as follows:

- `help` (help about commands)
- `cleanse` (delete all the data and reset the situation)
- `show-config` (show what configuration is to be created)
- `uninstall` (stop all processes and remove the managing process service)

And the service management commands are as follows:

- `hup` (send a service or all the hangup signals)
- `kill` (send a service or all the kill signals)
- `start`/`restart`/`stop` (send a service or all the commands)
- `status` (test and report the status of the service specified or all services)
- `tail` (watch the logs of all services)

Running the installer

Below we will show you how to run the omnibus-gitlab install on Debian Linux. Before we can run the package installer, we need to prepare some things:

1. We need to set the internationalization settings if we want to use US English and UTF8 and install some packages (curl, openssh-server en the default ssl root certificates):

   ```
   sudo apt-get update
   export LANGUAGE=en_US.UTF-8
   export LANG=en_US.UTF-8
   export LC_ALL=en_US.UTF-8
   sudo locale-gen en_US.UTF-8
   sudo apt-get install -y curl openssh-server ca-certificates
   ```

2. When using GitLab, it is also important to configure email for notifications. Usually, this is done via Postfix, but you can use another solution and point GitLab to it (external SMTP (Simple Mail Transfer Protocol)):

   ```
   sudo apt-get install -y postfix
   ```

3. The best option is to choose **Internet Site** when asked and use your external host name as mail name. For the rest, accept the defaults.

4. Add the GitLab package repository and install the package.

5. Using the following `curl` command, you install the GitLab package repository and initiate an installation by downloading a package:

   ```
   curl
   https://packages.gitlab.com/install/repositories/gitlab/gitlab-ee/script.deb.sh | sudo bash
   ```

6. The next step is to really execute the package install step. You can set the EXTERNAL_URL variable to the URL of your new GitLab instance. If you specify a https:// URL the installer will try to use Let's Encrypt for generating a certificate. This service is free to use (https://letsencrypt.org/), but requires a valid hostname (it is validated) and an incoming port 80, which is reachable from the internet. You can also specify a normal http:// URL in which case Let's Encrypt is not used. The install command is as follows:

   ```
   sudo EXTERNAL_URL="http://gitlab.example.com" apt-get install gitlab-ee
   ```

Browsing to the external URL and login

If it is the first time you are using it, you will be presented with a password reset form. You can specify the password for the initial admin account, and after the password is saved, you will be sent to the login screen. Log in with the admin credentials that you just chose.

Extensive information and instructions on what to do next and configuring GitLab are included in the following chapter.

Upgrade using the omnibus-gitlab package

Normally if you deploy the package on an existing installation it will automatically upgrade components that are installed. For GitLab 12 the PostgreSQL database will be automatically upgraded to version 10.7 unless you create a file called `/etc/gitlab/disable-postgresql-upgrade`. Always read the release notes for special instructions when upgrading. For version 12 they are here: `https://docs.gitlab.com/omnibus/update/gitlab_12_changes.html`.

Running from source

Before we dive into installing GitLab from source, please beware of the fact that using this method is *not* advised for production environments. It is very hard to maintain and reproduce a custom GitLab install. There are many components and it is much more efficient to use a package like Omnibus, where you get tried and tested software and dependencies.

It can however, prove useful in understanding how a GitLab installation is created.

When installing from source, make sure you have reviewed the latest installation guides for your platform for the GitLab branch you want (for example, 12-0). The instructions in this book will ultimately be out of date. Furthermore, if you run into an issue, you can try to find an answer on the GitLab forum: `https://forum.gitlab.com/c/troubleshooting`. If the problem turns out to be a bug or unwanted behavior by GitLab, you can open an issue at `https://gitlab.com/gitlab-org/gitlab-ce/issues`. The following sections will feature the exact installation instructions for a Debian version.

Operating system – Debian 10

Here, you will find the instructions for installing GitLab on Debian 10 code named `Buster`. Debian is one of the oldest Linux distributions and was first released in 1993, over 26 years ago. The foundation behind it has always had a firm principle to only include open source **General Public License (GPL)** software. The package management system in use, `apt`, combined with good package maintainers, ensured good quality of the software throughout the years. Their use the dependency management system (apt) to determine which components should be included created a very clean product.

Debian became a *basic* distribution that others *forked* and expanded upon. In 2016, there were about 125 Debian-based distributions.

Version 10 was released in July 2019 and will be supported up to 2022.

The following install instructions were created for and tested on Debian operating systems. For installing on **Red Hat Enterprise Linux (RHEL)** or its sister operating system, the **Community Enterprise Operating System (CentOS)**, we recommend using the omnibus packages.

The following instructions should work for most people. Many people run into permission problems because they have changed the location of directories or run services as a different user:

- First, we will start explaining which basic software packages you need to install in preparation for installing GitLab. Then, we'll touch on the installation of the required programming languages.
- Once, these steps are successful, we'll continue the installation by preparing the SQL database and the memory database for GitLab.
- Finally, we'll start the installation of the GitLab application components.

You will have to edit several configuration files as part of the installation. Make sure you have a working editor. The most common one is vim and we will use that in the examples of this book.

Required basic software packages

First, set the locale to your preference (I use US English UTF-8, which is 8-bit Unicode Transformation Format). These settings are by default not present on my Debian system:

```
export LANGUAGE=en_US.UTF-8
export LANG=en_US.UTF-8
```

```
export LC_ALL=en_US.UTF-8
sudo locale-gen en_US.UTF-8
```

Install the required software using the following command:

```
sudo apt-get install -y build-essential zlib1g-dev libyaml-dev libssl-dev
libgdbm-dev libre2-dev libreadline-dev libncurses5-dev libffi-dev curl
openssh-server libxml2-dev libxslt-dev libcurl4-openssl-dev libicu-dev
logrotate rsync python-docutils pkg-config cmake wget
```

Make sure the version of Git is 2.9.5 or higher:

```
git --version
```

If it is lower or not installed, install Git from source with these instructions:

- Make sure you have the build tools installed:

  ```
  sudo apt-get install -y libcurl4-openssl-dev libexpat1-dev gettext
  libz-dev libssl-dev build-essential
  ```

- Install the Perl compatible regular expressions tools:

  ```
  cd /tmp
  curl --silent --show-error --location
  https://ftp.pcre.org/pub/pcre/pcre2-10.33.tar.gz --output
  pcre2.tar.gz
  tar -xzf pcre2.tar.gz
  cd pcre2-10.33
  chmod +x configure
  ./configure --prefix=/usr --enable-jit
  make
  sudo make install
  ```

- Now download, check the `shasum` and build Git:

  ```
  cd /tmp
  curl --remote-name --location --progress
  https://www.kernel.org/pub/software/scm/git/git-2.22.0.tar.gz
  echo
  'a4b7e4365bee43caa12a38d646d2c93743d755d1cea5eab448ffb40906c9da0b
  git-2.22.0.tar.gz' | shasum -a256 -c - && tar -xzf
  git-2.22.0.tar.gz
  cd git-2.22.0/
  ./configure --with-libpcre
  make prefix=/usr/local all
  sudo make prefix=/usr/local install
  ```

- Install `graphicsmagick`:

  ```
  sudo apt-get install -y graphicsmagick
  ```

- Install a mail server, but don't use Exim. It makes more sense to use Postfix:

  ```
  sudo apt-get install -y postfix
  ```

- Then, select **Internet Site** and press *Enter* to confirm the hostname.

Required programming languages

GitLab needs several programming languages in order to function. You need to install them in order to use all the features.

Ruby

As GitLab is still mainly written in Ruby, we need to install that language. Remove the old Ruby 1.8 if present in the OS:

```
sudo apt-get remove ruby1.8
```

Download the latest Ruby, check the signature and compile it:

```
$ wget https://cache.ruby-lang.org/pub/ruby/2.6/ruby-2.6.3.tar.gz
$ shasum ruby-2.6.3.tar.gz
2347ed6ca5490a104ebd5684d2b9b5eefa6cd33c  ruby-2.6.3.tar.gz
$ tar xvzf ruby-2.6.3.tar.gz
..
$ cd ruby-2.6.3
$ ./configure --disable-install-rdoc
$ make
$ sudo make install
```

After installation is finished, check the version using the following command:

```
$ruby -v
ruby 2.6.3p62 (2019-04-16 revision 67580) [x86_64-linux]
```

Then, install the bundler gem:

```
$ sudo gem install bundler --no-document --version '< 2'
Fetching: bundler-1.17.3.gem (100%)
Successfully installed bundler-1.17.3
1 gem installed
```

Now, the basic installation of Ruby is complete.

Go

The newer parts of GitLab are written in Go (sometimes called Golang). These parts have been in GitLab since version 8.0, so we need this language compiler too in order to run newer versions of GitLab. It is best to download the latest version of Go here: `https://golang.org`. After download make sure the checksum is correct (for the linux-amd64 page for go 11.10 it is `aefaa228b68641e266d1f23f1d95dba33f17552ba132878b65bb798ffa37e6d0`. We install it in the `/usr/local/bin` location:

```
$ wget https://dl.google.com/go/go1.11.10.linux-amd64.tar.gz
$ shasum  -a256 go1.11.10.linux-amd64.tar.gz
aefaa228b68641e266d1f23f1d95dba33f17552ba132878b65bb798ffa37e6d0
go1.11.10.linux-amd64.tar.gz
$ sudo tar -C /usr/local -xzf go1.11.10.linux-amd64.tar.gz
$ sudo ln -sf /usr/local/go/bin/{go,godoc,gofmt} /usr/local/bin/
$ rm go1.11.10.linux-amd64.tar.gz

$ go version
go version go1.11.10 linux/amd64
```

Currently, Go supports eight different hardware instructions sets, so you have some choice. You can find downloads for platforms other than 64-bit Linux on the Go **Downloads** page, which is located at `https://golang.org/dl/`.

Node.js

GitLab uses Node.js to compile JavaScript, and Yarn is used for the dependency management of JavaScript components. Because these tools evolve quickly (there are regular new versions), you should really check the current requirements at `https://about.gitlab.com/`. As of April 2019, the supported version of Node.js should be ≥ 8.10.0, and Yarn should be ≥ v1.10.0.

Because the versions in the Linux distributions are typically behind, you should install from the source. The following code block shows how this is done:

```
$ curl --location https://deb.nodesource.com/setup_12.x | sudo bash -
$ sudo apt-get install -y nodejs
$ node -v
v12.6.0

$ curl --silent --show-error https://dl.yarnpkg.com/debian/pubkey.gpg |
sudo apt-key add -
  OK
$ echo "deb https://dl.yarnpkg.com/debian

/ stable main" | sudo tee \
/etc/apt/sources.list.d/yarn.list
$ sudo apt-get update
$ sudo apt-get install yarn
...

$ yarn -v
1.17.3
```

You can find more information about Yarn at https://yarnpkg.com/en/docs. The Node.js documentation can be found at https://nodejs.org/en/docs/.

System users

Create a Git user for GitLab that has no login shell and provide a common name in the GECOs field (GECOS = old Unix age printers):

```
$ sudo adduser --disabled-login --gecos 'GitLab user' git
Adding user `git' ...
Adding new group `git' (1001) ...
Adding new user `git' (1001) with group `git' ...
Creating home directory `/home/git' ...
Copying files from `/etc/skel' ...
```

The result is a user being added named git, with a group called git, an established home directory, and some template files copied to the home directory from /etc/skel.

SQL database

You really should use a PostgreSQL database, as explained in Chapter 1, *Introducing the GitLab Architecture*. For MySQL (a different SQL database), check the MySQL setup guide.

Install the database packages using the following command:

```
$ sudo apt-get install -y postgresql postgresql-client libpq-dev
postgresql-contrib
. . . .
Setting up postgresql-contrib (11+200+deb10u2) ...
Setting up postgresql (11+200+deb10u2) ...
Processing triggers for systemd (241-5) ...
Processing triggers for man-db (2.8.5-2) ...
Processing triggers for libc-bin (2.28-10) ...
```

Start the Database Engine:

```
$ sudo service postgresql start
```

Create a database user for GitLab:

```
$ sudo -u postgres psql -d template1 -c "CREATE USER git CREATEDB;"
CREATE ROLE
```

Create the pg_trgm extension (required for GitLab 8.6+):

```
$ sudo -u postgres psql -d template1 -c "CREATE EXTENSION IF NOT EXISTS
pg_trgm;"
 CREATE EXTENSION
```

Create the GitLab production database and grant all privileges on the database:

```
$ sudo -u postgres psql -d template1 -c "CREATE DATABASE
gitlabhq_production OWNER git;"
 CREATE DATABASE
```

Try connecting to the new database with the new user:

```
$ sudo -u git -H psql -d gitlabhq_production
Postgresql (9.4.22) Type "help" for help.
gitlabhq_production=>
```

Check whether the `pg_trgm` extension is enabled by pasting or typing this in the database console:

```
SELECT true AS enabled
FROM pg_available_extensions
WHERE name = 'pg_trgm'
AND installed_version IS NOT NULL;
```

If the extension is enabled, this will produce the following output:

```
enabled
-------
t
(1 row)
```

Now, we set the database password:

```
gitlabhq_production=> \password git
Enter new password: <type a password>
Enter it again: <type again this password>
gitlabhq_production=> \q
```

Quit the database console with `\q`. Save this password for later use for yourself when you configure the GitLab installation.

Create an entry in the PostgreSQL main configuration file:

```
$ vi /etc/postgresql/11/main/postgresql.conf
```

Change the listen address to `*`, or change the IP if it now says localhost and uncomment:

```
listen_addresses = '*'
```

Create an entry in the PostgreSQL host file:

```
$ sudo vi /etc/postgresql/11/main/pg_hba.conf
```

Add a line such as this:

```
host gitlabhq_production git <ip of gitlab server>/32 md5
```

After saving the host file, restart the database instance for the settings to take effect:

```
$ sudo service postgresql restart
```

The database is now ready for GitLab.

Redis memory database

In the previous chapter, we talked about Redis and how the program works.

We need at least v2.8 of Redis for the installation of GitLab. It can be easily installed on Debian with `apt`:

```
$ sudo apt-get install redis-server
```

Configure Redis to use sockets:

```
$ sudo cp /etc/redis/redis.conf /etc/redis/redis.conf.orig
```

Disable Redis listening on **Transmission Control Protocol** (**TCP**) by setting `port` to 0:

```
$ sudo sed 's/^port .*/port 0/' /etc/redis/redis.conf.orig | sudo tee
/etc/redis/redis.conf
```

Enable the Redis socket for the default path on Debian and similar distributions:

```
$ sudo echo 'unixsocket /var/run/redis/redis.sock' | sudo tee -a
/etc/redis/redis.conf
```

Grant permission to the socket to all members of the Redis group:

```
$ sudo echo 'unixsocketperm 770' | sudo tee -a /etc/redis/redis.conf
```

Create the directory that contains the socket (if it exists it's ok):

```
$ sudo mkdir /var/run/redis
$ sudo chown redis:redis /var/run/redis
$ sudo chmod 755 /var/run/redis
```

Persist the directory that contains the socket, if applicable:

```
echo 'd /var/run/redis 0755 redis redis 10d -' | sudo tee -a
/etc/tmpfiles.d/redis.conf
  fi
```

Activate the changes to `redis.conf`:

```
$ sudo service redis-server restart
```

Add Git to the Redis group:

```
$ sudo usermod -aG redis git
```

We now have a functional Redis server to be used with GitLab.

GitLab

We'll install GitLab in the home directory of the `git` user:

```
$ cd /home/git
```

Clone the source:

```
$ sudo -u git -H git clone https://gitlab.com/gitlab-org/gitlab-ce.git -b
12-2-stable gitlab
 Cloning into 'gitlab'...
remote: Enumerating objects: 1234071, done.
remote: Counting objects: 100% (1234071/1234071), done.
remote: Compressing objects: 100% (369844/369844), done.
remote: Total 1234071 (delta 937064), reused 1101079 (delta 849256)
Receiving objects: 100% (1234071/1234071), 529.69 MiB | 5.58 MiB/s, done.
Resolving deltas: 100% (937064/937064), done.
```

Go to the GitLab installation folder:

```
$ cd /home/git/gitlab
```

Copy the example GitLab config:

```
$ sudo -u git -H cp config/gitlab.yml.example config/gitlab.yml
```

Update the GitLab configuration file and follow the directions at the top of the file:

```
$ sudo -u git vi config/gitlab.yml
```

Copy the example secrets file:

```
$ sudo -u git -H cp config/secrets.yml.example config/secrets.yml
$ sudo -u git -H chmod 0600 config/secrets.yml
```

Make sure GitLab can write to the `log/` and `tmp/` directories:

```
$ sudo chown -R git log/
$ sudo chown -R git tmp/
$ sudo chmod -R u+rwX,go-w log/
$ sudo chmod -R u+rwX tmp/
```

Make sure GitLab can write to the `tmp/pids/` and `tmp/sockets/` directories:

```
$ sudo chmod -R u+rwX tmp/pids/
$ sudo chmod -R u+rwX tmp/sockets/
```

Create the `public/uploads/` directory:

```
$ sudo -u git -H mkdir public/uploads/
```

Make sure that only the GitLab user has access to the `public/uploads/` directory, now that files in `public/uploads` are served by GitLab-Workhorse:

```
$ sudo chmod 0700 public/uploads
```

Change the permissions of the directory where CI job traces are stored:

```
$ sudo chmod -R u+rwX builds/
```

Change the permissions of the directory where CI artifacts are stored:

```
$ sudo chmod -R u+rwX shared/artifacts/
```

Change the permissions of the directory where GitLab pages are stored:

```
$ sudo chmod -R ug+rwX shared/pages/
```

Copy the example Unicorn configuration:

```
$ sudo -u git -H cp config/unicorn.rb.example config/unicorn.rb
```

Find the number of cores:

```
$ nproc
```

Enable cluster mode if you expect to have a high load instance. Set the number of workers to at least the number of cores. For example, change the amount of workers to 3 for a 2 GB RAM server:

```
$ sudo -u git vi config/unicorn.rb
```

Copy the example Rack attack configuration:

```
$ sudo -u git -H cp config/initializers/rack_attack.rb.example
config/initializers/rack_attack.rb
```

Configuration of Git global settings for Git user `autocrlf` is needed for the web editor:

```
$ sudo -u git -H git config --global core.autocrlf input
```

Disable `git gc -auto` because GitLab already runs `git gc` when needed:

```
$ sudo -u git -H git config --global gc.auto 0
```

Enable packfile bitmaps:

```
$ sudo -u git -H git config --global repack.writeBitmaps true
```

Enable push options:

```
$ sudo -u git -H git config --global receive.advertisePushOptions true
```

Configure the Redis connection settings:

```
$ sudo -u git -H cp config/resque.yml.example config/resque.yml
```

Configure the GitLab database settings by copying the template for PostgreSQL to
database.yml:

```
$ sudo -u git cp config/database.yml.postgresql config/database.yml
```

Now, update config/database.yml:

```
$ sudo -u git vi config/database.yml
```

At the very least, the lines to change are as follows:

```
password: "<your secure password>"
host: <your postgres host>
```

"<your secure password>" is the password you created earlier, in the *SQL database*
section of this chapter! The host is the hostname or IP address of your PostgreSQL database
server.

Make config/database.yml readable to Git only:

```
$ sudo -u git -H chmod o-rwx config/database.yml
```

Install RubyGems (expect a lot of output):

```
$sudo -u git -H bundle install --deployment --without development test
mysql aws kerberos
. . .
```

The core GitLab application is now installed on the system. We need other components as
well, such as GitLab Shell, GitLab Workhorse, and Gitaly. They will be explained in the
next sections.

Installing GitLab Shell

GitLab Shell is SSH access and repository management software developed specially for GitLab. You can install it as follows:

```
$ sudo -u git -H bundle exec rake gitlab:shell:install
REDIS_URL=unix:/var/run/redis/redis.sock RAILS_ENV=production
SKIP_STORAGE_VALIDATION=true
```

By default, the gitlab-shell configuration is generated from your main GitLab configuration. You can review (and modify) the gitlab-shell configuration as follows:

```
$ sudo -u git vi /home/git/gitlab-shell/config.yml
```

Starting the service will be executed later.

Installing GitLab-Workhorse

GitLab-Workhorse uses GNU (Gnu's Not Unix) make. The following command line will install GitLab-Workhorse in /home/git/gitlab-workhorse, which is the recommended location:

```
$ sudo -u git -H bundle exec rake
"gitlab:workhorse:install[/home/git/gitlab-workhorse]" RAILS_ENV=production
```

Installing Gitaly

Fetch the Gitaly source with Git and compile with Go:

```
$ sudo -u git -H bundle exec rake
"gitlab:gitaly:install[/home/git/gitaly,/home/git/repositories]"
RAILS_ENV=production
```

Restrict Gitaly socket access:

```
$ sudo chmod 0700 /home/git/gitlab/tmp/sockets/private
$ sudo chown git /home/git/gitlab/tmp/sockets/private
```

Make sure Gitaly is started:

```
$ sudo -u git bash -c "/home/git/gitlab/bin/daemon_with_pidfile
/home/git/gitlab/tmp/pids//gitaly.pid /home/git/gitaly/gitaly
/home/git/gitaly/config.toml >> /home/git/gitlab/log/gitaly.log 2>&1 &"
```

Take a look at `/home/git/gitlab/log/gitaly.log` for errors and check whether Gitaly processes are in the `ps aux` process list. It should run.

Initializing the database and activating advanced features

Use the following command to initialize the database and activate advanced features:

```
$ cd /home/git/gitlab
$ sudo -u git -H bundle exec rake gitlab:setup RAILS_ENV=production
force=yes
```

When done, you will see the following:

```
'Administrator account created:'
```

You can continue the installation and eventually start GitLab, then the first person who accesses the login page will be given the option to supply a new admin password. This is probably not what you want, so there is a command to set this before starting. You have to supply the password, email, and variable to override the database check to make it work (answer yes to the prompt):

```
sudo -u git -H bundle exec rake gitlab:setup RAILS_ENV=production
GITLAB_ROOT_PASSWORD=yourpassword GITLAB_ROOT_EMAIL=youremail@gmail.com
DISABLE_DATABASE_ENVIRONMENT_CHECK=1
```

So, if you don't set the password (and it is set to the default one), please wait to expose GitLab to the public internet until the installation is done and you've logged into the server the first time.

Final steps for preparing the system

There are a few actions left before we start the GitLab application.

Back up your secrets file (where GitLab stores encryption keys):

```
sudo cp config/secrets.yml /to/somewhere/safe
```

Install the System V init script:

```
sudo cp lib/support/init.d/gitlab /etc/init.d/gitlab
```

Active GitLab at boot time:

```
sudo update-rc.d gitlab defaults 21
```

Make sure log files are rotated frequently (to safe disk space):

```
sudo cp lib/support/logrotate/gitlab /etc/logrotate.d/gitlab
```

Check whether GitLab and its environment are set correctly:

```
$ sudo -u git -H bundle exec rake gitlab:env:info RAILS_ENV=production
```

You will get an output such as the following:

```
System information
System: Debian 9.8
Current User: git
Using RVM: no
Ruby Version: 2.5.5p157
Gem Version: 2.7.6.2
Bundler Version:1.17.3
Rake Version: 12.3.2
Redis Version: 3.2.6
Git Version: 2.11.0
..
```

Everything on the system is configured to run GitLab and to make it survive a reboot.

Preparing to serve

We are almost ready to start GitLab. First, we need to prepare the frontend to serve content.

Compiling GetText PO files

Use the following command to compile GetText PO (portable object) files. This takes care of handling string values in different languages (you will see comparable output):

```
$sudo -u git -H bundle exec rake gettext:compile RAILS_ENV=production

Created app.js in /home/git/gitlab/app/assets/javascripts/locale/ja
Created app.js in /home/git/gitlab/app/assets/javascripts/locale/eo
Created app.js in /home/git/gitlab/app/assets/javascripts/locale/zh_HK
Created app.js in /home/git/gitlab/app/assets/javascripts/locale/fil_PH
Created app.js in /home/git/gitlab/app/assets/javascripts/locale/ar_SA
Created app.js in /home/git/gitlab/app/assets/javascripts/locale/en
..
```

Compiling assets

Use the following command to compile assets with Yarn (receiving similar output):

```
$sudo -u git -H yarn install --production --pure-lockfile
yarn install v1.17.2
[1/5] Validating package.json...
[2/5] Resolving packages...
...
Done in 48.37s.
```

Finally, use the following command to compile the last assets (similar output):

```
$sudo -u git -H bundle exec rake gitlab:assets:compile RAILS_ENV=production
NODE_ENV=production
warning Resolution field "ts-jest@24.0.0" is incompatible with requested
version "ts-jest@^23.10.5"
`yarn:check` finished in 4.2137985 seconds
Created app.js in /home/git/gitlab/app/assets/javascripts/locale/ja
...
```

Starting your GitLab instance

Use the following command to start your GitLab instance:

```
sudo service gitlab start
```

Or use the following command:

```
sudo /etc/init.d/gitlab restart
```

If you check the process list with `ps aux` you should be able to see some Unicorn and Sidekiq processes appear:

```
29073 ? Sl 0:16 unicorn_rails master -c /home/git/gitlab/config/unicorn.rb
-E production -D
29094 ? Sl 0:00 unicorn_rails worker[0] -c
/home/git/gitlab/config/unicorn.rb -E production -D
29096 ? Sl 0:00 unicorn_rails worker[1] -c
/home/git/gitlab/config/unicorn.rb -E production -D
29098 ? Sl 0:00 unicorn_rails worker[2] -c
/home/git/gitlab/config/unicorn.rb -E production -D
29112 ? Ssl 0:00 gitlab-workhorse -listenUmask 0 -listenNetwork unix -
listenAddr /home/git/gitlab/tmp/sockets/gitlab-workhorse.socket -
authBackend http://127.0.0.1:8080 -authSocket
/home/git/gitlab/tmp/sockets/gitlab.socket -documentRoot
29119 ? Ssl 0:00 /home/git/gitaly/gitaly /home/git/gitaly/config.toml
```

```
29132 ? Sl 0:01 ruby /home/git/gitaly/ruby/bin/gitaly-ruby 29119
/tmp/gitaly-ruby021668259/socket.1
29135 ? Sl 0:01 ruby /home/git/gitaly/ruby/bin/gitaly-ruby 29119
/tmp/gitaly-ruby021668259/socket.0
29143 ? Sl 0:14 sidekiq 5.2.7 gitlab [0 of 10 busy]
```

The main application is running, so now, we need to put NGINX in front as a reverse proxy.

NGINX

The role of this component in the GitLab architecture is well described in `Chapter 1`, *Introducing the GitLab Architecture*. It functions as a reverse proxy, and buffers HTTP requests from clients before they are sent to the Unicorn application server. The default NGINX that comes with Debian is too old for use with GitLab. That is why we have to install a newer one (> 1.12.1).

Now, install the latest NGINX:

```
$ sudo apt-get install -y nginx
```

Copy the GitLab custom NGINX configuration files that are in our GitLab installation folder to the NGINX configuration folder:

```
$ cd /home/gitlab/gitlab;sudo cp lib/support/nginx/gitlab
/etc/nginx/conf.d/gitlab.conf
```

Change settings if needed (for example, change the `server_name`
`YOUR_SERVER_FQDN` line to the DNS name of your GitLab application server):

```
$ sudo vi /etc/nginx/conf.d/gitlab.conf
```

Delete the default NGINX configuration files:

```
sudo rm -f /etc/nginx/conf.d/default*
sudo rm -f /etc/nginx/sites-enabled/default
sudo rm -f /etc/nginx/sites-available/default
```

Restart NGINX to activate the configuration:

```
sudo service nginx restart
```

In case of any errors, look in `/var/log/nginx/gitlab_error.log`. Now, you should find GitLab running.

Go to your new GitLab application server in your web browser for your first GitLab login. Remember that if you did not create a password earlier at `Run gitlab:setup`, you will be presented with a form to provide a password for the administrator account. The default `username = 'root'` can be changed later. You can set up the password now and log in again to start doing work!

The installation is finished!

Using it from Docker

The future is in containers. It has been said for years, and now it is almost fact. Running applications in containers provides many advantages. It requires much less operating system overhead because containers share the capacity of the underlying operating system. GitLab provides GitLab Docker images via Docker Hub, the central registry on the internet for official Docker images.

Both GitLab CE and EE are available and are called `gitlab/gitlab-ce` and `gitlab/gitlab-ee`. GitLab Docker images are feature complete images of GitLab and they run all the services in a single container.

Containers can run in different environments, but let's start with the following:

- Run the image in Docker Engine directly.
- Run GitLab using `docker-compose`.

Currently containers can be run on Linux, macOS and Windows (your mileage will vary).

In the following examples we will run Docker on Debian 10, so you will need `sudo` to run the Docker commands. If you run the examples on macOS, `sudo` is not needed.

You really need Docker software for this. See the official installation docs (`https://tuleap-documentation.readthedocs.io/en/latest/developer-guide/quick-start/install-docker.html`) for how to install it.

Docker is not officially supported on Windows. You might encounter problems with volume permissions and other unknown issues. Try at your own risk and maybe find help on **Internet Relay Chat (IRC)** in the forums.

Running the image directly

Before running the image, make sure you have a directory available for storing configuration, logs, and data (or be prepared to lose data). Normally, we create directories in our home folder, but a better idea is to use the **Filesystem Hierarchy Standard (FHS)**, a community supported standard of where to put stuff. `/src` seems perfect for storing container data (see `http://tldp.org/LDP/Linux-Filesystem-Hierarchy/html/srv.html`). GitLab also uses this convention in their samples.

The GitLab container uses host-mounted volumes to store persistent data:

Local directory	Container location	Purpose
`/srv/gitlab/data`	`/var/opt/gitlab/data`	For storing application data.
`/srv/gitlab/logs`	`/var/log/gitlab`	For storing logs.
`/srv/gitlab/config`	`/etc/gitlab`	For storing the GitLab configuration files.

Create them like this:

```
sudo mkdir -p /srv/gitlab/data
sudo mkdir -p /srv/gitlab/logs
sudo mkdir -p /srv/gitlab/config
```

If you want to use other local directories, that is fine, but the container locations are needed for GitLab to function correctly.

Now, run the `gitlab-ce` image:

```
sudo docker run \
  --hostname gitlab.joustie.nl \
  --publish 443:443 --publish 80:80 --publish 22:22 \
  --name gitlab \
  --volume /srv/gitlab/config:/etc/gitlab \
  --volume /srv/gitlab/logs:/var/log/gitlab \
  --volume /srv/gitlab/data:/var/opt/gitlab \
  gitlab/gitlab-ce:latest
```

Running it this way will run it in the foreground and you'll be able to see the console. You can add `--detach` to run the image in the background.

Starting with `--publish` (or `-p` for short) will make the ports required to access SSH, HTTP, and HTTPS available. All GitLab data will be stored as subdirectories of `/srv/gitlab/`.

Adding `--restart always \` as an option will make the container automatically start after a system reboot.

If you're on SELinux and don't want it cause permission problems, you can put `Z` after your volumes (`--volume /srv/gitlab/data:/var/opt/gitlab:Z`). Docker will then execute a shell command: `chcon -Rt svirt_sandbox_file_t` for that location.

When you execute the command you should see Docker fetching the image, this can take a while:

```
Unable to find image 'gitlab/gitlab-ce:latest' locally
latest: Pulling from gitlab/gitlab-ce
f7277927d38a: Downloading [=============================> ] 24MB/43.92MB
8d3eac894db4: Download complete
edf72af6d627: Download complete
3e4f86211d23: Download complete
340a842f7859: Downloading [======================> ] 11.77MB/26.26MB
357b5acafc50: Download complete
5f6d22e2dbb8: Download complete
5967b74e147b: Download complete
f703d2e0c343: Download complete
11b57921aaaa: Downloading [> ] 4.807MB/670.7MB
```

You can check whether the container is running with the following:

```
sudo docker ps
```

You should see a list of running containers, including one that is named `gitlab`. You can also see the unique identifier of the containers, this is called the `container_id`. In this example, you can now access this container at `http://gitlab.joustie.n`.

Configuring GitLab after startup

Because the containers provided by GitLab use the official omnibus package, all configuration actions are centered around the `gitlab.rb` file.

The software inside the container is provisioned using the omnibus GitLab install, so that means `/etc/gitlab/gitlab.rb` is used inside the container. You can edit the file by entering the container with a shell:

```
sudo docker exec -it gitlab /bin/bash
```

Another way is to directly edit the `gitlab.rb` file in a Docker command:

```
sudo docker exec -it gitlab vi /etc/gitlab/gitlab.rb
```

You will have to set `external_url` to something valid in the `gitlab.rb` file as well to make repository links in GitLab work correctly. When you are there, you can check other settings as well, such as enabling HTTPS, and very importantly, an SMTP server to use for mail. The Docker image does not have an SMTP server included.

When you are finished making the changes you want, you will have to restart the container to reconfigure GitLab (it does so every time at restart):

```
sudo docker restart gitlab
```

Starting the container with configuration settings as input

You can start the GitLab container and let it configure itself at startup by adding the `GITLAB_OMNIBUS_CONFIG` environment variable to the `docker run` command.

Put any settings from `gitlab.rb` in it that you'd like and they will be loaded in the container start procedure before the internal `gitlab.rb` file. Some examples from the omnibus-gitlab template are as follows and you can add it as argument to docker:

```
--env GITLAB_OMNIBUS_CONFIG="external_url '
external_url 'GENERATED_EXTERNAL_URL' \
gitlab_rails['smtp_enable'] = true \
gitlab_rails['smtp_address'] = "smtp.server" \
gitlab_rails['smtp_port'] = 465"
gitlab_rails['gitlab_shell_ssh_port'] = 2222
```

Here's an example that sets the external URL and sets the SMTP server address while starting the container:

```
sudo docker run --detach \
  --hostname gitlab.joustie.nl \
  --env GITLAB_OMNIBUS_CONFIG="external_url 'http://gitlab.joustie.nl';
gitlab_rails['smtp_address'] = "smtp.server" " \
  --publish 443:443 --publish 80:80 --publish 22:22 \
  --name gitlab \
  --restart always \
  --volume /srv/gitlab/config:/etc/gitlab \
  --volume /srv/gitlab/logs:/var/log/gitlab \
  --volume /srv/gitlab/data:/var/opt/gitlab \
  gitlab/gitlab-ce:latest
```

You can add more environment variables, which are documented here: `https://docs.gitlab.com/ee/administration/environment_variables.html`.

It can take some time for the container to be operational. After starting and configuring, GitLab is reachable via your browser at `https://localhost`.

The first time you see the GitLab login page, an admin password has to be set up. After you have chosen one and submitted it, you can use it to log in.

Upgrading GitLab

Even in a container, upgrading GitLab is sometimes necessary. The easy way is as follows:

1. Stop the currently active container:

   ```
   sudo docker stop gitlab (or container_id)
   ```

2. Remove the existing instance:

   ```
   sudo docker rm gitlab (or container_id)
   ```

3. Pull the new image:

   ```
   sudo docker pull gitlab/gitlab-ce:latest
   ```

4. Recreate the container in the same way as earlier:

   ```
   sudo docker run --detach \
   --hostname gitlab.joustie.nl \
   --publish 443:443 --publish 80:80 --publish 22:22 \
   --name gitlab \
   --restart always \
   --volume /srv/gitlab/config:/etc/gitlab \
   --volume /srv/gitlab/logs:/var/log/gitlab \
   --volume /srv/gitlab/data:/var/opt/gitlab \
   gitlab/gitlab-ce:latest
   ```

When the container starts again, it will reconfigure and update itself (it will perform a `gitlab-ctl reconfigure`).

Run GitLab CE on a different IP address

Using the same `--publish` mechanism, you can specify not only the port but also the IP address that Docker will use.

To run the latest GitLab CE on IP-address `192.168.1.1`, use the following command:

```
sudo docker run --detach \
 --hostname gitlab.joustie.nl \
 --publish 192.168.1.1:443:443 \
 --publish 192.168.1.1:80:80 \
 --publish 192.168.1.1:22:22 \
 --name gitlab \
 --restart always \
 --volume /srv/gitlab/config:/etc/gitlab \
 --volume /srv/gitlab/logs:/var/log/gitlab \
 --volume /srv/gitlab/data:/var/opt/gitlab \
 gitlab/gitlab-ce:latest
```

Now, GitLab is accessible at `http://192.168.1.1` and `https://192.168.1.1`. A `docker-compose.yml` example that uses different ports can be found in the *Install GitLab using Docker Compose* section.

Debugging the container

Sometimes, a container does not behave the way you expect it to. How can you debug this? First, you can check the container logs:

```
sudo docker logs gitlab
```

Enter the running container:

```
sudo docker exec -it gitlab /bin/bash
```

You now have root access to the GitLab container and you can view the situation as if you were in a VM running omnibus-gitlab.

Install GitLab using Docker Compose

Docker Compose is used to run multiple containers as a single service. By using this tool, you can easily manage your Docker-based GitLab installation. It can be used to configure, install, and upgrade the service. It is Python-based and can be installed from `https://docs.docker.com/compose/install/`.

If you have installed Docker Compose, or already have it on your system, you can build your service.

Create a `docker-compose.yml` file (or download an example):

```
web:
  image: 'gitlab/gitlab-ce:latest'
  restart: always
  hostname: 'gitlab.joustie.nl'
  environment:
  GITLAB_OMNIBUS_CONFIG: |
  external_url 'https://gitlab.joustie.nl'
  ports:
  - '80:8080'
  - '443:4443'
  - '22:2222'
  volumes:
  - '/srv/gitlab/config:/etc/gitlab'
  - '/srv/gitlab/logs:/var/log/gitlab'
  - '/srv/gitlab/data:/var/opt/gitlab'
```

Check the port settings. This is the same as using `--publish 80:9090` or `-p 2224:22` with pure `docker` and not `docker-compose`.

Make sure you are in the same directory as `docker-compose.yml` and run the following:

```
docker-compose up -d
```

GitLab will start and run an omnibus-gitlab reconfigure during boot to set up GitLab. To add more configuration settings at startup, follow the instructions mentioned previously to add directives to the `GITLAB_OMNIBUS_CONFIG` variable.

Updating GitLab using Docker Compose

We have seen several ways to run Docker containers. You can run them standalone (plain Docker), or create sets of containers that can work together with services (Docker Compose). The next step is to orchestrate containers.

Deploying GitLab using Kubernetes

After some years of uncertainty, Google's **Kubernetes** has emerged as the premier container orchestration tool. Every major cloud vendor has integration for its API. This does not automatically mean that it works the same everywhere. Because the product has been developing so quickly, you will notice differences.

The fastest way to deploy GitLab on a Kubernetes cluster is by using Helm charts. Avoiding the management of each separate resource on a cluster, **Helm** bundles these resources in an application model: a chart. It works like a package management system in which applications are registered. Information on how to install, configure, and upgrade this application is contained in this package.

Helm consists of a server called **Tiller**, which that lives in the Kubernetes cluster, and Helm, the command-line client that talks to the Tiller server.

GitLab Runner Helm chart

With this chart, you can create scalable GitLab Runners. It will use the Kubernetes executor. When it receives a new job to process from GitLab CI, a new pod will be created in a specified namespace.

First, add the Helm repository:

```
helm repo add gitlab https://charts.gitlab.io helm init
```

Before you can start this Runner, you need to create a .yml file with parameters (we named it values.yml). There is a template available at https://gitlab.com/charts/gitlab-runner/blob/master/values.yaml. The settings are explained in the template file.

The minimum you should fill in is as follows:

```
gitlabUrl: https://gitlab.home.joustie.nl/
runnerRegistrationToken:
"dE47NAgHgnFRpdd23RiDJ9JOSzBH40mxqLa1B42Ds5eb94ZWebhPydPt9n"
```

After the configuration of values.yml, you can start the deployment.

Deploying of a GitLab Runner to Kubernetes

Initiate the deployment with the following command (replace `yournamespace` with something you prefer):

```
helm install --namespace yournamespace --name gitlab-runner -f values.yml
gitlab/gitlab-runner
```

After a short time, you should find your Runner listed in the *Runners* section of the administration pages in GitLab.

GitLab Helm chart

This is the official and recommended way to install GitLab on a cloud native environment. This chart contains all the necessary components to get started, and you can scale up deployments easily. This specific chart is the optimal way to run GitLab in a Kubernetes cluster.

The default deployment includes the following:

- **Core GitLab components**:
  - **Unicorn**: The pre-forking Ruby on Rails web server
  - **GitLab Shell**: The Ruby wrapper around Git on the server, enabling **Git-over-SSH**
  - **GitLab Workhorse**: The smart reverse proxy, taking on big HTTP-requests
  - **Registry**: The GitLab container registry
  - **Sidekiq**: The backend services for GitLab, taking care of merge requests, emails, and other asynchronous jobs
  - **Gitaly**: The storage layer abstraction for Git operations
- **Extra optional dependencies**:
  - **Redis**: The caching key value store, database multi-tool can speed up processing
  - **Minio**: An object storage server with an Amazon S3 compatible interface

- **Bonus material**:
  - **An autoscaling, unprivileged GitLab Runner using the Kubernetes executor**: If you run GitLab through Kubernetes, a dedicated GitLab runner is part of the design.

- **Automatically provisioned SSL via Let's Encrypt**: When you provide Kubernetes with an administrator and a domain name, the Let's Encrypt automation builtin can setup SSL for you.

As with the GitLab Docker image, the GitLab chart is a feature completed for the core product and takes a few minutes to deploy. Deploying GitLab using the Helm chart takes 5 to 10 minutes depending on your hardware or service location. It is also possible to run certain components outside of the Kubernetes cluster; this is also what you do in production, normally. It is better to keep your application state out of the cluster.

These are the requirements for deploying GitLab to Kubernetes:

- You need Helm version >2.9 and `kubectl` >1.8 (about 1 minor release version difference with your cluster).
- A Kubernetes cluster using version >1.8 with a minimum of 6 vCPUs and 16 GB RAM.
- The cluster can be a Google GKE, Amazon EKS, or Microsoft AKS-based cluster, or a local one using Minikube, for example.
- You should be able to easily configure a wildcard DNS entry for your domain (for example, `*.example.com`) and an external IP.
- You can connect and log in to the cluster.
- A configured and initialized Helm Tiller running.

To make sure Helm is configured and initialized, run the following command:

```
$ helm repo add gitlab https://charts.gitlab.io/
$ helm repo update
```

Deploying GitLab to Kubernetes

To deploy GitLab, the following three parameters are required:

- `global.host.domain`: Should point to your wildcard DNS domain
- `global.hosts.externalIP`: The external IP address for the cluster
- `certmanager-issues.email`: The email address that is used for issuing certificates (Let's Encrypt)

So, when you only have a few parameters such as these, just run the command:

```
$ helm upgrade --install gitlab gitlab/gitlab \
--timeout 600 \
--set global.hosts.domain=home.joustie.nl \
```

```
--set global.hosts.externalIP=<your external ip> \
--set certmanager-issuer.email=admin@joustie.nl
```

You can also run a deployment using a `values.yml` file, just like the GitLab Runners chart. You can find examples at `https://gitlab.com/charts/gitlab/tree/master/examples`.

Monitoring the deployment

After running the `helm upgrade --install` command, it can take several minutes before output is returned. It should look a bit like the following:

```
Release "gitlab" does not exist. Installing it now.
NAME: gitlab
LAST DEPLOYED: Wed Jan 2 12:31:31 2019
NAMESPACE: default
STATUS: DEPLOYED
RESOURCES:
==> v1/PersistentVolumeClaim
NAME STATUS VOLUME CAPACITY ACCESS MODES STORAGECLASS AGE
gitlab-minio Bound pvc-fc207fb5-0e81-11e9-b9ef-025000000001 10Gi RWO
hostpath 9s
gitlab-postgresql Bound pvc-fc2158a3-0e81-11e9-b9ef-025000000001 8Gi RWO
hostpath 9s
gitlab-prometheus-server Bound pvc-fc2240b5-0e81-11e9-b9ef-025000000001 8Gi
RWO hostpath 9s
gitlab-redis Bound pvc-fc236cfb-0e81-11e9-b9ef-025000000001 5Gi RWO
hostpath 9s
```

Afterwards (or during the deployment in another session), you can issue a `helm status gitlab` command to see info about the deployment.

Initial login

If everything went well, you will find your installation by adding GitLab to your wildcard DNS name, in the case of our preceding example, `gitlab.home.joustie.nl`.

We have not yet specified a root password for the initial administrator user in GitLab. During the deployment on Kubernetes, a random password was automatically created. You can fetch this password with the following command from Terminal (replace `name` with your deployment name; for us, it is `gitlab`):

```
kubectl get secret <name>-gitlab-initial-root-password -
ojsonpath={.data.password} | base64 --decode ; echo
```

Outgoing email

If you do not specify it, there is no outgoing email enabled. You have to enable it by specifying some settings. The following is the `install` command if you set the options right away:

```
$ helm upgrade --install gitlab gitlab/gitlab \
--timeout 600 \
--set global.hosts.domain=home.joustie.nl \
--set global.hosts.externalIP=<your external ip> \
--set certmanager-issuer.email=admin@joustie.nl \
--set global.smtp.enabled=true \
--set global.smtp.address=smtp.xs4all.nl \
--set global.smtp.port=25
```

Also, make sure there is no firewall preventing traffic in between. Clusters on **Google Kubernetes Engine (GKE)** have their SMTP ports blocked by default.

Updating GitLab using the Helm chart

Once your GitLab chart is installed, configuration changes and chart updates should be done using the Helm upgrade.

If you would like to upgrade GitLab or change settings, use the following procedure:

```
#update the chart
helm repo add gitlab https://charts.gitlab.io/
helm repo update
#get the current values
helm get values gitlab > gitlab.yaml
```

Edit the `gitlab.yaml` file, looking at the possible values here: https://docs.gitlab.com/charts/installation/command-line-options.html.

Save and apply the settings file:

```
helm upgrade gitlab gitlab/gitlab -f gitlab.yaml
```

The command should return a lot of output, but it should mention the following:

```
STATUS: DEPLOYED
```

Uninstalling GitLab using the Helm chart

To uninstall the GitLab chart, run the following:

```
helm delete gitlab
```

You can run `helm status` afterwards to see if the action has been completed.

Creating droplets on DigitalOcean

DigitalOcean is a cloud provider, originating from New York. It has been a darling of developers for years. It offers an API, integrations, and affordable pricing to run your application workloads and VMs.

There are two ways of installing GitLab on DigitalOcean. You can create VMs (**droplets**) yourself and configure them using the omnibus installer or install them from source yourself. An even better way is to use the predefined GitLab droplet image that is already available on the site. When creating a droplet, you can specify this image.

When you log in to DigitalOcean, you can go to your droplets page and create a new one:

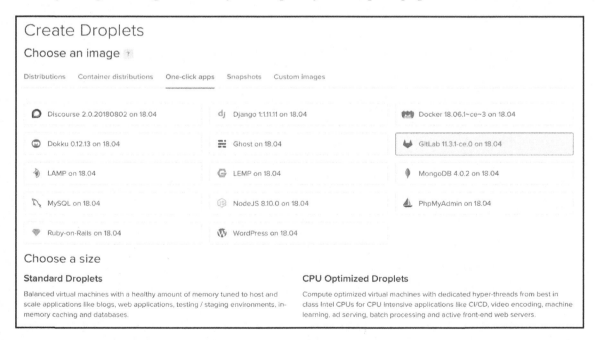

Determine the options for a droplet:

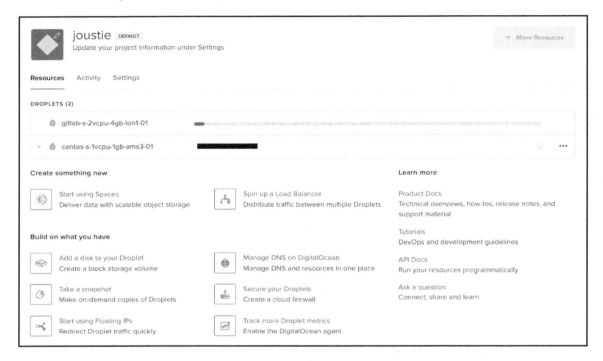

After logging in, you will be asked to set some options:

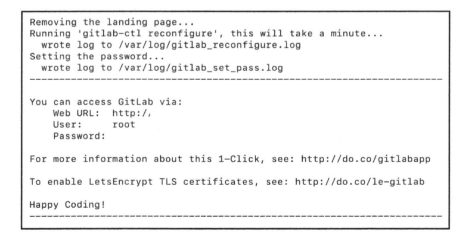

The droplet is ready. The system will reboot and reconfigure itself. If the login does not work, log in via SSH as a root to your droplet and execute the following command:

```
tail -100 /var/log/gitlab_set_pass.log
```

Take a look at this:

```
Could not create the default administrator account:
-> Password is too short (minimum is 8 characters)
```

If this is visible, we have to try to set the password again using one of the methods available in the omnibus package. Add the following line to the /etc/gitlab/gitlab.rb file:

```
gitlab_rails['initial_root_password'] = 'nonstandardpassword'
```

Then, execute the following in order to re-seed the database (it is empty, so that doesn't matter) and reset the admin password:

```
gitlab-rake gitlab:setup
```

After some time, you should receive the following output:

```
Administrator account created:
login: root password: You'll be prompted to create one on your first visit.
```

If you go to the URL of your new GitLab instance, you can set the password as shown:

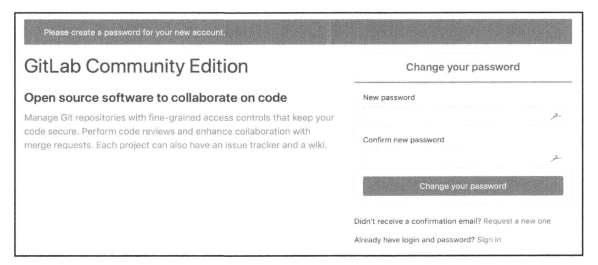

Enjoy your GitLab!

Summary

In this chapter, we discussed the different ways of installing GitLab. The Linux platform was the chosen OS for which we provided instructions and examples. We started with the recommended way of installing for most organizations, using the omnibus package.

It is also possible to install GitLab from scratch and to run it from source.

It is also possible to run GitLab from a Docker container. We also showed you how to update Docker-based GitLab installs and gave an example of using Docker Compose to create a multi-container installation. Finally, we talked about the fact that, when scaling, you probably would like several containers deployed and managed. We showed you how to achieve this with Kubernetes as the orchestration tool.

In the next chapter, we will dive into the process of configuring GitLab after the initial installation.

Questions

1. What is the recommended way of installing GitLab?
2. At the least, which ports do you need to open on your firewall?
3. On what platforms can you install GitLab using the omnibus package?
4. What is the basic administration command you use in an omnibus-based install?
5. What version of Git is the minimum you need on a source-based GitLab install?
6. What PostgreSQL extension do you need to enable for GitLab in a source-based GitLab install?
7. What is the name of the official GitLab CE Docker images?
8. What is the location of site-specific data according to **Linux Filesystem Hierarchy (LFH)**?
9. What programming language do you need to have installed to run Docker Compose?
10. What is the recommended way of deploying GitLab components to Kubernetes?

Further reading

- *Learn Docker - Fundamentals of Docker 18.x* by *Gabriel N. Schenker*: `https://www.packtpub.com/in/networking-and-servers/learn-docker-fundamentals-docker-18x`
- *Develop and Operate Microservices on Kubernetes* by *Martin Helmich*: `https://www.packtpub.com/in/virtualization-and-cloud/develop-and-operate-microservices-kubernetes-video`
- GitLab install documentation: `https://about.gitlab.com/install/`

3

Configuring GitLab Using the Web UI

After installing GitLab in the previous chapter, you probably have a running instance. But how can you manage it? You need to know how to configure the software. This chapter will explain how this is achieved for the different kinds of GitLab installations that are available.

The following topics will be covered in this chapter:

- Configuring GitLab settings at the instance level
- Configuring GitLab settings at the group level
- Configuring GitLab settings at the project level

Technical requirements

To manage omnibus installs, you need to use a central configuration file called `gitlab.rb`. You need to create it yourself or copy an example of one. A template of this configuration file is available at `https://gitlab.com/gitlab-org/omnibus-gitlab/blob/master/files/gitlab-config-template/gitlab.rb.template`. Please note that it isn't updated after upgrades. We will quote and discuss parts of this file in this chapter.

To follow along with the instructions in this chapter, please download this book's GitHub repository, along with the examples that are available, at `https://github.com/PacktPublishing/Mastering-GitLab-12/tree/master/Chapter03`.

Configuring GitLab settings at the instance level

When you log on to GitLab as an administrator, you will notice a tool icon in the top right of the menu:

When you click on that, the administrator page will load, which you can use to access instance-level settings. The base page provides an overview of active projects, users, and groups:

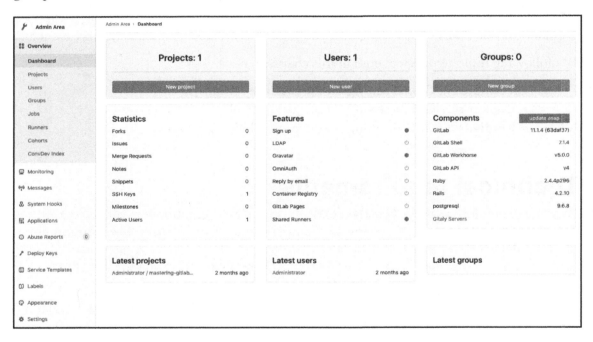

On the left-hand side, there are several global administration options. Let's go through them.

Menu options

The options are grouped, and some items can even be expanded:

- **Dashboard**: **Dashboard** gives you some insight into the number of projects, users, and groups that are in your GitLab instance. You can create new ones from this screen. There is also other interesting information in the form of statistics, where you can get an overview of active features and installed components. If you enabled exposing instance information to GitLab, it will also mention whether you should upgrade your instance to a newer version of GitLab.
- **Projects**: In the **Projects** pane, you can search for projects and create new ones. For the search option, there are some filters available.
- **Users**: The **Users** pane offers the same functionality as the **Projects** pane, that is, searching for users with advanced filtering and being able to create new users.
- **Groups**: The **Groups** pane is identical to the previous panes in terms of its features, but without fancy filters.
- **Jobs**: The **Jobs** pane offers you insight into **continuous integration/continuous deployment (CI/CD)** jobs that are pending, running, or finished.
- **Runners**: In this section of the administration page, options and views on CI/CD GitLab runners are available.
- **Gitaly servers**: By default, there is only one Gitaly server, and it is shown here. However, there could be more, depending on your setup.

Monitoring

The monitoring section offers interesting bits of information that are needed so that you can administer your GitLab instance:

- **System information**: CPU, memory, and other metrics.
- **Background Jobs**: GitLab integrated the Sidekiq statistics gem into the application, and it can be viewed here.
- **Logs**: In this section, you can view 2,000 lines of information from the most important GitLab log files (unicorn, gitlab-shell, Sidekiq, and so on).
- **Health check**: This is a very interesting page for sysadmins. Here, you will find endpoints that will give some insight into the health of the running GitLab instance. There is also a token present, which you will need to send as a parameter if your monitoring software wants to scrape the page.

- **Requests Profiles**: This is only interesting to developers or testers. Here, you can send a header to GitLab for use in request profiling.
- **Audit Log**: If you have an enterprise license, you can find audit events here and filter them.

Messages

Your GitLab instance has a facility where you can send messages to all of your users. These broadcasts can come in handy if you want to inform your users about system-wide events, such as upgrades and scheduled downtime. The following is the **Admin** page, which you can find in the side menu:

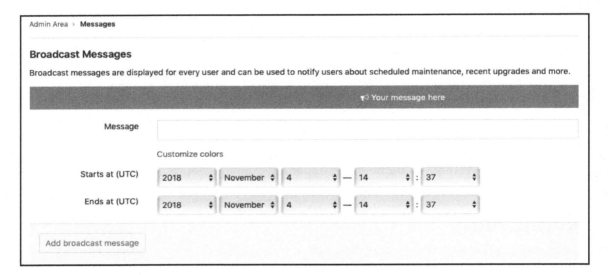

After you've scheduled a new message, it can be reused later as well:

System hooks

GitLab can perform HTTP POST requests on the system level and act on several events.

A standard event is raised when you're creating a new project or user. Additionally, it can send other types of events as well. Just add a destination URL and (optionally) a secret token:

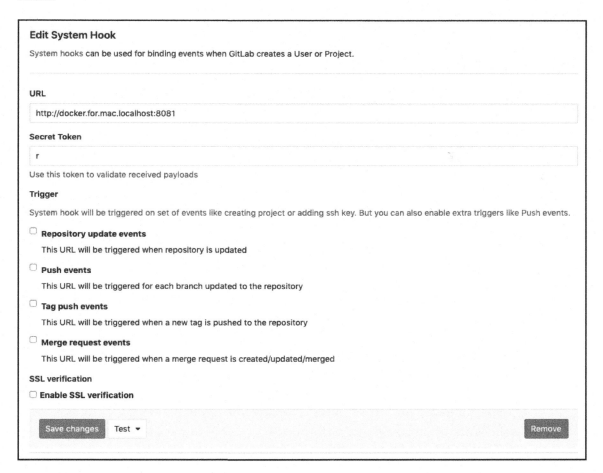

When you have configured your system hook, there is a drop-down list with a test to check whether it works by calling the URL.

Plugins

On this page, you also have the option to configure installed **plugins**. This basically fires a locally installed program instead of calling a URL with parameters.

It requires you to place the plugin code in `/opt/gitlab/embedded/service/gitlab-rails/plugins`, and it has to be written in a certain way. After installation, the plugin can be run as a hook.

Applications

In this section of the administration page, you have the option to register third-party applications in order to use GitLab as an OAuth authorization provider.

Open Authorization (OAuth) is an open standard for authorization. Users can give a program or website access to their private data that's kept on another website without revealing their username and password.

To register an application, you need to provide a name, callback URL, and set a few options.

Trusted means that a token is exchanged based on the already validated resource owner's credentials. The user authorization step is subsequently skipped for this application when it's used.

Some other scopes are also defined that allow a given application to perform various actions. These are as follows:

- **API**: Grants complete read and write access to the API, including all groups and projects.
- `read_user`: Grants read-only access to the authenticated user's profile through the `/user` API endpoint, which includes username, public email, and full name. It also grants access to read-only API endpoints under `/users`.
- `sudo`: Grants permission to perform API actions as any user in the system when authenticated as an admin user.

- `read_repository`: Grants read-only access to repositories on private projects using Git over HTTP (not using the API).
- `openid`: Grants permission to authenticate with GitLab using OpenID Connect. It also gives read-only access to the user's profile and group memberships.

> You can also revoke registration if you wish to. GitLab uses **doorkeeper-gem**, which can be found at `https://github.com/doorkeeper-gem/doorkeeper`, to provide this functionality.

Abuse reports

There are several places in the GitLab web interface where, as a user, you can file and report abuse. You can find buttons to file a report in the following sections:

- Comments
- Issues and merge requests
- The profile page of a user (refer to the following screenshot):

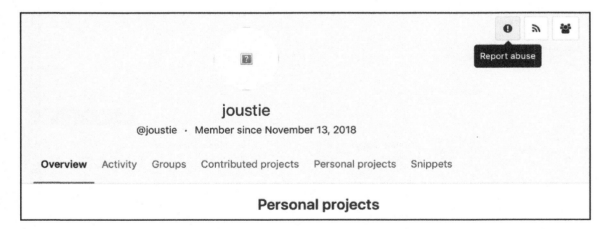

When you click the **Report abuse** button, the following form will appear:

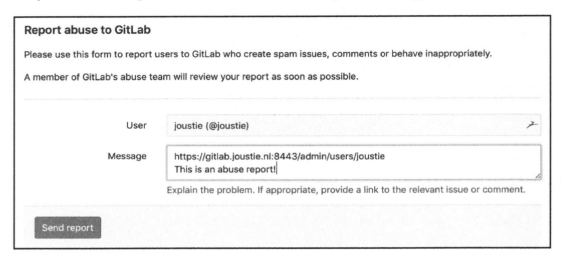

If you click on the **Send report** button, an administrator will be notified, and he or she will find the abuse report in the **Abuse Reports** section of the administration pages:

License

If you are using GitLab Enterprise Edition, this is the place where you manage your license. You can either upload a file or insert the appropriate license key. You can browse to GitLab to buy a new license.

Kubernetes

In this section, you can add an instance-wide Kubernetes cluster, which will be used to create deployment environments. We will discuss this option in `Chapter 11`, *The Release and Configure Phase*.

Push rules

In this section, you can define all kinds of rules that will allow or disallow Git pushes:

Admin Area › **Push Rules**

Pre-defined push rules.

Rules that define what git pushes are accepted for a project. All newly created projects will use this settings.

◌ **Committer restriction**
Users can only push commits to this repository that were committed with one of their own verified emails. This

◌ **Reject unsigned commits**
Only signed commits can be pushed to this repository. This setting will be applied to all projects unless overrid

◌ **Do not allow users to remove git tags with** `git push`
Tags can still be deleted through the web UI.

◌ **Check whether author is a GitLab user**
Restrict commits by author (email) to existing GitLab users

◌ **Prevent committing secrets to Git**
GitLab will reject any files that are likely to contain secrets. The list of file names we reject is available in the do

---

Geo

When you have an Enterprise license and want to configure replicas of your GitLab instance, this is the place to use. We will discuss Geo in `Chapter 22`, *Using Geo to Create Distributed Read-Only Copies of GitLab*.

Deploy Keys

In this section, you can register SSH keys, which are known as **Global Shared Deploy keys**. They allow read-only or read-write (if enabled) access to be configured on any repository in the entire GitLab installation. When the administrator has registered them here, you can assign them in your project, as shown in the following screenshot:

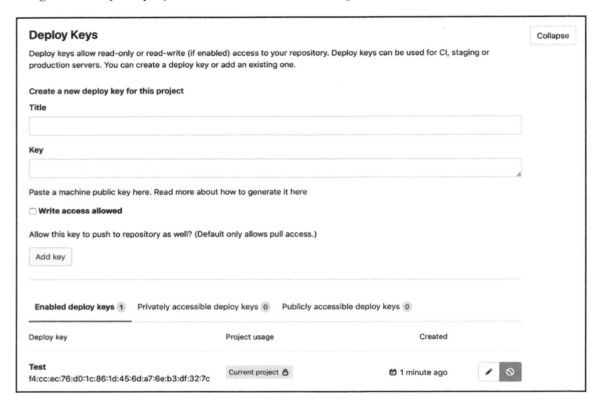

This feature can be used by a remote CI/CD server to check out code.

Service templates

Project services allow you to integrate GitLab with other third-party applications. They resemble plugins that you can find in other systems. They allow for a lot of freedom in terms of adding functionality to GitLab. In the **Service Templates** section, you can edit information for predefined templates. The repository owners then have to configure less information if they want to enable a service integration for their repository.

Appearance

You can define some cosmetic aspects of your GitLab instance on the **Appearance settings** page:

Admin Area › **Appearance**

Appearance settings

You can modify the look and feel of GitLab here

Navigation bar:

Header logo   [Choose File] no file selected
Maximum file size is 1MB. Pages are optimized for a 28px tall header logo

Favicon:

Favicon   [Choose File] no file selected
Maximum file size is 1MB. Image size must be 32x32px. Allowed image formats are '.png' and '.ico'.
Images with incorrect dimensions are not resized automatically, and may result in unexpected behavior.

Sign in/Sign up pages:

Title

Description

Description parsed with **GitLab Flavored Markdown**.

Logo   [Choose File] no file selected
Maximum file size is 1MB. Pages are optimized for a 640x360 px logo.

New project pages:

New project guidelines

Guidelines parsed with **GitLab Flavored Markdown**.

[Save]

If, for example, you want to greet your users with a nice logo on the front page, you can change the logo by uploading a new one. You can do this by clicking the **Choose File** button near the **Logo** section. After you have done this, log out. You will be redirected to the front page:

Settings

This section has a lot of detailed options, all of which we will discuss here.

General

This part of the administration panel deals with settings that are not easily put into a group.

Visibility and access controls

Here, you define the default authorizations and permissions for users. There are three basic options. For instance, you can make projects private, which means that only you or people you grant access to can see when you create a new project. The internal level means only logged-in users can see your project (read-only). Public is the widest access level and allows anyone to see your project (but not write to it). The same authorizations can be set for snippets and groups. You can also determine what sources can be imported.

There are a lot of import modules available, but maybe you want to limit those. Another import option is to allow projects to be exported. There are several functions that can help users with this. If this isn't something you would like to cater for, then you can disable it here. GitLab supports both Git client access protocols (SSH and HTTP). You can also disable them in this section if you want to. Finally, you can control what kind of SSH keys can be used for Git SSH. Is RSA too insecure? Just disable it.

Account and limit

In this section, you can set options such as session expiration (the default is 20 minutes), project limits, and maximum attachment sizes. The default project limit is set to 100,000, while the maximum size of a repository is not set by default. The attachment size is 10 MB. You can also enable Gravatars for accounts, which means that an image that is uploaded to `gravatar.com` can function as your personal icon. GitLab can act as an OAuth backend, and you can allow normal users to register new applications by using it.

You can also configure the way new users are handled. They can be defined as external users. This means that new users can only access specific projects that they are granted access to. They can't create new projects. Optionally, you can define exceptions for that rule with a regular expression. The final option is to enable a prompt to let users know that they haven't uploaded public SSH keys yet.

Diff limits

In this section, you can set the maximum size a diff patch can get to before it cannot be displayed in the normal diff view. If this size is reached, a link to a blob view will be presented.

Sign-up restrictions

In a default installation, a form is available on the GitLab login page so that you can sign up if you don't have an account. You can disable the signup pages here, as well as edit a whitelist and blacklist to deny access to certain domains upfront. You can also specify whether you want an email to be sent after the signup procedure.

Some text will be shown to the user after signup has completed.

Sign-in restrictions

These settings cover the following restrictions:

- Enable or disable logging in to the web interface with a password (without it, you need a third-party authentication provider such as Google)
- Enable or disable password authentication for Git over HTTPS (without it, a personal access token is needed)
- Enable or disable two-factor authentication (with a grace period that determines how long a user can wait during configuration)

It is possible to use a hardware token device as a second factor, as you can see in the following screenshot (this only works in Chrome):

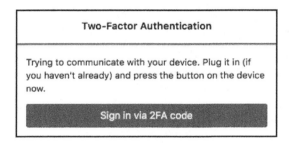

You can also choose to use a code generator app such as Google Authentication:

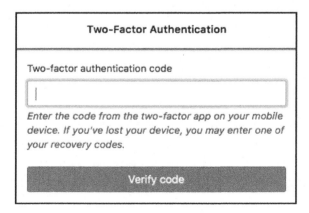

You can also set a home page URL here, which is where non-logged-in users will be redirected to. In the same way, you can define an after-sign-out path, where users will be led to when they sign out.

Finally, it's also possible to set a standard sign-in text to be visible on the login page.

Terms of service and privacy policy

If you use GitLab for an organization that uses strict terms, you can make sure that your users accept a policy that you can enter here, in a nice markdown-formatted text box.

External authentication

For some installations, it could be crucial to let external systems have more influence on the access policies in GitLab. For this, you can specify an external authorization service that checks the user's information and the classification label that has been given to a project. Based on that query, access may or may not be granted. If you enable this, all the pages that use cross-project data won't work anymore (such as snippets and activity).

Web Terminal

This is a recent feature, and is where you can access a terminal via a web browser (part of a pipeline). Here, you can set a timeout on the session time for this terminal. Keeping it to zero means that it will try the session indefinitely.

Web IDE

Web IDE is a feature that is also new and in full development. This book is actually typed in it, and it works better than most web editors. The main option that you can control from the settings page is the feature toggle, which allows client-side JavaScript projects to enable live preview functionality using CodeSandbox.

 For more information about project access, go to `https://codesandbox.io`.

Integrations

One of the ways to advance GitLab as a product is to offer several ways to integrate with other products. This also aligns with the Unix and open source philosophy of creating small, interoperable utilities. On a technical level, there are three ways to accomplish this:

- Using webhooks (event mechanisms, asynchronous, and so on. For more information, go to `https://gitlab.com/gitlab-org/gitlab-ce/blob/master/doc/web_hooks/web_hooks.md`).
- Using the GitLab API (proactively get information from GitLab).
- Using project integration (running from a repository in GitLab). In the settings, four options are available: Elasticsearch, PlantUML, Snowplow, and the ability to view third-party offers.

Elasticsearch

Only available in Enterprise edition, this search engine integration feature is really powerful, but is a subject on its own. It offers a full-text search option for GitLab so that you can search for text throughout your source code repositories. You will need to install the search program, which has a HTTP web interface on another server, and specify the connection settings (the URL):

You can also limit what will be indexed:

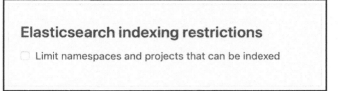

Another option is to connect to an Elasticsearch instance that you are running in the Amazon cloud. You can specify connection settings here as well if you have this set up:

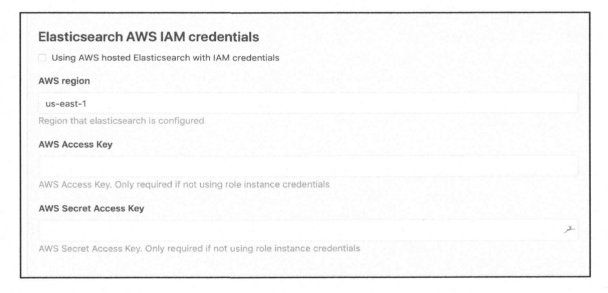

You can find more information on this at `http://elastic.co`.

PlantUML

Here, you can define the URL for PlantUML (this is an API integration).

Third-party offers

This setting lets you opt out of third-party offerings. An example of such an offer would be to get free Google Cloud credits so that you can use Google's Kubernetes platform.

Snowplow

Again, Snowplow is an Enterprise feature. Some companies want to track custom events in GitLab. With Snowplow, you can use this big data platform to collect and analyze data. If you enable this integration, you have to provide a collector URI, a site ID, and a cookie domain.

Repository

Here, you will find options that are generic for all repositories.

Repository mirror

With GitLab, you can create repository mirrors. This means that, after an initial synchronization, the content (and metadata, if possible) is kept up to date with the remote source. The sync job will be triggered automatically and will time out after 15 minutes. This setting determines whether a user can set up mirrors. If it's disabled, only administrators can perform this task.

Repository storage

The most important settings handle the way storage is used. Instead of using folder structures with names, you can use hashed values as directory names for projects. This way, when you're moving projects, the folder isn't moved on an OS level – the reference to the hash is changed in the database instead. Keeping a hash-based reference tree and searching is much faster than traversing a folder tree by name.

Secondly, you can specify alternate storage locations where new projects are stored. If there is more than one location, it will alternate between them in no particular order. The location that shows up in the chooser depends on what storage paths were defined in `gitlab.rb` (for omnibus installations) or `gitlab.ym` (source-based setups).

The settings for the storage circuit breaker are found here as well. This is used to handle failures of the underlying storage GitLab uses. When you're using network filesystems such as **Network File System** (**NFS**), locking issues can occur, which eventually make the whole system hang indefinitely.

Repository maintenance

Git has a special integrity checking feature called **fsck**. Just like the **Filesystem Consistency Check (fsck)** for filesystems, it can verify a structure and tell us whether it's compromised. The name of this Git function was chosen because Git was initially built as a filesystem. A filesystem is classed as a graph model, and Git implements this as tree and blob objects. Because all of the items are check-summed, fsck can verify the integrity of the objects and their relations. This graph is depicted in the following diagram:

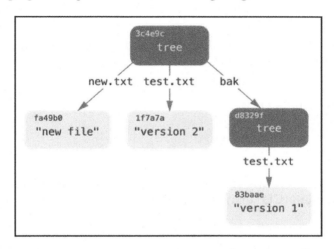

Changes between files in a repository are saved as deltas and packed together in pack files, which are then compressed. This also happens to other objects in the repository hierarchy. In short, this means that the graph model has been enhanced to make Git operations faster and more efficient on your computer, and to save disk space. Sometimes, after commit -- amend or git rebase, objects such as commits become unreachable (there's no parent SHA). All the preceding use cases are candidates for the Git garbage collection function: git gc (https://git-scm.com/docs/git-gc). It is recommended to run this function on your Git repositories regularly.

In the GitLab settings, you can control the two ways in which Git is being used on the GitLab server in order to maintain repository hierarchies. The first option is that you can enable periodic repository checks with git fsck. Letting GitLab do this ensures that you can spot and possibly repair disk corruption issues you wouldn't easily find normally if you were to process all the files.

GitLab can also do housekeeping. It should run periodically to prevent the corruption of repositories. Unfortunately, it can also generate false alarms.

The second option is that you can control the way housekeeping is done on the server in order to make Git repositories more efficient and fast. You can enable and control when `git gc` is performed on the GitLab server. Another option for `git pack` operations is to let them use bitmap indexes. This could result in much faster cloning (but more disk space being used). The parameters for housekeeping are the amount of times a repository is pushed before `git repack` (incremental), `git repack` (full), and `git gc` is performed.

Templates

From GitLab 11.x onward, you can define a special directory that will provide templates for all of GitLab. You can also create your own.

The custom project templates settings let you specify which group is the default group so that you can provide templates.

CI/CD

This page contains several configuration options for **Continuous Integration (CI)** and **Continuous Deployment (CD)** using GitLab.

Auto DevOps settings

As of GitLab 11.3, Auto DevOps is automatically enabled for all projects. When the build process is triggered for a project and a pipeline is created, the Auto DevOps feature will be disabled for the project if the pipeline fails. If an alternative `.gitlab-ci.yml` file is located in the project, it will use that instead. You can override the default Auto DevOps settings here and disable them:

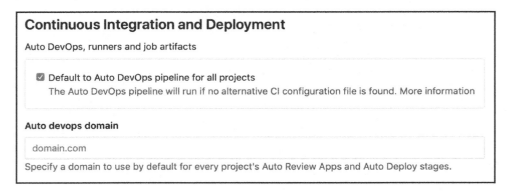

Shared runner settings

One of the key components of CI/CD is the runners. In this section, you can enable shared runners for all new projects, which means that any shared runner could end up building your code. There is a security aspect to this because shared runners could exist that aren't using a stateless mechanism. They could be running your job, and not clean up the artifacts, and get a new build job. This is probably is not what you want. Your data could be compromised by another build project.

Therefore, another option is to set some warning text for shared runners that communicate so that you can ensure your shared runners are under control:

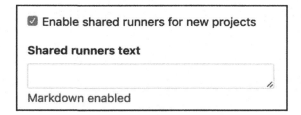

When runners build artifacts, the results can be uploaded and viewed after the pipeline has finished. You may want to set a certain limit on the size of the combined artifacts that get uploaded as a ZIP file to the GitLab CI.

You can also specify how long artifacts should stay available after the build. This is controlled by the default artifact expiration time:

When an artifact reaches this age, it is deleted in the periodic expiration task. As we can see in the following screenshot, it runs every hour:

Container registry

GitLab can also function as a container registry. By this, we mean it can store images that you create on your workstation or inside of GitLab runner pipelines. In this section of the admin area, you can specify how long an authorization token remains valid. The default is five minutes.

Reporting

Most people have an easy time identifying or explaining the term reporting. I personally don't understand how GitLab grouped certain options under this subject. To me, the first one, that is, spam and anti-bot protection, should belong to a security or privacy part of the settings.

Spam and anti-bot protection

GitLab is able to use reCAPTCHA and Akismet to handle abusive traffic. If you enable this setting, you need a site key and a private key, both of which can be generated at `http://www.google.com/recaptcha`. In this way, you raise another barrier against spammers creating users in an automated way. If you register, you have to prove you are a human by answering specific questions.

In a similar manner, Akismet can help you protect your issues in GitLab from spammers. With the advent of weblogs and the possibility to comment, a new spam technique emerged called comment spam. Spammers try to influence readers with massive amounts of comments. Akismet was established as an extra check (GitLab calls its API) to prevent automated comments (issues in GitLab).

As an extra security measure, there's the option to restrict simultaneous logins from multiple IPs. You can even set a maximum number of IPs a user can connect from by using an IP expiration time.

Abuse reports

Here, you can set an email address that abuse reports can be sent to. The option to create an abuse report is scattered throughout GitLab.

Error reporting and logging

In general, there are numerous log files for all kinds of services that GitLab is running. In this section, you can specify logging and reporting for clients (also known as browsers). The GitLab frontend JavaScript application that runs in your browser has the option to use Sentry (`https://sentry.io/welcome/`). By using this, you can monitor and proactively catch errors from your users and act accordingly.

Metrics and profiling

Administrators or owners of a GitLab system like to know how their system is performing – not only at an OS level, but also in terms of functionality. For instance, information about how long certain operations take to complete is very important. These metrics are available in GitLab, but you need to do some configuration to make these numbers available. There are several ways to retrieve this data from GitLab, and it's here where you can specify details about sources of information.

Metrics – InfluxDB

The first system that can operate as a backend store for metrics is InfluxDB. This is a special kind of database that stores time series data. Before you can use this feature, you will have to set up this database on a separate server. It is too heavy to run on the same GitLab machine. Instructions on how to configure this can be found at `https://docs.gitlab.com/ee/administration/monitoring/performance/influxdb_configuration.html`. When you enable InfluxDB metrics, it will set up a **User Datagram Protocol (UDP)** stream to the InfluxDB host that will carry all kinds of event information. You can fine-tune the connection pool size, the connection timeout, and so on to make sure that you don't generate too much data. After changing this setting, you will have to restart.

Metrics – Prometheus

The preferred time series database for GitLab as of 2018 is Prometheus. Its scraping endpoint for GitLab can be enabled here. You will need to restart GitLab after you change it. A Prometheus server is bundled in `omnibus-gitlab` itself.

Profiling – Performance Bar

Sometimes, you like to know how GitLab's performance is when it's running in a browser, or you want to see which part of a GitLab request takes the most time to complete. Enter `Profiling-Performance Bar`, which you can enable for certain groups. Once the **Performance Bar** is enabled, you will need to press the *P* + *B* keyboard shortcut to actually display it:

Usage statistics

In this section of the settings, you can enable or disable two sets of information that can be collected by GitLab by default. You can also choose to only let the information be viewable by instance admins. These types of information are as follows:

- Version check (you will see **Update ASAP** in the overview when a new version is available)
- Usage ping (to improve GitLab and its user experience)
- Can share data to the public or only admins
- Check the **Preview payload** button to view other data that's shared in this ping

Pseudonymizer data collection

When enabled, this option will make sure that GitLab writes anonymized information to a comma-separated values file. This file will then be uploaded to the S3 storage bucket that you specify in your configuration files (`gitlab.rb` for omnibus-gitlab installs and `gitlab.yml` for source-based installs).

Network

In this section, you can control some of the options that influence network performance and communication.

Performance optimization

Here, you can disable writing to an authorized keys file and let GitLab read authorized keys straight from the database instead of via a file. This helps speed up the authorization phase of Git SSH.

User and IP rate limits

Here, you can throttle for web and API requests. You also have the option to make a difference between authenticated and anonymous requests.

Outbound requests

By default, webhooks that are created in the system aren't allowed to go out of the local IP subnet. With this option, you can allow hooks to go out.

Geo

In this section, you can set some Geo preferences, such as the timeout after which the communication with a secondary instance is considered lost. Another setting that's available allows you to list the IPs and networks that can connect and pretend they are secondaries.

Preferences

These settings are general and are related to different subjects.

Email

In the email section, you can make emails come straight from originators, who, for instance, create issues or merge requests. The second option you can control is whether GitLab sends emails in HTML format.

Help page

You can also customize the way the **Help page** for GitLab is presented. There's the option to provide some custom text, which will be displayed on top of the **Help page**:

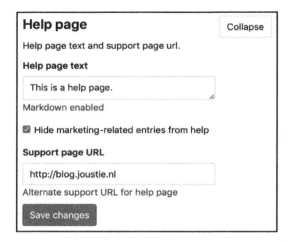

The following is a screenshot of the standard **Help page**:

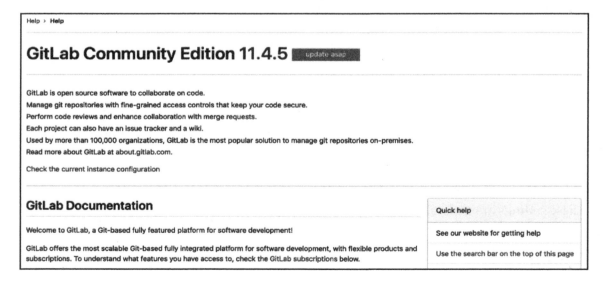

Let's make some changes by adding `This is a help page.`:

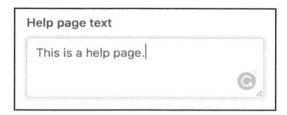

The result will be as follows:

Pages

If you use the GitLab Pages feature, you can specify the maximum size of pages. You can set it to zero if you want the size to be unlimited. You can also allow users to prove that they own a domain before you serve a page for it:

Real-time features

The GitLab web interface gives you the option to poll for real-time events, like it does when you press the **Merge** button on a merge request. You can set a multiplier for this here so that it polls less often (or more often, depending on what you want).

Gitaly

Regarding Gitaly, you can control some of its timings here. If Gitaly is being slow, you'll want it to time out for certain requests, because otherwise the operation can bring down the whole GitLab instance. Since Gitaly is the interface to the repositories, think of filesystems or nodes not responding. Very bad things can happen when locks occur or when network issues prevent data transfers. It's better to know when to cut the cord.

Localization

This is a big section of the settings since there are many localization settings for software products. The only one that is exposed in this screen is **Default first day of the week**:

This depends on your geographical location.

Configuring GitLab settings at the group level

The admin area is only accessible to users with the admin role, but other roles can configure settings too. If you, as a user, have been granted permission to *add groups*, you can change the settings of the groups you have created. If you navigate to **Your Groups** from the top-level menu, you can access the settings from the left-hand side menu.

Here, you will see a submenu with the items that you can configure. It looks a lot like the UI in the admin area but is, of course, scoped to the group:

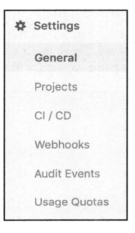

In GitLab 12.0, a new interesting feature has been added to the **General** pane for group settings: **Restrict address by IP address**. It is an Enterprise feature and, by using it, you can make sure that certain IP addresses aren't allowed to access group content. In the following screenshot, you can see that 192.168.1.0/24 is the only IP range that's allowed to see the group content:

Restrict access by IP address

192.168.1.0/24

This group, including all subgroups, projects and git repositories, will only be reachable from the specified IP address range. Example: `192.168.0.0/24` . Read more.

Large File Storage

Check the documentation.

☑ Allow projects within this group to use Git LFS
This setting can be overridden in each project.

For instance, you don't want software to be downloaded from a VPN.

Configuring GitLab settings at the project level

In the previous sections, we saw that we can adjust the settings at the instance level in the admin area, as well as at the group level. There are also options for setting an individual project. If you browse to one of your projects, you will see a **Settings** menu on the left:

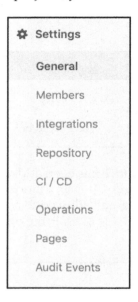

General

The **General** menu provides some specific settings that aren't found anywhere else. Let's look at the most important ones.

Naming, topics, avatar

Under the **General** settings, you can find the fields:

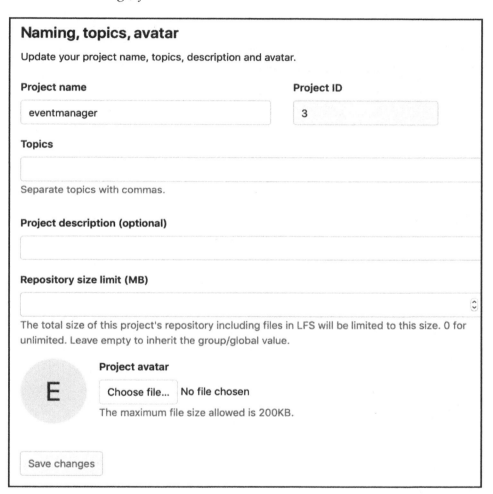

Visibility, project features, permissions

A very important part of these settings is the **Visibility, project features, permissions** sections. You can enable or disable certain features, as well as determine who is allowed to do what:

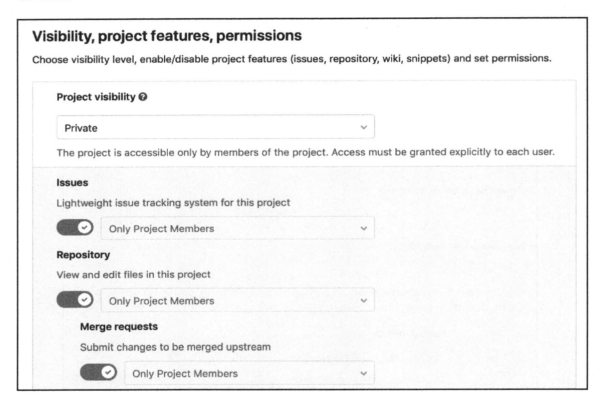

Merge requests

For an individual project, you can define merge request behavior. For example, you can define how GitLab will execute merges on the server. For every executed merge request, there is a Git session on the server running the same Git binary that you have on your workstation. For instance, you can specify that the server side never does a merge commit:

Merge requests

Collapse

Choose your merge method, options, checks, and set up a default merge request description template.

Merge method
This will dictate the commit history when you merge a merge request

● Merge commit
  Every merge creates a merge commit

○ Merge commit with semi-linear history
  Every merge creates a merge commit
  Fast-forward merges only
  When conflicts arise the user is given the option to rebase

○ Fast-forward merge
  No merge commits are created
  Fast-forward merges only
  When conflicts arise the user is given the option to rebase

Merge options
Additional merge request capabilities that influence how and when merges will be performed

☑ Merge pipelines will try to validate the post-merge result prior to merging
  Pipelines need to be configured to enable this feature. ❷

  ☑ Allow merge trains

☐ Automatically resolve merge request diff discussions when they become outdated

☑ Show link to create/view merge request when pushing from the command line

Merge checks
These checks must pass before merge requests can be merged

☐ Pipelines must succeed
  Pipelines need to be configured to enable this feature. ❷

☐ All discussions must be resolved

Default description template for merge requests ❷

Description parsed with GitLab Flavored Markdown

Save changes

In version 12.0 of GitLab, the concept of merge trains was added. If you enable this, all the merges must pass in sequence, and your merge will be a part of this train. The merges only succeed as a whole, and this use case is common in Enterprise environments where different teams work on the same product. In future versions, this feature will be enabled by default.

Summary

In this chapter, we discussed how to configure an existing GitLab application instance via the web interface. The administration pages of GitLab give you a lot of control over your instance. After going through those pages, we explained the various items that can be managed.

In the next chapter, we will take a look at configuring GitLab through a regular Terminal interface without a web browser.

Questions

1. What icon is used to represent the administration section?
2. Which three items feature prominently on the admin dashboard?
3. What is the maximum size of an uploaded logo image?
4. Which metrics backend can be configured?
5. What product is used to enable live preview functionality?
6. What UML tool can be integrated with GitLab?
7. What mechanism is used to prevent network storage from hanging GitLab?
8. What process can help preserve repository integrity?
9. Which CI/CD feature is enabled by default?
10. What value has to be set in GitLab Pages to enable unlimited size?

Further reading

- *Getting Started with Kubernetes - Third Edition,* by *Jesse White* and *Jonathan Baier*: https://www.packtpub.com/in/virtualization-and-cloud/getting-started-kubernetes-third-edition
- *Develop and Operate Microservices on Kubernetes,* by *Martin Helmich*: https://www.packtpub.com/virtualization-and-cloud/develop-and-operate-microservices-kubernetes-video
- *Docker Cookbook - Second Edition,* by *Neependra K Khare, Jeeva S. Chelladhurai,* and *Ken Cochrane*: https://www.packtpub.com/in/virtualization-and-cloud/docker-cookbook-second-edition

4
Configuring GitLab from the Terminal

After installing GitLab, you probably have a running instance. So, how do you manage it? In the previous chapter, we showed you the options that can be managed through the web interface. But there are many more options that can be set only through the configuration files on the server. You need to know how to configure the software in a regular terminal. This chapter will explain how this is achieved for the different types of GitLab installations.

The following topics will be covered in this chapter:

- Configuring omnibus installations from the terminal
- Configuring source installations
- Reconfiguring GitLab Docker containers
- Changing GitLab in a Kubernetes environment

Technical requirements

For managing omnibus installations, there is one central configuration file called `gitlab.rb`. You need to create it or copy an example. There is a template available. You can find it at `https://gitlab.com/gitlab-org/omnibus-gitlab/blob/master/files/gitlab-config-template/gitlab.rb.template`. It is not updated after upgrades. Throughout this chapter, we will quote and discuss parts of this file.

To follow along with the instructions in this chapter, please download the Git repository available at GitHub:
`https://github.com/PacktPublishing/Mastering-GitLab-12/tree/master/Chapter04`.

You will also need the following:

- **Docker**: https://www.docker.com
- **kubectl**: https://kubernetes.io/docs/tasks/tools/install-kubectl/

Configuring omnibus and GitLab installations from the terminal

You can find the template for `gitlab.rb` at https://gitlab.com/gitlab-org/omnibus-gitlab/blob/master/files/gitlab-config-template/gitlab.rb.template. It is not updated after upgrades.

You can also use omnibus or GitLab to implement **high availability (HA)** for your GitLab installation.

There is a part in `gitlab.rb` where you can define the role of the GitLab instance you are configuring. If there are no roles defined by default, omnibus will configure your server to host all the core components of GitLab.

For instance, add the following line of code if your instance will run as a Redis master, and have the Redis sentinel agent running:

```
roles ['redis_sentinel_role', 'redis_master_role']
```

The following roles are available:

- `redis_sentinel_role`: Enables the sentinel service only.
- `redis_master_role`: Enables Redis and monitoring, and allows you to configure the master password.
- `redis_slave_role`: Enables the Redis service and monitoring.
- `geo_primary_role`: Configures the database for replication and prepares the application server as `geo primary`.
- `geo_secondary_role`: Prepares the database for replication and sets the application up as `secondary geo`.
- `postgres_role`: Switches on the `postgresql`, `repmgr`, and `consul` services on the machine. Sets up only these components.
- `pgbouncer_role`: This role adds the PgBouncer software for the database load-balancing feature.

After editing, you have to issue a `gitlab-ctl reconfigure` to apply the settings.

Configuring source installations

The main configuration file to change is `gitlab.yml`, which is usually found in `/home/git/gitlab/config`. It follows the `.yml` standard and this has several implications. The first one is that indentation is very important. If you just copy and paste configuration, you will find that it can mess up the file contents. Another important feature that is used in the `gitlab.yml` file is utilizing anchors and aliases (**&base**) to specify different configuration targets. In practice, this means that the main configuration for all environments is specified in the `config` file (`production: &base`).

Below the `production: &base` target, the other environments are specified, and they refer to `&base` but override certain key-value pairs. How does GitLab know which environment information should be used? That is determined by the `RAILS_ENV` variable used when installing and starting GitLab.

We have put an example configuration file in repository of this book (`https://github.com/PacktPublishing/Mastering-GitLab-12/blob/master/Chapter04/config_gitlab.yml.example`).

The configuration file has several sections, and we'll run through them.

GitLab app settings

This section of the configuration file is mainly used to define the global settings for the whole GitLab application.

The first settings you will encounter are mainly for the web server component (Unicorn). You can specify which FQDN to use for the hostname, the port on which to listen to, and whether to use HTTPS:

```
host: localhost
 port: 80
 https: false
```

You can set the port to `443` and HTTPS to true if you want to use HTTPS. If you have a different `ssh_host` in your setup, you can specify it as well (If you want Git-SSH to run on the same server, that you don't need to specify this):

```
ssh_host: ssh.host_example.com
```

Furthermore, if you want to use relative URLs (/mygitlab/ for instance):

```
relative_url_root: /gitlab
```

You can also change the option regarding which OS-user to use for running the web server processes:

```
user: git
```

The next setting is about dates and times, and you can specify the timezone to be used throughout the entire application:

```
time_zone: 'UTC'
```

The next bundle of settings handles email. You can disable GitLab's use of email entirely or specify who the sender and the subject, among other things:

```
email_enabled: true
 email_from: example@example.com
 email_display_name: GitLab
 email_reply_to: noreply@example.com
 email_subject_suffix: ''
```

The next setting determines whether new users can create groups (be careful, as existing users retain this privilege).

```
default_can_create_group: false
```

If you want old users to be also stripped of this privilege, one way to do it is to use the Rails console:

```
irb(main):012:0> @users.each do |u|
 irb(main):013:1*   u.can_create_group= false
 irb(main):014:1> u.save
 irb(main):015:1> end
```

The next option allows you the option to change your username. This is generally not recommended if you use another system such as **Lightweight Directory Access Protocol (LDAP)** for account management:

```
username_changing_enabled: false
```

The next set of options determines the style to be used for GitLab; I suggest you try them all (1-10):

```
# default_theme: 1 # default: 1
```

A nice feature that can automate your development workflow very efficiently is the automatic closing of issues by issuing a commit to the default project branch. You can use the following pattern to make the automation work. If it matches, it will be closed. The pattern is quite complicated, so we will use the code provided:

```
issue_closing_pattern:
'\b((?:[Cc]los(?:e[sd]?|ing)|\b[Ff]ix(?:e[sd]|ing)?|\b[Rr]esolv(?:e[sd]?|in
g)|\b[Ii]mplement(?:s|ed|ing)?)(:?) +(?:(?:issues? +)?%{issue_ref}(?:(?:,
*| +and +)?)|([A-Z][A-Z0-9_]+-\d+))+)'
```

We could, for example, use the following commit message:

```
Fix #122 and Closes groupx/bestproject#1000.
Also  important for #10 and fixes #11, #229 and #188
and https://gitlab.example.com/group/mything/issues/9999.
```

In the preceding example, #122, #1000, #11, #229, #188, and #9999 will be automatically closed. Only #10 will not be touched, because it does not match the pattern.

In GitLab, in each project you have some default capabilities, such as the possibility to create issues or a wiki in the project space. There is an option to disable or enable them by default:

```
default_projects_features:
    issues: true
    merge_requests: true
    wiki: true
    snippets: true
    builds: true
    container_registry: true
```

The CI/CD component of GitLab relies heavily on webhooks as its primary eventing mechanism over network boundaries. On slow networks, you may want to increase the timeout value of them to make them try harder:

```
webhook_timeout: 10
```

You can download the contents of a project, which are combined in a ZIP file. This creation of a ZIP file needs some temporary disk space, which you can define here, the repository downloads directory (relative path to the Rails directory):

```
repository_downloads_path: shared/cache/archive/
```

GitLab can also utilize an email client, which can get mail from an IMAP server, and parse the mail contents for issues and merge request IDs. If you set this up correctly, you can allow users to reply to notification emails, and the result will be added to the issue or the merge request. The first part is where you enable or disable the function:

```
incoming_email:
  enabled: false
```

The second part is where you define the incoming email address that is used and what part of it is variable (every merge-request or issue number is a variable):

```
address: "gitlab-incoming+%{key}@gmail.com"
```

The other settings mainly concern the IMAP server that is used along with the credentials and connection settings:

```
user: "gitlab-incoming@gmail.com"
  password: "[REDACTED]"
  host: "imap.gmail.com"
  port: 993
  ssl: true
  start_tls: false
mailbox: "inbox"
  idle_timeout: 60
```

These settings together enable incoming email for your GitLab instance.

This concludes the section in the configuration file that covers some general settings. The next section is about storing different kinds of files.

Storing big files

The GitLab CI/CD components can build your software, and that results in build artifacts. They are sent back from the GitLab runners to the GitLab server. You can download them through the web UI. These artifacts are, by default, stored on the GitLab server in `shared/artifacts`. As the files can become quite large and numerous, it is also possible to store these artifacts somewhere else, where the GitLab server can fetch them when needed or redirect the request. You can set up object storage with Amazon S3, for example, to be used as a big bucket to store files.

By default GitLab it stores artifacts in the local shared path `shared/artifact` on the server where GitLab is installed:

```
artifacts:
  enabled: true
  path: shared/artifacts
```

When comparing operations during merge requests, the `diffs` files are normally saved in the database when enabled. But when set to `true`, GitLab will save them in a shared path:

```
external_diffs:
  enabled: true
  storage_path: shared/external-diffs
```

In the same manner as the build artifacts and `diffs`, GitLab can store Git **Large File Storage (LFS)** objects in a different place, out of the project repository. A reference to this place is then inserted as a substitute in the project repository. This is a Git client extension, for which the server side necessities have been implemented in GitLab. (More info about Git LFS can be found at `https://git-lfs.github.com/`.) It can be enabled and given a path:

```
lfs:
  enabled: true
  storage_path: shared/lfs-objects
```

Another possible use for object storage is to store `uploads`, such as attachments and avatars. We can enable this in GitLab to save space and use storage more efficiently:

```
uploads:
  base_dir: uploads/-/system
```

There are more options for storage than only local. You can also store things as an object somewhere else.

Using object storage

A more efficient way of storing artifacts is by utilizing object storage. It can currently be used for `artifacts`, `lfs`, `uploads`, and `external_diffs` for merge requests. The trick is to add an `object_store:` part, which can have several options:

```
object_store:
  enabled: true
  remote_directory: artifacts
```

A direct upload avoids saving the file in transit and directly uploads to AWS another chosen object storage provider:

```
direct_upload: true
```

The next setting after `remote_directory` can limit the uploading of artifacts somewhat if they are first saved in GitLab:

```
background_upload: false
```

If you set `proxy_download` to `false`, you will get redirected to object storage when downloading, instead of being sent through a proxy connection:

```
proxy_download: false
```

There are some other specific settings regarding the connection to object storage. It has to do with the provider type and specific attributes of this provider. The credentials and the region are settings that have to be defined for most providers. The AWS signature version is for creating signed URLs, and you have the option of v2 or v4. The endpoint is fixed for AWS, but it can differ according to the provider. The path style refers to the resolving of the files. If it is set to `true`, it will be like `host/bucket_name/object`, but if it is set to `false`, it will be like `bucket_name.host/object`.

All settings under the connection section will look as follows:

```
connection:
  provider: AWS
    aws_access_key_id: AWS_ACCESS_KEY_ID
    aws_secret_access_key: AWS_SECRET_ACCESS_KEY
    region: us-east-1
    aws_signature_version: 4
    endpoint: 'https://s3.amazonaws.com'
    path_style: true
```

So far, we have seen the different storage options for big files that can be part of CI jobs or repositories.

As you can see, there are many options to store different kinds of files. You can also publish certain files as web content using pages, and that is the subject of the next section.

GitLab pages

GitLab pages is an extension of CI/CD where web content can be automatically built and deployed to a web server. You can publish static websites directly from a repository. There are several options to consider. To use the feature, but also if access control should be enabled and the path where the pages are stored.

The extension uses the GitLab pages daemon, which is written in Go and serves up content from the shared location. If you run it on the same server, you ideally run it on page 80 or 443, in case you have to add an IP to the GitLab server. It is possible to run it on a separate server, but you need to export the path from the GitLab server over the network to the host, which will run the GitLab pages daemon.

> More information can be found at `https://gitlab.com/gitlab-org/gitlab-pages`.

The first settings concerning GitLab pages are to enable or disable it completely, to enable or disable `access_control`, and you can set a path to the shared pages:

```
pages:
    enabled: false
    access_control: false
    path: shared/pages
```

The following settings determine the properties of the server for GitLab pages:

```
host: example.com
port: 80
https: false
artifacts_server: true
external_http: ["1.1.1.1:80", "[2001::1]:80"]
external_https: ["1.1.1.1:443", "[2001::1]:443"]
```

The last setting defines the location of a socket for admin access:

```
admin:
    address: unix:/home/git/gitlab/tmp/sockets/private/pages-admin.socket #
TCP connections are supported too (e.g. tcp://host:port)
```

The settings for GitLab pages are complete.

Mattermost

There are many integrations for GitLab available, but one very interesting one is **Mattermost**, a Slack-like chat collaboration tool. It was acquired by GitLab in 2017, and is now even integrated in the omnibus GitLab install. You can enable the ChatOps operation with this tool. In the settings, you can enable the specific button in GitLab:

```
mattermost:
   enabled: false
   host: 'https://mattermost.example.com'
```

By enabling this, you can use the **Add** button in GitLab in the service settings.

Gravatar

The following code block defines settings for using avatars, which is by default `gravatar.com`. **Gravatar** is a **Globally Recognized Avatar**. An *avatar* is an image following you from site to site, and the Gravatar service originated from WordPress, where it was used for blogs. You can set the HTTP and HTTPS URL here:

```
gravatar:
plain_url: "http://www.gravatar.com/avatar/%{hash}?s=%{size}&d=identicon"
ssl_url: "https://secure.gravatar.com/avatar/%{hash}?s=%{size}&d=identicon"
```

Another example would be to set it to point to an Office 365 URL (you must be authenticated to Office 365 to use it):

```
gravatar: plain_url:
"http://outlook.office365.com/owa/service.svc/s/GetPersonaPhoto?email=%{ema
il}&size=HR120x120"
ssl_url:
"http://outlook.office365.com/owa/service.svc/s/GetPersonaPhoto?email=%{ema
il}&size=HR120x120"
```

 Another service that offers these services is **Libreavatar**. You can find more info about this at `https://wiki.libravatar.org/api/`.

Sidekiq

The **Sidekiq** component of GitLab takes care of background jobs, and you can find more information about it in `Chapter 1`, *Introducing the GitLab Architecture*. Most of the configuration is done in the configuration file of Sidekiq itself, but there are some options in the `gitlab.yml` file you can define.

For instance, you can only define the `log_format` here and the cron jobs that will be run in Sidekiq:

```
## Sidekiq
 sidekiq:
   log_format: default # (json is also supported)
```

In the Sidekiq background processing, there is also a job scheduler integrated, which, by default, runs a couple of jobs. The format of the schedule is just like cron on Unix systems. The most import jobs are listed as follows:

- `stuck_ci_jobs_worker`: Set stuck jobs to state failed.
- `pipeline_schedule_worker`: Execute scheduled triggers.
- `expire_build_artifacts_worker`: Remove expired build artifacts.
- `repository_check_worker`: Periodically run `git fsck` on all repositories.
- `ci_archive_traces_cron_worker`: Archive live traces that have not been archived yet.
- `admin_email_worker`: Send admin emails.
- `repository_archive_cache_worker`: Remove outdated repository archives.
- `pages_domain_verification_cron_worker`: Verify custom GitLab pages domains.
- `schedule_migrate_external_diffs_worker`: Periodically migrate `diffs` from the database to external storage.

For GitLab **Enterprise Edition** (**EE**), several extra jobs are available, mainly ones that handle Geo synchronization and LDAP sync.

GitLab Registry

GitLab can function as a fully fledged container registry for Docker containers. You can set options for it in the following section.

The first option is basically the on or off switch:

```
enabled: true
```

The next option is the hostname, which it will set:

```
host: registry.example.com
```

You can also define the network port it will listen on:

```
port: 5005
```

There is an internal address you can define that GitLab itself will connect to:

```
api_url: http://localhost:5000/
```

The GitLab registry uses a keypair, the `rootcertbundle`, here is the private key location:

```
key: config/registry.key
```

Set the path that is used for storage:

```
path: shared/registry
```

Set the name of the issuer of the certificate:

```
issuer: gitlab-issuer
```

 Further options can be found at https://docs.gitlab.com/ee/administration/container_registry.html.

GitLab CI settings

GitLab **CI** used to be a separate software component but is now firmly integrated into the GitLab backend.

There are three options to configure in the `gitlab.yml`:

- `all_broken_builds`: Only send an email if a build broke.
- `add_pusher`: Also, add the user pushing the last version of the repository to the recipient list.

- `builds_path`: The location where the build traces are stored.

```
gitlab_ci:
 all_broken_builds: true
 add_pusher: true
 builds_path: builds/
```

Further configuration of GitLab CI is done from the web interface as you have seen in the previous chapter.

Auth settings

There are several authentication providers available for GitLab. The main on-premise one is the **LDAP** interface (to Active Directory, OpenLDAP).

The first part is the enabling of the feature:

```
ldap:
    enabled: false
```

The next part is the declaration of servers:

```
servers:
  main:
    label: 'LDAP'
    host: '_your_ldap_server'
    port: 389
    uid: 'sAMAccountName'
    bind_dn: '_the_full_dn_of_the_user_you_will_bind_with'
    password: '_the_password_of_the_bind_user'
```

As you can see, we define a `label` and set up a `host` and `port`. We also give the `uid` attribute to use and a `password` and `bind_dn` (object or user used to attach to LDAP).

You can set options for SSL to enhance security:

```
encryption: 'start_tls'
 verify_certificates: true
 ssl_version: 'TLSv1_1'
```

Next up are some settings that belong to how login actions are handled and how timeouts are handled:

```
timeout: 10
 active_directory: true
 allow_username_or_email_login: false
 block_auto_created_users: false
```

GitLab needs to know where it can find users from in your LDAP tree and how to distinguish them from other objects or persons. You can set the LDAP base and a filter:

```
base: 'ou=People,dc=gitlab,dc=example' or 'DC=mydomain,DC=com'
 user_filter:
'(&(objectclass=user)(|(samaccountname=momo)(samaccountname=toto)))'
```

In the next part, you can determine which LDAP attributes you want to use in GitLab. It maps LDAP objects to GitLab objects:

```
username: ['uid', 'userid', 'sAMAccountName']
email:    ['mail', 'email', 'userPrincipalName']
name:       'cn'
first_name: 'givenName'
last_name:  'sn'
lowercase_usernames: false
```

If you have an enterprise license, you are entitled to define more than one LDAP server, which is often the case in a corporate environment. You can add a main label to a block of settings we filled in the preceding code block and create a new block with a new label:

```
label:
    host:
```

Besides LDAP, you can authenticate users with OAuth-enabled cloud providers. The first section of the settings deal with some general options, such as enabling the feature, how to handle information from those providers, and other behavioral aspects of the mechanism. The comments in the configuration file are very detailed about what the possibilities are.

The second part of the section allows you to define an OmniAuth provider. There are several examples mentioned, such as GitHub and Facebook and Auth0 (https://auth0.com/) (an identity management platform). Again, the configuration file offers a lot of explanation regarding how to configure this.

At the end of this configuration file section, there are two settings that are, in my opinion, not Auth settings, but they are important.

You can define a shared file storage path. GitLab uses shared file storage for some operations:

```
shared:
    /mnt/gitlab
```

Here, you define settings for the Gitaly service. If you run it from the source, you should mention where you ran it from:

```
gitaly:
    client_path: /home/git/gitaly/bin
    token:
```

Advanced settings

I am not sure why there is an advanced section such as this in `gitlab.yml`, but the first options deal with repository settings. The main thing here is that you specify the path to the repositories shown as follows:

```
storages:
 default:
 path: /home/git/repositories/
 gitaly_address: unix:/home/git/gitlab/tmp/sockets/private/gitaly.socket #
 gitaly_token: 'special token'
```

There is always a `default` entry, and you can specify a `path` and a `gitaly_address` here (also in the form of `tcp://`). You can override the global `gitaly_token` here.

GitLab has a backup or restore facility. It is in the form of a rake task. For example, you can invoke a backup task like this:

```
sudo -u git -H bundle exec rake gitlab:backup:create
```

The former command has options you can set via the configuration file. Once again, you can use the cloud to store files. GitLab imports cloud drivers for AWS, Google, OpenStack Swift, Rackspace, and Aliyun as well. A local driver is also available. The following is an example entry in `gitlab.yml`:

```
## Backup settings
backup:
 path: "tmp/backups"
```

The GitLab shell is the primary component to provide Git-SSH connections, and when run from the source, you have to specify the path where it is installed. There is also a path set for hooks, which can execute when an event like a git push is fired (you can create your own hooks):

```
gitlab_shell:
 path: /home/git/gitlab-shell/
 hooks_path: /home/git/gitlab-shell/hooks/
```

You also have to define the file which contains a secret. It is to be used when GitLab shell connects to the rails backend to verify access of the user that tries to do Git-SSH operations:

```
# File that contains the secret key for verifying access for gitlab-shell.
 # Default is '.gitlab_shell_secret' relative to Rails.root (i.e. root of
the GitLab app).
 secret_file: /home/git/gitlab/.gitlab_shell_secret
```

In the following code block, you see the definition of the key that is used by GitLab Workhorse to get access to the rails application.

```
workhorse:
 secret_file: /home/git/gitlab/.gitlab_workhorse_secret
```

It is defined in the file .gitlab_workhorse_secret as follows TJEf6HQcgkBjcLGVdZ4h6Y2PB89X1RGs/RsJ7FIfg6s=.

You have the option of changing to another Git version:

```
## Git settings
git:
 bin_path: /usr/bin/git
```

The webpack program is used to compile and serve frontend assets such as **Cascading Style Sheets (CSS)**, only to be used in development:

```
## Webpack settings
webpack:
 dev_server:
 enabled: true
 host: localhost
 port: 3001
```

The Prometheus endpoint that is built in also gathers data about Unicorn performance. It will sample the Unicorn Unix socket for that. Here, you can define the sampling rate. You can also define a whitelist for IPs allow to connect to the metrics endpoint:

```
# Built in monitoring settings
monitoring:
 unicorn_sampler_interval: 10
 ip_whitelist:
  - 127.0.0.0/8
```

Another built-in metrics provider, a `sidekiq` Prometheus exporter, is controlled from here:

```
sidekiq_exporter:
 enabled: true
 address: localhost
 port: 3808
```

As you can see, the topics that are handled in this section are quite different, and I am not sure whether they should reside under advanced settings. There is also a final section in the `gitlab.yml` file called **extra customization**. The most important part here is `rack_attack`.

Rack Attack

An import part of internet security nowadays are built-in throttling mechanisms to counter denial-of-service attacks. GitLab uses the Rack Attack Gem that can keep an eye on the number of requests coming from individual IPs. You can disable it here and set a whitelist and some thresholds:

```
rack_attack:
   git_basic_auth:
    enabled: true
     ip_whitelist: ["127.0.0.1"]
```

You can limit the number of Git HTTP authentication attempts:

```
maxretry: 10
```

After 60 seconds, the auth attempt counter will be reset:

```
findtime: 60
```

You can also ban an IP for one hour (3,600 seconds); for example, after too many auth attempts:

```
bantime: 3600
```

We have reached the end of the `gitlab.yml` file. After restarting GitLab, the changes will become active. There are other ways of running GitLab. In the next section, we will take a look at configuring an instance in a Docker container.

Reconfiguring GitLab Docker containers

The official containers from GitLab use the `omnibus-gitlab` package, so all the configuration is managed through the unique configuration file, `/etc/gitlab/gitlab.rb`.

Once the container is started, you can connect to it by starting a Bash session:

```
docker exec -it gitlab /bin/bash
```

You can now edit `/etc/gitlab/gitlab.rb` inside the Docker container. Then you can run `gitlab-ctl reconfigure` after that to apply the changes.

A second way to configure the container is to start it up with a environment variable, `GITLAB_OMNIBUS_CONFIG`. This variable can contain the contents of a `gitlab.rb` file. These settings will not be persisted to the real file.

You could use the following code:

```
sudo docker run  \
  --hostname gitlab.joustie.nl \
  --env GITLAB_OMNIBUS_CONFIG="external_url 'http://gitlab.joustie.nl/';
gitlab_rails['lfs_enabled'] = true;" \
  --publish 443:444 --publish 80:81 --publish 22:2222 \
  --volume /srv/gitlab/config:/etc/gitlab \
  --volume /srv/gitlab/logs:/var/log/gitlab \
  --volume /srv/gitlab/data:/var/opt/gitlab \
  gitlab/gitlab-ce:latest
```

The container start-up process will always run `gitlab-ctl reconfigure`. This means the omnibus template settings you specify during container startup need to be explicitly set every time you spin up the container; otherwise, your container will reconfigure and you will lose the settings.

Changing GitLab in a Kubernetes environment

Since GitLab for Kubernetes is configured by Helm charts, you need to configure all settings through that.

The options can be found here: `https://gitlab.com/charts/gitlab/blob/master/doc/installation/command-line-options.md`.

For each set of options, some are required, and those that are not required have a default value.

In the next section, we will pick some of the options to change in a Kubernetes environment.

Basic configuration

There are two required settings here: `global.hosts.domain` and `global.hosts.externalIP`. These should point to the host and IP where GitLab is to be served from. Another interesting set of these are as follows:

- `global.psql.host`
- `global.psql.password.secret`
- `global.psql.password.key`

These contain information that point to an external Postgres instance.

Other options can be found in the command-line options URL at `https://gitlab.com/charts/gitlab/blob/master/doc/installation/command-line-options.md`.

Configuring TLS

These options control the TLS configuration that is activated for GitLab. There are no required options, but if you don't want to use Let's Encrypt, set `global.ingress.configureCertmanager` to false.

Configuring outgoing emails

For outgoing email, there are several options such as the host of the incoming mail server—for example:

```
global.smtp.address (e.g. smtp.joustie.nl) with
global.smtp.authentication="" (disable smtp authentication)
```

To set this configuration setting and enable it, you use the following command line:

```
helm upgrade   gitlab gitlab/gitlab \
    --timeout 600 \
    --set global.hosts.domain=kicks-ass.net \
    --set global.hosts.externalIP=82.161.132.207 \
    --set certmanager-issuer.email=joustie@gmail.com \
    --set global.smtp.enabled=true \
    --set global.smtp.address=smtp.joustie.nl \
    --set global.smtp.authentication=""
```

If your SMTP server requires authentication, you need to add the credentials as an –set option and deploy the password also as a secret with the following:

```
kubectl create secret generic smtp-password --from-
literal=password=yourpasswordhere
```

After you have issued the `helm upgrade` command, the `unicorn` and `sidekiq` components will automatically restart in the Kubernetes cluster.

Other settings

Many other settings are available, and you can view them at https://gitlab.com/charts/gitlab/blob/master/doc/installation/command-line-options.md.

Here are some examples:

- **Incoming Email configuration**: GitLab can also handle incoming mail for the service desk feature.
- **GitLab shell**: You can provide settings for the GitLab shell.
- **RBAC settings**: You can describe Kubernetes **Role Based Access Control (RBAC)**.

- **Advanced nginx ingress configuration**: Change the default ingress nginx settings for the cluster.
- **Advanced in-cluster Redis configuration**: Change the settings for the Redis cluster.
- **Advanced registry configuration**: Change the settings for the Docker registry that is running as a microservice.
- **Advanced MinIO configuration**: Change the settings for the MinIO object storage microservice.
- **Advanced GitLab configuration**: Change the advanced settings in GitLab.

Summary

In this chapter, we discussed configuring an existing GitLab application instance. As we have seen in earlier chapters, the options are different, depending on the installation path you have chosen. An omnibus GitLab installation is relatively easy to configure. Just change the setting in `/etc/gitlab/gitlab.rb` and run `gitlab-ctl reconfigure`. Changing the settings in an installation from source requires a bit more attention, because the dependencies between the GitLab components aren't managed as they are with omnibus GitLab. Configuring the GitLab instance running inside the Docker containers is the same as the way you manage the omnibus GitLab installations.

In the next chapter, we will be exploring settings that should be altered in your GitHub and in GitLab to understand the procedure of importing and running the project.

Questions

1. What services are enabled when the `postgres_role` is chosen in `gitlab.rb`?
2. Where is `gitlab.yml` usually found?
3. What protocol is used for the incoming mail feature?
4. What does LFS stand for?
5. Which Open Source chat tool is tightly integrated with GitLab?
6. What license is needed to support LDAP groups?
7. What mechanism does GitLab provide to throttle web requests?
8. What tool do you need, besides Helm, to configure Kubernetes?

Further reading

- *Getting Started with Kubernetes - Third Edition* by *Jesse White* and *Jonathan Baier*: https://www.packtpub.com/virtualization-and-cloud/getting-started-kubernetes-third-edition
- *Develop and Operate Microservices on Kubernetes [Video]* by *Martin Helmich*: https://www.packtpub.com/virtualization-and-cloud/develop-and-operate-microservices-kubernetes-video
- *Docker Cookbook - Second Edition* by *Jeeva S. Chelladhurai, Ken Cochrane, Neependra Khare*: https://www.packtpub.com/virtualization-and-cloud/docker-cookbook-second-edition

Section 2: Migrating Data from Different Locations

2

Depending on which platform the reader currently uses, the path to a successful migration to GitLab is explained and demonstrated.

This section comprises the following chapters:

5
Importing Your Project from GitHub to GitLab

In the first section, we explained the GitLab architecture and how to install and configure GitLab in several ways. In this part of the book, we will look at several ways of migrating source projects from third parties to GitLab. We will start with GitHub, which resembles GitLab a lot and which was the inspiration to develop it. After years of development, the two products still share the same basic functionality, but have diverged in additional features. There are several ways you can import projects from GitHub.

In this chapter, the following points will be covered:

- Using the GitHub integration feature in GitLab (also known as the GitHub importer)
- Using a GitHub token—create this in GitHub for third party application integration
- Using a GitLab rake task—you need access to a GitLab instance that can run rake tasks, and when you possess administrator rights

For each method, we will present what you have to configure and prepare in GitHub and GitLab. Finally, we will run the import for each method.

Technical requirements

In order to manage omnibus installs, you need to use a central configuration file called `gitlab.rb`. You need to create it or copy an example of one. Fortunately, a template is available, which you can find at `https://gitlab.com/gitlab-org/omnibus-gitlab/blob/master/files/gitlab-config-template/gitlab.rb.template`. It isn't updated after upgrades. Later on in this chapter, I will quote and discuss parts of this file.

To follow along with the instructions in this chapter, please download the GitHub repository, along with the examples available on the GitHub repository, at `https://github.com/PacktPublishing/Mastering-GitLab-12/tree/master/Chapter05`.

You will also need a GitHub account, as well as a GitLab account in the cloud or on premise.

In regards to user matching, you want to make sure that the GitHub users associated with the repository have the following:

- A GitLab account that uses OAuth-based login using the GitHub icon
- A GitLab account with an email address that is identical to their public email address in GitHub

Using the GitHub integration feature

To export things from GitHub, the proper authorizations must be set. This can be done using GitHub integration with OAuth registration, where GitLab authenticates with GitHub to access a list of projects for the user.

The best result of mapping authors and assignees from GitHub to GitLab is achieved when using the GitHub integration features that are available in GitLab instead of using a single personal access token from GitHub.

The integration covers all the import items we just mentioned and tries to keep all the references intact. For instance, the importer will try to find the GitHub authors and assignees of issues and pull requests. This means that GitLab integration has to be enabled in your GitLab instance.

Preparing GitHub for export

To register GitLab as an application that can connect to GitHub, you have to log in to your GitHub account. To do this, go to `https://github.com/settings/developers` and register GitLab as an OAuth application:

Fill in the form using the following data:

- Application name (the name of your application)
- Homepage URL (the full URL to your application)
- Application description (general description)

- Authorization callback URL (the most important setting, the URL to send to after authentication):

After the registration has succeeded, an overview is presented with two very important pieces of information: the client ID and client secret are shown, and also how many users have used the OAuth link to connect GitHub repositories. The client ID and client secret are needed later to configure GitLab for integration.

The following screen appears after a successful registration:

You now have GitHub configured and can move on to the *Preparing GitLab for import* section.

Preparing GitLab for import

To finish the setup for the GitHub integration, we have to set up our GitLab instance so that we can connect as a registered OAuth application to GitHub. We do this by adding an `omniauth_provider` to the GitLab configuration. Remember the client ID and the client secret? We will need these here.

For GitLab omnibus installations, we need to create a section in `/etc/gitlab/gitlab.rb` like the following one. `app_id` is the client ID, while `app_secret` is the client secret. The name that is provided isn't important. After the file has been saved, you have to use `gitlab-ctl reconfigure`:

```
gitlab_rails['omniauth_providers'] = [
    {
      "name" => "github",
      "app_id" => "dd1c6d6aed110b2cce8e",
      "app_secret" => "f6ddd6059c694ecfc1a96f962fa20b6c3f7c8c4a",
      "args" => { "scope" => "user:email" }
    }
  ]
```

For GitHub Enterprise, you can specify the URL of your GitHub instance as well:

```
"url" => "https://github.example.com/",
```

For GitLab installations from source, we edit the `config.yml` file, as follows. and restart GitLab after saving it:

```
- { name: 'github',
      app_id: 'dd1c6d6aed110b2cce8e',
      app_secret: 'f6ddd6059c694ecfc1a96f962fa20b6c3f7c8c4a',
      url: "https://github.com/",
      verify_ssl: true,
      args: { scope: 'user:email' } }
```

See `https://github.com/gitlabhq/omnibus-gitlab/blob/master/files/gitlab-config-template/gitlab.rb.template` for more information on settings you can set in the `gitlab.rb` file. Also see `Chapter 2`, *Installing GitLab* about this subject.

Running the import

Follow these steps to learn how to run the import:

1. In GitLab, choose to create a new project and use the **Import project** tab to find the **GitHub** icon:

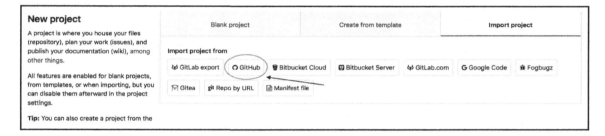

2. After clicking on the **GitHub** icon, you will find a page where you can click **List your GitHub repositories**:

3. When GitHub integration is enabled, the next step will be to authorize GitLab to access your projects:

4. If authorization succeeds, a list of projects that can be migrated is shown. Select the projects to be migrated, and click **Import**:

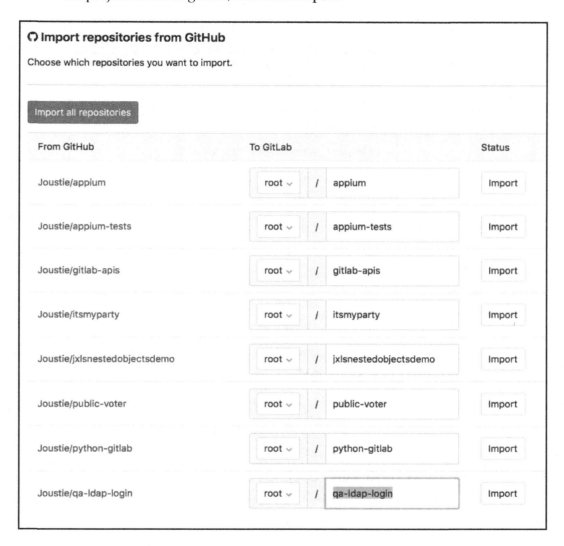

Make sure that you don't have projects with the same name already in GitLab in your namespace, otherwise you will receive a 422 error, as shown in the following screenshot:

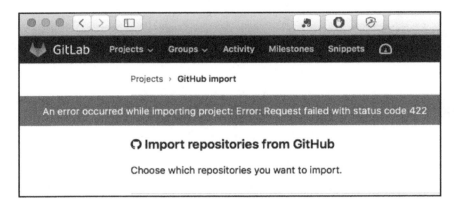

When the import is finished, you will receive a message:

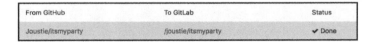

The project has been successfully imported!

Using a GitHub token

When using a GitHub token to import, there's nothing special to configure in GitLab – you can enter it immediately, as you will see later.

Preparing GitHub for export

A personal token can be used as delegated authorization from your GitHub account. Let's get started:

1. You create one via `https://github.com/settings/tokens`:

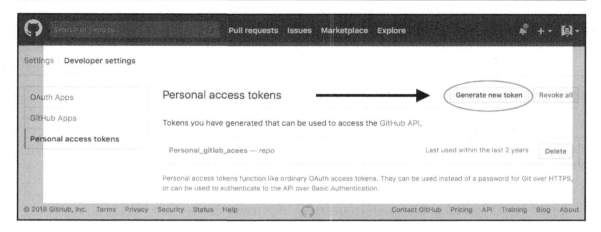

2. Make sure you set a meaningful token description and choose the **repo** scope only. We want the GitLab importer to access these objects:

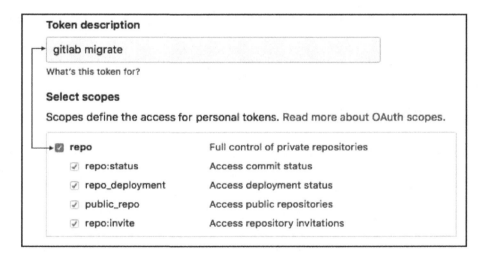

3. Once the token has been created, make sure to record the token somewhere because it won't be shown again, and losing it means that you have to recreate it:

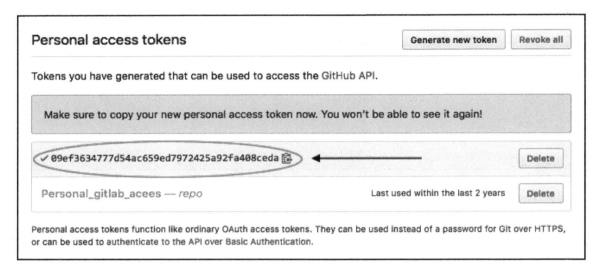

You now have a GitHub token and can choose to use it directly in the GitLab web interface.

Running the import

Let's get started and learn how to prepare GitLab for import:

1. In GitLab, create a new project and use the import tab to find the **GitHub** icon, as shown in the following screenshot:

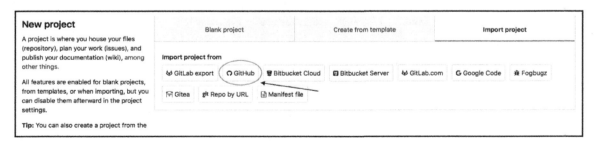

2. If GitHub integration is disabled, the next screen won't have an option for you to list your GitHub repositories. To choose a project to migrate, you have to enter the personal token you created on `https://github.com/`:

3. Again, if authorization succeeds, a list of projects that can be migrated is shown. Select the projects to be migrated and click **Import**:

4. When the import is finished, you will receive a message:

From GitHub	To GitLab	Status
Joustie/itsmyparty	/joustie/itsmyparty	✔ Done

The project has successfully been imported using the token.

Using a GitLab rake task

In order to retrieve and import GitHub repositories, you will need a GitHub personal access token, as demonstrated earlier.

Preparing GitLab for import

For importing projects using a rake task, there is only one option to configure in GitLab beforehand: the number of Sidekiq resources. You will notice that for big projects, it can take quite some time to import all the data. To speed up this process, assign more Sidekiq workers to the following queues:

- `github_importer`
- `github_importer_advance_stage`

For GitLab omnibus installations, these queues are part of the default Sidekiq process. Giving more threads to Sidekiq will mean that there will be more workers:

```
# sidekiq['concurrency'] = 25
```

 See `https://github.com/gitlabhq/omnibus-gitlab/blob/master/files/gitlab-config-template/gitlab.rb.template` for more information on settings you can set in the `gitlab.rb` file. Also, see `Chapter 2`, *Installing GitLab* about this subject.

Running the import

The GitLab rake task can import a single project or multiple projects at once. It is invoked from the command line, so you need administrator access to the machine where the GitLab application is running.

When specifying a GitHub repository as the fourth argument to the rake task, you can directly import it.

To import a specific GitHub project (named `joustie/github_repo` here), do the following:

- **Omnibus installations**:

```
sudo gitlab-rake "import:github[<personal_access_token>,<gitlab
user>,<namespace/project>,<source_namespace/github_repo>]"
```

- **Installations from source**:

```
bundle exec rake "import:github[<personal_access_token>,<gitlab
user>,<namespace/project>,<source_namespace/github_repo>]"
RAILS_ENV=production
```

To import a project from the list of your available GitHub projects, do the following:

- **Omnibus installations**:

```
sudo gitlab-rake "import:github[<personal_access_token>,<gitlab
user>,<namespace/project>]"
```

- **Installations from source**:

```
bundle exec rake "import:github[<personal_access_token>,<gitlab
user>,<namespace/project>]" RAILS_ENV=production
```

It is also possible to specify subgroups such as `<groupname/groupname/project>`.

For my example project, you will see the following results:

```
[root@gitlab:/# gitlab-rake "import:github[09ef3634777d54ac659ed7972425a92fa408ceda,root,root/itsmyparty]"
ID: 48487555    Name: Joustie/appium
ID: 55003607    Name: Joustie/appium-tests
ID: 93713892    Name: Joustie/gitlab-apis
ID: 158928269   Name: Joustie/itsmyparty
ID: 71631927    Name: Joustie/jxlsnestedobjectsdemo
ID: 88996033    Name: Joustie/public-voter
ID: 140297528   Name: Joustie/python-gitlab
ID: 9371605     Name: Joustie/qa-ldap-login
ID? 
```

The GitHub importer obtained a list of projects with your GitHub personal access token. When you want to specify one particular project, use the ID:

```
ID? 158928269
This will import GitHub Joustie/itsmyparty into GitLab root/itsmyparty as Administrat
Permission checks are ignored. Press any key to continue.
```

The importer will ask for confirmation after that:

```
Starting the import (this could take a while)
Import finished. Timings:   0.450000   0.060000   0.510000 (  9.831726)
```

The rake tasks will run synchronously and perform the import. After the import operation, a summary of the timings is given:

When you log in to your GitLab instance, you will find the imported project.

Summary

We started this chapter by explaining what items can be migrated from GitHub to GitLab, and what the possibilities are. There are three options regarding migrating your data, and which ones you can use depend on how your GitLab instance is configured. The recommended way is to use the GitHub importer. This mechanism presents the most user-friendly and complete migration path.

GitHub and GitLab are very comparable, but in the next chapter, we will take a look at CVS and how it compares to Git as a versioning tool, and how to migrate it.

Questions

1. What is the equivalent of a pull request in GitLab?
2. Which ways exist to import GitHub projects into GitLab?
3. What is needed to display the authors correctly?
4. Which authentication mechanism is used to connect to GitHub?
5. What is the secret called that's needed to connect to GitHub?
6. What scope do you need for a token to import as much as possible from GitHub?
7. What is the name of the two queues that process the import?
8. Where can you find the import button for GitHub in GitLab?
9. What is the name of the rake task to import from GitHub?
10. Is it possible to import one particular project only?

Further reading

- *GitHub Essentials – Second Edition*, by *Achilleas Pipinellis*: https://www.packtpub.com/web-development/github-essentials-second-edition

6
Migrating from CVS

For a long time, the **Concurrent Versions System** (**CVS**) was the standard in versioning software. It is, in essence, a client-server revision control system for software. CVS was written in 1986 by Dick Grune of the University of Amsterdam as a collection of shell scripts called **RCS**. RCS can only do version management on separate files, so this was a big step forward. In 1989, Brian Berliner made an implementation in C, which has been developed further since; it is a piece of open source software that's distributed under the GNU **General Public License** (**GPL**).

In the 2000s, there was a shift to subversion and to decentralized version control software such as Git.

In this chapter, we will compare both versioning systems. After that, we will prepare and run a migration from CVS to Git.

The following topics will be covered in this chapter:

- CVS versus Git
- Preparation for migrating from CVS to Git
- Running the conversion
- Cleaning up after migration

Technical requirements

To follow along with the instructions in this chapter, please download this book's GitHub repository, along with the examples: `https://github.com/PacktPublishing/Mastering-GitLab-12/tree/master/Chapter06`.

The other requirements so that you can follow along with this chapter are as follows:

- CVS binary: `http://www.nongnu.org/cvs/`
- npm/Node.js binaries to create a JavaScript example: `https://nodejs.org`
- `cvs-fast-export` binary: `http://www.catb.org/~esr/cvs-fast-export`
- `cvs2git` binary: `https://www.mcs.anl.gov/~jacob/cvs2svn/cvs2git.html`

CVS versus Git

Centralization versus decentralization – this is the biggest difference between CVS, which is centralized, and Git's distributed design. With CVS, all developers pull from a centralized repository, thereby creating a single point of failure. Git uses a decentralized model, where every developer has a full-blown code repository locally available. By using push and pull requests, the decentralized repositories share code.

The following diagram depicts using push and pull on shared and distributed repositories:

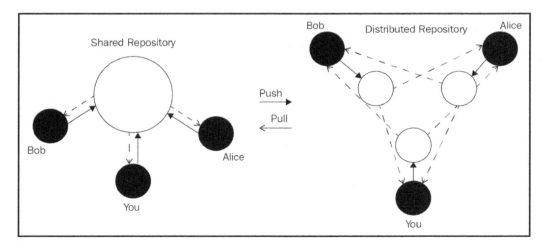

With Git, there are different options in regards to the network protocol and system settings. In particular, you have the decision to communicate with remote services over SSH or HTTP. By utilizing SSH, you can generate your SSH keys and set them up for use with Git. After this, you can use Git to clone/push or pull from SSH locations. You can also use Git to use HTTP as a protocol, which generally requires basic HTTP authentication, after which the Git operations can occur. Some Git clients have built-in caching mechanisms to help you avoid typing in your HTTP password every time.

Publishing your work in this context is done by committing your changes to the central repository. CVS uses a specific protocol, called pserver, which is unencrypted and in plain text by default. Another option is to use the **remote shell** (**rsh**) on the remote server. To enhance security, you can also tunnel the pserver protocol through SSH or use SSH as the rsh executable.

The authorization model that's used in CVS systems is very simple. If you want to write something, you need to commit access to a repository. There is no facility to accept patches from people who are not authorized. The merge requests with all the facilities that modern Git servers provide have to be executed by the committer themselves. So, from a development engineering perspective, Git offers more complex workflows and is tailored for a world where many people contribute to a software project.

Besides the infrastructural difference, there are also several differences between your local CVS/Git client.

Filesets versus changesets

CVS and Git have a different way of representing changes on a meta level. CVS uses filesets, so changes are recorded per file. Git, on the other hand, uses changesets, so changes are recorded against the *whole* repository. The advantage of this is that you can revert a change easily; however, this means that it is almost impossible to do a partial checkout (if you want to do this).

Git branching

When using Git, it is very easy and cheap to create new branches – they're just pointers (a SHA-1 ID) to a specific commit. You create them on the fly, and that is how it should be, especially in agile development and with many collaborating developers.

The following diagram illustrates how Git uses branching:

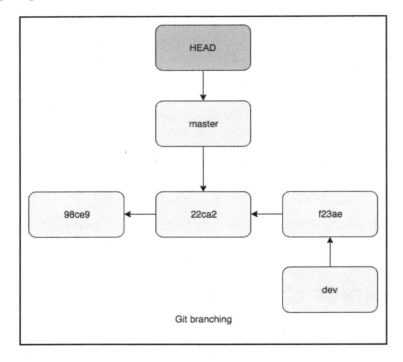

Notice the hash values shown in the preceding objects (98ce9, 22ca2, and f23ae) – these are the SHA values that uniquely identify a commit.

CVS also uses branches, but because it is file-based, a new branch gets you a copy of all the files in a new directory, which is much less efficient. This situation is depicted in the following diagram:

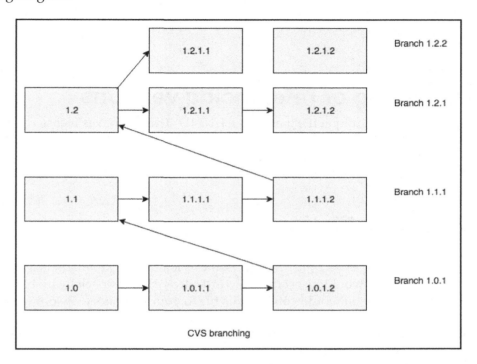

The way branches and file structures are handled is one of the most fundamental differences between these two systems.

Creating repositories

When using CVS to create repositories, you have to set up a CVSROOT location where versioning data is stored. Then, you have to import projects into that location and create a working copy somewhere else. This is much easier and more logical with Git since you just implement `git init && git add . && git commit` in an existing directory only once a `.git` directory is created with repository meta information.

Atomic operations

The basic idea of CVS is that it operates on files and not on snapshots. This means that when changes are processed and the operation is interrupted, the repository as a whole is inconsistent. This differs to Git, where changes succeed as a whole, or they fail without the changes combined.

Object naming or referencing versions

In Git, every object has a unique ID, that is, a SHA-1 ID. This ID makes it easier to reference in the future (you can also use a shortened version if you so desire). In CVS, every file has its own version number. This number also reflects how many times it's been altered. In CVS, to reference changes to the project as a whole, you need to use tags.

Keyword substitution

CVS supports the substitution of certain keywords in source code. For example, `$Author$`, `$CVSHeader$`, and `$Id$`. Developers have used this feature frequently (some still do). To use this mechanism, you would insert the keyword – let's call it a special variable – in your text or source file. Then, you would commit this file to your repository. By doing this, CVS will substitute this variable with the value in the CVS context during the commit. A lot of people use the `$Id$` string in their C source code. You can turn off this behavior completely in CVS by specifying `-ko` on the command line.

As an example, let's say I add a keyword to a source file, as follows:

```
{
  "name": "cvsproject",
  "version": "1.0.0",
  "description": "something",
  "main": "index.js",
  "scripts": {
  "test": "echo \"Error: no test specified\" && exit 1"
  },
  "keywords": [],
  "author": "$Author$",
  "license": "ISC"
  }
```

Then, I would commit this change:

```
$ cvs commit -m "Added author keyword"
 cvs commit: Examining .
 cvs commit: Examining images
 /Users/joostevertse/cvsroot/cvsproject/cvsproject/package.json,v <--
 package.json
 new revision: 1.3; previous revision: 1.2
```

After the commit, the keyword has been substituted by my username:

```
"author": "$Author: joostevertse $",
```

Git has a very limited set of keywords, and this is because changes are per repository and not per file. Also, Git avoids modifying files that didn't change when switching to another branch or rewinding to another point in time.

Binary blobs

Git and CVS handle binary files differently. In CVS, it is harder to handle them since you have to explicitly label them as binary. If you don't, you run the risk of corrupting the file with unwanted LR/LF conversions or keyword substitutions. Git, on the other hand, can automatically detect whether your file is of the binary kind. It uses the same mechanism as GNU Diffutils.

Let's create a simple binary from source and add a reserved keyword. Then, we will compile it with GCC and run it:

```
$ cat hello.c
 #include <stdio.h>
 int main()
 {
    // printf() displays the string inside quotation
    printf("Hello, World!$Author$");
    return 0;
 }

$ gcc hello.c -o hello

$ ./hello
 Hello, World!$Author$
```

So, let's copy the binary to the CVS project that we used previously:

```
$ cp hello /Users/joostevertse/cvs/cvsproject/cvsproject/
$ cd $HOME/cvs/cvsproject/cvsproject

$ cvs add hello
 cvs add: scheduling file `hello' for addition
 cvs add: use `cvs commit' to add this file permanently

$ cvs commit -m "binary with keywords inside"
 cvs commit: Examining .
 cvs commit: Examining images
 /Users/joostevertse/cvsroot/cvsproject/cvsproject/hello,v <-- hello
 initial revision: 1.1

$ ./hello
 Segmentation fault: 11
```

What happened? Well, keyword substitution added the author name in the binary! It corrupted it. If you run the `cat` command, you will find the following line in the file:

```
1jE???H??]??%?L??AS?%q?h?????Hello, World!$Author: joostevertse $P44{4
```

Fortunately, you can fix this with `cvs admin`:

```
$ cvs admin -kb hello
$ cvs update -A hello
$ cvs commit -m "make it binary" hello
$ ./hello
Hello, World!$Author$
```

Amending commits

One frequently used feature of Git is the ability to amend to a commit. This is possible because, in Git, there is a difference between creating and publishing a commit. This won't inconvenience users compared to CVS, where it would. If you make a typo in your commit message in Git, you can use `git commit --amend` to correct it. It's also technically possible in CVS, but it would be hard to implement:

```
$ echo "This is the last line FOR REAL" >> README.md
$ git log
commit 499beb6dd81ee62e90b05ee8e9aa3ccced7a4fd2 (HEAD -> new-readme)
Author: Joost Evertse <joustie@gmail.com>
Date:   Thu Dec 6 21:18:32 2018 +0100

    A new line was added
```

Let's pretend I forgot to add something to my README.md file (a text file in my repository). The following code shows you how to add it to the last commit:

```
$ echo "This is the last line FOR REAL" >> README.md
$ git add README.md
$ git commit -m "A new line was added FOR REAL" --amend
$ git log
commit 9c527dfe0ac2ce04b6cd1be6085bac00c7f31e6c (HEAD -> new-readme)
Author: Joost Evertse <joustie@gmail.com>
Date:    Thu Dec 6 21:18:32 2018 +0100

    A new line was added FOR REAL
```

By doing this, you can add to a commit, but this is only reflected in your local Git copy. You still have to push your changes to remote servers if you want others to see your changes.

A central repository

CVS as a centralized system has one place of origin. Git is a distributed versioning system, which means that each developer has its own copy of the repository. They have a private one and they can push changes to a public one or merge changes from other remotes. In larger organizations, it is common to have a central place to aggregate projects. With Git, there is no need to have a single central place where you store your changes. Each developer can have their own repository (or better repositories, that is, a private one in which they undertake development, and a public bare one where they publish parts that are ready), and they can pull/fetch from other repositories in a symmetric fashion.

In the Git world, there is no single source of truth like there is in the CVS server. There can be several truths, and because it is so easy to integrate changes from others, this works.

Accompanying toolset

Git provides a lot of tools that you can work with (Git bisect for one), which makes for a more productive way of working.

Detecting file renames

The ability to rename a file is not supported in CVS, and being able to restore the state of the project when renames have happened is hard. Git uses heuristic rename detection so that it can analyze whether the content or filename are similar. You can also configure this detection in order to copy files.

Commit before merge

A side effect of Git, when using a local repository, is that it changes the way commits are handled in the system. With CVS, you will need to handle conflicts first (if someone else changed something before you pull to update your working directory and resolve issues). Having done this, you can commit your changes to the CVS repository. This is called **merge-before-commit**. Git works entirely differently, since commits are always done in the local repository. This commit-before-merge strategy means that you merge changes after the commit, and it is also possible to ask the other developer to merge and resolve issues. It can get harder to distinguish changes between commits if there are many merges, but to retain a nice linear history, it is also possible to mimic CVS behavior by using the Git *rebase* mechanism (`git pull --rebase`) in which you apply changes on top of the updated state.

The last big difference is in the way people collaborate with each other. Some developers only need a read-only copy of the original software, but they need anonymous read-only access to the source code. Both CVS and Git can accommodate this. Things become different if people want to contribute something back to the project. With CVS, one way of doing this (like with the Linux kernel) is by sending patches via email. This is done by people who change a small amount of code. With Git, it is actually very easy to execute your changes on top of an existing upstream version and then generate an email with `git format-patch`. With bigger contributions, the functionality and ease of a pull request become important, and this was what Git was designed for. All of this happened because of the snapshot paradigm.

Preparing to migrate from CVS to Git

In the next section, we will look at two tools that can help us migrate repositories.

Preparing for a conversion using cvs-fast-export

This migration tool was created by Eric S. Raymond, a very well-known writer/developer who wrote the famous essay *The Cathedral and the Bazaar* about open source software. He is also the author of fetchmail (an early open source POP3-client). Let's get started.

For this tool, `cvs-fast-export`, I will create a CVS project from scratch that we will convert. Let's get started:

1. Create a CVS root. This is where the CVS database will reside:

   ```
   $ cvs -d ~/cvsroot init
   ```

2. Add some variables for CVS to your environment:

   ```
   $ echo "export CVSROOT=~/cvsroot; export CVSEDITOR=vim" >>
   ~/.bash_profile
   $ source ~/.bash_profile
   ```

3. As an example, we will create an empty JavaScript project and add it to CVS. First, create a project:

   ```
   $ mkdir ~/cvs
   $ cd cvs
   $ mkdir cvsproject
   $ cd cvsproject/
   imac:cvsproject joostevertse$ npm init --yes
   ```

4. Now, let's add the project to CVS:

   ```
   $ cd ..
   $ cvs import -m "Example javascript project" cvsproject Joost
   start
   cvs import: Importing
   /Users/joostevertse/cvsroot/cvsproject/cvsproject
   N cvsproject/cvsproject/package.json

   No conflicts created by this import
   ```

5. Now, the project is present in CVSROOT:

   ```
   $ ls ~/cvsroot
   CVSROOT       cvsproject
   ```

6. Now, we need to completely erase `~/cvs/cvsproject` because we're going to check it out as a CVS working directory:

```
$ rm -rf cvsproject/
```

7. The next step is checking out the project in CVS, which will create a CVS working copy:

```
$ cvs checkout cvsproject
cvs checkout: Updating cvsproject
cvs checkout: Updating cvsproject/cvsproject
U cvsproject/cvsproject/package.json
```

8. Looking into the directory reveals a CVS directory structure:

```
$ tree
.
├── CVS
│   ├── Entries
│   ├── Repository
│   └── Root
└── cvsproject
    ├── CVS
    │   ├── Entries
    │   ├── Repository
    │   └── Root
    └── package.json

3 directories, 7 files
```

9. Let's create an image directory and add it to the repository:

```
$ mkdir images
$ cvs add images
Directory /Users/joostevertse/cvsroot/cvsproject/cvsproject/images
added to the repository
```

10. With the `cvs status` command, we can check which files have changed:

```
$ cvs status
cvs status: Examining .
===============================================================
File: package.json      Status: Locally Modified

    Working revision:    1.1.1.1 2018-12-04 23:01:21 +0100
    Repository revision: 1.1.1.1
/Users/joostevertse/cvsroot/cvsproject/cvsproject/package.json,v
    Commit Identifier:    xmczkBNhTpkbWw2B
```

```
Sticky Tag:      (none)
Sticky Date:     (none)
Sticky Options: (none)

cvs status: Examining images
```

11. Let's commit these changes into our CVS repository:

```
$
ls
cvs commit: Examining .
cvs commit: Examining images
/Users/joostevertse/cvsroot/cvsproject/cvsproject/package.json,v
<-- package.json
new revision: 1.2; previous revision: 1.1
```

12. With the `cvs log` command, we can see what has changed in more detail:

```
$ cvs log
cvs log: Logging .

RCS file:
/Users/joostevertse/cvsroot/cvsproject/cvsproject/package.json,v
Working file: package.json
head: 1.2
branch:
locks: strict
access list:
symbolic names:
start: 1.1.1.1
Joost: 1.1.1
keyword substitution: kv
total revisions: 3; selected revisions: 3
...
```

Now, we have a CVS repository that's been prepared for migration with `cvs-fast-export`.

Preparing for a conversion using cvs2git

Now, let's take a look the second tool, `cvs2git`. For this conversion, I took a copy of a project I have used before (**itsmyparty**: https://github.com/Joustie/itsmyparty), like so:

```
$ git clone git@gitlab.com:joustie/itsmyparty_gitlab.git
Cloning into 'itsmyparty_gitlab'...
imac:git joostevertse$ cd itsmyparty_gitlab
```

```
imac:itsmyparty_gitlab joostevertse$ tree
.
├──── attendees.rb
├──── attendees.yml
├──── atttendees.yml
├──── itsmyparty.rb
....
1 directory, 12 files
```

Then, I imported the source code into a CVS repository (I deleted the `.git` directory first):

```
$ cvs import -m "dir structure" cvsexample joost start
N cvsexample/machines.yml
N cvsexample/itsmyparty.rb
N cvsexample/presence.yml
N cvsexample/atttendees.yml
.....
No conflicts created by this import
```

As you can see, no conflicts were created by this import, which is great. We are now ready to run the conversions.

Running the conversion

There are a couple of ways to convert data from a CVS repository into a Git one. After you have converted the repository, you need to push this new Git repository to a GitLab server.

Converting data using cvs-fast-export

Perform the following steps for Converting data using `cvs-fast-export`:

1. First, download the source from Eric Raymond's site: `http://www.catb.org/ ~esr/cvs-fast-export`:

```
$ wget
http://www.catb.org/~esr/cvs-fast-export/cvs-fast-export-1.44.tar.g
z
$ tar xvzf cvs-fast-export-1.44.tar.gz
$ cd cvs-fast-export*
```

2. Then, build the software:

```
$ make cvs-fast-export
$ cp cvs-fast-export /usr/local/bin; chmod +x /usr/local/bin/cvs-
fast-export
```

3. Go to your cvsroot directory and run the tool in a pipe with find and output the results to a file:

```
imac:cvs-fast-export-1.44 joostevertse$ cd $HOME/cvsroot
imac:cvsroot joostevertse$ find . |cvs-fast-export   >../cv.fi
```

4. Then, initiate an empty Git repository:

```
$ cd $HOME/git
$ mkdir cvsproject
$ cd cvsproject
$ git init
 Initialized empty Git repository in
/Users/joostevertse/git/cvsproject/.git/
```

5. Now, it's time to use git fast-import to populate our empty Git repository with information from the old CVS project:

```
$ cat ../../cv.fi |git fast-import
 Unpacking objects: 100% (19/19), done.
 /usr/local/Cellar/git/2.15.1_1/libexec/git-core/git-fast-import
statistics:
 . . .
```

6. Now that all the meta information has been converted, the only thing left to do is checkout the code from Git:

```
$ git checkout
$ git status
 On branch master
 nothing to commit, working tree clean
$ ls
 hello           package.json
```

The CVS project is now available as a Git repository.

Converting data using cvs2git

Let's take a look at converting data using `cvs2git`:

1. The first step is to migrate the CVS data structure to something that could be imported with `git fast-import`:

```
$ ./cvs2git --blobfile=/tmp/git-blob.dat \
  --dumpfile=/tmp/git-dump.dat "--username=Firstname Lastname"
~/cvsroot/cvsexample

Writing temporary files to
'/var/folders/sf/rdjwj43j4kx63xxng1gkgd040000gn/T/cvs2git-ElawtZ
...
```

2. The first pass (`CollectRevsPass`) went through all the version files and analyzed them for revisions. The next 14 passes will transform all kinds of data from CVS and convert it:

```
----- pass 2 (CleanMetadataPass) -----
Converting metadata to UTF8...
Done
...
```

3. Now the tool is will display statistics about the import:

```
cvs2svn Statistics:
------------------
Total CVS Files: 50
Total CVS Revisions: 50
Total CVS Branches: 0
.....
```

4. The next step is to create a skeleton Git repository, where we could import the converted data:

```
$ mkdir itwasmyparty
$ cd itwasmyparty/
$ git init
 Initialized empty Git repository in
/Users/joostevertse/git/itwasmyparty/.git/
```

5. Then, we start the import, with the blobs being imported first (`git-blob.dat`):

```
$ git fast-import --export-marks=/tmp/git-marks.dat < /tmp/git-
blob.dat

Unpacking objects: 100% (48/48), done.
git-fast-import statistics:
....
```

6. Then, we import the Git metadata (`git-dump.dat`):

```
$ git fast-import --import-marks=/tmp/git-marks.dat < /tmp/git-
dump.dat

Unpacking objects: 100% (23/23), done.
git-fast-import statistics:
....
```

7. Now, all we need to do is checkout the data:

```
$ git checkout
$ git status
On branch master
nothing to commit, working tree clean
```

Now you have a migrated CVS repository.

Cleaning up after migration

Usually, after a migration of some sort, you will need to clean up afterwards. How this will take place in this situation depends on your use case. If it is a one-off migration, you should make a tarball of the old CVSROOT and put it on a DVD. You can also choose to let the repository systems coexist and even perform updates on the CVS repository from Git. There are also ways to create bidirectional communication (prepare for some shell scripting).

What definitely needs to happen if you migrated the CVS repository to Git is that you will need to add a remote that is pointing to your GitLab server. This will be the platform where pull requests (or, in GitLab speak, *merge requests*) are created.

Here, you need create an empty project in your GitLab server and then add the remote, as follows:

```
git remote add gitlab url-to-gitlab-repo
git push gitlab master
```

Your old CVS repository will have been converted and pushed to your GitLab server.

Summary

In this chapter, we discussed the origins of CVS. We compared CVS to Git in a variety of way. The basic difference between the two is that CVS is a centralized versioning system while Git is of a distributed nature. Afterwards, we set up a basic CVS project and prepared to migrate it to GitLab. Then, we made a copy of an existing project to be used with the second tool. Finally, we looked at two different ways of performing conversion to migrate the repositories.

In the next chapter, we will take a look at what many people consider the *enhanced* successor of CVS: subversion. It already incorporates features that are also present in Git.

Questions

1. What is the biggest difference between CVS and Git?
2. What is the network protocol that's used with CVS called?
3. CVS uses changesets. (True | False)
4. How does Git implement versioning numbers?
5. How can you easily correct a typo in a commit message in Git?
6. Is it possible to rename a file in CVS?
7. What is the command to initialize a new CVS database on your machine?
8. What is the command to initialize a new Git project?
9. Who created the `cvs-fast-export` tool?
10. How do you import your migrated repository into GitLab?

Further reading

- cvs-fast-export: http://www.catb.org/~esr/cvs-fast-export
- cvs2git: https://www.mcs.anl.gov/~jacob/cvs2svn/cvs2git.html
- *Git Version Control Cookbook - Second Edition* By *Kenneth Geisshirt, Emanuele Zattin, Rasmus Voss,* and *Aske Olsson*: https://www.packtpub.com/in/application-development/git-version-control-cookbook-second-edition

Switching from SVN

7

The shortcomings of CVS have led to the development of other systems, with one of the most well-known being **Apache Subversion** (**SVN**). In addition to the improvements it has brought, it was specially ensured that is has high compatibility with CVS. It is also open source licensed (with an Apache license, not GNU). It was started in 2000 by Collabnet Inc., but changed to an Apache project in 2009. You can find it at `https://subversion.apache.org`.

In this chapter, will we cover the following topics:

- The difference between SVN and Git
- Mirroring SVN with GIT
- Using svn2git to migrate in one cut

Technical requirements

To follow along with the instructions in this chapter, please download this book's GitHub repository, along with the examples from `https://github.com/PacktPublishing/Mastering-GitLab-12/tree/master/Chapter07`.

Some example will be executed on macOS and some on Debian 10.

The other requirements for this chapter are as follows:

- **Git**: `http://git-scm.org`
- **SVN**: `https://subversion.apache.org/packages.html`
- **Git LFS**: `https://git-lfs.github.com`
- **SubGit**: `https://subgit.com`
- **svn2git**: `https://github.com/nirvdrum/svn2git`

The difference between SVN and Git

Like CVS, the biggest difference between Git and SVN is that SVN follows a centralized architecture, while Git uses a distributed network. There is one SVN server, and as a client you communicate your changes with it. This in different to Git, where there can be many local copies, and one copy can reside on a central server. This architecture is depicted as follows:

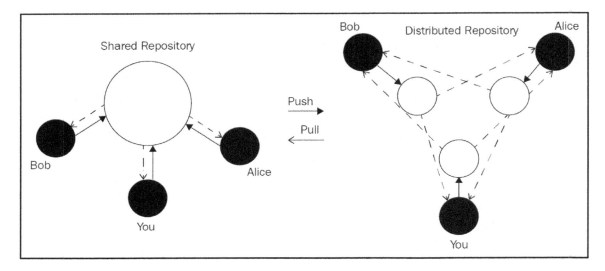

With Git, there are several options to choose from regarding protocol and network settings. Most importantly, you have the choice to communicate with remotes over SSH or HTTP. Using SSH, you wrap Git commands, possibly using certificate authentication, and with HTTP, you implement Git actions using WebDAV and basic HTTP authentication.

SVN has a networking layer that is abstracted, which means that clients exhibit the same behavior, no matter what sort of server they are operating against.

There are several different server options available, as follows:

- **The svnserver server**: This one is easy to set up, does not need system accounts on a server, and is faster than WebDAV (which extends the HTTP protocol with filesystem access). One big disadvantage is that communication using this server is unencrypted by default.

- **svnserver through SSH**: This has all the advantages we mentioned previously, but is protected with SSH encryption. It works by tunneling the svnserver traffic through an SSH session.
- **The Apache web server with module dav_svn**: In this situation, all traffic on the network layer is carried out over HTTP. The famous Apache web server has support for WebDAV operations, and there is a specific Apache module that handles SVN traffic (`dav_svn`). It is noticeably slower because of the overhead in the HTTP protocol, but is had the added bonus that repositories are browse-able through a web browser.

Besides their infrastructural difference, there are also several differences between your local SVN/Git client.

Security and access control

With SVN, you can set up your server to grant or deny permissions to users. You can even define finer-grained access rules based on paths. All of this is configured in a central location. With Git running on your client, there is no access control by default. Your server implementation or central repository that's running Git must do that for you. GitLab has this functionality.

The repository's change history is kept centrally on the server in the SVN world, and to change it you need to gain access to this central place.

Because Git is a distributed versioning system, every developer can make changes to any part of their local repository history. Although pushing a changed history is heavily discouraged, it is possible. This can wreak havoc if other developers are depending on particular changes.

For Git users, the complete history of a repository is saved locally and updated from and to remotes, so there is always a local copy.

Making regular backups is smart to do with both Git and SVN. Even with a central server and several distributed copies, you need to stay in sync to keep all the data available.

Space requirements and references

One of the things SVN can do compared to Git is that you can check out parts of the repository. In Git, the repository can only be cloned as a whole.

In Git, every object has a unique ID, that is, a SHA-1; for instance, 921103db8259eb9de72f42db8b939895f5651422.

This makes it easier to reference. You can also use a shortened version (921103d):

```
$ git rev-parse --short 921103db8259eb9de72f42db8b939895f5651422
921103d
```

In SVN, a file is always the newest version. To reference changes to a file, you need to use *revisions*. That revision points to the whole repository.

SVN working directories contain two copies of each file, which is why Git repositories are generally much smaller – they only contain one copy. A directory with a cloned Git repository contains a small index file with approximately 100 bytes of index data per tracked file.

If a project has a lot of files, the difference in size between SVN and Git can become quite large! A thing most people don't realize is that SVN can track empty directories, while Git cannot! Only file contents are tracked by Git, so empty directories will not show! The following diagram shows the way SVN handles changes:

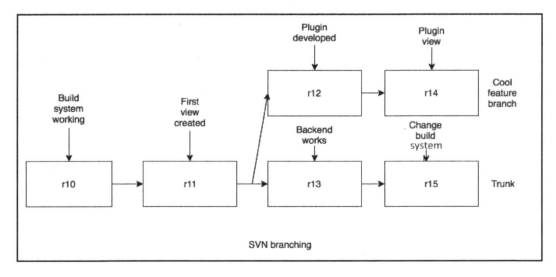

Git, on the other hand, uses the graph model, which is as follows:

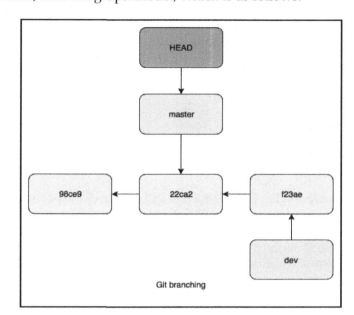

As we can see, the difference in size and the ways of referencing between SVN and Git is very large!

Branching

Both Git and SVN support the use of branches. However, for SVN, branches are part of a possible workflow and style, while for Git the use of branches is built into the command palette and standard way of working.

One of the major disadvantages of SVN is the way of branching and merging. It can take a long time if you have large repositories. If you create a new branch in SVN, you create a completely new directory within the repository, which means there is repetition in that structure. When the branch is ready or no longer needed, you commit back to the trunk.

A big technical difference between Git and SVN versions before 1.5 is that Git used three-way merges as standard, while SVN used two-way merges. It couldn't perform three-way merges because it didn't store merge information. Git, by using its graph database, can check where the code bases share a common state and then merge from the diversion point, which is then technically a three-way merge. In the latest version of SVN, this is also incorporated because the meta information about branches and merges is kept after merging. Unfortunately, the basic problem still exists – a branch is a full copy (not a reference).

At the same time, there can be changes on the trunk already. Your version of it won't have the changes that are in the branches of developers. This means that you could have conflicting changes, files, or structures that are missing in your branch.

The main reason developers like Git so much is the power of the branching model. Comparing it to the many repetitions in SVN, Git only creates references to a specific commit, so there's less repetition and less waste of space and I/O. Instantiating the reference by creation, deletion, or changing a branch will not affect the commits. Want to try something? Fix a bug quickly? Just create a branch, edit files, and push the commits to the central repository, then delete the branch. Create them lightheartedly!

Handling binaries with SVN and Git

Speed is often recited as the main advantage Git has over SVN. This is not exactly the case when handling binary files. If developers checkout full repositories every time and they contain changing binary files, you lose this speed advantage.

In SVN, only the working tree and the latest changes are checked out to the local system. When many changes are made to binary files, checking them out in SVN takes less time than with Git.

Of course, there are workarounds for storing binary files in Git repositories, the most famous being Git LFS (`https://git-lfs.github.com/`). This is a solution that was developed by GitHub and is an extension to Git. With it, you store a pointer inside your repository instead of in a big binary file. Still, every developer action leads to a pile of changed history data. This is going to make operations perform slower.

GitLab also supports Git LFS operations. Depending on how you or your administrator configured GitLab, the location of LFS uploaded data can be on the GitLab server itself, or on shared server storage that's connected to you GitLab server. Alternatively, it can be stored on an S3-compatible service.

You can install Git LFS on several platforms (`https://github.com/git-lfs/git-lfs/wiki/Installation`). The main requisite is that you have installed Git version 1.8.2 or higher.

Let's try using `git-lfs`:

1. We will try this on macOS and install it with `brew`:

```
$ brew install git-lfs
 ==> Downloading
https://homebrew.bintray.com/bottles/git-lfs-2.6.1.high_sierra.bott
le.tar.gz
 ==> Downloading from
https://akamai.bintray.com/0d/0daf04ca0a32e208be0e6df07c42a1ab049a3
e50c962b04ea650a626a97920bb?__gda__=exp=1545082825~hmac=321540978a3
2b9bda7e114cc68cdddb1c772d02d8c93ed919a0d04bff4075377&respo
#############################################################
##### 100.0%
 ==> Pouring git-lfs-2.6.1.high_sierra.bottle.tar.gz
 ==> Caveats
```

2. Update your Git configuration to finish the installation:

```
$ git lfs install
$ git lfs install --system
```

3. When you have Git LFS installed, you need to enable the functionality for your local repository:

```
$ git lfs install
Updated git hooks.
Git LFS initialized.
```

4. Tell Git which kind of files you consider large. After this, add the `.gitattributes` file to the commit:

```
$ git lfs track "*.dmg"
Tracking "*.dmg"
$ git add .gitattributes
```

5. The next step it to just add and commit your changes:

```
$ git add .
$ git commit -m "Testing lfs"
 [master eb9ed7c] Testing lfs
  2 files changed, 4 insertions(+)
  create mode 100644 .gitattributes
  create mode 100644 OpenRA-release-20180923.dmg
```

6. Now, when you push the repository to the remote server, you will notice a different behavior. Git LFS is handling part of the upload:

```
$ git push
 Locking support detected on remote "origin". Consider enabling it
with:
    $ git config
lfs.https://gitlab.com/joustie/itsmyparty_gitlab.git/info/lfs.locks
verify true
 Uploading LFS objects: 100% (1/1), 35 MB | 979 KB/s, done
 Counting objects: 4, done.
 Delta compression using up to 16 threads.
 Compressing objects: 100% (3/3), done.
 Writing objects: 100% (4/4), 487 bytes | 0 bytes/s, done.
 Total 4 (delta 1), reused 0 (delta 0)
 To gitlab.com:joustie/itsmyparty_gitlab.git
    6b64bcc..eb9ed7c  master -> master
```

So, even with SVN handling files faster, if you use Git LFS, you get the same advantages.

If you compare Git LFS with SVN on a basic level, then SVN is faster when it comes to handling binary files. If you use additional Git LFS for Git, they perform approximately the same.

Mirroring SVN and GIT

In order to mirror SVN with Git, we will use the SubGit tool (https://subgit.com/), which is maintained and sold by TMate software. You can download a version for your operating system or choose the basic one, which is a multiplatform Java binary. If you unzip the package you downloaded, the SubGit tool can be found in the bin directory.

SubGit should be set up on your Git server. It will scan the settings for the remote SVN repository you specify, then download SVN revisions and convert them into Git commits. SubGit keeps both repositories synchronized. When a user pushes a new commit to Git, SubGit converts and tries to update SVN. It also gets new revisions from SVN as soon as they appear. SVN and Git users see each other's commits as if they were all working on the same versioning system. SubGit makes sure that possible conflicts don't occur between the systems and maintains the integrity of the mirror.

Keep in mind that for this sync to work, your GitLab server should not use hashed storage. Hashed directory names are not very usable in this context.

Furthermore, the following examples will be executed on a Debian 10 machine, which is why the `apt-get` package manager is used.

Running SubGit in mirror mode requires that you register the software at TMate software. Registration is free for open source, academic, and start-up projects:

1. First, create an empty project in GitLab:

2. Then, open a Terminal on the machine where your GitLab instances are running and create the following environment variables. `SVN_PROJECT_URL` should contain a link to the SVN project you want to copy/convert/mirror:

```
$ export GIT_REPO_PATH=$HOME/git/pdf.git
$ export SVN_PROJECT_URL=svn://svn.riscos.info/pdf/trunk/
```

3. Make sure that you have Java configured on the machine:

```
$ apt-get install openjdk-8-jdk
Reading package lists... Done
Building dependency tree
Reading state information... Done
...
...
Setting up openjdk-8-jdk:amd64 (8u191-b12-0ubuntu0.16.04.1)
...
```

4. Now, we can start the first run of the SubGit tool, which configures everything in order for the mirroring or one-time migration to succeed (I have copied the `subgit` binary from the package to `/opt/subgit/bin`):

```
$ /opt/subgit/bin/subgit configure --layout auto  $SVN_PROJECT_URL
$GIT_REPO_PATH
 SubGit version 3.3.5 ('Bobique') build #4042

 Configuring writable Git mirror of remote Subversion repository:
     Subversion repository URL : svn://svn.riscos.info/pdf
     Git repository location   : /var/opt/gitlab/git-
data/repositories/root/pdf.git

 Git repository is served by GitLab, hooks will be installed into
'custom_hooks' directory.

 Peg location detected: r35 trunk
 Fetching SVN history... Done.
 Growing trees... Done.
 Project origin detected: r1 trunk
 Building branches layouts... Done.
 Combing beards... Done.
 Generating SVN to Git mapping... Done.

CONFIGURATION SUCCESSFUL
```

To complete SubGit installation and have it running continuously, do the following:

1. Adjust Subversion to Git branch mapping if necessary in the following file:

   ```
   /var/opt/gitlab/git-data/repositories/root/pdf.git/subgit/config
   ```

2. Define at least one Subversion credential in the default SubGit password file, as follows:

   ```
   /var/opt/gitlab/git-data/repositories/root/pdf.git/subgit/passwd
   ```

   Alternatively, you can configure SSH or SSL credentials in the `[auth]` section of the following root:

   ```
   /var/opt/gitlab/git-data/repositories/root/pdf.git/subgit/config
   ```

3. Optionally, add custom authors mapping to the `authors.txt` file(s) in the following file:

   ```
   /var/opt/gitlab/git-data/repositories/root/pdf.git/subgit/authors.txt
   ```

4. Run the `subgit install` command:

   ```
   $ subgit install /var/opt/gitlab/git-data/repositories/root/pdf.git
   ```

If you query the process list, you will see that the SubGit daemon is running:

```
$ ps ax |grep subgit |grep -v grep
  17314 ?        Ssl    0:00 /usr/lib/jvm/java-8-openjdk-amd64/jre/bin/java
-noverify -client -Djava.awt.headless=true -Djna.nosys=true -cp
/var/opt/gitlab/git-
data/repositories/root/pdf.git/subgit/lib/subgit-3.3.5_4042_fat.jar
org.tmatesoft.translator.SubGitDaemon test --svn /var/opt/gitlab/git-
data/repositories/root/pdf.git --limit 1544992584093
```

If you view the project in GitLab directly after the installation done with SubGit, you will find that there is still nothing visible. This is because of caching the user interface. So far, we have done operations on the filesystem and we need to flush the Redis cache.

You can use the following command on the GitLab server to do this:

```
$ gitlab-rake cache:clear
```

Now, the imported project should be visible:

We now have two source code repositories that are in sync. Sometimes, you only need one-way conversion, and this is what we will be covering in the next section.

No sync, just convert

You can also use the SubGit tool to do a one-time migration. You don't need a license for this, and it's free. Just download the tool and run it.

So, instead of using `install`, which enables synchronization, just use `import` as an argument:

```
$ /opt/subgit/bin/subgit import $GIT_REPO_PATH
  SubGit version 3.3.5 ('Bobique') build #4042
```

```
Translating Subversion revisions to Git commits...

    Subversion revisions translated: 35.
    Total time: 9 seconds.

IMPORT SUCCESSFUL
```

After this has completed, you can refresh the cache to see the changes being reflected in the web UI.

A one-time conversion is an easy operation to perform compared to a sync, but there is another tool that can do this as well.

Using svn2git to migrate in one cut

As you have seen with SubGit, it is possible to create a syncing solution between SVN and Git. In reality, most of the time, when you want to migrate to a new system, you will want to do it in one go. It decreases the margin of error and is easier to reason about. So, when you do such a hard cut over, make your developers use the new repository. Setting up syncing will not help you migrate in the long run. In comparison to SubGit, you can use your own workstation to do the conversion.

You can use a tool such as svn2git (`https://github.com/nirvdrum/svn2git`) to do a conversion in one step. On your workstation, you can install it as a Ruby Gem if you already have Ruby and Git installed:

```
$ sudo gem install svn2git
```

On Debian-based Linux distributions, you can install the native packages:

```
$ sudo apt-get install git-core git-svn ruby
```

If you need the authors in your project to display correctly, you can make sure that mapping the authors from SVN to Git is performed correctly as part of the conversion. It depends on whether you create an authors file or not. If you choose not to, then no mapping will be performed. In some situations, this can be an issue, while some users don't care at all. If you want to map users, make sure you map every author in the SVN repository. Failing to do so will result in a failed conversion, and you will have to start again.

By using the following command, you will get a list of authors that are present in the repository. Run the following in the SVN source repository. I have done so on my workstation:

```
$ svn log --quiet | grep -E "r[0-9]+ \| .+ \|" | cut -d'|' -f2 | sed 's/
//g' | sort | uniq
 cgransden
 peter
```

In this case, there are only two authors. Use the following output to create the authors.txt file and map authors line by line:

```
cgransden = cgransden <cgransden@gitlab.joustie.nl>
 peter = peter <peter@gitlab.joustie.nl>
```

The repository we are converting has a reasonable default structure. It has a trunk, branches, and tags. If your SVN repositories are more complicated, you have to use more options. You can find these in the svn2git documentation on the home page shown earlier, or use svn2git --help.

Make sure that you run the svn2git conversion command in an empty directory.

The default format of the svn2git command line is
https://svn.example.com/path/to/repo --authors /path/to/authors.txt.

In my example, we are not changing authors, so we'll leave them out. If your SVN repository is protected by a username and password, you can add the --username 'password' and --password 'password' options as well:

```
$ svn2git svn://svn.riscos.info/pdf
 Initialized empty Git repository in /Users/joostevertse/svn/pdf.git/.git/
 r1 = 154856522ddf7c81f34dc80b11a41b963dcc2c13 (refs/remotes/svn/trunk)
    A    !PDF/!sprites22,ff9
    A    !PDF/Documents/Help.html,faf
    A    !PDF/Documents/Licences/Copying
    A    !PDF/Documents/Licences/BSDLicence
    A    !PDF/Documents/Licences/README
 ...
```

The next step is to finish the conversion by pushing your migrated repository to GitLab. It's best to create an empty project in GitLab and fetch the projects HTTP or SSH location. Then, you can add it as a remote to your local repository and push it. This will contain all the commits and branches.

When the conversion is complete, you can import the project into GitLab by creating a new remote locally and push the repository:

```
$ git push --all origin
 Counting objects: 1009, done.
 Delta compression using up to 16 threads.
 Compressing objects: 100% (414/414), done.
 Writing objects: 100% (1009/1009), 1.39 MiB | 0 bytes/s, done.
 Total 1009 (delta 591), reused 1009 (delta 591)
 remote: Resolving deltas: 100% (591/591), done.
 To https://gitlab.joustie.nl:8443/root/pdf.git
  * [new branch]      master -> master
```

If you have tags, don't forget to push them, too:

```
$ git push --tags origin
 Everything up-to-date
```

This finalizes the conversion using svn2git, the second tool that you can use to perform a one-off migration of SVN to Git.

Summary

In this chapter, we started by tracing the origins of SVN and why it rose to popularity. Afterwards, we made a comparison between SVN and Git on certain aspects that are relevant for versioning systems, such as architecture, branching methods, and how to deal with binary files.

The second part of this chapter deals with ways to migrate SVN projects to Git. The first tool we discussed was SubGit. It is capable not only of migration projects from SVN to Git, but can also act as a proxy and let both repositories coexist. The second tool we talked about was svn2git, which does a migration in one cut. The other notable difference between these tools is that SubGit is installed on your GitLab server, while svn2git can be run from your workstation.

In the next chapter, we will take a look at another type of source control system. This one is created by Microsoft and not open source.

Questions

1. What is the home page of the SVN project?
2. What is the biggest difference between SVN and Git?
3. Name the three different ways to run a SVN server.
4. With SVN, where is the history of a project saved?
5. Git uses SHAs, but what does SVN use?
6. What type of merge did SVN versions before 1.5 perform?
7. What version of Git is needed for Git LFS?
8. Name two ways that GitLab implements LFS as storage backend.
9. What two mechanisms does SubGit support for migration?
10. When you use svn2git, what is the last step of migrating to GitLab?

Further reading

- **SubGit**: https://subgit.com/
- **svn2git**: https://github.com/nirvdrum/svn2git
- **SVN redbook**: http://svnbook.red-bean.com/
- **SVN documentation**: https://subversion.apache.org/docs/

Moving Repositories from TFS

Team Foundation Server (TFS) is the collaboration platform and foundation of Microsoft's **Application Life Cycle Management (ALM)** solution, which comes with code version management (including package management (NuGet, Maven, and so on)), work item management, extensive reporting and dashboard capabilities, automated build and release management, and test management. Through extensive integration with development tools such as Visual Studio, TFS is used to communicate and collaborate with the process of designing, building (continuous integration), testing, and deploying (continuous delivery) the software, which should ultimately be used to increase productivity and team output, improve quality, and gain more insight into the application life cycle.

In this chapter, we will compare TFS to Git, and then we will migrate a TFS repository to Git that is in the old TFVC (Team Foundation Version Control) format. Note that, nowadays, Microsoft has standardized on Git for version management, so TFVC is not widely used anymore.

In this chapter, we will cover the following topics:

- TFS versus Git
- The git-tfs tool

Technical requirements

To follow along with the instructions in this chapter, please download this book's GitHub repository, along with the examples, from `https://github.com/PacktPublishing/Mastering-GitLab-12/tree/master/Chapter08`.

The other requirements for this chapter are as follows:

- Git: `http://git-scm.org`
- Azure DevOps account: `https://azure.microsoft.com/nl-nl/services/devops/`

- Git-tfs: `https://github.com/git-tfs/git-tfs`
- GitLab account: (`https://gitlab.com` or on premise)

TFS versus Git

Microsoft created TFS as a product to help teams create software.

It has the following features:

- Source code management
- Requirements management
- Lab management
- Reporting
- Project management (for Agile software and waterfall development)
- Automated builds
- Testing
- Release management capabilities

The solution was created to help across the entire life cycle of the product (ALM). It can cooperate with several **Integrated Development Environments** (**IDEs**), but works best with Microsoft's own Visual Studio, which nowadays is multiplatform.

It has been around for some time, but currently the focus is on getting customers to use the Cloud version of TFS: Azure DevOps. You get all the features of TFS on premise, but it is much more scalable.

For source code management, two different kinds of repositories are supported. Originally, the default was **Team Foundation Version Control** (**TFVC**), which resembles SVN and is very much a centralized **Version Control System** (**VCS**). The other choice is Git. Over the past few years, Git has been adopted as the default VCS within Microsoft. You probably won't find a team that doesn't use Git within Microsoft (well, maybe the team that's responsible for TFS).

If you want to migrate your TFS Git repository to GitLab, it's very easy. For instance, you can move a repository to a new one in an on-premise GitLab:

```
cd existing_repo
git remote rename origin old-origin
git remote add origin https://gitlab.example.com/me/newprojectingitlab.git
git push -u origin --all
git push -u origin --tags
```

Migrating a TFVC project takes a bit more effort, which I will explain later. First, let me explain the differences between TFVC and Git. We will start with the most important one: whether it is centralized or decentralized.

Centralized or decentralized

The basic design of TFVC is that of a centralized repository on a server with authorized clients connecting to it to exchange information. Git's distributed nature is the complete opposite, with no central authority by default and the possibility to freely push and pull changes with others. Of course, you can create a central server that harbors a copy of the Git repository that everyone agrees is the newest version. This difference can be seen in the following diagram. The Git repository can exist in a local TFS or the Azure instance, while the TFVC one can only exist in one central place:

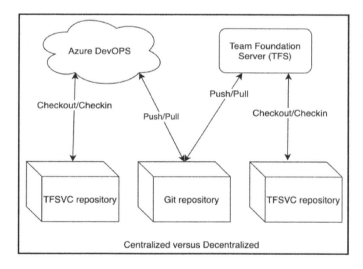

Centralized versus Decentralized

Handling changes

The best tool that you can use to work with TFVC is without a doubt Visual Studio. Let's discuss some points regarding the way it handles changes in your files.

Branching and merging capacity

Compared to branches in Git, which are repository scoped, TFVC branches are path scoped and not as lightweight. Generally speaking, team members create additional workspaces for each branch they are working on. Changes are branch-independent, so to avoid chaos at integration time, you need to forward-integrate as many times as possible. The standard merge with TFVC uses a two-way merge (baseless).

Set your bar for creating branches high and only branch when you have a need for code or release isolation. It's more resource-intensive to use branches in TFVC. As the number of your feature branches increases, so do your storage requirements and branch hierarchy visualization fuzziness. In the following screenshot, you can see the situation as a developer; you can't merge because of conflicts:

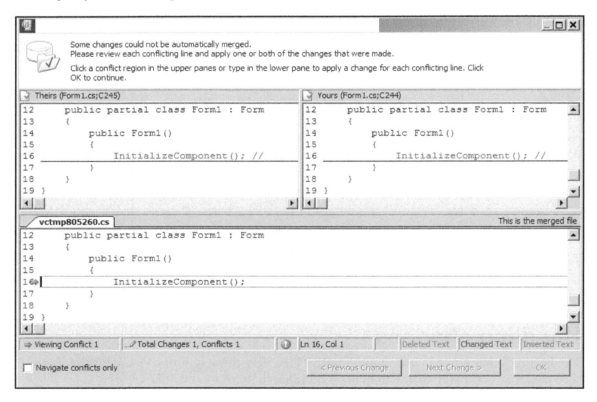

In Git, a branch is only a pointer to a commit. The default diff in Git uses three-way merging, which also helps developers merge back.

History

Because of the centralized nature of TFVC, some pieces of information are not available when you are not connected. File history is not replicated to the client's development machine and can only be viewed when you are online with the server. This information is viewable via Visual Studio and the web portal. Via the context menu of an item, you can annotate files to see who changed a line, and when they changed it. The following screenshot shows what sort of information is given in the web portal:

Contents	History	Compare	**Annotate**		✎ Edit	☰ Rename	🗑 Delete	↓ Download

```
5        Joost Evertse        Thursday    1  using System;
                                          2
                                          3  namespace MovingToGitlab
                                          4  {
                                          5      class Program
                                          6      {
                                          7          static void Main(string[] args)
                                          8          {
6        Joost Evertse        Thursday    9              Console.WriteLine("Hello World! I am moving to GitLab");
5        Joost Evertse        Thursday   10          }
                                         11      }
                                         12  }
                                         13
```

With Git, file history is replicated on the client's development machine. You can also view it when there is no connection to the TFS server. You can view history in Visual Studio and on the web portal, as well as on the specific Git server you are using, such as GitLab. By using Git's command option, you can find out who changed which lines in a file, and why. It can be a useful tool for identifying changes in your code as annotation is in TFVC. See the following `git blame` command:

```
$ git blame BSDLicence
e2cc9eb2 (peter 2010-01-08 20:35:51 +0000  1) The files
e2cc9eb2 (peter 2010-01-08 20:35:51 +0000  2)
e2cc9eb2 (peter 2010-01-08 20:35:51 +0000  3) !PDF.Res
e2cc9eb2 (peter 2010-01-08 20:35:51 +0000  4) !PDF.Sprites
e2cc9eb2 (peter 2010-01-08 20:35:51 +0000  5) !PDF.Sprites22
e2cc9eb2 (peter 2010-01-08 20:35:51 +0000  6) !PDF.Messages
e2cc9eb2 (peter 2010-01-08 20:35:51 +0000  7) !PDF.Documents.Help/html
e2cc9eb2 (peter 2010-01-08 20:35:51 +0000  8) !PDF.Documents.Help/txt
```

We can see that `peter` changed this file.

Traceability

For some use cases, it is of the utmost importance to have good traceability. Think of companies such as banks and insurance companies who have to adhere to strict policies because of legislation. Since TFVC is a centralized repository type, its traceability is quite good out of the box. All change operations are recorded on the server and performed only by authorized individuals. There are direct links between issues, bugs, boards, and backlog items.

With Git, it is possible to setup the same system, but you need to make sure that your centralized repository enforces some extra checks and handles linking between entities (issue tracking in GitLab, for instance). By default, anyone can change the history of a Git repository, so out of the box, the traceability in Git is not very good.

File handling

Another big difference between Git and TFVC is when it comes to handling changes. This is connected to the fact that TFVC uses a central repository and Git is, by its nature, distributed. TFVC, with its central server, keeps all the files in a project under a single root path. Within this context, it is possible to apply permissions at a file level or lock files on the central server. By default, this is not possible with Git or with the basic GitLab configuration since there is no central place where you can enforce these authorizations. You can lock files somewhere, but a developer can happily continue developing locally and change code.

On the other hand, with Git, you can have multiple repositories in a GitLab project and have protection on a branch level or repository level. You have the option to define multiple remotes to which you can push code. This means that you can store code in GitLab and also on Windows Azure. The following screenshot shows the menu that you can use to lock a file in TFVC:

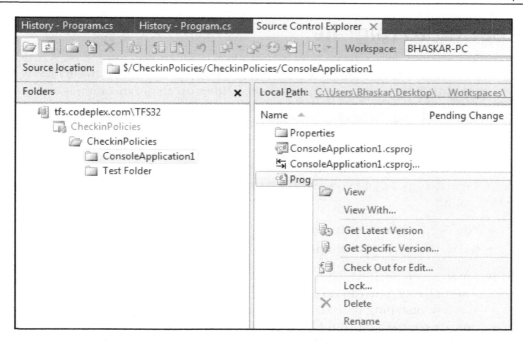

With TFVC, the files are all under one path and under control while in Git, there can be many branches and files spread over different remote servers. It's hard, if not impossible, to enforce centralized control.

The git-tfs tool

There are several ways to migrate data from TFVC to Git. The simplest way is to do the migration in TFS itself. You can use their own import/export tools from the https://docs. microsoft.com/en-us/azure/devops/repos/git/import-from-tfvc?view=azure-devops tabs=new-navviewFallbackFrom=vsts website.

There is also another tool that can be used for migration. It is possible to have a bi-directional gateway between TFS and Git, just like there is with git-svn. It can put TFS commits into a Git repository, and allows you to push back changes to TFS.

The existence of these tools is caused by the fact that Microsoft internally switched to Git years ago and they have contributed a lot of source code to the codebase of Git. That is why it is standard (especially with Azure) to create new repositories using the Git format nowadays.

Preparing to migrate

In this section, we will demonstrate how to migrate a TFVC project located on Azure DevOps. First, we will locate our project on Azure DevOps. You can do this by navigating to your organization at `https://dev.azure.com`. Setting up an organization is outside the scope of this book, but it is quite easy and free if you are a small company or an open source project. You can read more about this on the Azure page, here: `https://azure.microsoft.com/nl-nl/services/devops/`.

The project page for the git-tfs migration tool can be found on GitHub (`https://github.com/git-tfs/git-tfs`). Before you install git-tfs, there are a few prerequisites you need to take into account:

- You need a Windows machine to install it with.
- It has to have Git for Windows.

The git-tfs binaries can be downloaded from `https://github.com/git-tfs/git-tfs/releases`. Alternatively, you can do a managed install with chocolatey (`https://chocolatey.org/`). Installing with such a package manager takes care of the necessary details for you. Of course, you could build the package yourself because the source is also available. For these examples, we will use a basic Windows machine I already have set up. Let's get started:

1. It's easy to install Git using chocolatey:

```
Administrator: Command Prompt - choco install gittfs                    —    □    ×

Microsoft Windows [Version 10.0.10240]
(c) 2015 Microsoft Corporation. All rights reserved.

C:\Windows\system32>choco install gittfs
Chocolatey v0.10.11
Installing the following packages:
gittfs
By installing you accept licenses for the packages.
Progress: Downloading git 2.20.1... 100%
Progress: Downloading git.install 2.20.1... 100%
Progress: Downloading gittfs 0.29.0... 100%

git.install v2.20.1 [Approved]
git.install package files install completed. Performing other installation steps.
Using Git LFS
Installing 64-bit git.install...
```

2. The next step is to install git-tfs using the `gittfs` package:

3. In order to perform the migration, we need to create a new project in our GitLab instance so that we have a destination for our Azure DevOps project:

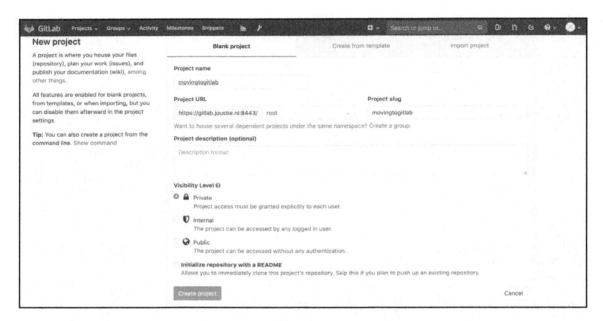

4. Now, we will use the git-tfs tool to clone the test project we created in Azure DevOps. It will bring up an authentication window:

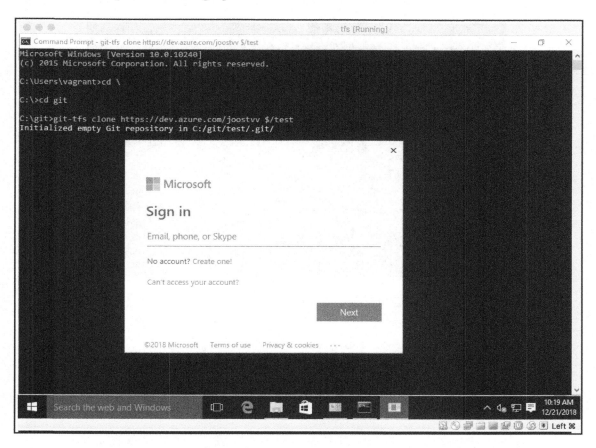

5. It will automatically search through change sets and convert them into Git:

```
Command Prompt

Microsoft Windows [Version 10.0.10240]
(c) 2015 Microsoft Corporation. All rights reserved.

C:\Users\vagrant>cd \

C:\>cd git

C:\git>git-tfs clone https://dev.azure.com/joostvv $/test
Initialized empty Git repository in C:/git/test/.git/

info: no TFS root found !

PS:perhaps you should convert your trunk folder into a branch in TFS.
Fetching from TFS remote 'default'...
C2 = 73ee984c3fe6bd811635710142b75e5c815d5737
C3 = 82b32a380e2b81cccae5f69596b914b10cc5cd90
C4 = cd77bad0fde65e938e9597c064d9bc3268a614e7
C5 = f3a57963ec07264d1aa34f2042b70b618cc39dc1
C6 = e220994c0a0af5efecec3c44018642aed2ab4b1b


C:\git>_
```

6. To copy this local Git repository to our GitLab project, we need to create a remote entry:

```
C:\git\MovingToGitlab>git remote add origin
https://gitlab.joustie.nl:8443/root/movingtogitlab.git
```

7. Then, we will use `push -u` to push it to GitLab. Git for Windows will present you with a login screen, which you can authenticate against `gitlab.joustie.nl`:

```
C:\git\MovingToGitlab\MovingToGitlab>git push -u origin master
Enumerating objects: 13, done.
Counting objects: 100% (13/13), done.
Delta compression using up to 2 threads
Compressing objects: 100% (8/8), done.
Writing objects: 100% (13/13), 1.33 KiB | 1.33 MiB/s, done.
Total 13 (delta 2), reused 8 (delta 1)
To https://gitlab.joustie.nl:8443/root/movingtogitlab.git
 * [new branch]      master -> master
Branch 'master' set up to track remote branch 'master' from 'origin'.
```

8. When the migrations are finished, you can log in to your GitLab project. Here, you will find the pushed code:

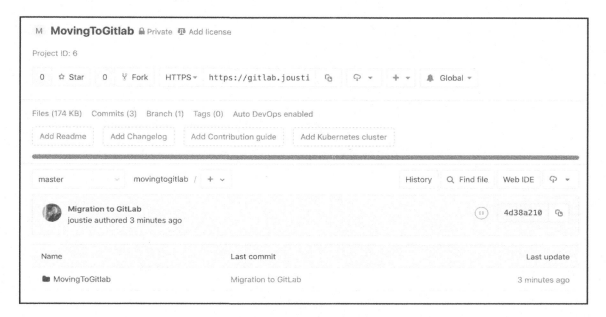

9. You can view the commit history in Git with `git log`:

```
C:\git\MovingToGitlab>git log
commit d653c16bd4a9d7bf3850b8c7b9fd143f9a086bf6 (HEAD -> master, tfs/default)
Author: Joost Evertse <joostvv@hotmail.com>
Date:    Thu Dec 20 14:53:58 2018 +0000

    Changed default output

    git-tfs-id: [https://dev.azure.com/joostvv]$/test/MovingToGitlab;C6

commit 4473f8142aa7cecaaf6f4b91698ba4331abcbeaf
Author: Joost Evertse <joostvv@hotmail.com>
Date:    Thu Dec 20 14:52:00 2018 +0000

    Initial check-in of module MovingToGitlab

    git-tfs-id: [https://dev.azure.com/joostvv]$/test/MovingToGitlab;C5
```

10. If you compare it with the history in TFVC, you will find it to be the same:

By using the git-tfs tool, it is relatively easy to migrate your existing TFVC to Git.

Summary

This chapter explained what TFS is and where its place is in the Microsoft product gamma. First, we compared TFVC and Git in terms of their architecture, as well as the way they handle branching and merging. We also took a look at how they treat history and the traceability of changes.

From there, we learned that there are different ways to migrate from TFS to Git. For one, you can export from the server itself. There's also a tool that you can use to create a mirror between a TFS and a Git repository that's called git-tfs. The most logical reason for this tool to exist is because, nowadays, Git relies heavily on Git repositories and needs to convert TFVC projects into Git format internally.

This chapter ends the part of this book about migrating data from other systems to GitLab. In the next part, we will extensively discuss the ways of connecting to GitLab.

Questions

1. What is TFS used for in Microsoft's ALM suite?
2. What is the biggest difference between TFVC and Git?
3. TFS is part of what product in Azure?
4. How do you migrate a TFS Git repository to GitLab?
5. How are branches scoped in TFVC?
6. Where is history kept with TFVC?
7. What tool resembles git-tfs?
8. What tool on Windows makes it easy to install Git?

Further reading

- *Microsoft Team Foundation Server 2015 Cookbook* by *Tarun Arora*: https://www.packtpub.com/networking-and-servers/microsoft-team-foundation-server-2015-cookbook
- *Implementing DevOps with Microsoft Azure* by *Mitesh Soni*: https://www.packtpub.com/networking-and-servers/implementing-devops-microsoft-azure
- TFS site: https://visualstudio.microsoft.com/tfs/
- Git-tfs: https://github.com/git-tfs/git-tfs

3
Section 3: Implement the GitLab DevOps Workflow

In this section, you'll gain an understanding of, and able to implement, all of the features GitLab provides in a workflow, or pick the required parts of the workflow.

This section comprises the following chapters:

9
GitLab Vision - the Whole Toolchain in One Application

This chapter is intended to provide more insight into the background against which GitLab has arisen. The product was literally created to help solve a number of problems that the Agile movement experienced. We will talk about the history of development methodologies and the rise of Agile as the dominant way to develop software. The Agile methodologies spilled over to the traditional operations department, which then led to the DevOps movement. Finally, we will summarize a number of tools that are part of the DevOps way of working.

In this chapter, we will cover following topics:

- The Agile Manifesto
- **Extreme Programming (XP)**
- The DevOps movement
- The toolchain

Technical requirements

To follow along with the instructions in this chapter, please download the Git repository with examples available from GitHub at `https://github.com/PacktPublishing/Mastering-GitLab-12/tree/master/Chapter09`.

The Agile Manifesto

Some people in the 1990s had a problem with the classic engineering mindset of comparing software development to build engineering. Instead of trying to keep the requirements stable and not let them get out of hand through requirements creep or scope creep, they looked for a process that did not depend on the stability of requirement. Those people came up with a number of different ideas in response, and those methods are commonly known as lightweight methods. All of these form the Agile movement, together with lean manufacturing methods, and have grown very popular over time.

Now, what is it about Agile that everyone says nowadays? For some, it's way of life and of looking at things. In IT, according to Google, it is a method of project management, used especially for software development, that is characterized by the division of tasks into short phases of work and the frequent reassessment and adaptation of plans.

Officially, Agile is not a method, but a collective term. Agile was born from several other methods to develop products (mostly software). Examples include XP, Scrum, the **Dynamic Systems Development Method (DSDM)**, Adaptive Software Development, and Crystal. These methods share the common characteristic that they all aim for less bureaucracy during product and software development, and embrace change. In the 1980s and 1990s, these separate methods were developed by various experts, who eventually set up the Agile Manifesto in 2001. These were mainly intended to prevent problems with the application of traditional waterfall methods.

All of the big names from different Agile disciplines eventually decided to come together informally and discuss ways to help IT improve. The Agile Manifesto was drawn up during this meeting of 17 software developers. It took place from February 11 to February 13, 2001, at The Lodge in Snowbird, Utah. The name Agile was also chosen here. Word has it that the name lightweight method was on the table, but Agile was eventually chosen.

The initial model – waterfall

When people talk about the origins of the waterfall model, it is often said that W. W. Royce introduced it in 1970 in the paper, *Managing the Development of Large Software Systems* (`http://www-scf.usc.edu/~csci201/lectures/Lecture11/royce1970.pdf`). Royce himself actually believed in the iterative approach to software development and did not even use the term waterfall. Royce described the waterfall model as a method he thought was too extreme – and even an proposition doomed to fail: *"I believe in this concept, but the implementation described above is risky and invites failure"*, Royce wrote.

In 1970, Royce thought that the waterfall method had to be seen as an initial concept, as he felt there were errors in the method. He published a document examining how the initial concept could be developed into a repeated method. In this enhanced model, there was more feedback between each phase than the previous phase, as we now often see in the current methods. Annoyingly for Royce, only the initial method got attention, and the criticism he had on this method was largely ignored.

Royce's intention was to transform the model from the paper into an iterating model; still, the original method has been widely used and idealized. However, people who oppose this model think it is too basic and has no real practical use. The following diagram illustrates the waterfall model:

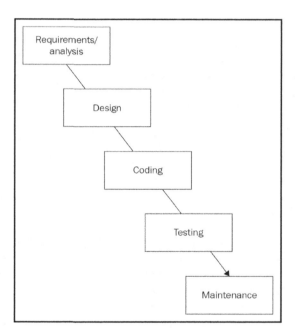

The waterfall model consists of the following phases:

- **Definition study/analysis (Requirements/analysis)**: In this phase, the only goal is to search for requirements. Some research is done to clarify the purpose of the software.
- **Basic design (Design)**: In this phase, what has emerged during the first phase becomes clearer. The customer wishlist is put on paper and the user interface of the program is already being considered. Generally speaking, in this phase, it is recorded what the future system must do.

- **Technical design/detail design (Design)**: A prototype or minimal program can already be built using the basic design. During this phase, consideration is given to the possibilities of achieving the desired functionality technically. The options are already grouped in modules, functions, or programs.
- **Construction/implementation (Coding)**: In the construction phase, the actual source code is written for the program.
- **To test (Testing)**: In the testing phase, it is checked whether the software is built properly according to the design. Here, errors can also emerge that have already been made in earlier stages. In the theoretical model, this should not happen.
- **Integration (Testing)**: The system should now be ready and tested. However, it should also work with other pieces of software or hardware. There are special tests for this that make sure the integration works.
- **Management and maintenance (Maintenance)**: In order to ensure that the system continues to operate and function according to specification, maintenance will have to be carried out.

To summarize, the waterfall model consists of different phases. Each phase has its own level that also determines the sequence. The highest level is executed first before the following, lower phases. This is equal to the natural effect of a waterfall, hence the name.

To mitigate the cons of the original method, several enhanced forms were developed.

Royce's model

Royce's model describes a different waterfall model that can go back to previous phases. Often, it will become apparent at a particular phase that something went wrong in a previous phase (this will most commonly surface in testing phases). It should then be possible to go back to a previous phase easily. 99% of the time, changes to the design have to be made – nobody is perfect, so this model is more realistic. Nevertheless, Royce continued to emphasize the importance of good documentation for proper phase transitions.

The following diagram illustrates Royce's model:

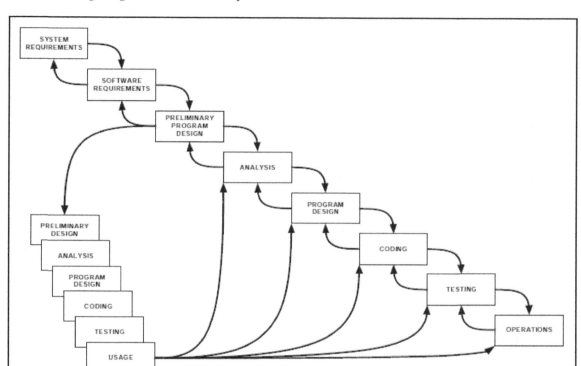

The sashimi model

The sashimi model, designed by Peter Degrace, is one of the models discussed in the book, *Wicked Problems, Righteous Solutions: A Catalog of Modern Software Engineering Paradigms*. This model assumes the same phases as the waterfall model, but that they can overlap (even more than once). This way of working means that fewer resources are wasted. In the following diagram, you can see how the phases can overlap. What matters is that there are no hard endings of phases or gateways. You can see the current time as an example. Another aspect of this figure is that, in contrast to the waterfall model, the lead time is also included in the model. This is to indicate that you can already start designing, even if the analysis is not yet complete. It also means that you can go back to the analysis in the design phase.

The following figure illustrates the sashimi model:

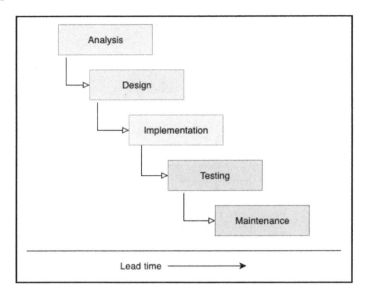

The V-model

The V-model shows the phase transitions within software development, which offers the possibility of QA. For every phase transition, the developers and the customer make quality agreements about, for example, the designs. The V shape illustrates that at the bottom of the shape, after real implementation, there will be an ever-growing understanding of the problem that is being solved, and that initial ideas and requirements are tested against reality.

The following diagram illustrates the V-model model:

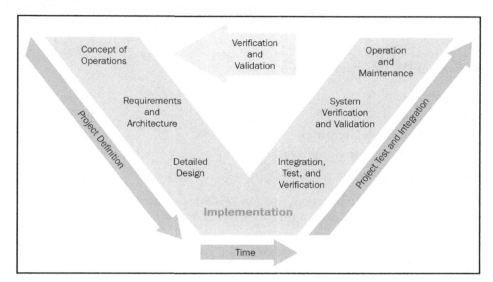

The sequential way of working that is presented here in these methods fits classic engineering methods. For a long time during the 1970s and 1980s, it was believed that software engineering as a discipline should work in a similar way to how engineers build skyscrapers. Skyscrapers are built by first creating a detailed architectural plan before construction workers can carry out the building phase. To create an architecture and a plan in such a way, you need a very clear understanding of what needs to be built. What is important here is that the upfront requirements are clearly outlined and do not change along the way. If the expectations of real-world engineering projects changed as rapidly as they do in software, however, nothing would get built.

DSDM

The DSDM is derived from the linear **Software Development Methodology (SDM)** model, which originated in the 1990s. It was an answer to the problem that, in linear methods, the functionality to be developed is often available too late as a whole. If the functionality to be delivered can be divided into sub-functionalities, these sub-functionalities can be delivered separately. We call this incremental system development or step-by-step development. In the beginning you want to find out which functionality can be split off. This means that the first two phases from the waterfall approach are completed, but only when the partial functionalities are clear can these be developed step by step in parallel.

DSDM is more than just applying iterations at development stages. All of the remaining phases after analysis are iterative. In addition, the division of phases looks slightly different. In contrast to the linear development model, it is also possible to go back to previous phases.

The phases within DSDM are structured as follows:

- Feasibility study
- Business analysis
- Functional model iteration
- Design and construction iteration
- Implementation

Timeboxing is one of the core practices used in DSDM to control each stage, which is combined with better prioritization with MoSCoW. We will explain this in the following section.

Timeboxing

In order to ensure that a project can be of service to the organization in time, timeboxes are used. For example, the functionality with the highest priority should always be delivered within a timebox. If there is time and space left, then there will be room for functionalities with a lower priority. A timebox is a time interval in which an intermediate product is delivered. During the project, the precise functionality is refined further. Due to growing insights and changing circumstances, the specifications of a functionality can also change.

A timebox is prepared, in which must-haves, should-haves, and (possibly) could-haves are defined. This layout allows you to create room for manoeuvre without affecting the end time of the timebox. In other words, in the case of changing insight or emergencies, you will be able to re-prioritize. This may be at the expense of should-have and could-have system requirements. By applying MoSCoW, you make these choices explicit.

With this technique, you can keep constant focus on functional requirements with the highest priority, monitor your time and budget, and still be able to act when insights change. Using this technique enables you to give priority to the system requirements that give a company the most benefit, and lower the priority for requirements that were derived from situations that may never occur. This also makes systems simpler in design—something that improves their maintainability.

The classification of requirements and wishes based on the MoSCoW classification also helps users to visualize the support for a project within an organization. There are now authors who think that you should consider projects as clusters of micro-projects. Every micro-project is a requirement or a wish with a certain priority. In many projects, the support from stakeholders starts to crumble when people are confronted with changes. If a project includes many must-haves, this risk will be smaller than when it largely consists of would-haves.

MoSCoW

It often happens that a project is hindered by too many wishes from the user organization. However, a development strategy that provides feedback to the customer can prevent over-demanding the development organization. DSDM counteracts this by dividing the functional requirements and wishes into a number of categories in which the priority is indicated for each functionality.

DSDM uses the MoSCoW rules to determine the priorities for requirements and wishes.

MoSCoW stands for:

- **Must-have**: This category has the highest priority, is guaranteed to be delivered, and counts as the engine of the information system.
- **Should-have**: A necessary requirement where a (temporary) workaround is possible.
- **Could-have**: A requirement with a clear added value, but without it there is still a usable system.
- **Would-have (or want to have but won't have this time around)**: This requirement can be missed, although it does not mean that it is not relevant; in the next increment, it can be a **must-have**.

Nowadays, DSDM is not extensively used. The last decade has seen other methods gain a lot more popularity, especially Agile methods such as Scrum, which we will discuss next.

Scrum

The next lightweight model we will touch upon in this book is called Scrum, which, as of 2018, has been widely adopted outside the IT realm. It is not a method such as DSDM and can be better described as a framework. It uses the paradigm of a sports team (rugby, to be exact), where a group of people work together to achieve a goal. In the rugby game, a scrum drives the ball into the game. The scrum group consists of five to eight players who operate as a unit. In the IT world, it is a group of people who create business value through close cooperation and coordination.

In Rugby, each player has a unique position; they play both roles in attack and defense, and they work as a team to get the ball to the other side. It can be compared to a situation in IT, where the degree of success of a scrum team depends on the different disciplines within the team and how they work together and coordinate with each other.

The Rugby comparison originates from a 1986 article from the Harvard Business Review, *The New Product Development Game,* where the authors Takeuchi and Nonaka introduced the term scrum in the context of product development. They argued that it would bring more speed and flexibility, and they based it on case studies done in several industries, notably the automotive industries.

In the early 1990s, Ken Schwaber and Jeff Sutherland started using scrum techniques in their companies, and eventually in 1995, they presented a paper describing the Scrum framework at a software design conference.

Scrum sets out the following values:

- **Commitment**: The members must fully commit themselves to the project; it is not a part-time job.
- **Focus**: embers should focus on what needs to be done in each sprints.
- **Openness (Transparency)**: People must keep each other well informed about progress and possible problems.
- **Respect**: Members must respect those with a different background and expertise and trust each other's good intent.
- **Guts**: Members must have the courage to say things, ask questions, and come up with new solutions.

Scrum works with multidisciplinary teams who prefer to work in one room so that consultation is easy. The team is supervised by a scrum master, who has a facilitating role. The product owner is the customer or a client, or a representative thereof. He or she specifies the desired results, usually in the form of user stories. These user stories are kept in a list, the product backlog, or the work stock. The product owner sorts the work stock for priority. The most important user stories are at the top.

In Scrum, you work in sprints or iterations. These usually last from about a week to a month, with a duration of two weeks as the most common. Sprints are timeboxed. In other words, it is certain in advance how long a Sprint will last for and when it will end. At the beginning of a sprint, the user stories for that Sprint are determined and recorded in the sprint backlog.

Sprints provide results that are as tangible as possible. This means that the software development will provide usable code, including integration, tests, and documentation, that is understandable for the customer or end user.

At the end of a sprint, a sprint review takes place, where the result is shown to the product owner. In addition, an evaluation takes place within the team.

Crystal methods

A Crystal method is a lightweight method with characteristics such as emphasis on people instead of processes and products, fast communication (preferably by working together in one room), the quick delivery of products, frequent and automatic testing, and regular evaluations.

Unlike some other software development processes, Crystal is not a software development method, but a collection of methods and processes. This collection is called the Crystal Family. Crystal was invented and described by Alistair Cockburn. Each member of the Crystal Family is indicated with a color representing the weight of a method, where the following applies: the darker the color, the heavier the method. The color of the method is chosen on the basis of the size and severity of the project. The size is determined by the number of people participating in the project, and the severity is determined by the risk that choosing the method could cause systemic damage. The colors are, like real crystals, sorted from light to dark. Crystal clear is the smallest and lightest, followed by yellow, orange, orange web, red, maroon, blue, violet, and so on.

Although the Crystal methods differ from each other, they do have some similarities, which is why they are also called a family. They have three common priorities: safety, efficiency, and usability. Furthermore, they also have common characteristics, the three most important of which are the frequent delivery of (intermediate) products, feedback on improvements, and good communication.

We have already discussed a team-based approach to product development with certain process steps, and now with Crystal methods, a lightweight Agile method that focuses on people within the team itself. There are also more radical methods that focus not only on people and process, but also on tooling and technical quality. We will discuss these XP methods in the following section.

XP

One of the most important subcultures of the Agile movement is XP. The main founders of XP are Kent Beck, Ken Auer, Ward Cunningham, Martin Fowler, and Ron Jeffries. They developed XP during the **Chrysler Comprehensive Compensation** (C3) system project in 1996. It is very popular nowadays, and this is reflected in the culture of software development but also in its ways of working and the toolset it uses. We believe GitLab is, in many ways, the tool once imagined for XP. It is, in fact, so profound that we have decided to dedicate an entire chapter to it to explain its relevance for GitLab.

XP takes its name from the fact that a number of proven development principles (so-called best practices) are carried through to the extreme. The optimal power of XP stems from the application of the 12 best practices of software development. The best practices are grouped into four groups: fine feedback, continuous process, shared knowledge, and the well-being of the developers.

Fine-scale feedback

One of the most important principles in XP is the usage of feedback mechanisms and trying to keep the feedback loops as small as possible. This starts at the planning stage, because feedback from a customer at this stage can already limit wasted time.

The fine-scale feedback group in XP includes four practices: planning game, pair programming, **test-driven development** (TDD), and whole team. We will discuss the feedback loop for each practice in the following sections.

Planning game

The planning takes place at the beginning of each iteration and consists of both release planning and iteration planning.

Release planning determines which functionality will be realized in which release. Both the developers and the users are present.

Release planning consists of the following three phases:

- **Exploration phase**: Here, the users make a shortlist of the most important requirements for the new system. This happens in the form of user stories.
- **Commitment phase**: Here, it is decided which user stories will be included in the next release and when this release will be.
- **Steering phase**: Here, the plan can be modified, and new stories added and others removed.

Iteration planning is when user stories included in the release schedule for an upcoming Sprint are divided into tasks for the developers. No users are involved, only developers.

Iteration planning also consists of three phases; they are as follows:

- **Exploration phase**: Here, the stories are translated into tasks, which are then written on cards called task cards.
- **Commitment phase**: Here, the time taken to realize the tasks is estimated and the tasks are assigned to the developers (pairs).
- **Steering phase**: Here, the tasks are carried out, and the result is compared with the original time schedule of the user story.

The purpose of this kind of planning is to ensure that a product can be delivered. It is not so much about delivering exact data as about delivering the product.

Release planning

During this part of the planning game, customers and developers try to find out what will be included in the next release of the software and when this will take place. The focus is on creating user stories.

This part of the game consists of the following three phases:

- **Exploration phase**: This is the process of gathering requirements and estimating the amount of time it will take to realize them. Activities in this phase includes the following:
    - **Writing a story (user story)**: Here, the users come up with a problem or wish; during a consultation, the developers will try to fully understand this problem. On this basis, a user story is written. This is done by the users, indicating what they expect from a system. It is important that developers do not interfere.
    - **Estimating the user story (estimating a story)**: The developers estimate how much time it will take to make this. The developers can now also designate short examinations, called spikes, to investigate parts of the problem or the solution direction. These spikes are used to achieve better time estimates and are thrown away as soon as the problem and/or the solution is clear to everyone.
    - **Splitting a user story**: In this phase, the story must be completely clear and all ambiguities must be cleared up before iterative planning can be started. If the developers cannot give a time estimate for the story due to lack of clarity, the story must be split. If the users have described all their wishes, they can continue with the concept of decision-making, which is known as the commitment phase.
- **Commitment phase**: In this phase, we will find out what the costs are, what the benefits are, and what schedule consequences they have. We create four different lists based on the way we sort the items, which are as follows:
    - **Sorting by value**: Users put the user stories in order of what they consider important. They make the following three stacks:
        - **Critical**: Without these stories, the system cannot work or has no value.
        - **Important**: User stories that are important to the company.
        - **Nice to have**: User stories in which less important characteristics are realized.

- **Sorting according to risk**: Here, the developers give an estimate of the risks and sort the story accordingly. All values for the user story are added together, giving the user story a accumulated risk value of low (0-1), medium (2-4), or high (5-6). The following is an example of this:

Completeness (do we have all the details about the table?)

- Full (0)
- Incomplete (1)
- Unknown (2)

Vulnerability (are changes likely?):

- Low (0)
- Medium (1)
- High (2)

Difficulty (how difficult is it to realize?):

- Simple (0)
- Standard (1)
- Difficult (2)

- **Determining the development speed (velocity)**: Here, the developers determine at what speed they can execute a project and sort items accordingly.
- **Scope**: Here, it is determined which user stories will be realized in the coming release. This is the final sort. On this basis, the release date is determined. The sort should be according to the value for the users (business value).

- **Steering phase**: In this phase, the developers can steer the process together with the users. In other words, they can still change something, whether that be an individual user's story, or the importance of another particular story.

Iteration planning

Depending on the speed of the team, it can be determined how many story points the team can do per iteration. Iterations can last from one to three weeks. The focus here is on creating tasks and prioritizing them. The iterations also have the same phases as the earlier release planning, as follows:

- **Exploration phase**: During the research phase of iteration planning, the user stories are divided into tasks, and how long a task will take is estimated. The main activities in this phase include the following:
  - Translating the user story into tasks and writing them on task cards.
  - Adding or splitting tasks; in other words, if the developer cannot properly estimate how long a task will last because it is too big or too small, something will need to be altered.
  - Estimating the task, where an estimation of a task's execution is produced.

- **Commitment phase**: In the assignment phase of iteration planning, the following tasks are distributed among the developers:
  - A developer (programmer) accepts a task: Each developer takes a task for which they then become responsible.
  - The developer gives a time schedule: Because the developer is now responsible, they are now best able to give a time estimate.
  - The effective working time is determined, outlining the number of hours that a developer or programmer can develop during an iteration. (For example, in a 40-hour working week, in which five hours of meetings are held, the effective working time becomes 35 hours.)
  - Balancing: Once all the tasks have been assigned, the number of hours each developer has received is also compared to how many hours they actually have available (this is also known as the load factor). The tasks may then be redistributed to ensure that each developer has roughly the same amount of work. If a developer has too much work, something will have to shift.

- **Steering phase**: The execution of tasks is done during the execution, or steering phase, of iteration planning. There is a bit of a game element to this, but the following steps are advised:
  - **Taking a task card**: Here, the developer gets a card with the description of one of the tasks they have registered for.

- **Finding a partner**: The developer looks for a partner to develop the task with.
- **Designing the task**: If necessary, in this stage, a (short) design will be made.
- **Writing the unit test**: Before any programming, all tests must be ready. Preferably, these are automatic tests because they often have to be done every time source code is checked in.
- **Writing the code**: Here, the programmer or developer makes the program.
- **Testing the program**: The unit tests are performed.
- **Refactoring**: In this step, the refactoring rules are applied and the developers ensure their code meets the standards.
- **Doing functional and integration tests**: After the unit test, all possible other tests are run, such as integration tests, regression tests, and so on. The code must be adjusted in this step until the test succeeds.

Pair programming

XP states that, ultimately, everything revolves around code when software is crafted. So, if it is a good thing for developers to review code together, software should always be developed in pairs. In other words, pair programming can be defined by two people working behind one computer. Pair programming is often considered one of the most extreme and controversial aspects of XP because it is thought to be slower. However, research has shown that peer review and code inspection are the most powerful weapons against bugs—and these are much more powerful than systematic testing. These techniques are only used sparsely and often drum up great resistance among the programmers themselves, as well as managers who are afraid of an increase in working hours.

By enforcing the rule that all software development is carried out in pairs, which also change composition regularly, a collective sense of ownership arises, and peer review and code inspection become a natural part of the software process. As a result, the system ultimately delivered no longer consists of a collection of pieces of code tied together with strings, which are poorly maintainable.

There is another advantage to this way of working: there are always at least two people who fully understand every piece of code. The transference of knowledge to new colleagues happens more naturally, and a continuous training on the job takes place.

Some of the benefits of pair programming include the following:

- **Better quality code**: Activities such as reading code out loud and discussing the thought process behind it helps others to understand its complexity, as well as giving developers the opportunity to clarify any details and prevent irrevocable choices from being made.
- **Better knowledge-sharing within a team**: This is particularly useful when one of the developers is not yet familiar with the software component cooperates with someone who is.
- **Improved knowledge transfer**: This is helped by developers automatically learning new techniques and skills from experienced team members.
- **Less management overhead**: This is aided by less individual control because developers are working in teams of two or more.
- **Continued focus**: Pair programming can be particularly helpful if one member of the pair has their work interrupted for any reason.

So, are there any drawbacks to pair programming? Currently, it is not known exactly what the costs and benefits of pair programming are, but initial research indicates that the duration of a task increases by an average of 15% when a pair is working over an individual. Whether that cost can be justified by higher code quality is debatable.

Test Driven Development

In **Test Driven Development (TDD)**, testing is carried out before any programming. TDD relies on the premise that if testing is good, the test code should be written before a line of code (functionality) is.

Within XP, the writing of automatic unit tests occupies an important place, as writing unit tests is done before an actual program is started. In TDD, the programmer makes one or two tests, writes a piece of the program, makes an additional test case, reworks the program until the new test passes, the designs a new test, and so on.

The advantage of this process is that the programmer is obliged to think about the functionality and the exceptions that their program should take into account; they think about what the program should do first and how the program will work second. In other words, the tests capture the required functionality. It is therefore important that every program only has enough functionality to make the test work. If all tests pass, the program meets the previously-defined requirements, which are defined in the written and successful unit tests.

When refactoring is required, the already-written unit tests are therefore a guarantee that changes will not cause undesirable side effects in the operation of a program.

Should it be necessary to expand a program with new functionality, the first thing to do is to start writing new unit tests that will define the new functionality to be written. This new functionality is only realized when both the new and the old unit tests all succeed.

If a bug is found at a later stage during a functional test, writing a unit test that brings this bug to light is the first port of call. A bug is therefore not a fault in the program, but rather the result of an insufficient test.

To summarize, a software development project that is carried out using TDD does the following:

- Starts with one unit test that describes one feature of the program
- Runs the test, which should ultimately fail because there is no code
- Utilizes the minimum amount of code needed to make a test pass
- Rewrites code to make it simpler
- Repeats the process with more tests

Using this approach, the defect rate should go down after time, despite more time being needed to get things started. Most teams report that once they have reached the end stages of a project, the upfront testing cost is paid back and they work quicker in a project's final phases. Code that is developed this way tends to be of higher quality than otherwise, because for testing to work, you are forced to create code that is high in cohesion but low in coupling. This keeps code that works on the same behavior and keeps properties in the same class, as well as keeping modules as isolated as possible with clear interfaces to other code.

This approach may sound quite simple, but in practice, it's quite hard, as developers may forget to run tests. However, this problem can be easily fixed by setting up a project template in a CI/CD environment with pre-configured tests, where tests are run at every commit or push. If there are software engineers who are prone to overdo testing, it is a good idea to agree on the number of tests, and how far they will go, beforehand. Don't test constructs that are simple, such as accessors, for instance. On the other hand, be careful not to over-simplify your tests, such as by creating tests but no assertions.

Team culture and agreements are very important for testing. If some team members aren't on board, you will have conflicts. Also ensure that any test-templating, automation, or suites are well supported, or your tests will break. (This also means that several people should have knowledge of these products.)

In essence, TDD can really improve the quality of your software. This is especially true if all tests are automated via a continuous process, which we will discuss in the following section.

Continuous processes

Continuous processes are a group of processes that are envisioned to run all the time with no interruptions. There is also no need for batching, which often slows down XP as a whole.

Continuous integration

If integration and integration tests are important, then code should be integrated as often as possible – preferably, several times a day. This will prevent your team from working with different copies locally and encourages them to work alongside each other. Any integration problems will also become immediately visible. GitLab CI was created for this reason, and was introduced in Chapter 1, *Introducing the GitLab Architecture.*

One of the key reasons CI is used is to prevent integration problems, which can occur if developers work on their own for too long. Imagine the phenomenon of integration hell, where at the last minute before release, a developer merges a big chunk of code that then introduces conflicts.

Continuous integration has always been coupled with TDD in the XP world. Before integration tests are run, it helps if code is thoroughly tested locally, preferably by using unit tests. This way of testing code in your local environment helps uncover bugs before they break other people's code. Note that you can also hide features that are not yet complete by using feature toggles, which disable certain behaviors in code.

In some cases, build servers are used for other parts of the software **Quality Assurance (QA)** process, including running additional security tests, measuring performance, and even generating documentation. This behavior of shifting responsibilities to the build server means that a lot of QA work that was traditionally done after development work can instead be performed during development, with the bonus of immediate feedback. This feedback loop is a big driver of the continuous process of developing a software product, with the other being automation.

Automation has been further extended to create **Continuous Delivery (CD)**, by making the deployment of software part of the automation. To make this possible and run quickly without issue, the code in the main trunk or branch should always be in a state so that it can be deployed.

Every element of building a software product that can also be automated is eligible to be part of the CI process, especially when it's particularly complex. Automating these stages is one of the reasons CI/CD exists.

Refactoring

An important technique that differentiates XP from traditional development methods is refactoring, which is the continuous rewriting of program code in small, precisely-measured steps without affecting any visible functionality. In short, refactoring adds nothing to the functionality, but simplifies the design. By regularly executing rewriting steps, the overall effect is often astonishing.

In the meantime, some 70 rewrite rules have been discovered and documented. They carry names such as introduce null object, replace temp with query, and replace conditional with polymorphism. The preconditions for the successful application of refactoring is that there are unit tests available that can be carried out automatically after every rewriting step to ensure that the functionality has not changed. For example, for Smalltalk, there is now a refactoring browser, with which rewriting rules can be applied automatically and without the user having to worry too much about accuracy. Refactoring is often used in preparation for implementing an extension or a change in functionality.

What is not meant with refactoring is the rewriting of code, bug-fixing, or changing the user interface. Another danger of refactoring is that with the absence of good automated tests, you may introduce regression errors.

After some time and experience using this technique, teams report considerable improvements in the length of the code, less duplication, better coupling and cohesion, and reduced cyclomatic complexity. For people new to your software, this makes it easier to learn. For teams, it helps to think collectively about the general design of a project, and to understand why certain decisions have been made. Usually, this also relies on the introduction of certain reusable components and modules.

Short iterations

Software is regularly delivered to the customer for review in releases of limited size; if short iteration strokes are good, you should therefore make them very short. We're talking seconds, minutes, or hours, instead of weeks, months, and years. An average iteration of XP takes two weeks, although according to extremeprogramming.org, it can vary from one to three weeks.

The XP cycle consists of six phases: Exploration, Planning, Iterations to Release, Production, Maintenance, and Death.

For Agile projects, an iteration is a specific time period during which development takes place. This is called timeboxing. This period varies from project to project, but is usually between one and four weeks, and is often defined for each project. A typical Agile approach would be that a project consists of several iterations, with a short phase of planning at the beginning and a closing phase at the end.

Iterations are mostly classified in work weeks that start on a Monday and end on a Friday. After a while, the fixed term of the iteration makes it easier to assess how long a project will take.

The iteration timebox in the Scrum methodology is called a Sprint, which is of course a reference to Rugby. In XP, they are called weekly cycles. To most people, the word iteration means repetition or even multiple repetitions; when used in the Agile context, it means a repeated process.

Everybody owns the code

Note that every developer has equal rights to all aspects of a program's code. If the design is good, make it part of everyone's daily work and improve the design step by step as soon as the need arises. If architecture is so important, let everyone work on developing it. This concept encourages everyone to contribute and take responsibility.

Shared understanding

The values in a group are mostly to do with perception. To be efficient and effective as a group, you have to agree on certain points and share values and a common understanding.

Coding standards

To have a shared understanding you need to have some rules. There are coding standards that are known and used by everyone. It really helps if source is consistently formatted. That way everyone can read it and change it. Speak the same language in your code files. It will also help in ensuring collective ownership of the codebase.

Simple design

If the code belongs to all developers in a group and everyone can change everything, it should be possible for them to do so. Keep the design as simple as possible. XP works a lot with the **Keep It Short and Simple (KISS)** principle. In other words, for a system to be easy to change, the design should be as simple as possible. This is easier said than done, however.

Traditional development methods have learned to think ahead and to always think about functionality in a design that might have to be realized in the future, but these methods are based on the assumption that costs for changes increase exponentially. This is why XP is always trying to choose the simplest design to enable a functionality that must now be realized. Ideally, any future expansions can be implemented with XP without the usual extra costs. It also turns out that, all too often in the realization of a well thought-out design, it does not reflect current requirements. This may happen either because certain details have been overlooked during analysis and design, or because requirements have been adjusted. With XP, design does not come first, but instead follows the code.

System metaphor

All team members, including developers and users or customers, share a common view on the system (known as a metaphor); everyone must be able to describe the system in simple words. The use of naming conventions should also contribute to this.

As we have discussed, the final takeaway is that when working with XP, the human element is still the most important one. Is everyone talking about the same things, for example? Do they all think the right priorities are set? Are they able to create software that works and is understandable? This human element is also one of the driving forces behind DevOps, the spillover of Agile thinking from software development to IT operations.

The DevOps movement

The term DevOps originated in Belgium around the end of the last decade, as a result of the so-called DevOps days. These days were meant to bring together IT experts from both development and management operations. A DevOps team was initially defined as a multidisciplinary team that is fully responsible for the management and CD of a service. Think of Amazon and Google as companies that use these kinds of teams; they release dozens of changes every day.

This way of working is not yet standardized in big organizations—ITIL and PRINCE2 still reign, and the Information Technology (IT) department is desperately trying to deliver services with value. The way in which these services are provided is difficult to maintain in the current situation where IT is still often seen as a cost item. This is caused by the following:

- The way of organizing organizations as a collection of independent silo's
- A focus on creating process excess (too many rules set in stone)
- Not defining clear **Key Performance Indicators** (**KPIs**) for measuring performance.

The technologies in these silos are not compatible, whereas for a successful business-IT alignment, one coherent chain is needed.

In addition, we are now seeing that customers are increasingly asking for the fast delivery of a new functionality. This includes the quick resolution of incidents, short lines of communication, and excellent quality requirements in their IT organization. Using the old ways of organizing IT in an organization, processes, working methods, attitude, behavior, and the required performance and results are not being sufficiently realized. A famous quote attributed to Albert Einstein, that *"the definition of insanity is doing the same thing over and over again and expecting a different result"*, seems to increasingly apply to IT. It is time, therefore, to fundamentally reconsider the setup of its organizations.

The following diagram illustrates the DevOps process:

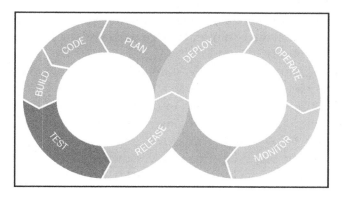

History of the movement

The term DevOps still causes a lot of confusion in many places. As a movement, it is still young, but it is largely based on common sense and experiences from the past. DevOps teams appeared from an effort by companies to respond to changes in the market. The new DevOps approach has been further developed with the aim of releasing higher-quality software to customers faster and more frequently. A brief timeline of DevOps is as follows:

- **2007**: During the migration of a data center for the Belgian government, Patrick Debois is frustrated by the many conflicts between developers and system administrators. This makes him think.
- **2008**: At the Agile Conference in Toronto, software developer Andrew Shafer is poised to give a session about Agile infrastructure. He decides to skip it because he thought there were no attendees, but Debois was going to attend. Later, Debois tracks down Shafer for a wide-ranging hallway conversation. Based on their talk, they form the Agile Systems Administration Group.
- **2009**: Two Flickr employees, John Allspaw and Paul Hammond, make the case to test, build, and deploy responsive, fresh software in a bid to make operations and development integrated and transparent. The first DevOps days take place in Gent, Belgium. The conference takes place on October 30 with an impressive collection of developers, system administrators, experts, and others. When the conference ends, ongoing discussions move over to Twitter. To create a memorable hashtag, Debois shortens the name to #DevOps.

- **2010**: This is when the first ever DevOps days were organized in the US, carried out with the help of John Willis (author of the famous book, *The Phoenix Project*), along with early proponents of DevOps. The event soon becomes a global series of conferences that are community-organized and are the major force driving the DevOps community forward.
- **2011**: The community of DevOps starts to use open source tools, such as Vagrant, that can leverage technologies such as Chef and Puppet.
- **2012**: The presentation development segment grows rapidly and becomes focused on innovation. There are now various DevOps days that suddenly pop up in a number of countries.
- **2014**: Some of the biggest companies worldwide begin to use the DevOps method in their organization, including LEGO and Nordstrom.

Today, DevOps is embraced across the world by a number of businesses; small, big, and private businesses benefit from DevOps. DevOps can bring out the best results in the long-run for any business and contribute to its success.

However, an organization is not able to switch over to DevOps quickly – changing processes in an organization can have a major impact on its culture and needs time. A good way to find out where you might be in this journey is to use a maturity model. When using a model to represent reality, you can start to simplify the problem, instead of being overloaded by the amount of solutions and tools that are available. If you know where you are in the maturity model, you can determine where you want to be, and then plan your journey.

Four Quadrant Model

The original maturity model is the Capability Maturity Model invented at **Carnegie Mellon University (CMU)**. It is a bit heavy to fully utilize, so simplified, more lightweight versions of it are preferable. One such version is the Four Quadrant Model put forward by Brian Dawson (`https://techbeacon.com/devops/how-map-your-devops-journey`). It is derived from real-world DevOps transformations and offers a flexible way to assess maturity.

In the Four Quadrant Model, the values on the x axis consist of the different phases in the cycle of software development. You can recognize the **Software Development Life Cycle (SDLC)** in this:

- Define
- Plan
- Code

- Build
- Integrate
- Test
- Release
- Deploy
- Operate

You see there is quite some overlap with the DevOps lifecycle phases that are proposed by GitLab.

The cycle is divided into two halves: **Agile Upstream** (which includes a definition, planning, coding, and building) and **Agile Downstream** (which includes integration, testing, release, implementation, and methods such as continuous deployment and continuous delivery).

On the y axis, there is the level of adoption of Agile and DevOps practices in an organization. At the lower end, there is the team level, which moves on to the workgroup level, and finally the enterprise level. In the original CMMI model, there are usually different levels of maturity. The following figure illustrates the 4 Quadrant model:

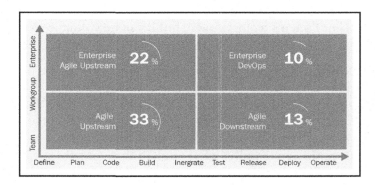

Agile Upstream means that in a software life cycle, the development side of the product is done with Agile methodologies. Agile Downstream is all about the deployment and operational side of the SDLC.

Each team must strive to implement the Four Quadrant Model because it enables them to innovate faster, increase productivity, respond to market changes, gain a competitive advantage, and increase employee satisfaction and retention.

Another way of measuring maturity is to look at competencies. How strong are you in certain aspects, for example?

Four levels of competence

One way to test competence is by using the model mentioned by Mike Kavis' paper in Forbes. He describes a model that is based on the *Four stages of learning* used by Noel Burch in the 1970s.

The basic idea is that an individual goes through the following four stages while acquiring a new skill:

- **Stage 1: unconscious incompetence**: A person may not recognize that they need a certain skill. The first step in changing or growing is to recognize this deficit and to acknowledge the skill as is.
- **Stage 2: conscious incompetence**: Gradually, it becomes apparent that a necessary skill is lacking. This is learned by making mistakes.
- **Stage 3: conscious competence**: After several iterations or tries, the person acquires the skill and knowingly applies it. It won't succeed every time, and doing so takes serious effort.
- **Stage 4: unconscious competence**: The skill has become so natural or logical, that it can be applied unconsciously. It can even by taught to others.

Davis claims that this model can be applied to organizations that are trying to grasp the DevOps concept. It is not scientifically proven, but it can be valuable to make the following comparison:

- **Stage 1: Nothing there**: The organization initially seems averse to change. The term DevOps is described as a hype and is not applicable. This usually means that people don't really understand what DevOps is about. People are trapped in the old silo thoughts and think that development should take over operations, or vice versa.
- **Stage 2: Recognition**: Finally, it has sunk in that something has to change. In this stage, there will be mistakes. For instance, automation is introduced but the development silo may still think it is responsible for writing everything. A new silo (the DevOps silo) emerges, where developers are only creating automation for operations. These developers are not knowledgeable in networking or security and compliance or other operational issues. Similar problems occur if the Operations department silo is converted to 'the' DevOps engineer. With limited knowledge about engineering, untested and unmanageable shell scripts may appear. However, at this stage, an organization is still learning and will eventually proceed to the next stage if the inevitable growing pains are managed.

- **Stage 3**: **Coming of age**: After learning from their mistake, the management of an organization has taken up interest and recognized the added value of changing people and processes. In the previous stage, the aim was to integrate the silos of development and operations. Now that this has succeeded through trial and error, cooperation has expanded to include legal departments, compliance, and audit. The first signs of productivity are visible, with the creation of specialized platforms, a framework, or a template for deploying standardized enterprise applications from idea to production. Platforms begin to have everything baked in, such as compliance and quality control.

- **Stage 4**: **100% business driven**: At this stage, multiple business units in an organization deploy several times a day and are able to easily enhance the process and share their knowledge via the platform. In the most optimal form, the business unit is in complete control and has become a multi-disciplined team that can advise and collaborate with dedicated platform specialists.

Of course, these models are quite theoretical, but they can help in the process of organizational change. Fortunately, several tools have emerged to help organizations bridge these gaps between the stages of maturity, which we'll discuss in the following sections.

The toolchain

Although we have learned that DevOps is more than just tools, there are a number of tools that are commonly used in the enterprise, such as the following:

- **A source code repository**: Computer source code has become a very valuable asset. It is usually stored in a repository with advanced version management features. The repository manages the many versions of code that are checked in, so developers can collaborate on each other's projects. This concept is not new and has been around for 30 years, but is a big part of continuous integration because it is where the source code is kept. Popular source code repository tools include the following:
    - Git on the client
    - GitLab
    - GitHub
    - Subversion
    - TFS
    - CVS

All of these repository tools are explained in detail in Chapter 4, *Configuring GitLab from the Terminal,* Chapter 5, *Importing Your Project from GitHub to GitLab,* Chapter 6, *Migrating From CVS,* and Chapter 7, *Switching from SVN.*

- **Build server**: Building software used to be done on the individual developer's workstation, but for the CI pipeline, a dedicated build server is used to compile source code from the source code repository into executable artefacts. Modern build servers do not just build, but also provide advance testing functions. Popular tools include the following:
  - **GitLab Runners**: The build tool for GitLab.
  - **Jenkins**: A fork of the Hudson project and a CI platform. This platform is primarily intended for the repeated execution and monitoring of build tasks, as well as the automated building and testing of applications. The many freely available plugins make it very easy to further expand the functionality of Jenkins. This software is only available as a distributed service to use on the cloud and is tightly integrated with GitHub as a source code repository.
- **Configuration management**: For CI/CD, you need to control the environment where it takes place. For this, there are configuration management tools that describe and automate large parts of your infrastructure. Popular tools include the following:
  - **Puppet**: Management software which can control large numbers of servers. This concerns both the management of configuration files (the settings of servers) and the management of the installed software (packages). It uses a declarative language and has a steep learning curve.
  - **Chef**: Also configuration management software, Chef supports slightly fewer platforms than Puppet and is not a declarative language. Chef uses pure Ruby code that indicates what you want to do on your servers. You have more freedom to create your own program data structures and functions. It is used by GitLab to manage the omnibus package.

- **Virtual infrastructure**: Infrastructure on which software runs has always been virtual, and an operating system is already several layers of abstraction. In the cloud, virtual infrastructure is an extra layer of abstraction that represents entire machines (such as networks, nodes, and storage). There is also an orchestration layer that manages the infrastructure. This provides easy up- and down-scaling and can use all resources efficiently. The first real, large-scale virtual infrastructure that became available as a service was Amazon Web Services. The other major tech companies soon followed with Google Cloud and Microsoft Azure. These infrastructures can be managed with their own orchestration tools, but also have APIs that can be used by configuration management tools, including the following:
  - Ansible
  - Puppet
  - Chef
  - Google Cloud

Governments often have special requirements regarding their data. This is called data sovereignty and this is why specialist clouds have arisen for governments. According to Garter, these clouds could be the next legacy system, after government infrastructure was moved like-for-like to the cloud without being decomposed into elastic, efficient, and cost-effective cloud components.

Not everyone is able to run their software and data on public clouds, even if they have special agreements. If you run a private or hybrid cloud, for example, you are essentially using abstractions that exist on the internet in your own data center. Even without the elasticity of Amazon or Azure, it can be very beneficial to apply cloud techniques yourself. The accompanying automation tools make integration with existing systems easier, and a lot less people are needed for managing the system. There are also private clouds; for example, VMware has vCloud. It is quite easy to extend your existing VMware infrastructure to create cloud-like environments.

- **Test automation**: Testing is all about ensuring confidence in your product. When the product reaches deployment time in your pipeline, it should be tested for certain defects automatically before it has reached that point. There are several tools available to perform all kinds of testing and integrate nicely with a lot of other pipeline products; they include the following:
  - **Selenium**: Selenium is an application that allows you to automate browsers. What you do with this depends on your goal. You can automate repetitive administrative tasks, but Selenium is also used for browser testing.

- **Cucumber**: This is a test tool for **Behavior-Driven Development (BDD)**. The primary goal of BDD is to let people communicate, and close the gap between technical and business people. You can write tests in a human-readable format.
- **Apache JMeter**: JMeter is an open source tool that performs load, performance, and stress tests. It is a simple but effective application where different types of scripts show exactly what the result of the test is. These scripts are used for HTTP websites and provide a simulated test environment. In addition to applications, JMeter is also suitable for checking services on the web and various databases.
- You can also utilize GitLab Runners and write your own tests.

- **Pipeline orchestration**: The pipeline refers to an automated number of steps to get your code from inception to production after it has been checked into version control. It's based on the idea of a manufacturing assembly line.

To manage things along the way in a CI/CD process, pipeline orchestration tools were introduced. Some of these tools include:

- **Kubernetes**: Kubernetes is, essentially, a platform for the roll-out and management of containers on a large scale. Kubernetes, Greek for helmsman or pilot, is the second name for the project, which originally saw the light of day in the big halls of Google as Project Seven of Nine. Project Seven of Nine was an external version of Borg, the task scheduler that drives the services of Google, and the operation of which was a Google secret for a long time.
- Built as an extension to the Docker API, orchestration using Swarm also became popular a couple of years ago. It can easily convert a loose group of Docker containers in a managed virtual Docker engine. This makes it very easy to start running container workloads at scale from scratch.
- **Mesos/Marathon Apache**: Mesos is a distributed kernel and is the backbone of DC/OS. It abstracts CPU, memory, storage, and other computer resolutions. It has APIs for resource management, planning in data centers, and cloud environments. It can scale up to 10,000 nodes. It can therefore be extremely suitable for large production clusters. It supports container orchestration with Marathon.

All of the aforementioned tools can be integrated with GitLab, and you can use GitLab for all parts of a pipeline. You can use runners for testing, building, or deploying your product, and you can utilize Kubernetes to orchestrate your workloads.

It's up to you which part of the pipeline is used in GitLab, but it can support you in all stages of the DevOps life cycle, illustrated as follows:

We have now explained the basic setup of a CD pipeline in DevOps. GitLab offers close to 100% of all the stages, but can integrate with existing components as well.

Summary

This chapter was intended to provide more background on the origins and development of GitLab. A tool does not arise from the void. In the 1990s, it became clear that in different parts of the world, people came to the same conclusion: linear software development is not the right approach for all projects. The solution to this problem has finally reached the operations department after 10 years through DevOps. DevOps is a way of working and a culture with accompanying tools for which GitLab has been built. In the next chapter, we will see how GitLab can contribute to a better DevOps experience.

Questions

1. What is an SDLC?
2. How many participants were at the Agile Manifesto conference in Utah?
3. When was the waterfall model first mentioned?
4. Where was XP programming born?
5. What does MoSCoW mean?
6. Where and when did the first DevOps days take place?
7. What is Agile Upstream?
8. Name two configuration management tools.

Further reading

- *The Agile Maturity Model:* https://info.thoughtworks.com/rs/thoughtworks2/images/agile_maturity_model.pdf
- *DevOps maturity model:* https://techbeacon.com/devops/how-map-your-devops-journey
- *What is DevOps?* http://radar.oreilly.com/2012/06/what-is-devops.html
- *The Agile Developer's Handbook,* by *Paul Flewelling:* https://www.packtpub.com/web-development/agile-developers-handbook
- *DevOps: Continuous Delivery, Integration, and Deployment with DevOps,* by *Sricharan Vadapalli:* https://www.packtpub.com/virtualization-and-cloud/devops-continuous-delivery-integration-and-deployment-devops
- *Practical DevOpsm,* by *Joakim Verona:* https://www.packtpub.com/in/networking-and-servers/practical-devops
- *Wicked Problems, Righteous Solutions: A Catalogue of Modern Software Engineering Paradigms,* by *DeGrace, Peter,* and *Stahl, Leslie Hulet,* pp. 116, 117, 127. Reprinted with permission of Prentice Hall, Englewood Cliffs, New Jersey, 1990.
- *Managing the development of large systems: Concepts and techniques,* by W. W. Royce In: 9th International Conference on Software Engineering. ACM. 1970. p. 328-38.

10
Create Your Product, Verify, and Package it

In this chapter, we will try to compare the theory from the previous chapter with its implementation in GitLab. As GitLab was born from a need to have a collaboration platform with advanced features, it has grown organically to its current form. It was built with agility in mind. We will present a use case where a small company wants to build a software product, and we will use GitLab to evolve the idea into a product.

In this chapter, we will be covering following topics:

- The GitLab workflow
- Managing your ideas
- Planning your feature
- Creating it
- Verifying your product
- Packaging it for use

Technical requirements

To follow along with instructions in this chapter, please download the Git repository, along with the examples, from GitHub: `https://github.com/PacktPublishing/Mastering-GitLab-12/tree/master/Chapter10`.

You will need an Amazon account if you want to try the examples.

You also need **AWS Command Line Interface (AWS CLI)**: `https://docs.aws.amazon.com/cli/latest/userguide/cli-chap-install.html`

The GitLab workflow

Remember we introduced the DevOps pipeline as seen by GitLab in previous chapter. This screenshot shows the various GitLab stages:

In this chapter, we will present several aspects of the entire pipeline as we try to use it in our example project. The first phase is defined as **Manage**, and it sounds a bit weird as the first part, but it is a continuous process spanning the entire pipeline, and GitLab provides tools for it. The next stage will be **Plan**, in which you refine and prioritize and set timelines. Then you start the **Create** phase where the tasks are executed to produce solutions. After creating your product, you need to test different aspects of it in the **Verify** phase. After verifying the product you will package it for deployment.

To explain the GitLab workflow in more detail, we will present a use case that is going to be used throughout this chapter to demonstrate features in GitLab. For some features you will need the most comprehensive GitLab license.

Imagine a company called *Event Horizon*. They want to build a solution for managing events (for humans). For instance, you can use their solution to arrange invitations to a party.

We introduce User1, who is a backend engineer, and is tasked with creating a backend for this solution. Then we also have User2, who is currently product owner of this product. They are both part of the IT department of the company. Then we have User3, who is part of the marketing department.

User1 and User2 have both been made members of the IT group in GitLab. User3 is a member of the marketing group, but has reporter access to IT.

Let's help them create this product (minimally) and demonstrate how they can use GitLab for this.

In the meeting where both users and developers are present (the Release planning in XP, or Sprint 0 when using Scrum) it is decided that these are following requirements:

1. We want to build an app to help organize events.
2. It needs to use email to communicate.
3. We are creating a list of invitees in advance.
4. Invitees can interactively indicate if they will attend.
5. Non-functional requirement: documentation is very important.
6. Non-functional requirement: we want to automate as much as possible.
7. Non-functional requirement: the tool used should enhance collaboration.
8. Non-functional requirement: the code used should be reviewed by at least one other person.

At the end of the meeting, the requirements are prioritized and the developers talk without the customers about the possibilities with GitLab as a product. This phase is the subject of the next section.

DevOps phase – manage your ideas

Instead of creating big designs up front we have learned that iterative development is the way to go. But even for projects using Agile methodologies there are some considerations before your coding goes off to start. This stage in the DevOps life cycle is called *Manage* and it comprises the *whole life cycle*. It is the beginning of an Agile iteration but also the end and in between. You will manage your solution from the beginning and it never stops. An import part of managing is knowing how you are doing. You can analyze this in GitLab, as shown in the next section.

Cycle analytics

One of the most important metrics in developing software through an Agile method is the cycle time. This **Key Performance Indicator** (**KPI**) is best described as the total time that has elapsed from the time work has started until completion of the task. Or in IT, the time it takes to get an idea implemented on production.

Before Agile project management, tools such as Microsoft Project were used to keep track of time. Nowadays, *guesstimates* are not entered in a project anymore, but other things such as risk and velocity are calculated in story points and they are used to plan some weeks ahead.

In GitLab, there is a place to measure cycle times: cycle analytics. It means you have to use GitLab's project management features and it is available in all editions. The following image is an example of cycle analytics for the GitLab CE project. Notice that it takes about a month for an idea to go into production (which corresponds nicely with its actual release cycle):

We can use cycle analytics later in the project to check how well GitLab is used and what velocity the development team has.

DevOps phase – plan your feature

The next stage in the DevOps life cycle that GitLab is envisioning is *Plan*. For this phase, we will explore all the steps needed to prepare for the coding and building of the solution. In GitLab, there are several tools that can help you in this phase, regardless of which development methodology you prefer (Agile or waterfall). Where to begin? We always begin with creating an issue. We will discuss this in the next section:

Issues

What is an issue? Well, it can be many things. It could be a new business idea, a technical problem, a cry for help. An issue is like starting a new discussion, and it is a way to express your thinking. It should change along the way as other people get involved. It is the atomic, basic, first thing in GitLab that everything else is derived from. It always a good idea to start looking in the existing list of issues to see if your problem or wish is already part of an existing issue.

GitLab, as a product, facilitates this discussion and offers ways to manage it and flows to verify assumptions.

An issue has several attributes and concepts, which we will look at.

Content

Of course, an issue has content, so how is it structured? The issue has a title and a description. It is also possible to insert tasks into the issue using markdown formatting. What also counts as content are the accompanying comments and events/activities that are linked and viewable through the issue. Within the content you can also insert quick actions, which will be discussed later in this chapter.

Status of the issue

There are several states an issue can be in. Of course, it can be open or closed. Another aspect of state is the confidentiality of the issue. If there is sensitive information, an issue can be marked as confidential. The visibility of the issue is then limited to members of the group who have at least reporter permissions.

Meta information

Every issue has an author, and that information is prominently displayed, along with the current assignee. Other meta information consists of well-known project management data, such as: milestones, due dates, and weight.

Let's try to make this clear, based on our example. The *Event Horizon* company is about to start the first Scrum sprints. They want to use GitLab issues for project management.

User1 creates an issue in which he asks which technology we are going to use. That could be an example of the first issue, as shown in the following screenshot:

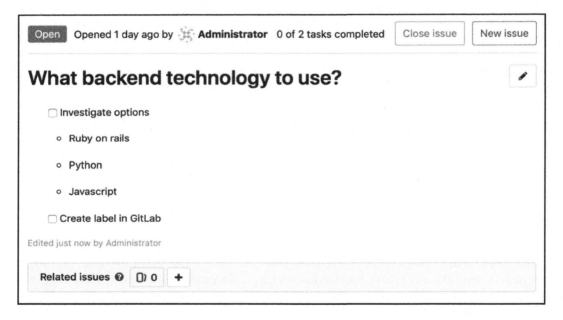

You will see that there is a list with tasks defined.

User2 creates an issue regarding which documentation style to use for the project, as shown in the following screenshot:

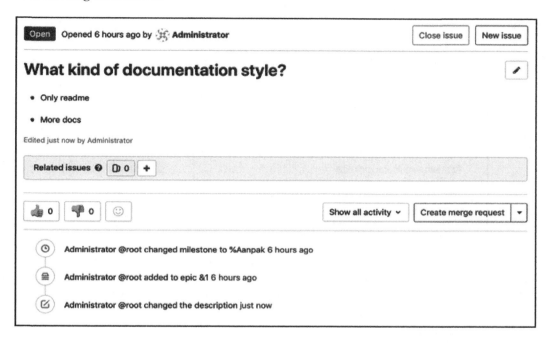

Both are valid questions to ask, and to start a discussion about, and we will see how this continues when an issue evolves to the next level, a discussion. We will talk about this in the next section.

Discussions

This a very important part of GitLab and is the next step in issue discovery. It is possible to give feedback in the form of comments in the context of an issue, and also in the following:

- Epics
- Merge requests
- Snippets
- Commits
- Commit diffs

It is also possible to create a threaded discussion or to transform a comment into one. You can use markdown to format your text and use quick actions (as described in the *Quick actions* section in this chapter). The default comment form is shown in the following example:

If you have set up your GitLab for incoming email, you can respond to emails that are sent as comment notification emails. Replying to those will create a new comment or discussion item. In the following screenshot, you will find a discussion for an issue in the Event Horizon web application:

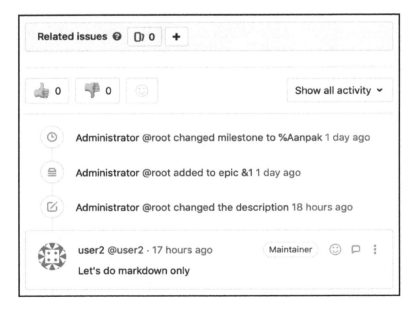

As mentioned, it is also possible to add a discussion to an epic, which we will discuss later. The following example is the screenshot for adding any discussion to an epic:

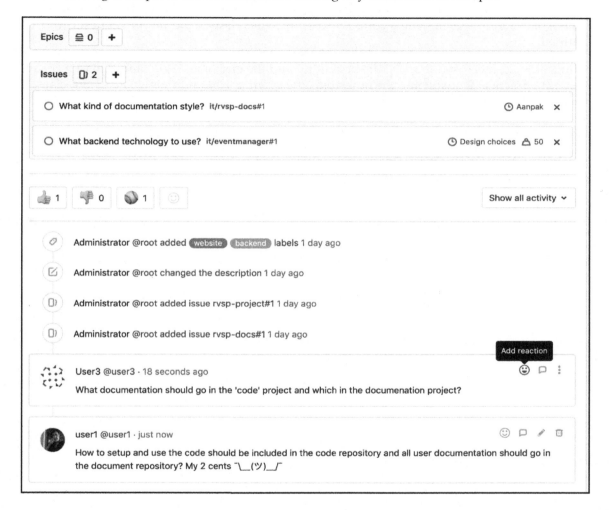

Using these discussions, the idea evolves, as does the understanding of it.

Milestones

Milestones can have different functions in a project, but are used in GitLab to indicate where one stands in achieving a common goal for which issues and merge requests are defined.

A milestone can be used to mark the beginning and the end of an Agile iteration or a sprint. It's quite practical to just name the milestone after your sprint and then you can associate issues to the milestone to add work.

At GitLab, they are used as one release cycle. For instance, when they go from release 11.8 to 11.9, all the work contained in that release will be represented by a milestone, and that will be labeled 11.9. Each piece of work is represented in an issue, for instance, the problems you need to solve, the conversation. All these issues work together towards one large milestone.

For the Event Horizon project, there are three milestones defined: **mvp 1**, **MVP3**, and **mvp2**. You can see them as follows:

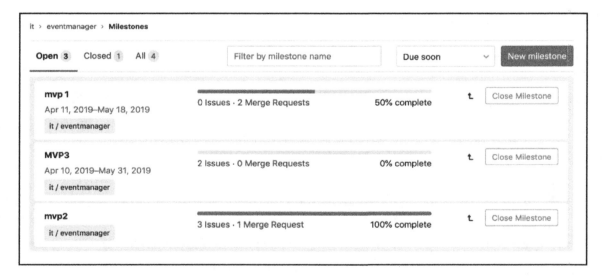

If we open a milestone, it has the following characteristics:

Project milestones can only be linked to issues and merge requests in the project context. You can view a list of milestones by going to **Issues** and then **Milestones**. Group milestones can be linked with issues and merge requests on the group context, which means you can link it to several projects that are part of the group. The list of those can be found via the **Issues** and then **Milestones** links in the group. A general view of all milestones is via the dashboard milestones list, or via the top navigation link, **Milestones**.

Epics

If you have GitLab EE, you can create epics. An epic is an extensive user story that still has to be broken down into a set of smaller user stories. Usually, an epic describes a defined piece of functionality or product property, but needs to be worked out in more detail before the team can commit to this feature to be realized within one sprint. It's like a theme among issues.

For big organizations that work with long-running project management programs, there is also the option to have multi-level epics so that you can link and coordinate efforts. There is a button (+) for it in the creation form of the epic.

Epics very much resemble issues in that you have the same editing functions and state. The same formatting is applicable, and also the same quick actions. Maybe more importantly for epics is the option to set due dates. Big projects that cover multiple business domains are still more date driven, so we can imagine that these fields are more appropriate here then in Agile-drive smaller projects.

From the epic, you can navigate to the linked issues. Also, when issues become too big and are misrepresented epics, it is also possible to promote an issue to an epic.

For the Event Horizon project, the Product Owner User3 can create an epic to track the progress of the two different projects and the issues that were created earlier. The following screenshot shows the tracking progress for the projects:

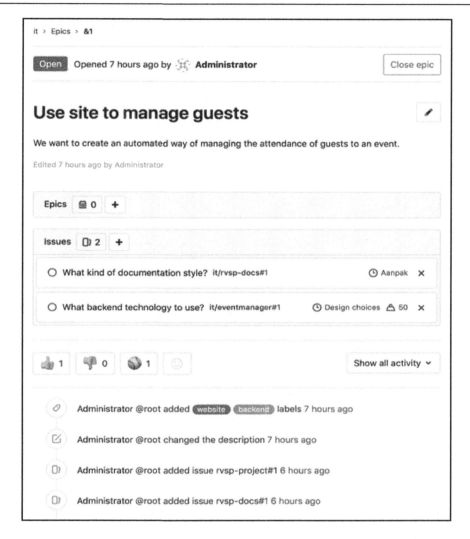

The ability to use epics to group issues is necessary for keeping control over multiple discussions and issues and projects that together work towards a solution.

Time tracking

With this feature, you can track how much time is being spent on issues and merge requests. You can also track what was estimated, to see where you stand. It is part of GitLab Core.

In the following screenshot, we can see that for an issue in the eventmanager project some time has been estimated and spent:

In the body of an issue or merge request, and in comments, you can use quick actions to enter the estimated and spent time for the issue. It can only be done by team members.

As seen in the following screenshot, you can use `/estimate`, followed by the unit of time. If something will take five days and four hours, you would write `/estimate 5d 4h` in a comment and, after that, press **Comment**. There can only be one estimate. You can also remove it by using `/remove_estimate`. Here's the screenshot for reference:

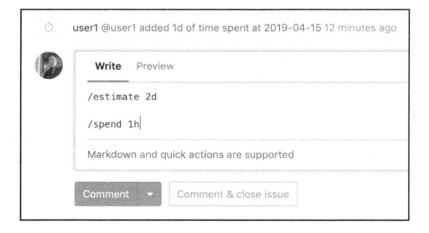

In the same manner, you can record how much time has been spent on the issue. Members of the project can use a quick /spent action in issues and merge requests to add time to a total amount of time that is dedicated to an issue. For example, if two hours have been spent, you issue /spent 2h, and it will show in the right panel. You can even remove time spent by using negative numbers, for instance, /spend -1h. It won't go below 0, but will reset the number. You can remove the total at once with /remote_time_spent.

Quick actions

A very handy feature in GitLab is the quick action. You can use a / with certain keywords to trigger a command on issues, epics, merge requests, and commits, just like you can with something like IRC chat. It is faster than using GitLab's web buttons or other controls. Remember to put each *command* on a separate line, otherwise it will be parsed incorrectly. Once they are parsed and executed, they will be removed from the text and nobody can see them. There is, of course, an audit trail for the action executed.

Some samples of quick action are as follows:

- /todo: Add a todo item from the comment
- /done: Mark the todo as done
- /close: Same as clicking the close button
- /assign me or @someone else
- /milestone %milestone: Set a milestone from the comment
- /estimate <1w 3d 1h 10m>: Add a time estimation
- /due <in 1 day>: Set a due date
- /approve: Approve a merge request
- Special quick action for commit messages: /tag v1.5 – Tag immediately a commit with a message of choice

> You can find all quick actions here: https://docs.gitlab.com/ee/user/project/quick_actions.html

The Project Issue board

Hidden in GitLab is a very nice project management feature. It is called the *Project Issue board*. It can be used to implement a workflow by using visualization and can help to plan and organize. It does not enforce one way of working. You have to organize and form your own process. The boards are heavily dependent on labels, which are used to group issues into lists.

If you go to the issues in the left navigation bar, you will find the option **Boards**. By default, you get a board called **Development** that offers basic lanes such as **Open, To Do, Doing**, and **Closed**. You can drag issues from lane to lane, indicating a change in state. For instance, if an issue is done, you drag it to **Closed**. What happens is that the issue will automatically get the label **Closed**. The following screenshot is an example of the project issue board for the eventmanager project:

If you use GitLab Enterprise Edition, you can even have multiple issue boards, which can mean several things:

- A board can be shared by multiple teams: Group Issue boards.
- Each team can have its own boards.
- There are several views for projects, based on the scope of the board (milestone, label, assignee and weight).

In the following screenshot, you can see how to create a new issue board by clicking on the drop-down list saying **Development**. The default board is as follows:

When you click on **Create new board** you will be presented with a form to enter the name of the new board, and the scope of the board. As with a label, it is just an attribute of an issue that is used to group or aggregate. Let's choose to focus on milestones, and choose the milestone **MVP3**, which is the minimum viable product coming out of sprint 3, which is shown as follows:

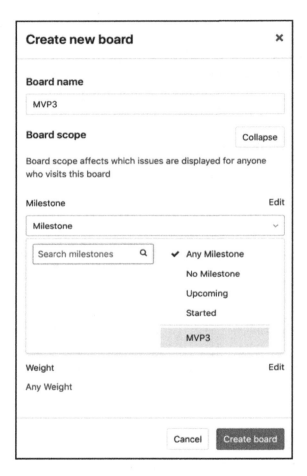

After creation, you will be presented with an issue board including the issues that are already assigned to a milestone. You can add issues (which then are coupled to the milestone) with the **Add Issues,** which is shown in the following example:

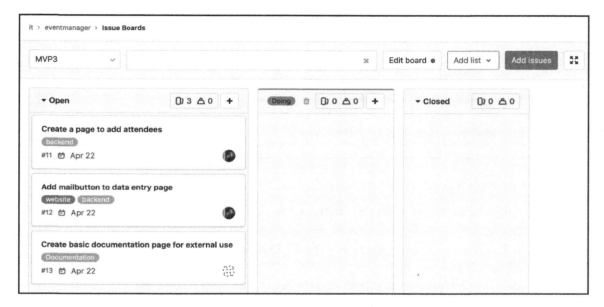

Issue boards can function as information radiators for teams, it organizes issues in the way you want and can be the subject of conversation for a team meeting.

Todos

A planning feature that is useful for the individual user is *todo*. Notification emails can pile up in your inbox and get messy. An easy-to-use todo list, where you can view your tasks sorted chronologically, is more focused. You will find them at the top of your navigation bar, as follows:

When you have clicked the todo item, you will see a list of your todos with the option to sort in different fields, as shown in the following example:

The following items could trigger a todo item:

- An issue or merge request is assigned to you.
- Being `@mentioned` in an issue, merge request, commit, or epic.
- A failed job in one of your project CI/CD pipelines that has been marked *not allowed to fail*.
- When in an automatic pipeline, a merge request has a conflict.

DevOps phase – create it

Now that the project has been planned by creating issues, milestones and so on, it is time to really start building. The next phase is *Create*, and GitLab provides several tools to help you with this. Before you start building, you should make sure your project and group structure is adequate for cooperation.

Projects and groups

The *Event Horizon* company has created two groups in GitLab. One group is called **it** and another **Marketing,** as shown in the following screenshot:

We have created two separate projects in this context. The first one is called eventmanager, which will hold the source code for the technical solution. You can create this project by clicking on **New Project** if this is your first project, or click on the **+** icon in the top navigation bar. The form to create a new project appears as follows:

The title of the project is eventmanager, and it will also appear in the URL. Take a good look at the first part of the URL. This is the namespace that defaults to your own, but we want this project to be in the **it** group. When you do that, you will notice that visibility is automatically set to **Private**. This is because the group **it** has this as default.

Finally, we want this project to be accompanied by a README, so we need to choose to automatically create it. Don't worry about what the project will look like, we will iterate on it in the sprint.

Next, there is a second project called eventmanager-documentation, which will consist of the documentation. We will use GitLab pages as a technology to build our user documentation, and will choose **Pages/Plain HTML** as a template. This is shown in the following screenshot:

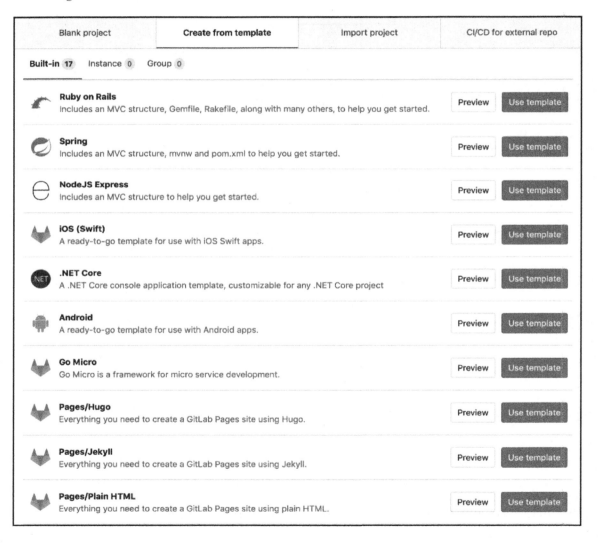

You have to enter the **Project name** and **Project slug** and determine the visibility, as per the following example:

If you click on projects you will see a list of two projects, as shown in the following example:

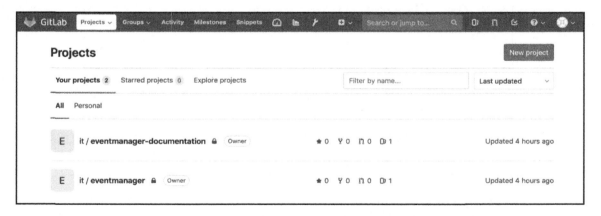

Now we have our project and group structure ready, let's deal with other features that promote cooperation.

Snippets

If you have worked with GitHub as a developer, you will have seen *gists* before. These are little pieces of code that are usable for more than one goal. Often they could exist in several code repositories, but they are available as gists to be reused. In GitLab this concept is known as *snippets*. They are also used as examples to be discussed about, and so on. The following example is a screenshot of a new snippet:

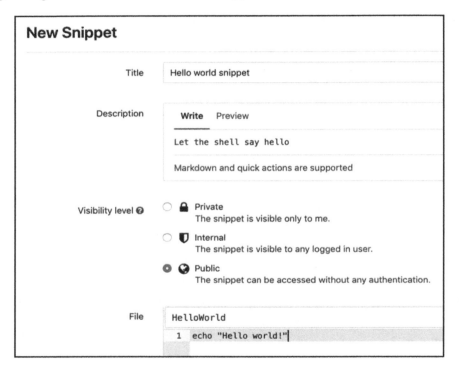

You can create snippets on a personal and project level. They can be made public, and there is even an option to embed them in your own site, as shown in the following example:

Snippets can be used to share information, and using them could help to fulfill the requirement for the platform to enhance collaboration.

Web IDE

As of GitLab 10.4, an enhanced web editor is available in GitLab that gives you the ability to work on code online from the web. It offers many different features, including syntax highlighting for the most common languages (PHP, Ruby, Shell, Python, Java, C) and markup languages (XML, Markdown, and HTML). It is based on the Monaco editor which you can find here: `https://microsoft.github.io/monaco-editor/`.

The Event Horizon company can also develop their software in the Web IDE. It, of course, has support for Ruby, the language in which GitLab is mostly written.

In the following screenshot, you will see a file from the eventmanager project shown in the web IDE:

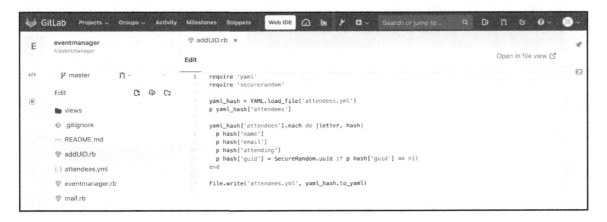

Use of this tool would also enhance collaboration within Event Horizon.

Wiki

While we have created a separate project to provide documentation for our new software product, GitLab also has a system for creating documentation by default. It is the Wiki feature. Every project can easily enable this feature and you will then have a full-blown wiki system available.

When you navigate to the **Wiki** through the left navigation bar in your project you will be presented with the following screen:

If you create a new wiki, you will have to provide a title, the markup language used, and then you can start adding content. As all the information is itself saved in an accompanying Git repository, you can give the **Commit message**, because saving the page is creating a new commit, as shown in the following screenshot:

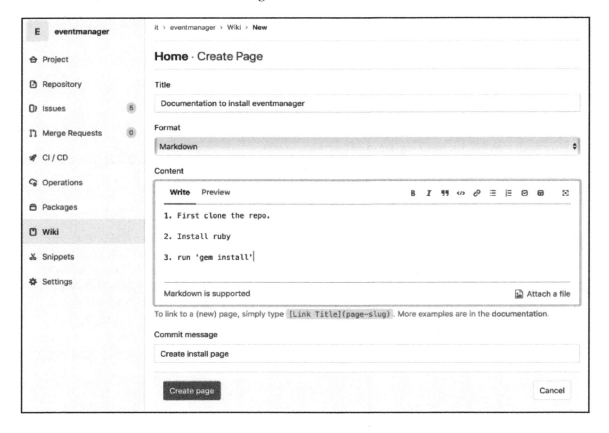

Once created, you will see the page if you click on **Wiki** the next time. You can now create more pages (even a page hierarchy if you want) and you can view the page history (everything is versioned), as shown in the following example:

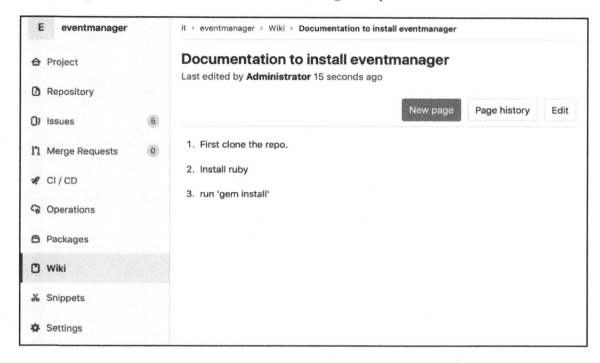

As you can see, Wiki is another feature that enhances collaboration between employees.

Protected branches

Because in Git it is possible to rewrite the entire history, GitLab has some mechanisms built in to help mitigate this risk. You can use *protected branches*.

Protected branches have the following characteristics:

- Before GitLab 11.9 you could not create a protected branch, only *Maintainers* could (as of 11.9 Developers can create them).
- Only Maintainers can push directly to a protected branch.
- It is prohibited to use force push to a protected branch.
- A protected branch cannot be deleted.

The only way to accept changes into a protected branch is to use merge requests. By default, the master branch is a protected branch. The following example is the screenshot for the protected branch:

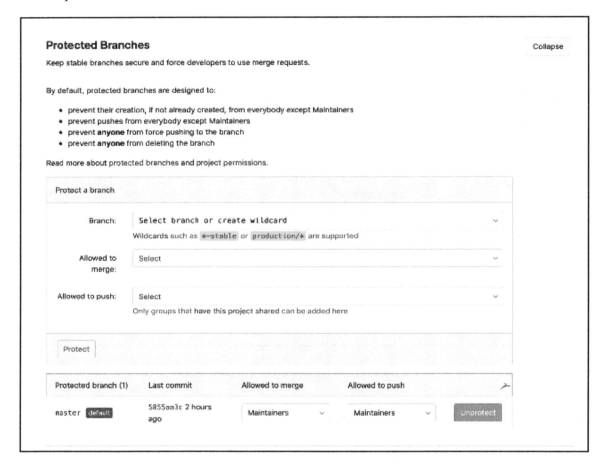

Using a protected branch forces the use of code reviews, which is a requirement for the eventmanager project.

Merge requests

So, the first version of eventmanager is almost ready. User1 has uploaded the latest changes to branch MVP1, and is ready to create a merge request, as shown in the following screenshot:

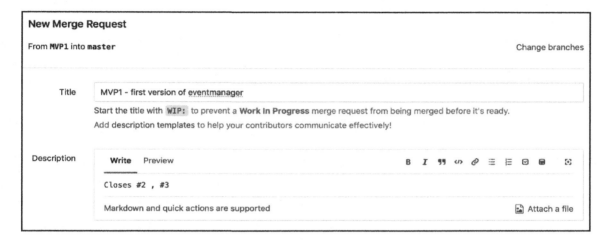

You can see the usage of quick actions by specifying `Closes #2, #3` in the **Description** field.

If you scroll down, you will see there is a section to view in which changes are introduced to the master branch when you accept this merge request. It shows you how many changes (**6**) are in our example, which files are changed, and what was changed. This is shown in the following screenshot:

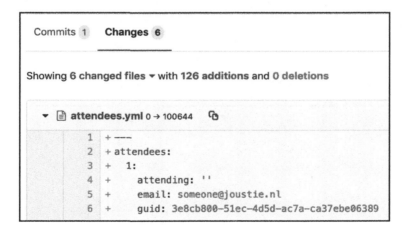

You can see **User3** has been added as merge request approver, so he or she has to review the changes, as shown in the following screenshot:

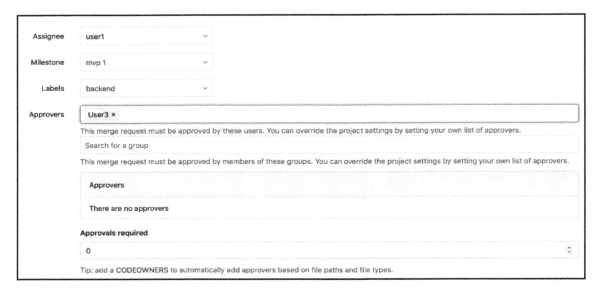

At the bottom of the screen, you can see which branches will be merged by this merge request, and you can specify to delete the originating branch and/or squash the changes (which means all changes are placed under one commit). This is shown in the following example:

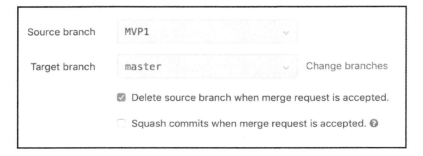

If User3 logs in, he will have a todo item for reviewing this merge request. As an example, let's pretend User3 did a review and placed some comments. Let's look at part of the `index.erb` file that is used in the eventmanager app to display a message saying that someone is invited to an event. You can find the file in the code examples (`https://github.com/PacktPublishing/Mastering-GitLab-12/tree/master/Chapter09/eventmanager`). Here's the snippet of code that is picked by the reviewer as troublesome:

```
<p>You are invited to my event on December 15!</p>
```

User3 thinks the text `You are invited to my event on December 15!` is too specific. Better to keep the text simple. He wants to suggest changing the text to `You are invited to my event!`. He can add a suggestion using a quick action in markdown format in the review comment, shown as follows:

After saving the comment, it looks like the following example:

User3 can finish his review now. User1 gets a notification that the merge request has been reviewed. As he logs in and navigates to the review comment in the merge request, he will discover the suggestion made by User3 with a button to apply the suggestion. The comment will automatically be marked as resolved, as shown in the following example:

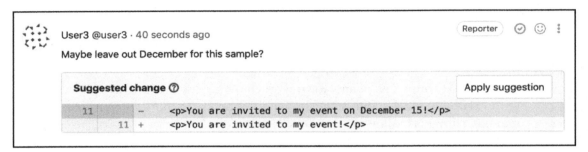

There is another comment by User3 about an entry in the `attendees.yml` file, shown in the following code:

```
attendees:
  1:
    attending: ''
    email: someone@joustie.nl
    guid: 3e8cb800-51ec-4d5d-ac7a-ca37ebe06389
    name: Someone
  10:
    attending: 'NO'
    email: anotherone@joustie.nl
    guid: 1070d08f-c5ea-4247-95b1-ee7a3ca4a342
    name: Anotherone
  11:
    attending: 'NO'
    email: organiser@joustie.nl
    guid: c7d49f48-2f05-468d-9d2e-9609e8311f3c
    name: Organiser
```

There are no sample entries in `attendees.yml` with a YES, so Users3 suggests to change one entry, as shown in the following screenshot:

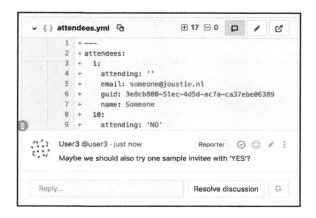

Unfortunately, the customer who attends the demo at the end of the sprint was not informed about the possibility to have an entry with No. There are also no real tests defined, so User1 decides to push this comment as an issue for the next iteration of the product, as shown in the following example:

When all discussion points are resolved, the merge request can be approved by User3, as shown in the following screenshot:

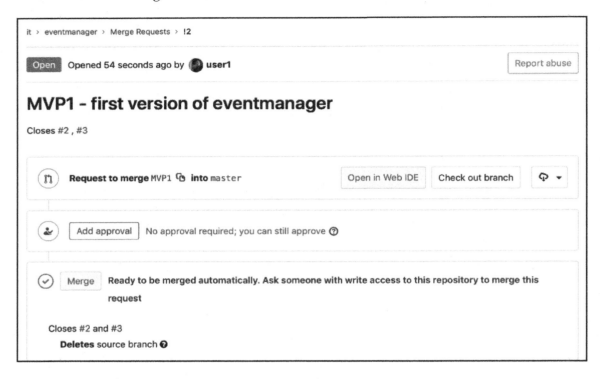

The merge request feature is one of the most important reasons to use GitLab. You can merge code or text in a project and cooperate on it.

DevOps phase – verify your product

The next phase in the DevOps life cycle is *Verify*. After building your product in the create phase, you need to verify whether the product meets the requirements, is secure, and that the quality in general is OK. This can all be done from within GitLab, by using the **continuous integration (CI)** features. In the following sections, we will discuss a number of components of the CI pipeline.

Code Quality reports

A nice feature that verifies code quality is a quality scan with CI/CD in GitLab. It makes use of the open source and free Code Climate engines (https://codeclimate.com/). It is embedded in a special Docker container that you can run within your GitLab runner. The following code is an example of a .gitlab-ci.yml file that runs such a scan:

```
code_quality:
 image: docker:stable
 variables:
 DOCKER_DRIVER: overlay2
 allow_failure: true
 services:
 - docker:stable-dind
 script:
 - export SP_VERSION=$(echo "$CI_SERVER_VERSION" | sed
's/^\([0-9]*\)\.\([0-9]*\).*/\1-\2-stable/')
 - docker run
 --env SOURCE_CODE="$PWD"
 --volume "$PWD":/code
 --volume /var/run/docker.sock:/var/run/docker.sock
 "registry.gitlab.com/gitlab-org/security-products/codequality:$SP_VERSION"
/code
 artifacts:
 paths: [gl-code-quality-report.json]
```

When the jobs runs, the following logging is produced:

```
Running with gitlab-runner 11.7.0 (8bb608ff)
   on test-runner 97YoGmXL
...
```

After downloading the Docker container, it will start scanning the code. When the scanning is complete a report is generated, as follows:

```
Uploading artifacts...
 gl-code-quality-report.json: found 1 matching files
 Uploading artifacts to coordinator... ok            id=403
responseStatus=201 Created token=ngLDxFmF
 Job succeeded
```

To view the report, download the artifact from the right, where there are links to it. The following example shows the screenshot of the **Job artifacts** tab:

If you open the report with an editor to properly format it, it will show warnings or high or critical findings. In the case of the eventmanager project, it found an unused variable, as follows:

```
"type": "Issue",
"check_name": "Rubocop/Lint/UnusedBlockArgument",
"description": "Unused block argument - `letter`. If it's
necessary, use `_` or `_letter` as an argument name to indicate that it
won't be used.",
"categories": [
    "Style"
],
"remediation_points": 50000,
"location": {
    "path": "addUID.rb",
...
```

Please notice the `"remediation_points": 50000,` entry, which scores the finding. This is different depending on the category finding, and can be used to compare total scores of several scans, showing you the progress (or decline) of total quality.

There follows the block of code that was mentioned in the report:

```
yaml_hash['attendees'].each do |letter, hash|
 p hash['name']
 p hash['email']
 p hash['attending']
 p hash['guid'] = SecureRandom.uuid if p hash['guid'] == nil
end
```

You can see that in the first line there is a `letter` variable that is unused in the loop. If we change `letter` to `_letter` the test should not report it as a warning anymore. Unused variables are reported as a warning, you can suppress the warning with an underscore.

After the next run of the CI pipeline, the code quality scan will show that nothing was found, the report will be empty.

You can use Code Quality reports as well in merge requests. It can run before merge and you can compare remediation points. If there are likely to be critical findings, the job would show as failed and in red. Now that we have verified that the application is of minimum quality, we also want to verify if the app or website is OK for users. We can build review versions on which to perform manual tests. This is our next section.

Review apps

The ultimate verification of your software product is to run all tests available and even mimic production. In GitLab, this can be accomplished by using GitLab CI and GitLab runners. For this to work, we will show an example using the eventmanager documentation site. One of the requirements of the project is, of course, creating documentation. We also created a separate project for it called **eventmanager-documentation**. There are already web pages present, so let's automate the review process (also one of the requirements: more automation). We are going to use an Amazon S3 bucket, which has been enabled to act as a webserver (you can find information about how to configure them here: `https://docs.aws.amazon.com/AmazonS3/latest/dev/HowDoIWebsiteConfiguration.html`).

To upload files to a S3 bucket, you need to authenticate with AWS. We can add secret variables to the project that contain the credentials for AWS that are needed. You can find them under **Project | Settings | CI/CD | Environment variables**, as shown in the following screenshot:

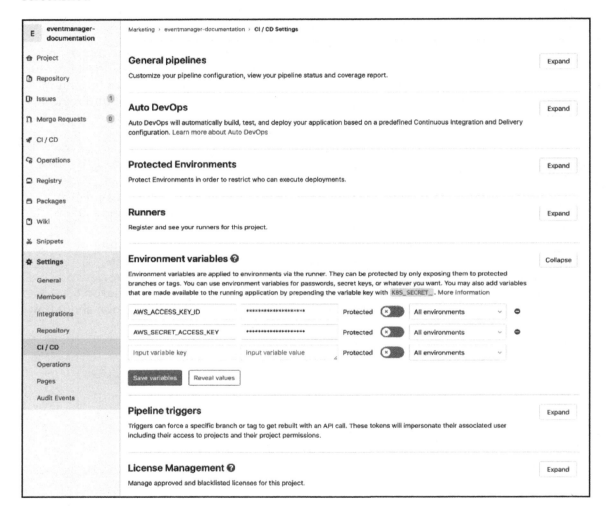

When the `AWS_ACCESS_KEY_ID` and `AWS_SECRET_ACCESS_KEY` variables are present, you can execute aws-cli actions within GitLab CI/CD pipelines. The `.gitlab-ci.yml` file that is used to deploy review apps is shown as follows:

```
review apps:
 variables:
   S3_BUCKET_NAME: "joustie-1"
 image: python:latest
 environment: review
 script:
  - pip install awscli
  - aws s3 cp public/*.html s3://$S3_BUCKET_NAME/
```

The job is called review apps, as seen on the first line. Then, after that, a variable is declared, the S3 bucket name. Next is the Docker image name that is used, which in this case is an image with Python installed, so we can make use of the Python-based AWS CLI utility that is installed in the script section. The last line contains the AWS CLI command to copy a file to an S3 bucket, and it authenticates through the environment variables that we have set.

After saving this file, the job will run, and if all goes well the HTML files are uploaded to your bucket. If you follow the job log you will see the following.

1. First, it gets the container:

    Pulling docker image python:latest ...

2. Then it clones the repository:

    Checking out 5625d409 as master...

    It installs the Amazon CLI tool:

    $ pip install awscli
    Collecting awscli

3. Then it uploads the HTML files to the S3 bucket:

```
$ aws s3 cp public/*.html s3://$S3_BUCKET_NAME/  Completed 617
Bytes/617 Bytes (2.1 KiB/s) with 1 file(s) remaining
```

When the job succeeds, the review environment will be created in GitLab. You can click on the **review** link, as shown in the following example:

The next page will show a list of deployments in the review environment, as follows:

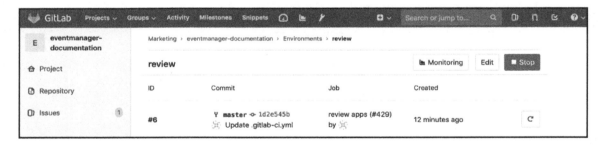

You can add the URL to the environment manually via edit, as follows:

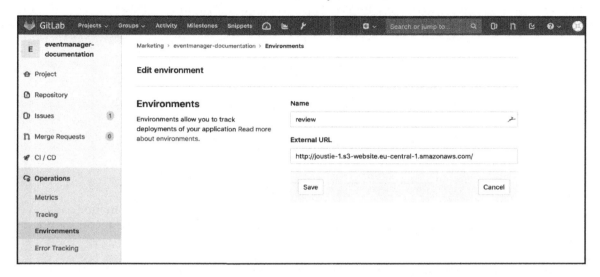

After adding the URL to the environment, a button **View deployment** is available, as follows:

If you click **View deployment**, you will be taken to the review app, as follows:

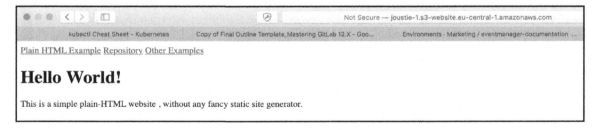

As of version 12.0 of GitLab, you will have a 'review button' next to 'view app' in the pipeline view. It will then run the review app with a little form in the corner where you can enter feedback. This input will be directly inserted into the issue.

So, to verify our project we have used Code Quality reports for the eventmanager code. We learned that, initially, there was a warning that a variable was not used. We recommended a fix and we ran the pipeline again, and the warning went.

We have demonstrated the use of a review app for the documentation project. Using this review app we could verify that our initial requirements were met.

Both methods of automation implemented in your pipeline will greatly enhance your Agility and DevOps capabilities. When you find errors, you can correct them and run the pipeline again.

DevOps phase – package it for use

GitLab use Docker containers in their products for several purposes. To store container images that were custom built for projects they also added Docker Container Registry functionality to GitLab. By using this, you avoid having to store images in a remote location that is maybe not safe enough. The container registry is the subject of the next section.

GitLab container registry

If you have the container registry enabled in GitLab, you can store Docker images that are built in your CI/CD process. To enable this GitLab feature, you have to reconfigure your GitLab instance and enable the registry functionality. When enabled, there will be a registry menu item on the left for each project. If you click on it, you can view the contents of the registry and instructions on how to use it, as shown in the following screenshot:

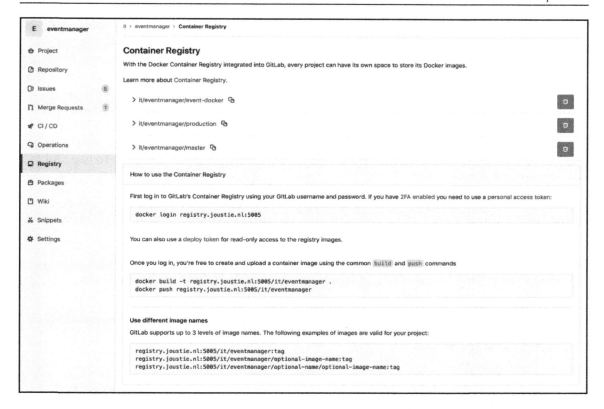

To store images in it for later use you have to edit your CI/CD configuration file in the root of your project. Here's an example for the eventmanager project:

```
build:
image: docker:stable
  services:
    - docker:dind
  variables:
    DOCKER_HOST: tcp://docker:2375
    DOCKER_DRIVER: overlay2
  stage: build
  script:
    - docker login -u $CI_REGISTRY_USER -p $CI_REGISTRY_PASSWORD
$CI_REGISTRY
    - docker build -t $CI_REGISTRY/it/eventmanager:latest .
    - docker push $CI_REGISTRY/it/eventmanager:latest
```

To summarize the file, it defines a build job. On the second line, the image to use is defined as `docker:stable`. Because this image will build a docker container itself, it uses the `docker:dind` service, which enables Docker in Docker functionality. Then, in the variables section, there are two Docker variables defined: the Docker host to connect to (which is the docker engine and it will build a container itself) and the Docker storage driver to use, which is overlay2. The stage defined is build. Then, in the scripts section, the actual script is given, which is really a basic Docker build, which is preceded by a login to the GitLab Docker registry and followed by a push to that location. You can see variables that start with `$CI_REGISTRY`. These are predefined variables available within GitLab to use and make use of one time tokens.

When you save this file in the Web IDE, or push it to GitLab, the new pipeline will run immediately. If it does not run, or says there is no runner available, check if your runner is running in privileged mode. It needs this to run `docker:dind`.

After the image is finished, it is pushed to the GitLab registry with the latest tag. If this is successful the job has succeeded and will be green, as shown in the following code:

```
$ docker push $CI_REGISTRY/it/eventmanager:latest
 The push refers to repository [registry.joustie.nl:5005/it/eventmanager]
 4fef5b78d890: Preparing
 2cf71380877f: Preparing
 . . .
latest: digest:
sha256:346123861d2c745902e3e2aae3101c0fb3c17414467c74204119f17c2c0cfc9c
size: 1786
 Job succeeded
```

You can verify afterwards that the container is present in the registry by navigating to the registry page of your project, as follows:

The registry is a secure way to store image artifacts from the CI/CD pipeline. In the DevOps pipeline, it is part of the Package phase.

Summary

This chapter has tried to explain the GitLab flow using an example. Going through the first phases of the model with the eventmanager example demonstrates why GitLab is a tool that has sprung from the Agile revolution. From idea to implementation, every step can be automated and is very customizable. In the next chapter, we will continue the pipeline by looking at the Release and Configure phases.

Questions

1. What is the first phase of the DevOps cycle?
2. What is the most important unit of information in GitLab?
3. Why is it possible to turn comments into a discussion?
4. How can you give an estimate of four days for an issue?
5. How can you enforce a review mechanism in GitLab?
6. What kind of setting does a GitLab Runner need to run a Code Quality scan?
7. How can you enable the link to a deployed environment?
8. What do you need to do to enable the Registry link in a project?

Further reading

- *Comprehensive Ruby Programming* by *Jordan Hudgens*: https://www.packtpub.com/application-development/comprehensive-ruby-programming
- *Learn Docker - Fundamentals of Docker 18.x* by *Gabriel N. Schenker*: https://www.packtpub.com/networking-and-servers/learn-docker-fundamentals-docker-18x
- *AWS Automation Cookbook* by *Nikit Swaraj*: https://www.packtpub.com/virtualization-and-cloud/aws-automation-cookbook
- *Effective DevOps with AWS - Second Edition* by *Yogesh Raheja, Giuseppe Borgese,* and *Nathaniel Felsen*: https://www.packtpub.com/virtualization-and-cloud/effective-devops-aws-second-edition

The Release and Configure Phase

11

In this chapter, we will take automation one step further than before. We will start by showing you how to deploy your code to a staging environment after testing and ultimately to production. This is a basic concept in the DevOps transition. We will finish this chapter by explaining about Auto DevOps, a way to fully automate the deployment to a Kubernetes cluster with integrated testing, security scanning, and even performance tests. This is considered the optimal DevOps path by GitLab.

In this chapter, we will cover the following topics:

- Continuous Deployment with deployment to Amazon Web Services
- Auto DevOps with the use of a Kubernetes cluster in Google Cloud

Technical requirements

To follow along with the instructions in this chapter, please download this book's GitHub repository, along with the examples, at `https://github.com/PacktPublishing/Mastering-GitLab-12/tree/master/Chapter11`.

Here, in the `Chapter11` directory, you will find two applications that are used for the examples in this chapter.

To run certain automation scripts, you need an **Amazon Web Services (AWS)** account, which can be created here: https://aws.amazon.com/free/.

For the instructions on how to create a cluster on the **Google Kubernetes Engine (GKE)**, you also need a Google account that you can use with Google Cloud, which you can create here: https://cloud.google.com/products/search/apply/.

Continuous Deployment

Continuous Deployment, as explained in Chapter 9, *GitLab Vision – The Whole Toolchain in One Application,* is an extension of Continuous Integration, aiming at minimizing cycle time; that is, the time it takes to produce one new line of code by a development team and it being deployed in the production environment. We will demonstrate this practice by deploying the eventmanager Ruby code to Amazon Elastic Beanstalk, a service for deploying and scaling web applications and services that have been developed with a multitude of languages on different platforms.

There is also the option to create Ruby environments running a Puma web server. Let's log in to the AWS web console (https://console.aws.amazon.com/console/) and click on the **Services** tab. We can use the search option to find something within the huge range of services that are available within the Amazon Cloud:

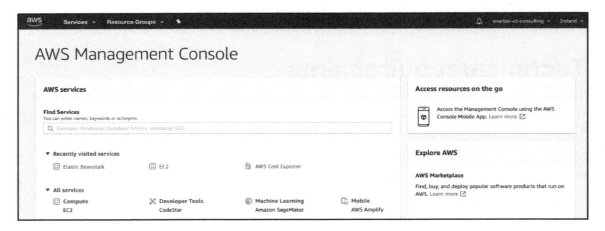

Type beanstalk into the **Find Services** widget and click the link it finds. Choose to create a new environment:

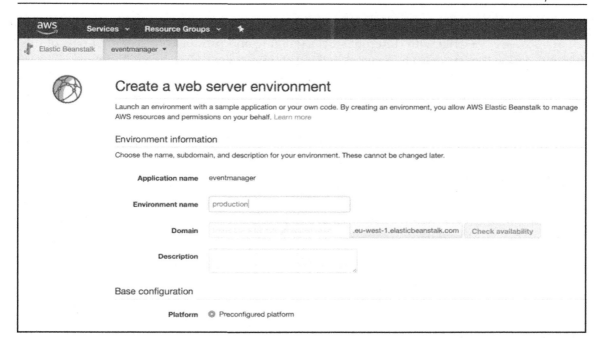

The environment will deploy. When it's finished, you can view it in the dashboard:

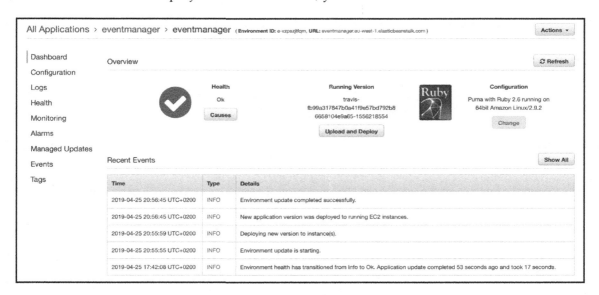

We are going to use CI/CD for our Continuous Deployment strategy. First, we will create a `.gitlab-ci.yml` file with different stages (staging and production). The first part of this file will define the variables to be used in the different stages. Here, we will define a `S3_BUCKET_NAME`, which will be used to copy a deployment package to, a `REGION` to specify where the service will be hosted, and finally an `APPNAME`, which corresponds to the app name in Amazon Beanstalk:

```
variables:
    S3_BUCKET_NAME: "elasticbeanstalk-eu-west-1-513361393569"
    REGION: "eu-west-1"
    APPNAME: "eventmanager"
```

We need to run our tests before we can advance to the next stage. In the following code, on the second line, we specify a Docker image with Ruby installed to run our tests. In the script section, run the default `rspec` tests:

```
test:
    image: ruby:latest
    stage: test
    script: "bundle install;rspec"
```

This step will use the dpl tool (`https://github.com/travis-ci/dpl`) to interface with Amazon Beanstalk and deploy to the staging environment:

```
deploy_staging:
    stage: deploy
    script:
      - echo "Deploy to staging server"
    image: ruby:latest
    environment:
     name: staging
     url: http://staging.gbnfcg9st9.eu-west-1.elasticbeanstalk.com
    script:
     - echo "Deploying to staging"
     - gem install dpl
     - dpl --provider=elasticbeanstalk --access-key-id=$AWS_ACCESS_KEY_ID -
-secret-access-key=$AWS_SECRET_ACCESS_KEY --app=$APPNAME --
env=$CI_ENVIRONMENT_NAME --region=$REGION 13  --bucket_name=$S3_BUCKET_NAME
    only:
     - cd
```

As you can see, we also need to get AWS credentials from somewhere ($AWS_ACCESS variables). We can define these variables in the CI/CD environment variables section of the settings of the eventmanager project. Now, we will use a feature called *multiproject pipelines*, which has been available since GitLab 11.8. We are going to define a *bridge job*, which will run the default pipeline in the eventmanager-documentation project:

```
deploy_documentation:
    stage: deploy
    variables:
      ENVIRONMENT: staging
    trigger: marketing/eventmanager-documentation
```

We also want to deploy to production. We created a separate Beanstalk instance for that with an environment named production. But what if we want the last step to remain a manual one? Then we need to define a control structure with when:manual, which means that the step has to be manually initiated:

```
deploy to production:
    stage: deploy
    environment: production
    when: manual
    image: ruby:latest
    script:
     - echo "Deploying to production"
     - gem install dpl
     - dpl --provider=elasticbeanstalk --access-key-id=$AWS_ACCESS_KEY_ID
--secret-access-key=$AWS_SECRET_ACCESS_KEY --app=$APPNAME --
env=$CI_ENVIRONMENT_NAME --region=$REGION 10  --bucket_name=$S3_BUCKET_NAME
    only:
     - cd
```

If you save this .gitlab-ci.yml file (and commit and push it), it will start a deployment. If you click on the pipeline, you will get an overview of the jobs:

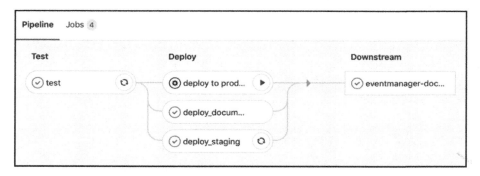

In the preceding screenshot, you can see the stages. First, there's the test stages, which run the rspec tests. The deploy_documentation job triggers a downstream pipeline (eventmanager-documentation). Simultaneously, the deployment to the staging area starts. Let's click on the job that starts:

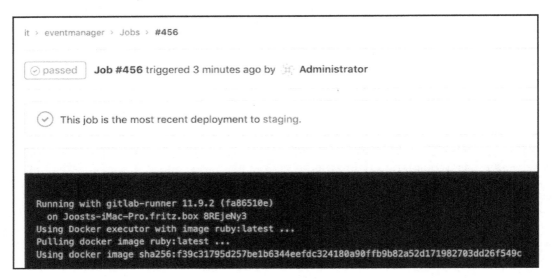

By looking at the log file of the deployment to the staging area, you will find the following code:

```
Running with gitlab-runner 11.9.2 (fa86510e)
   on Computer1 8REjeNy3
Using Docker executor with image ruby:latest ...
Pulling docker image ruby:latest ...
Using docker image
sha256:f39c31795d257be1b6344eefdc324180a90ffb9b82a52d171982703dd26f549c for
ruby:latest ...
Running on runner-8REjeNy3-project-3-concurrent-0 via Joosts-iMac-
Pro.fritz.box...
Reinitialized existing Git repository in /builds/it/eventmanager/.git/
Clean repository
Fetching changes...
fatal: remote origin already exists.
Checking out 2dbf81c9 as cd...
...
Skipping Git submodules setup
$ echo "Deploying to staging"
Deploying to staging
```

The container installs the dpl dependency:

```
$ gem install dpl
  Successfully installed dpl-1.10.8
  1 gem installed
```

It then runs the deployment:

```
dpl --provider=elasticbeanstalk --access-key-id=$AWS_ACCESS_KEY_ID --
secret-access-key=$AWS_SECRET_ACCESS_KEY --app=$APPNAME --
env=$CI_ENVIRONMENT_NAME --region=$REGION --bucket_name=$S3_BUCKET_NAME
```

The dpl tool only runs if the Git repository is clean:

```
Preparing deploy
  Cleaning up git repository with `git stash --all`. If you need build
artifacts for deployment, set `deploy.skip_cleanup: true`. See
https://docs.travis-ci.com/user/deployment#Uploading-Files-and-skip_cleanup
.
  No local changes to save
Deploying application
No stash found.
Job succeeded
```

There is no feedback about the upload except for the message stating that the application has been deployed. You can verify this deployment by visiting the URL that is mentioned in the Beanstalk environment that was created with the AWS console.

You can manually trigger the deploy job to production from the diagram, which is where we saw the play button.

In GitLab, you can go to **Operations** | **Environments** | **Production** to view the deployments. You can also roll back to an earlier release:

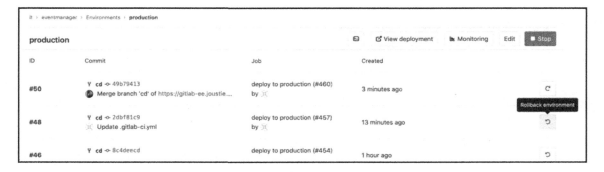

In this section, we have showed you how to implement a deployment pipeline using Gitlab CI and GitLab runners. You can create them just by using shell scripts and make them as elaborate as you want by using multiproject pipelines and advanced syntax.

Auto DevOps

By default, Auto DevOps is turned on for every project. It is essentially a very elaborate .gitlab-ci.yml file, which outlines the entire DevOps pipeline from the creating phase onward.

It fits in the GitLab vision of providing one application to collaborate on the entire DevOps life cycle of an application.

Configuring Auto DevOps

As we mentioned earlier, Auto DevOps is enabled by default for every project, but if you want to disable it or configure it differently, you need to go into the settings, which you can find by going to **Settings** | **CI/CD** | **Auto DevOps**:

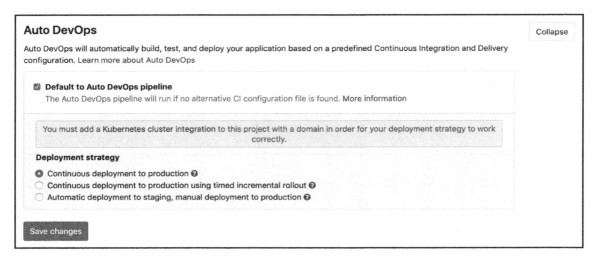

As you can see, you need to configure a Kubernetes cluster to make this all work.

Another setting you can manage here is the deployment strategy. The default setting is that the pipeline deploys up to production. This might not be the strategy you want for your enterprise. You can use an incremental rollout as well.

You should also note that a deployment pipelines is fully automated until the last step, which is production. You can choose to leave that as a manual step.

To control the individual steps in the pipeline, you can view the **Operations** menu on the left-hand side. The following is a screenshot of the available operations:

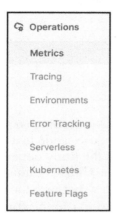

When the first piece of code is pushed to the repository, an Auto DevOps pipeline is created. For the `eventmanager` project, this looks as follows:

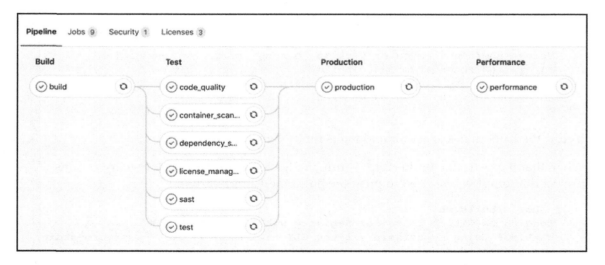

Let's evaluate each step of the Auto DevOps pipeline from the preceding screenshot.

Build step

The main idea is that, in the build phase, you prepare your code to run in a packaged way – in a Docker container that you built using a Dockerfile – via Heroku build packs.

For the `eventmanager` app, `user1` created the following Dockerfile:

```
FROM ruby:2
COPY . /var/www/ruby
WORKDIR /var/www/ruby
RUN bundle install
CMD ["ruby","eventmanager.rb"]
EXPOSE 5000/tcp
```

As you can see from the first line of the preceding code, it pulls a basic Ruby-enabled Debian Linux image. It copies all the source code to a directory and goes there. Then, a bundle install is run, which installs all the Ruby dependencies that are needed. Finally, it starts the `eventmanager` app using the CMD command and exposes port 5000 to the outside world. It has to expose port 5000 because the default Helm chart that is used to deploy to Kubernetes assumes this port to run the application. It will be wired to port 80 or 443 after deployment.

The following code is for the log when the build phase is started:

```
Running with gitlab-runner 11.8.0 (4745a6f3)
   on runner-gitlab-runner-7fd79f558b-2wx96 _drEv8rS
 Using Kubernetes namespace: gitlab-managed-apps
 Using Kubernetes executor with image registry.gitlab.com/gitlab-
org/cluster-integration/auto-build-image/master:stable ...
 Waiting for pod gitlab-managed-apps/runner-drev8rs-project-3-
concurrent-0fvjtb to be running, status is Pending
 ...
```

It runs the Kubernetes executor and waits for a pod to be available.

When that happens, the build script is run. First, a login to the GitLab registry for this project is attempted (we need to push the build there afterwards):

```
$ /build/build.sh
 Logging to GitLab Container Registry with CI credentials...
 WARNING! Using --password via the CLI is insecure. Use --password-stdin.
 Login Succeeded
 ...
```

Then, the build of the Docker image will start:

```
Building Dockerfile-based application...
 Sending build context to Docker daemon  113.7kB

 Step 1/6 : FROM ruby:2-alpine
 2-alpine: Pulling from library/ruby
 ...
```

The built container image is pushed to the Docker registry for the `eventmanager` project:

```
Successfully built 5bd173d74f67
 Successfully tagged
 ...
 Job succeeded
```

When the Docker container image is stored in the registry, the subsequent phases will use the image and pull it. This concludes the build step. The next step is to run the code quality scan.

Code quality scan

In this phase of the pipeline, a GitLab runner is used to scan your code for quality. You can find more information and an example of this in `Chapter 10`, *Create Your Product, Verifying It, and Packaging It.*

Container scanning

The next phase is still a part of the test stage. In this stage, a container instance is instantiated from your image and is scanned for vulnerabilities using clair (`https://github.com/coreos/clair`).

It will log in to the `eventmanager` Docker registry:

```
Running with gitlab-runner 11.8.0 (4745a6f3)
 ...
 $ container_scanning
 Logging to GitLab Container Registry with CI credentials...
 ...
```

Then, it will try to get a container with the scan tool in it:

```
Unable to find image 'arminc/clair-db:latest' locally
latest: Pulling from arminc/clair-db
...
```

When the container is running, it will start the scan:

```
2019/04/28 14:08:08 [0;32m[INFO] > Start clair-scanner
2019/04/28 14:08:37 [0;32m[INFO] > Server listening on port 9279
2019/04/28 14:08:37 [0;32m[INFO] > Analyzing
9cab74319993fe94abc345fa8933c789f4482b9644f9cb1d9758d31575ed1367
----------------------------------------------------------+
| STATUS | CVE SEVERITY | PACKAGE NAME | PACKAGE VERSION | CVE DESCRIPTION
|
| Unapproved | High CVE-2018-6551 | glibc | 2.24-11+deb9u4 | The malloc
implementation in the GNU C Library (aka |
...
```

The default Ruby images uses a Debian image, which apparently has a lot of open vulnerabilities.

If you switch the basic image your Dockerfile uses to `ruby:2-alpine`, you will have a more basic Linux container, which should not give all of these errors. You will have to restart the pipeline (click retry in the list):

```
Waiting for clair daemon to start
...
contains NO unapproved vulnerabilities
```

When no vulnerabilities are found, the report is uploaded as an artifact and the job will succeed:

```
Uploading artifacts...
gl-container-scanning-report.json: found 1 matching files
..
Job succeeded
```

The created Docker image is now scanned for known vulnerabilities. When you want to whitelist anything that's found, you can add them to a file called `clair-whitelist.yml` and add it to your repository.

Dependency scanning

This part of the pipeline scans your code for known security vulnerabilities in dependencies of your software. An example would be if you rely on third-party libraries that have known security issues. This will be explained in detail in the next chapter.

When this scan is complete, you will know whether the dependencies you use in your code are safe or not. It is also useful to know which licenses are used by dependencies because this can have a lot of consequences. We will explain this in the next section.

License management

An issue that's often overlooked by organizations is how to manage your **intellectual property rights (IP)**. There are different open source licenses around; for example, there ones that are classified as *permissive* such as X11, Apache, and the BSD licenses. You also have the *copyleft* kind, such as the GPL, which are more restrictive and could make you share your derivative works. By using the license scanner, you ensure that you're not using dependencies that have a negative impact on your intellectual property rights.

You will see the following output when the jobs runs:

```
Running with gitlab-runner 11.8.0 (4745a6f3)
   on runner-gitlab-runner-7fd79f558b-2wx96 _drEv8rS
 Using Kubernetes namespace: gitlab-managed-apps
 Using Kubernetes executor with image registry.gitlab.com/gitlab-
org/security-products/license-management:$CI_SERVER_VERSION_MAJOR-
$CI_SERVER_VERSION_MINOR-stable ...
```

This scan is run from a container, but that runs code and parses your project:

```
$ license_management
 mesg: ttyname failed: Inappropriate ioctl for device
 Added development to the ignored groups
 Added test to the ignored groups
 Fetching gem metadata from https://rubygems.org/.........
```

This will analyze and upload a report artifact:

```
Running license_finder  in /it/eventmanager
 LicenseFinder::Bundler: is active
 Uploading artifacts...
 gl-license-management-report.json: found 1 matching files
 Uploading artifacts to coordinator... ok          id=478
responseStatus=201 Created token=HjYg-s1y
 Job succeeded
```

The result is also viewable from the merge request widget.

As you can see, the inclusion of a license check in the pipeline can be very useful. Is it better to know as early as possible whether you are using dependencies that affect the way you can distribute your software. In the same parallel step of the pipeline, static security tests are conducted.

Static application security testing (sast)

This part of the pipeline scans your code for known security issues, and is known as a static application security test. This will be explained in more detail in the next chapter. The final parallel step in the test stage is running the actual tests that are defined by your code.

The final test step

In this pipeline, a specific container is started that clones the source code:

```
Running with gitlab-runner 11.8.0 (4745a6f3)
   on runner-gitlab-runner-7fd79f558b-2wx96 _drEv8rS
 Using Kubernetes namespace: gitlab-managed-apps
 Using Kubernetes executor with image gliderlabs/herokuish:latest ...
```

It will try to detect the language that's used. In our case, it finds a Ruby application, which is correct:

```
$ setup_test_db
 $ cp -R . /tmp/app
 $ /bin/herokuish buildpack test
 -----> Ruby app detected
 -----> Setting up Test for Ruby/Rack
 -----> Using Ruby version: ruby-2.5.3
 -----> Installing dependencies using bundler 1.15.2
```

After installing the necessary dependencies, it will run the rake test task:

```
 -----> Running test: bundle exec rspec
 ...
 Finished in 0.03197 seconds (files took 0.22688 seconds to load)
 3 examples, 0 failures
```

In our case, no errors were detected. You can check which tests are run in your tests folder.

Of course, the tests that are run are written by yourself, so you determine how much value they have. When they are finished, the next stage is to deploy to production, which is covered in the next section.

Production

The default Auto DevOps pipeline will deploy your code to production after it finishes the test stage. Various environment variables are available that you can set that will control the autoscaling of your replica pods. The heavy lifting in this phase is performed by the auto-deploy-app Helm chart. You can also provide your own chart by adding it to a .chart directory in your project or by setting AUTO_DEVOPS_CHART combined with the AUTO_DEVOPS_CHART_REPOSITORY environment variable with the URL to your custom chart. It will create several things:

- A deploy token
- A Prometheus monitoring instance that's wired for your application

Let's run the following code through the log file:

```
Running with gitlab-runner 11.8.0 (4745a6f3)
  on runner-gitlab-runner-7fd79f558b-2wx96 _drEv8rS
Using Kubernetes namespace: gitlab-managed-apps
Using Kubernetes executor with image alpine:latest ...
```

This checks the artifacts of the previous jobs and performs a check on the Kubernetes domain. It will install dependencies for minimal Helm execution:

```
Checking out 08222854 as master...
 Skipping Git submodules setup
 Downloading artifacts for code_quality (477)...
 Downloading artifacts from coordinator... ok        id=477
responseStatus=200 OK token=zxQGxCFW
 Downloading artifacts for license_management (478)...
 Downloading artifacts from coordinator... ok        id=478
responseStatus=200 OK token=HjYg-s1y
 Downloading artifacts for container_scanning (481)...
 Downloading artifacts from coordinator... ok        id=481
responseStatus=200 OK token=hErz9aWj
 $ # Auto DevOps variables and functions # collapsed multi-line command
 $ check_kube_domain
 $ install_dependencies
```

The next step is to download the required chart (auto-deploy-app chart or custom):

```
$ download_chart
```

Next, we need to ensure that a namespace is defined (which is usually the Kubernetes cluster name you used):

```
$ ensure_namespace
```

Now, it's time to initialize tiller (the Helm server):

```
initialize_tiller
```

Here, a secret to access the registry is created:

```
create_secret
```

Finally, the deployment can start:

```
$ deploy secret "production-secret"
deleted secret/production-secret replaced
Deploying new release...
Release "production" has been upgraded.
Happy Helming! ...
```

After the deployment, you will see feedback about the URL where the application is running. The name is created by appending the namespace to the project name and the domain wildcard where the cluster is running:

```
NOTES:
 Application should be accessible at:
http://it-eventmanager.kubernetes.joustie.nl
 Waiting for deployment "production" rollout to finish: 0 of 1 updated
replicas are available...
 deployment "production" successfully rolled out
 $ delete canary
 $ delete rollout
 $ persist_environment_url
 Uploading artifacts...
 environment_url.txt: found 1 matching files
 Uploading artifacts to coordinator... ok          id=482
responseStatus=201 Created token=koT8yujj
 Job succeeded
```

If you have configured `kubectl` to use the context of your GKE cluster, on the command line, you can verify whether your deployments took place:

```
Joosts-iMac-Pro:Part3 joostevertse$ kubectl get pods --all-namespaces
```

The list of pods should show you the pods that were started:

```
NAME                                              READY   STATUS
RESTARTS    AGE
  eventmanager          production-6b9db68f6f-hrwzv
1/1     Running     0           11h
  eventmanager          production-postgres-5b5cf56747-xngbk
1/1     Running     0           11h
```

By default, a `postgres` instance is started as well, and you can fine-tune your installation to use it if you need it. You can find more information about that here: `https://docs.gitlab.com/ee/topics/autodevops/#postgresql-database-support`. There are also other pods in the list, and they are all part of the deployment:

```
certmanager-cert-manager-6c8cd9f9bf-8kbf8                 1/1     Running
0           11h
  ingress-nginx-ingress-controller-ff666c548-n2s84        1/1     Running
0           11h
  ingress-nginx-ingress-default-backend-677b99f864-bnk8c  1/1     Running
0           11h
  runner-gitlab-runner-7fd79f558b-2wx96                   1/1     Running
0           11h
  tiller-deploy-6586b57bcb-t6zql                          1/1     Running
0           11h
```

The `eventmanager` application can be viewed by going to `http://it-eventmanager.kubernetes.joustie.nl`:

Now, we have a running application that is being tested and monitored. The next and final step is to run a performance check on the production environment. Again, we can use our Kubernetes cluster to spawn a test container for it and run performance tests on it, which is the subject of the next section.

Performance

In the log file for the performance job, you can see that Kubernetes is again used to spawn an instance to use:

```
Running with gitlab-runner 11.8.0 (4745a6f3)
   on runner-gitlab-runner-7fd79f558b-2wx96 _drEv8rS
 Using Kubernetes namespace: gitlab-managed-apps
```

The job connects to GitLab.com and verifies the version of the image it should pull. It uses the sitespeed.io container to do this (https://hub.docker.com/r/sitespeedio/sitespeed.io/):

```
$ performance
 Connecting to gitlab.com (35.231.145.151:443)
 index.js              100% |******************************|  1614
0:00:00 ETA

 Unable to find image 'sitespeedio/sitespeed.io:6.3.1' locally
 6.3.1: Pulling from sitespeedio/sitespeed.io
 ...
```

Inside the container, it tries to measure browser performance with Chrome and Firefox:

```
Google Chrome 63.0.3239.132
 Mozilla Firefox 54.0.1
 [2019-04-25 21:42:41] INFO: Versions OS: linux 4.14.91+ nodejs: v8.9.4
sitespeed.io: 6.3.1 browsertime: 2.1.4 coach: 1.2.0
```

It will do a subsequent number of runs:

```
[2019-04-25 21:42:41] INFO: Starting chrome for analysing
http://it-eventmanager.kubernetes.joustie.nl 3 time(s)
 [2019-04-25 21:42:41] INFO: Testing url
http://it-eventmanager.kubernetes.joustie.nl run 1
 [2019-04-25 21:42:51] INFO: Testing url
http://it-eventmanager.kubernetes.joustie.nl run 2
 [2019-04-25 21:43:00] INFO: Testing url
http://it-eventmanager.kubernetes.joustie.nl run 3
 [2019-04-25 21:43:09] INFO: 2 requests, 586 bytes, backEndTime: 39ms
(±1.87ms), firstPaint: 119ms (±2.43ms), firstVisualChange: 0ms (±0.00ms),
DOMContentLoaded: 103ms (±3.06ms), Load: 104ms (±3.06ms), speedIndex: 0
(±0.00), visualComplete85: 0ms (±0.00ms), lastVisualChange: 0ms (±0.00ms),
rumSpeedIndex: 119 (±2.25) (3 runs)
 [2019-04-25 21:43:13] INFO: HTML stored in /sitespeed.io/sitespeed-results
 [2019-04-25 21:43:13] INFO: Finished analyzing
http://it-eventmanager.kubernetes.joustie.nl
 ...
```

The results will be saved as a HTML report artifact, as well as a JSON file:

```
Uploading artifacts...
 performance.json: found 1 matching files
 sitespeed-results/: found 64 matching files
 Uploading artifacts to coordinator... ok          id=483
responseStatus=201 Created token=w-R8qzFw
 Job succeeded
```

The following code is a part of the JSON file:

```
[
    {
        "subject": "/",
        "metrics": [
            {
                "name": "Transfer Size (KB)",
                "value": "0.6",
                "desiredSize": "smaller"
    ...
```

A nice HTML report is available too, which is part of the artifacts.

Auto DevOps is a very handy concept. It can give you a complete pipeline if your application stays close to standards and is not very complex. If you need more customization, you can use the template and fine-tune it to your needs.

Summary

This chapter demonstrated the potential of GitLab and the role it plays in the operations phase of a software product. You can develop your solution, test it, and eventually run it in an environment. Along the way, you can automate as much as possible. If you use the Auto DevOps feature, you will reach the full potential of the DevOps concept, which is currently a sought-after skill.

In the next chapter, we will look at the monitor and secure phases, which are the final phases in the DevOps pipeline.

Questions

1. In which file do you define your deployments?
2. What is the dpl tool?
3. What is the GitLab vision for Auto DevOps?
4. Where are the build artifacts stored at the end of the build phase (using Dockerfile)?
5. What is the name of the container scanner that's used in Auto DevOps?
6. What is the name of the deployment Helm chart that's used in Auto DevOps?
7. How many pods are deployed for a production deploy?
8. What is the name of the performance container?

Further reading

- *Advanced Infrastructure Penetration Testing* by Chiheb Chebbi: https://www.packtpub.com/networking-and-servers/advanced-infrastructure-penetration-testing
- *Learn Docker - Fundamentals of Docker 18.x* by Gabriel N. Schenker: https://www.packtpub.com/in/networking-and-servers/learn-docker-fundamentals-docker-18x
- *AWS Automation Cookbook* by Nikit Swaraj: https://www.packtpub.com/virtualization-and-cloud/aws-automation-cookbook
- *Hands-On Kubernetes on Azure* by Gunther Lenz and Shivakumar Gopalakrishnan: https://www.packtpub.com/virtualization-and-cloud/hands-kubernetes-azure

12
Monitoring with Prometheus

In this chapter, we will explore how to monitor using the Prometheus time series, and we will also run some automated security tests. The built-in security tests in GitLab are only available when running with a GitLab Ultimate license on-premises or with a Gold subscription on `http://gitlab.com`.

In this chapter, we will cover following topics:

- Setting up Prometheus
- Customizing monitoring
- The static analysis of security vulnerabilities
- **Dynamic Application Security Testing (DAST)**
- Dependency checking

Technical requirements

To be able to manage Omnibus installs, there is one central configuration file required, called `gitlab.rb`. You need to create this file or copy an example. There is a template available at `https://gitlab.com/gitlab-org/omnibus-gitlab/blob/master/files/gitlab-config-template/gitlab.rb.template`. This file is not updated after upgrades. Throughout this chapter, we will quote and discuss elements of this file.

To follow along with the instructions in this chapter, please download the Git repository with examples, available at
GitHub: `https://github.com/PacktPublishing/Mastering-GitLab-12/tree/master/Chapter12`.

You will also need to have Python installed to create the Python sample exporter.

Setting up Prometheus

Prometheus is an open source monitoring system inspired by Borgmon, Google's production monitoring system. Since it was introduced in 2012, the project has built up an active community and has already been used by many companies. It is an example of a TSDB, a time-series monitoring database. This means that time is a deliberate X-axis in all of your measurements. Every new entry is an insert and not an update of a data-row.

This is best visualized in a table:

Time(x)	Key	Value
12.01.33	ping-latency	0.234556
12.03.33	ping-latency	0.223344

The two main advantages of this approach are as follows:

- **Scalability**: These databases are tuned to ingest data and do so very efficiently.
- **Usability**: They provide all kinds of tools and functions, for example, data retention and continuous queries.

Whereas most monitoring systems focus on measuring external system behaviors through health checks, Prometheus emphasizes measuring internal system behaviors by requesting metrics from the software itself. With Prometheus, you can set up monitoring dynamically, making it a valuable tool for gaining insight into distributed setups, such as software on a Kubernetes cluster.

The Prometheus project provides client libraries that make it easier to export metrics from software. These libraries enable you to integrate monitoring as part of your software. It opens a port to metrics inside your application, so to speak.

You can also use functions and objects from client libraries to expose the metrics inside your application.

Another method is to run separate smaller programs that gather data that will be scraped by the Prometheus server. Some officially endorsed exporters are available in the Prometheus group on GitHub: `https://github.com/prometheus`.

GitLab is packaged with both methods. When enabled, it can expose metrics from within GitLab itself, but the omnibus package can also deliver extra exporter instances that are able to monitor a number of components. The monitoring architecture is as follows (as you can see, the functionality runs on the GitLab application server):

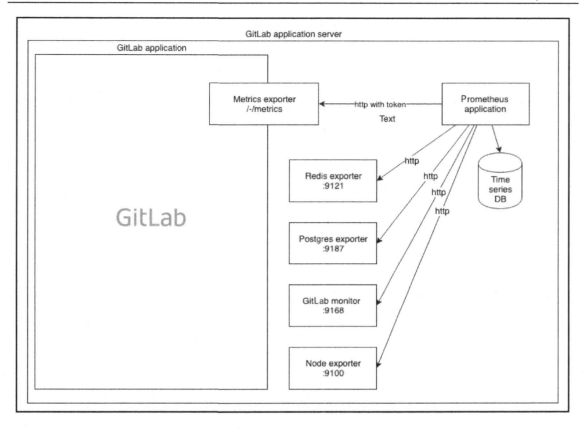

You can see several exporters in the image; let's go through them:

- The (GitLab) Metrics Exporter: GitLab has incorporated the client functions into itself and can expose metrics if the setting is enabled. You can find this feature in the **Admin** I **Settings** I **Metrics and profiling** I **Metrics Prometheus**, as shown in the following screenshot:

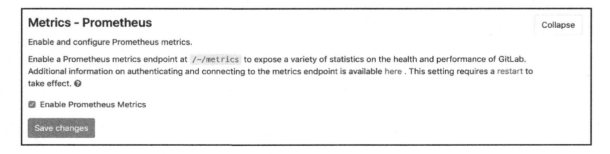

This works by allowing you to view the exporters' output on `http://{your gitlab url}}/-/metrics?token=something`. An example is given on the Health Check page via **Monitoring | Health check,** as shown in the following screenshot:

Make sure that you append the token to the request otherwise you won't see any data. An example output shown when visiting the URL is as follows:

```
# HELP gitaly_controller_action_duration_seconds Multiprocess metric
# TYPE gitaly_controller_action_duration_seconds histogram
gitaly_controller_action_duration_seconds_bucket{controller="RootController",action="index",gitaly_service="commit_service",rpc="find_commit",le="+Inf"} 42
gitaly_controller_action_duration_seconds_bucket{controller="RootController",action="index",gitaly_service="commit_service",rpc="find_commit",le="0.005"} 21
gitaly_controller_action_duration_seconds_bucket{controller="RootController",action="index",gitaly_service="commit_service",rpc="find_commit",le="0.01"} 38
gitaly_controller_action_duration_seconds_bucket{controller="RootController",action="index",gitaly_service="commit_service",rpc="find_commit",le="0.1"} 42
gitaly_controller_action_duration_seconds_bucket{controller="RootController",action="index",gitaly_service="commit_service",rpc="find_commit",le="1"} 42
gitaly_controller_action_duration_seconds_bucket{controller="RootController",action="index",gitaly_service="commit_service",rpc="find_commit",le="10"} 42
gitaly_controller_action_duration_seconds_bucket{controller="RootController",action="index",gitaly_service="commit_service",rpc="get_tree_entries",le="+Inf"} 7
gitaly_controller_action_duration_seconds_bucket{controller="RootController",action="index",gitaly_service="commit_service",rpc="get_tree_entries",le="0.005"} 7
gitaly_controller_action_duration_seconds_bucket{controller="RootController",action="index",gitaly_service="commit_service",rpc="get_tree_entries",le="0.01"} 7
gitaly_controller_action_duration_seconds_bucket{controller="RootController",action="index",gitaly_service="commit_service",rpc="get_tree_entries",le="0.1"} 7
gitaly_controller_action_duration_seconds_bucket{controller="RootController",action="index",gitaly_service="commit_service",rpc="get_tree_entries",le="1"} 7
gitaly_controller_action_duration_seconds_bucket{controller="RootController",action="index",gitaly_service="commit_service",rpc="get_tree_entries",le="10"} 7
gitaly_controller_action_duration_seconds_bucket{controller="RootController",action="index",gitaly_service="ref_service",rpc="find_default_branch_name",le="+Inf"} 7
gitaly_controller_action_duration_seconds_bucket{controller="RootController",action="index",gitaly_service="ref_service",rpc="find_default_branch_name",le="0.005"} 4
gitaly_controller_action_duration_seconds_bucket{controller="RootController",action="index",gitaly_service="ref_service",rpc="find_default_branch_name",le="0.01"} 7
gitaly_controller_action_duration_seconds_bucket{controller="RootController",action="index",gitaly_service="ref_service",rpc="find_default_branch_name",le="0.1"} 7
```

- The Redis Exporter: This is an external program you can find at `https://github.com/oliver006/redis_exporter/blob/master/README.md#whats-exported`. It is a Go binary that exposes metrics about Redis, the in-memory database and cache that GitLab uses for storing background job queues, and session state and UI caching.

When used together with Grafana, dashboards can be quickly set up, as shown in the following screenshot:

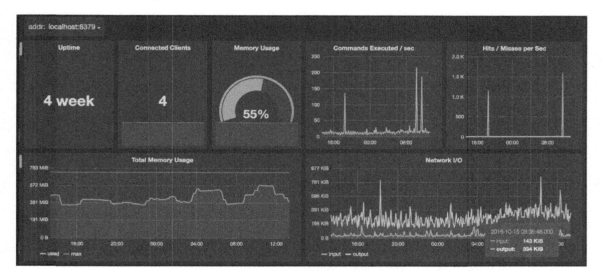

- The Postgres Exporter: Again, this is a Go binary and external project available at: `https://github.com/wrouesnel/postgres_exporter`.

- The GitLab Monitor: This exporter is a bit different in that it is built-in with Ruby and exposes metrics with the Sinatra web server gem. The project page is `https://gitlab.com/gitlab-org/gitlab-monitor`.

When you query the GitLab Monitor, you can provide different parameters, which represent the kind of metric you want to scrape; they include the following:

- **Database**: Provides information about tables, rows, and CI build
- **Git**: Provides information about Git pulls
- **Process**: Provides information about CPU, process count, sidekiq stats, and more

- The Node Exporter: This is perhaps one of the best-known exporters for Prometheus. It consists of a lot of basic metrics for an application node. Again, this exporter is written in Go and is available at `https://github.com/prometheus/node_exporter`.
- To enable the built-in Prometheus server on the GitLab application server, edit the `/etc/gitlab/gitlab.rb` file. Search for `prometheus['enable']`, uncomment it, and set it to `true`. There are several other options, but just enabling it will already deliver you a working instance.

The part of the `gitlab.rb` file you should change is as follows:

```
###############################################################
############
## Prometheus
##! Docs:
https://docs.gitlab.com/ce/administration/monitoring/prometheus/
###############################################################
############
prometheus['enable'] = true
# prometheus['monitor_kubernetes'] = true
# prometheus['username'] = 'gitlab-prometheus'
# prometheus['uid'] = nil
# prometheus['gid'] = nil
```

After changing `gitlab.rb`, you should run a reconfiguration to activate the changes. You will see messages explaining that certain exporters and the Prometheus server have been started.

You can navigate to the Prometheus console by going to the address configured in `prometheus['listen_address']`. You will be presented with a query interface. If you click the drop-down list, you should see a list of metrics that can be queried, as shown in the following screenshot:

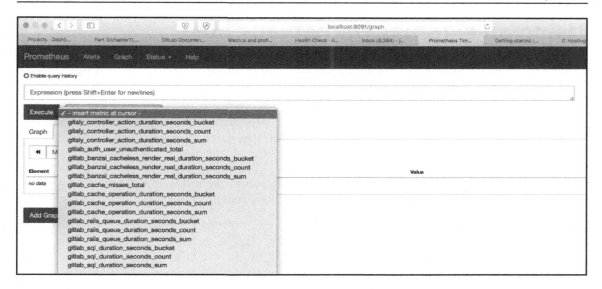

Once you have chosen a metric, it will display all values it has recorded in the database (including data that was actively scraped from Prometheus exporters). In this case, the chose view mode was probably **Console**. You can also view the data as a graph by clicking on **Graph**, as shown in the following screenshot:

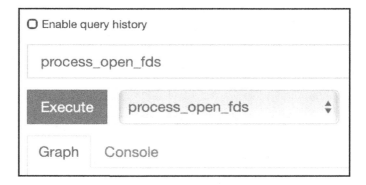

Using an external Prometheus host

If you are not using the omnibus package to manage GitLab or insist on using an external Prometheus server, the picture will be a bit different. You should be aware that the default security model that Prometheus uses is rather simple; it assumes that anyone can view the stored time series data, and the server provides no authentication, authorization, or encryption. If you need these features, you should prepare a reverse proxy in front of the Prometheus server to help. More information about this can be found at `https://prometheus.io/docs/operating/security/`.

The monitoring architecture for this situation is shown in the following diagram (as you can see, some functionality is running on a separate server):

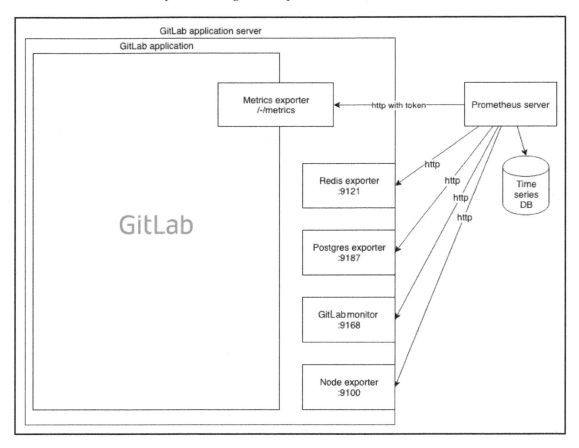

Now we have to make sure we have an external Prometheus host configured that is ready to scrape the data. As we've previously mentioned, Prometheus is a single Go binary. To specify which configuration file to load, use the `--config.file` flag. This configuration file has to have the YAML format. How a single Prometheus server monitors the GitLab Metrics Exporter embedded in GitLab is shown in the following `prometheus.yml` example:

```
- job_name: 'git-metrics'
params:
token: [ gitlab_health_check_access_token ]
metrics_path: /-/metrics
scrape_interval: 5s
scheme: https
tls_config:
insecure_skip_verify: true
file_sd_configs:
- files:
- /etc/prometheus/sd/gitlab_metrics_exporter_sd.yml
```

The `gitlab_metrics_exporter_sd.yml` file contains the following code:

```
- targets: ['gitlab.joustie.nl']
labels:
app: gitlab
```

If you put both files in `/tmp`, or elsewhere, and run Prometheus as a Docker container (as seen in the following example), you should have an external Prometheus ready for action. Of course, you can also install it from source and run it on a dedicated server somewhere else if preferred.

```
docker run -it --name my-prometheus \
-v /tmp:/etc/prometheus \
--publish 9090:9090 \
prom/prometheus
```

You now know how Prometheus runs on the GitLab application server itself, as well as on a separate server.

Enabling the external dashboard link

Since GitLab 12.0 it also possible to enable a link to an external dashboard from inside of GitLab.

1. Go to **Settings** | **Operations** and navigate to **External dashboard**
2. Insert the location to your external dashboard and click on **Save Changes**:

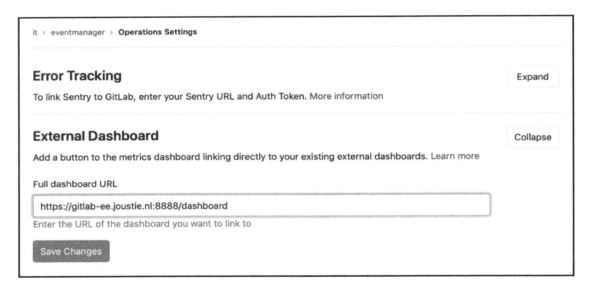

Customizing monitoring

There are several ways to create custom monitoring scripts that will supply time series data to your Prometheus server. As noted earlier in the *Setting up Prometheus* section, there are many client libraries available, such as `https://github.com/prometheus/client_python`.

In the following screenshot, you can see that the preceding project is not very big but does have stars on GitHub.

To use this library, install it using pip (a Python package manager for modules) with the following code:

```
$ pip install prometheus_client
Collecting prometheus_client
matplotlib 1.3.1 requires nose, which is not installed.
matplotlib 1.3.1 requires tornado, which is not installed.
Installing collected packages: prometheus-client
Successfully installed prometheus-client-0.6.0
```

You can also create a simple exporter by running the following code from a Python interpreter or via a file:

```
from prometheus_client import start_http_server, Summary
import random
import time
# Create a metric to track time spent and requests made.
REQUEST_TIME = Summary('request_processing_seconds', 'Time spent
processing request')
# Decorate function with metric.
@REQUEST_TIME.time()
def process_request(t):
"""A dummy function that takes some time."""
time.sleep(t)
if __name__ == '__main__':
# Start up the server to expose the metrics.
start_http_server(8000)
# Generate some requests.
while True:
process_request(random.random())
```

The exporter will start on `localhost`, on port 8000, and the following page will appear when called:

```
# HELP python_info Python platform information
# TYPE python_info gauge
python_info{implementation="CPython",major="2",minor="7",patchlevel="10",version="2.7.10"} 1.0
# HELP request_processing_seconds Time spent processing request
# TYPE request_processing_seconds summary
request_processing_seconds_count 21.0
request_processing_seconds_sum 9.778127431869507
# TYPE request_processing_seconds_created gauge
request_processing_seconds_created 1.550842945378787e+09
```

You can add this exporter to your Prometheus server by adding the following code to `prometheus.yml` and restarting Prometheus with `gitlab-ctl restart prometheus` on an omnibus-installed GitLab application server, or you can use `service prometheus restart` on an externally-installed Prometheus:

```
job_name: 'python_gitlab'
# Override the global default and scrape targets from this job every 5
seconds.
scrape_interval: 5s
static_configs:-
targets: ['localhost:8000']
```

You now have the option to modify your own Python application to report metrics, or you can create Python code that gathers metrics from your system. For instance, you may want to parse a log file for certain patterns and accumulate the relevant metrics.

The static analysis of security vulnerabilities

Static Application Security Testing (SAST) is used to analyze source code or binaries and to detect holes or weak points in security. When automated, this contributes to making your DevOps methodology resemble DevSecOps, where security testing and awareness is part of the DevOps life cycle.

GitLab, in its Ultimate license model, provides automated testing as part of the development of your application.

Currently, the following languages and frameworks are supported:

Language/Framework	Scan tool
.NET	Security Code Scan
C/C++	Flawfinder
Go	gosec
Groovy (Gradle and Grail)	find-sec-bugs
Java (Maven and Gradle)	find-sec-bugs
JavaScript	ESLint security plugin
Node.js	NodeJsScan
PHP	phpcs-security-audit
Python	bandit
Ruby on Rails	brakeman
Scala (sbt)	find-sec-bugs
Typescript	TSLint Config Security

First, you need GitLab Runner with a Docker-in-Docker executor.

This is a normal Docker executor, but it runs in privileged mode. This means it can run its own Docker daemon and therefore run containers itself.

You enable this functionality by changing the GitLab Runner configuration file (config.toml), making sure it has privileged = true. After changing this, restart the runner as follows:

```
[[runners]]
executor = "docker"
[runners.docker]
privileged = true
```

Secondly, you need a specific .gitlab-ci.yml in your GitLab project folder to make the actual coupling, as shown in the following snippet:

```
sast:
 image: docker:stable
 variables:
 DOCKER_DRIVER: overlay2
 allow_failure: true
 services:
 - docker:stable-dind
 script:
 - export SP_VERSION=$(echo "$CI_SERVER_VERSION" | sed
's/^\([0-9]*\)\.\([0-9]*\).*/\1-\2-stable/')
 - docker run
 --env SAST_CONFIDENCE_LEVEL="${SAST_CONFIDENCE_LEVEL:-3}"
 --volume "$PWD:/code"
 --volume /var/run/docker.sock:/var/run/docker.sock
 "registry.gitlab.com/gitlab-org/security-products/sast:$SP_VERSION"
/app/bin/run /code
 artifacts:
 reports:
 sast: gl-sast-report.json
```

As an example, we downloaded the following code from https://github.com/CSPF-Founder/JavaVulnerableLab into our own project. We added .gitlab-ci.yml to run a scan. When the code was pushed, the workflow started and prepared for the scan:

```
[0KRunning with gitlab-runner 11.7.0 (8bb608ff)
[0;m[0K on Joosts-MBP.fritz.box gGEycKK-
[0;m[0KUsing Docker executor with image docker:stable ...
[0;m[0KStarting service docker:stable-dind ...
[0;m[0KPulling docker image docker:stable-dind ...
[0;m[0KUsing docker image
```

```
sha256:5b626cc3459ad077146e8aac1fbe25f7099d71c6765efd6552b9209ca7ea4dc1 for
docker:stable-dind ...
 [0;m[OKWaiting for services to be up and running...
 [0;m[OKPulling docker image docker:stable ...
 [0;m[OKUsing docker image
sha256:73d492654a095a2f91078b2dfacd0cfe1a1fe25412fac54b4eb2f5a9609ad418 for
docker:stable ...
 [0;msection_start:1550847640:prepare_script
 [OKRunning on runner-gGEycKK--project-1-concurrent-0 via Joosts-
MBP.fritz.box...
 section_end:1550847642:prepare_script
 [OKsection_start:1550847642:get_sources
```

In the next stage, the repository containing the code to be scanned is cloned, shown as
follows:

```
 [OK[32;1mCloning repository...[0;m
 Cloning into '/builds/mastering_gitlab/JavaVulnerableLab'...
 [32;1mChecking out 157b6e94 as master...[0;m
 [32;1mSkipping Git submodules setup[0;m
 section_end:1550847644:get_sources
 [OKsection_start:1550847644:restore_cache
 [OKsection_end:1550847646:restore_cache
 [OKsection_start:1550847646:download_artifacts
 [OKsection_end:1550847647:download_artifacts
 [OKsection_start:1550847647:build_script
 [OK[32;1m$ export SP_VERSION=$(echo "$CI_SERVER_VERSION" | sed
's/^\([0-9]*\)\.\([0-9]*\).*/\1-\2-stable/')[0;m
 [32;1m$ docker run --env
SAST_CONFIDENCE_LEVEL="${SAST_CONFIDENCE_LEVEL:-3}" --volume "$PWD:/code" -
-volume /var/run/docker.sock:/var/run/docker.sock
"registry.gitlab.com/gitlab-org/security-products/sast:$SP_VERSION"
/app/bin/run /code[0;m
```

In the next step, the run tries to get a specific Docker image for the scan. It will not find that
locally and will instead try to get it from `gitlab.org`, as follows:

```
 Unable to find image 'registry.gitlab.com/gitlab-org/security-
products/sast:11-7-stable' locally
 11-7-stable: Pulling from gitlab-org/security-products/sast
 3f0edbe59eaa: Pulling fs layer
 3f0edbe59eaa: Download complete
 3f0edbe59eaa: Pull complete
 Digest:
sha256:d31cbb2bfd200b60543ef99fa03638c2335a52597e0966b7347f896dbe4e78e7
 Status: Downloaded newer image for registry.gitlab.com/gitlab-
org/security-products/sast:11-7-stable
```

After successfully downloading the image, it will start the scan, as follows:

```
2019/02/22 15:00:52 Copy project directory to containers
2019/02/22 15:00:52 [bandit] Detect project using plugin
2019/02/22 15:00:52 [bandit] Project not compatible
2019/02/22 15:00:52 [brakeman] Detect project using plugin
2019/02/22 15:00:52 [brakeman] Project not compatible
2019/02/22 15:00:52 [gosec] Detect project using plugin
2019/02/22 15:00:52 [gosec] Project not compatible
2019/02/22 15:00:52 [find-sec-bugs] Detect project using plugin
2019/02/22 15:00:52 [find-sec-bugs] Project is compatible
2019/02/22 15:00:52 [find-sec-bugs] Starting analyzer...
```

After 10 minutes, the results should be as follows:

```
Downloaded from central:
https://repo.maven.apache.org/maven2/com/google/collections/google-collecti
ons/1.0/google-collections-1.0.jar (640 kB at 882 kB/s)
[INFO] Changes detected - recompiling the module!
[WARNING] File encoding has not been set, using platform encoding UTF-8,
i.e. build is platform dependent!
[INFO] Compiling 15 source files to /tmp/app/target/classes
[INFO] ------------------------------------------------------------------
-----
[INFO] BUILD SUCCESS
[INFO] ------------------------------------------------------------------
-----
[INFO] Total time: 11.988 s
[INFO] Finished at: 2019-02-22T15:24:25Z
[INFO] ------------------------------------------------------------------
-----
```

The scan will report on which plugin or module can be use (in other words, it checks project compatibility), as follows:

```
Warnings generated: 49
2019/02/22 15:24:33 [find-sec-bugs-gradle] Detect project using plugin
2019/02/22 15:24:33 [find-sec-bugs-gradle] Project not compatible
2019/02/22 15:24:33 [find-sec-bugs-sbt] Detect project using plugin
2019/02/22 15:24:33 [find-sec-bugs-sbt] Project not compatible
2019/02/22 15:24:33 [find-sec-bugs-groovy] Detect project using plugin
2019/02/22 15:24:33 [find-sec-bugs-groovy] Project not compatible
2019/02/22 15:24:33 [flawfinder] Detect project using plugin
2019/02/22 15:24:33 [flawfinder] Project not compatible
2019/02/22 15:24:33 [phpcs-security-audit] Detect project using plugin
2019/02/22 15:24:33 [phpcs-security-audit] Project not compatible
2019/02/22 15:24:33 [security-code-scan] Detect project using plugin
2019/02/22 15:24:33 [security-code-scan] Project not compatible
```

```
2019/02/22 15:24:33 [nodejs-scan] Detect project using plugin
2019/02/22 15:24:33 [nodejs-scan] Project not compatible
```

You should now see a report of the findings, as in the following example (which is not entirely complete):

```
+------------------------------------------------------------------------
------------+
| Severity | Tool | Location |
+------------------------------------------------------------------------
-------------+
| High | Find Security Bugs |
src/main/java/org/cysecurity/cspf/jvl/controller/LoginValidator.java:64 |
| |
| HTTP cookie formed from untrusted input |
+------------------------------------------------------------------------
-------------+
| High | Find Security Bugs |
src/main/java/org/cysecurity/cspf/jvl/controller/AddPage.java:45 |
| |
| Relative path traversal in servlet |
+------------------------------------------------------------------------
-------------+
```

As you can see in the following snippet, a lot of security issues were discovered:

```
Uploading artifacts...
gl-sast-report.json: found 1 matching files
Uploading artifacts to coordinator... ok id=4 responseStatus=201 Created
token=Sy_pRf1e
Job succeeded
```

The scan finally finishes by uploading the report.

Essentially, SAST tries to analyze your code and applies plugins based on which code could be scanned. It will look for security hazards in your code. The scan is done in a special container delivered by GitLab. After scanning, a report is available.

Dynamic Application Security Testing

Dynamic Application Security Testing (DAST) runs PEN tests like scans of your application.

The test uses OWASP ZAProxy (`https://github.com/zaproxy/zaproxy`) to scan a running instance in your web application. It runs a passive scan, which means it only tries to discover your application by exploring links, will not find links created dynamically, and will not attack your application actively.

Before GitLab 12.0, this scan also used the Docker-in-Docker mechanism, but now it just retrieves and runs a container and the test. This means the image is cached on GitLab runners, and after retrieving the image for the first time, the security test will run faster.

As with SAST, you control how scanning happens through the `.gitlab-ci.yml` file, as follows:

```
dast:
image: registry.gitlab.com/gitlab-org/security-products/zaproxy
variables:
website: "https://blog.joustie.nl"
allow_failure: true
script:
- mkdir /zap/wrk/
- /zap/zap-baseline.py -J gl-dast-report.json -t $website || true
- cp /zap/wrk/gl-dast-report.json .
artifacts:
reports:
dast: gl-dast-report.json
```

When you push code to the repository, the DAST scan will start preparing, as shown in the following snippet. First, it will try to find the ZAProxy Docker container and pull it.

```
Running with gitlab-runner 11.7.0 (8bb608ff)
on host gGEycKK-
Using Docker executor with image registry.gitlab.com/gitlab-org/security-
products/zaproxy ...
Pulling docker image registry.gitlab.com/gitlab-org/security-
products/zaproxy ...
Using docker image
sha256:cd12d3ce5fc66ef0c6b2cf0e6b745876b666aed7f9e859451eaef884b92cefa7 for
registry.gitlab.com/gitlab-org/security-products/zaproxy ...
```

The scan will start as follows:

```
Running on runner-gGEycKK--project-2-concurrent-0 via Joosts-
MBP.fritz.box...
Fetching changes...
Removing zap.out
HEAD is now at 6024894 Update .gitlab-ci.yml
From http://192.168.178.82/root/unsecure
6024894..e6b26fe master -> origin/master
Checking out e6b26fe5 as master...
Skipping Git submodules setup
$ mkdir /zap/wrk/
$ /zap/zap-baseline.py -J gl-dast-report.json -t $website || true
2019-02-22 15:50:26,650 Params: ['zap-x.sh', '-daemon', '-port', '40096',
'-host', '0.0.0.0', '-config', 'api.disablekey=true', '-config',
'api.addrs.addr.name=.*', '-config', 'api.addrs.addr.regex=true', '-
config', 'spider.maxDuration=1', '-addonupdate', '-addoninstall',
'pscanrulesBeta']
Feb 22, 2019 3:50:34 PM java.util.prefs.FileSystemPreferences$1 run
INFO: Created user preferences directory.
```

It will try to scan the whole website, as shown in the following example:

```
Total of 251 URLs
PASS: Cookie No HttpOnly Flag [10010]
PASS: Cookie Without Secure Flag [10011]
PASS: Incomplete or No Cache-control and Pragma HTTP Header Set [10015]
PASS: Content-Type Header Missing [10019]
PASS: Information Disclosure - Debug Error Messages [10023]
PASS: Information Disclosure - Sensitive Information in URL [10024]
PASS: Information Disclosure - Sensitive Information in HTTP Referrer
Header [10025]
PASS: HTTP Parameter Override [10026]
PASS: Information Disclosure - Suspicious Comments [10027]
PASS: Viewstate Scanner [10032]
PASS: Secure Pages Include Mixed Content [10040]
PASS: CSP Scanner [10055]
PASS: Weak Authentication Method [10105]
PASS: Session ID in URL Rewrite [3]
PASS: Script Passive Scan Rules [50001]
PASS: Insecure JSF ViewState [90001]
PASS: Charset Mismatch [90011]
PASS: WSDL File Passive Scanner [90030]
PASS: Loosely Scoped Cookie [90033]
```

It will then report vulnerabilities immediately, as shown in the following snippet:

```
WARN-NEW: Web Browser XSS Protection Not Enabled [10016] x 112
  http://blog.joustie.nl/
  http://blog.joustie.nl/robots.txt
  http://blog.joustie.nl/sitemap.xml
  http://blog.joustie.nl
  http://blog.joustie.nl/atom.xml
WARN-NEW: Cross-Domain JavaScript Source File Inclusion [10017] x 108
  http://blog.joustie.nl/
  http://blog.joustie.nl
  http://blog.joustie.nl/tags/personal/
  http://blog.joustie.nl/2019/01/12/2018-05-29-personalblog/
  http://blog.joustie.nl/2018/05/29/2018-05-20-met-zn-allen-1-wereld/
  .....
FAIL-NEW: 0 FAIL-INPROG: 0 WARN-NEW: 7 WARN-INPROG: 0 INFO: 0 IGNORE: 0
PASS: 19
```

After scanning, the report is created and uploaded as an artifact, as follows:

```
$ cp /zap/wrk/gl-dast-report.json .
Uploading artifacts...
gl-dast-report.json: found 1 matching files
Uploading artifacts to coordinator... ok id=6 responseStatus=201 Created
token=LbTRyRU-
Job succeeded
```

As you can see from the preceding examples, by utilizing GitLab Runners with Docker, it is very easy to start a dynamic security scan.

Dependency checking

Known vulnerabilities in third-party components or dependencies are very common. They could even be part of the OWASP Top 10 List of Using Components with Known Vulnerabilities. The OWASP Web Malware Scanner (see `https://www.owasp.org`) is a malware scanner for web applications. It can be used to scan a web application by using signatures from a community build and a managed database. It works by testing each file of the web application for known signatures of malware.

These known vulnerable components should be identified at an early development stage. It is also good practice to perform vulnerability scanning of the dependency components not only in the development stage but also in the production stage on a regular basis.

Again, the dependency scan in your GitLab workflow is controlled through the `.gitlab-ci.yml` file. It also uses the Docker-in-Docker technique, as follows:

```
dependency_scanning:
  image: docker:stable
  variables:
  DOCKER_DRIVER: overlay2
  allow_failure: true
  services:
  - docker:stable-dind
  script:
  - export SP_VERSION=$(echo "$CI_SERVER_VERSION" | sed
  's/^\([0-9]*\)\.\([0-9]*\).*/\1-\2-stable/')
  - docker run
  --env DEP_SCAN_DISABLE_REMOTE_CHECKS="${DEP_SCAN_DISABLE_REMOTE_CHECKS:-
  false}"
  --volume "$PWD:/code"
  --volume /var/run/docker.sock:/var/run/docker.sock
  "registry.gitlab.com/gitlab-org/security-products/dependency-
  scanning:$SP_VERSION" /code
  artifacts:
  reports:
  dependency_scanning: gl-dependency-scanning-report.json
```

For this test, we used the same code (https://github.com/CSPF-Founder/JavaVulnerableLab) as we did in the SAST scan to show our results. Here, you can see the job as it prepares after being pushed some new code. It should pull the `stable-dind` image, as follows:

```
Running with gitlab-runner 11.7.0 (8bb608ff)
on host gGEycKK-
Using Docker executor with image docker:stable ...
Starting service docker:stable-dind ...
Pulling docker image docker:stable-dind ...
Using docker image
sha256:5b626cc3459ad077146e8aac1fbe25f7099d71c6765efd6552b9209ca7ea4dc1 for
docker:stable-dind ...
Waiting for services to be up and running...
Pulling docker image docker:stable ...
Using docker image
sha256:73d492654a095a2f91078b2dfacd0cfe1a1fe25412fac54b4eb2f5a9609ad418 for
docker:stable ...
```

Running the image will execute the dependency scan, as shown in the following snippets:

```
Running on runner-gGEycKK--project-2-concurrent-0 via Joosts-
MBP.fritz.box...
Fetching changes...
HEAD is now at e6b26fe Update .gitlab-ci.yml
From http://192.168.178.82/root/unsecure
e6b26fe..3aa3162 master -> origin/master
Checking out 3aa3162f as master...
Skipping Git submodules setup
$ export SP_VERSION=$(echo "$CI_SERVER_VERSION" | sed
's/^\([0-9]*\)\.\([0-9]*\).*/\1-\2-stable/')
$ docker run --env
DEP_SCAN_DISABLE_REMOTE_CHECKS="${DEP_SCAN_DISABLE_REMOTE_CHECKS:-false}" -
-volume "$PWD:/code" --volume /var/run/docker.sock:/var/run/docker.sock
"registry.gitlab.com/gitlab-org/security-products/dependency-
scanning:$SP_VERSION" /code
...
```

The technology used was formerly called Gemnasium. It was bought by GitLab in 2018, as you can see in a statement at https://docs.gitlab.com/ee/user/project/import/gemnasium.html.

```
Downloaded from central:
https://repo.maven.apache.org/maven2/org/codehaus/plexus/plexus/2.0.6/plexu
s-2.0.6.pom (17 kB at 621 kB/s)
[INFO] Gemnasium Maven Plugin
[INFO]
[INFO] Project's dependencies have been successfully dumped into:
/tmp/app/gemnasium-maven-plugin.json
[INFO] -----------------------------------------------------------------
-----
[INFO] BUILD SUCCESS
[INFO] -----------------------------------------------------------------
-----
[INFO] Total time: 5.504 s
[INFO] Finished at: 2019-02-23T11:45:49Z
[INFO] -----------------------------------------------------------------
-----
```

As you can see in the following code, some vulnerabilities in the MySQL library used were found:

```
+--------------------------------------------------------------------
---------------+
| Severity | Tool | Identifier |
+--------------------------------------------------------------------
---------------+
| Unknown | Gemnasium | CVE-2015-7501 |
| |
| InvokerTransformer code execution during deserialization in commons |
| collections/commons-collections |
| Solution: Upgrade to the latest version |
| In pom.xml |
+--------------------------------------------------------------------
---------------+
| Unknown | Gemnasium | CVE-2017-3523 |
| |
| Vulnerability in the MySQL Connectors in mysql/mysql-connector-java |
| Solution: Upgrade to the latest version |
| In pom.xml |
+--------------------------------------------------------------------
---------------+
2019/02/23 11:45:51 [gemnasium-python] Detect project using plugin
2019/02/23 11:45:51 [gemnasium-python] Project not compatible
2019/02/23 11:45:51 [retire.js] Detect project using plugin
2019/02/23 11:45:51 [retire.js] Project not compatible
Uploading artifacts...
gl-dependency-scanning-report.json: found 1 matching files
Uploading artifacts to coordinator... ok id=7 responseStatus=201 Created
token=1cdLFEJP
Job succeeded
```

The job ends by uploading the scan report.

Just like the other scans, dependency checking uses the same technique of running a specific scan program from inside a Docker container. In this case, the scan program in use is Gemnasium, which was taken over by GitLab last year. If a problematic dependency is found, it is displayed in the output and in the resulting report.

A nice feature of GitLab 12.0 is that after your conducted your dependency scan, the resulting list of dependencies is saved in your project. This is a much wanted feature by security/compliance teams to keep track of what dependencies are used throughout the enterprise:

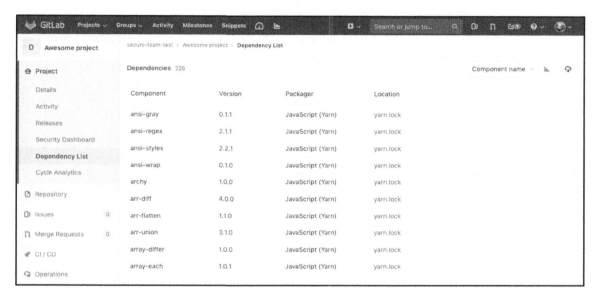

Summary

In this chapter, we discussed the use of monitoring in the workflow, and the possibility to immediately integrate security monitoring. GitLab provides out-of-the-box opportunities to set up such things. In this chapter, we also looked at Prometheus and ways to write custom monitoring for it. In the next chapter, we will discuss integration options for GitLab, in case you need to connect to other tools.

Questions

1. On which system is Prometheus inspired?
2. What is the name of the Prometheus clients?
3. On what path is the GitLab Metrics Exporter normally found?
4. What language was used for the GitLab Monitor Exporter?
5. How do you enable the built-in Prometheus server in the omnibus package?
6. What does SAST mean?
7. What does DAST mean?
8. Which file is used to control security testing?

Further reading

- Prometheus site: https://prometheus.io
- OWASP scan: https://www.owasp.org
- *Practical Site Reliability Engineering,* by *Pethuru Raj Chelliah, Shreyash Naithani,* and *Shailender Singh*: https://www.packtpub.com/virtualization-and-cloud/practical-site-reliability-engineering
- *Hands-On Security in DevOps,* by *Tony Hsu*: https://www.packtpub.com/in/networking-and-servers/hands-security-devops
- *Industrial Internet Application Development,* by *Alena Traukina, Jayant Thomas, Prashant Tyagi,* and *Kishore Reddipalli*: https://www.packtpub.com/in/application-development/industrial-internet-application-development

13
Integrating GitLab with CI/CD Tools

In this chapter, we will cover some of the integrations that are possible with GitLab. Most of the time, companies will not use one tool for their complete DevOps journey. GitLab encourages this for small to midsize companies, but the reality is that big enterprise customers use a mix of different tools and technologies. We will connect Jira to GitLab, as this tool is in use in a big portion of the enterprise market. Of course, the venerable Jenkins server has to be mentioned and tried, and modern organizations use Slack/Mattermost or other chat tools for real-time collaboration. We will finish this chapter with an example of how to utilize a basic webhook.

In this chapter, we will cover the following topics:

- Using Jira with GitLab
- Connecting with Jenkins
- Integrating with Mattermost
- Using webhooks for events

Technical requirements

For managing omnibus installs, there is one central configuration file called `gitlab.rb`. You need to create it or copy an example. There is a template available that you can find at `https://gitlab.com/gitlab-org/omnibus-gitlab/blob/master/files/gitlab-config-template/gitlab.rb.template`. It isn't updated after upgrades. In large parts of this chapter, I will quote and discuss parts of this file.

The code examples for this chapter are available in this book's GitHub repository at `https://github.com/PacktPublishing/Mastering-GitLab-12/tree/master/Chapter13`.

Using Jira with GitLab

Jira is an IT project management tool that was created by Atlassian in 2002 and was first created as software for developers.

Jira was originally an issue tracking tool, that is, a tool to list and manage tasks. A *task* can be anything: a problem that needs to be solved, a simple TODO, an application, and so on. However, you can also go much further and put your products, customers, companies, and so on into this tool.

JIRA is also a *workflow engine*. This means that you can define *workflows* (in other words, processes) that your tasks must follow. This way, you can impose different processes per project or per task. An example of a simple workflow for a task of the TODO type is OPEN | IN PROGRESS | READY.

For a different type of task, for example, an application to do something, you can set up this workflow: OPEN | CONFIRMED | APPROVED | READY.

Through its integrations, GitLab can interface with Jira. Although GitLab already offers a lot of the project management features that Jira provides, in larger organizations, it can help integrate these tools. For instance, when overall project management is done in Jira, you can make sure that specific links are accessible in the GitLab workflow through commit messages, merge requests, and so on.

As an example, let's create a project in Jira:

1. We created an account on the Cloud offering from Atlassian (`https://www.atlassian.com/enterprise/cloud`). When you have set up your instance in the Atlassian Cloud or on premise, continue to create a new project:

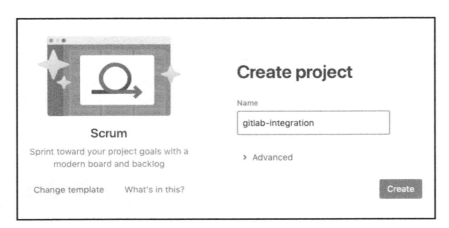

2. When your project has been created, you will see the following screen:

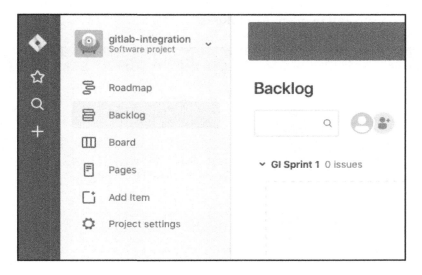

3. The next step is to create an issue in this project. Let's do that with minimal information and call it `Integrate GitLab and Jira`. You will see it create an issue with an ID of `GI-1`. We now have an issue in our project management tool, which we like to link to our GitLab instance:

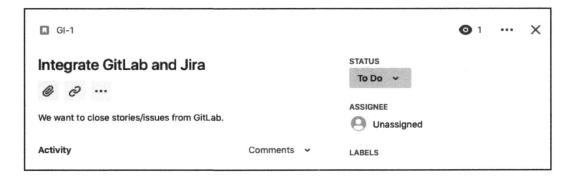

4. Now, we will create a special token in Jira, which we will use in GitLab to update the issue. Please visit `https://id.atlassian.com`, click **Security**, and then click **Create and manage API tokens**:

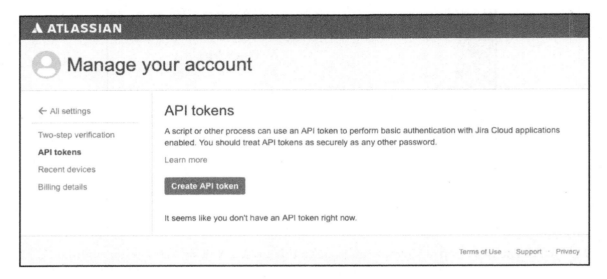

5. Click **Create API token**:

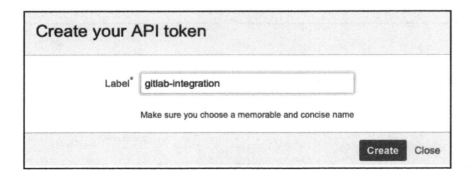

6. After you have given it a nice name and clicked **Create**, it will appear in the list:

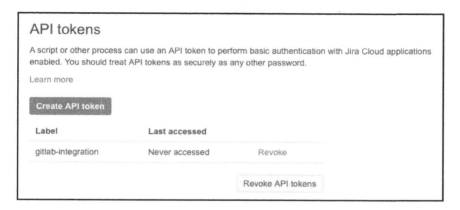

7. Now, we need to head over to our GitLab instance to create the project that we want to connect to Jira:

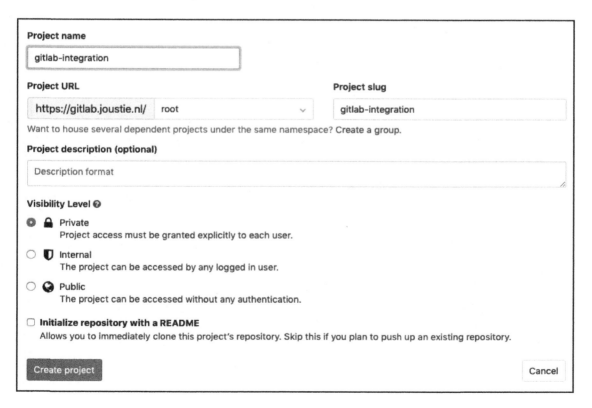

8. When the project has been created, go to the settings for this project and look for Jira in integrations:

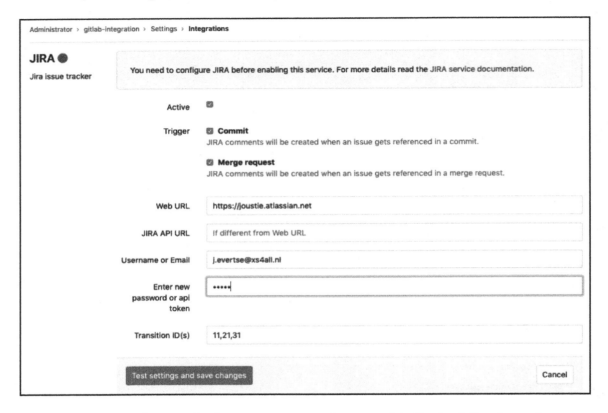

9. You can choose whether comments can be created in Jira by following references in a **Commit** or a **Merge request**. You need to give the web URL for your Jira instance, which in our case is `https://joustie.atlassian.net`.

Your username is the email address, and you can fill in your token that you created in Jira earlier.

Now comes the harder part. When you change a Jira issue to another state, you need to provide a transition ID. In our example, this is `11`, `21`, `31`. Now, what is that and where do we find it? This is a good question, and all you need to do is call Jira's API. They represent the state an issue can be in, and you need to know this state in order to change them.

In the following example, we called
`https://joustie.atlassian.net/rest/api/2/issue/GI-1/transitions`.

When you've found those IDs and saved the changes, Jira will test them, and hopefully, you'll receive the following feedback:

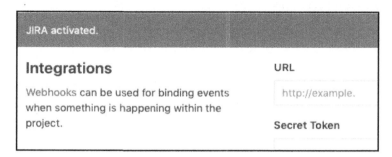

If you go back to the **Integrations** page, note that the Jira integration is green. Green is good:

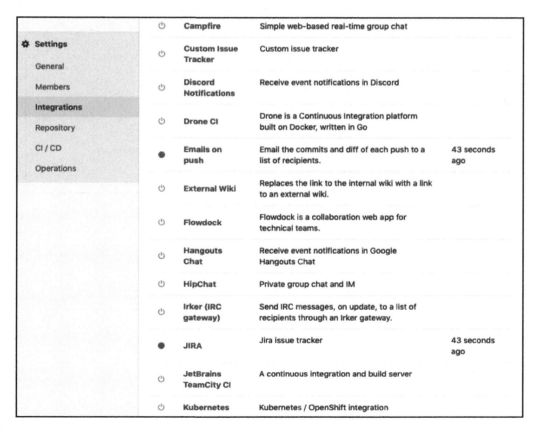

If something goes wrong or you would like to know more about these calls, you can consult `integrations_json.log` in the rails log directory. For instance, the successful call to activate Jira integration is as follows:

```
{"severity":"INFO","time":"2019-03-02T16:48:49.466Z","correlation_id":"28a6
7335-4f3d-40ed-826d-8ca0d6d34f84","service_class":"JiraService","project_id
":12,"project_path":"root/gitlab-integration","message":"Successfully
posted","client_url":"https://joustie.atlassian.net"}
```

Now, you can resolve an issue in Jira through GitLab:

```
Joosts-iMac:gitlab-integration joostevertse$ git commit -m "Initial
commit: Resolves GI-1"
[master (root-commit) 0418211] Initial commit: Resolves GI-1
1 file changed, 0 insertions(+), 0 deletions(-)
create mode 100644 test.txt
```

In the project overview, you will find that the issue has moved to **Done**:

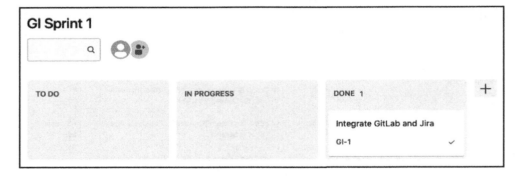

If you look in the issue itself, you will find that is has a status of **Closed**:

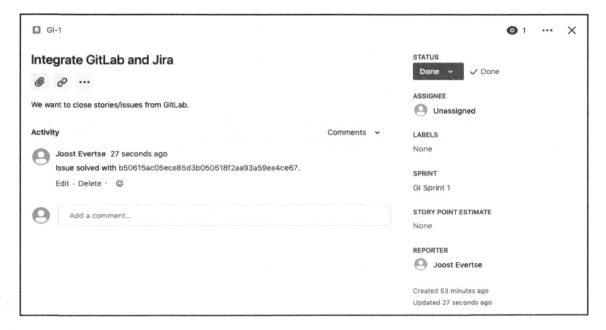

As you can see, it is possible to integrate project management tools like Jira with GitLab and keep issues in sync. In this section, we have demonstrated how to integrate a cloud-based Jira offering with a local on-premise GitLab installation. Now, let's move on and connect with Jenkins.

Connecting Jenkins to GitLab

Jenkins (a fork of the Hudson project) is a Continuous Integration platform. The platform is primarily intended for the repeated execution and monitoring of build tasks, as well as the automated building and testing of applications. The many freely available plugins make it very easy to expand the functionality of Jenkins. An example of this is its integration with other systems (such as Sonar, Jira, or CloudBees) or changing its look and feel. It is possible to build a complete Continuous Delivery pipeline by using the right plugins.

There is also a GitLab plugin available to integrate Jenkins in a GitLab workflow. You can download and host Jenkins yourself, or buy capacity in the cloud.

As an example, we have used a local Jenkins container and pulled a container from `https:/ /hub.docker.com/_/jenkins`. Let's get started:

1. When your Jenkins container has been configured and started, you need to make sure that the GitLab plugin has been installed:

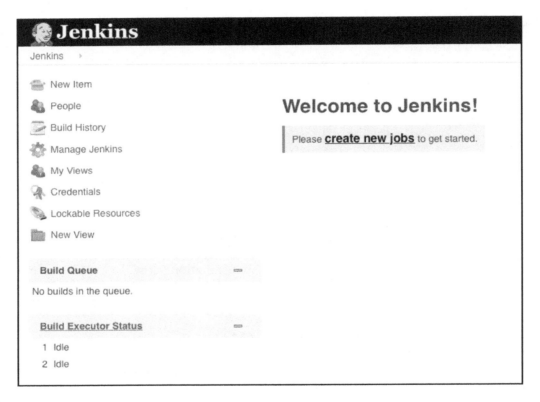

2. Click on **Manage Jenkins** | **Manage Plugins**:

3. If you click on the **Available** tab and filter for GitLab, you can choose the **GitLab** plugin:

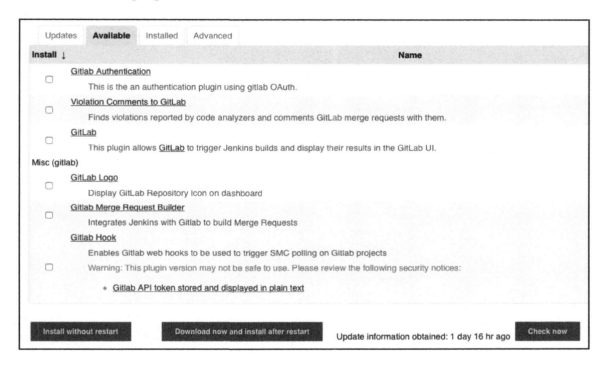

4. When it has been installed, you will see it appearing as a **Success**:

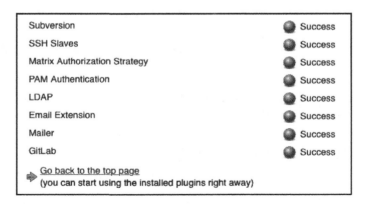

5. Now, go back to the **Manage Jenkins** page, click **Configure System**, and scroll to the **GitLab** section.

6. Give the connection a name of your choice, provide the correct URL, and click **Add** to get a GitLab API token. This API token can be generated in GitLab in the settings:

7. You only need to fill in the API token here:

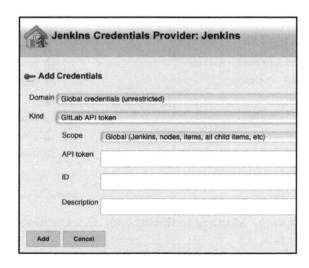

8. The next step is to create projects in Jenkins and GitLab (for this example). For this occasion, we chose a freestyle project and named it `petclinic`:

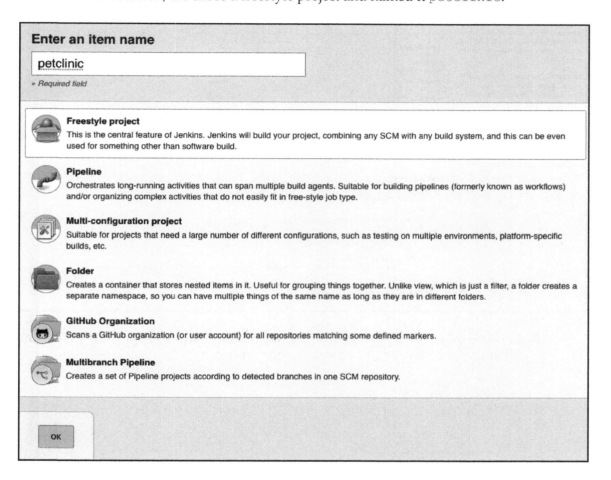

9. We did the same for GitLab:

10. In your Jenkins project, scroll down to the **Source Code Management** section and fill in the URL of your GitLab source code repository:

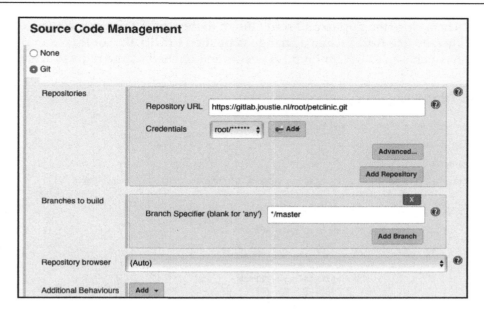

11. Next, click **Add** to add credentials. You need to add a username and password to connect to your HTTP Git repository (or an SSH user/key or an API key):

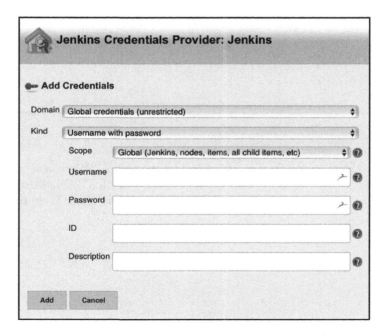

12. Then, close the popup and scroll down to the **Build Triggers** section. You can then enable **Build when a change is pushed to GitLab**. For this example, we have chosen to trigger on push events and opened merge request events:

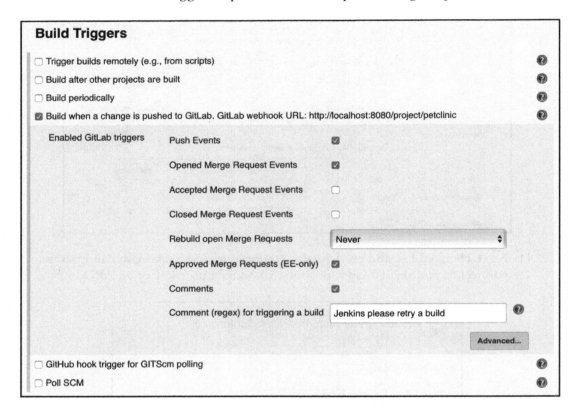

13. Click on **Save** to save your settings.

For testing and fast development, I recommend using ngrok. This is a secure tunnel program that you can use to connect a localhost to a dynamic URL hosting service. You can find the tool at `http://ngrok.com`. Download the binary and place it on the local path.

We can use it to tunnel from the internet (where our GitLab lives in a cloud container) to our local Docker container running Jenkins.

Start ngrok to connect an internet URL to our local Jenkins running on 8080 in Docker:

```
Joosts-iMac:images_chapter12 joostevertse$ ngrok http 8080
```

After starting ngrok, you will be presented with the following output:

```
grok by @inconshreveable

ession Status                online
ession Expires               7 hours, 59 minutes
ersion                       2.2.8
egion                        United States (us)
eb Interface                 http://127.0.0.1:4040
orwarding                    http://5d388e86.ngrok.io -> localhost:8080
orwarding                    https://5d388e86.ngrok.io -> localhost:8080

onnections                   ttl     opn     rt1     rt5     p50     p90
                             0       0       0.00    0.00    0.00    0.00
```

Now, change some code in the repository and push the code to GitLab:

```
Joosts-iMac:petclinic joostevertse$ git push -u origin master
 Enumerating objects: 130, done.
 Counting objects: 100% (130/130), done.
 Delta compression using up to 16 threads
 Compressing objects: 100% (119/119), done.
 Writing objects: 100% (130/130), 352.91 KiB | 12.17 MiB/s, done.
 Total 130 (delta 26), reused 0 (delta 0)
 remote: Resolving deltas: 100% (26/26), done.
 To https://gitlab.joustie.nl/root/petclinic.git
 * [new branch] master -> master
 Branch 'master' set up to track remote branch 'master' from 'origin'.
 Joosts-iMac:petclinic joostevertse$
```

You will notice the hook being triggered in ngrok:

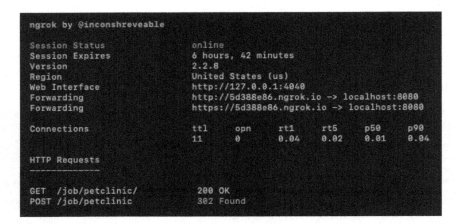

By going to Jenkins, you will see that it receives an event and starts building the project:

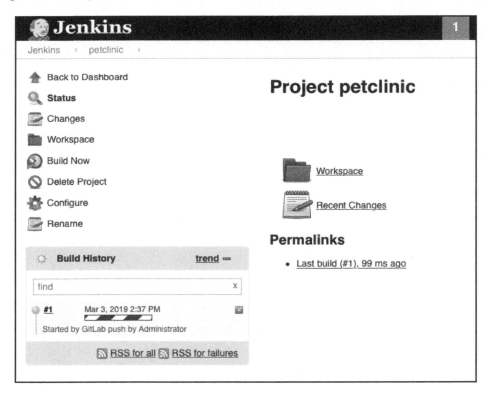

As you can see, it's quite easy to connect Jenkins to GitLab. You can choose to let Jenkins react to different kinds of events in GitLab.

Integrating with Mattermost

Mattermost is the number one open source Slack alternative, and can be hosted on a proprietary platform that you manage yourself.

When teams use these tools, they can become more productive because of direct communication via chat in specialized channels. There, they can exchange quick information bits – even files (images/video, anything) and datafiles that are used by applications.

You can use Mattermost via a browser, or use the platform-specific app on your mobile device. No specific personal data is used other than your email address.

What is also one of its killer features is that it easily connects to third-party applications and systems such as GitLab, Jira Jenkins, Nagios, Zabbix, Kopano, and many more! The company has actually been bought by GitLab, and Mattermost is part of the omnibus installation. In other words, you can easily enable it and run it together with GitLab. ChatOps has been supported since GitLab Ultimate 10.6, but came to GitLab Core in 11.9.

As an example, we will set up a new Mattermost server to integrate with a GitLab instance in order to use slash commands.

Because Mattermost is part of the GitLab omnibus package, you can enable/install it by editing the `gitlab.rb` file, and use `gitlab-ctl` afterwards to reconfigure your instance.

The configuration key to change in `gitlab.rb` is as follows:

```
mattermost['enable'] = true
```

After Mattermost has been started, you can go the integrations page of the settings of your project and search for the Mattermost slash command service. Click on **Add to Mattermost**. This will only work automatically on Mattermost 3.4, so make sure that your omnibus package isn't too old.

If Mattermost isn't installed on your server, you can pull a simple Mattermost image from Docker Hub. `mattermost/mattermost-preview` will do fine. Let's get started:

1. When you log in for the first time in your container (by default, this is via `http://localhost:8065`), you have to create a user:

Mattermost

All team communication in one place, searchable and accessible anywhere

Let's create your account

Already have an account? Click here to sign in.

What's your email address?

    joustie@gmail.com

Valid email required for sign-up

Choose your username

    joustie

Username must begin with a letter, and contain between 3 to 22 lowercase characters made up of numbers, letters, and the symbols '.', '-' and '_'

Choose your password

    ········

Create Account

By proceeding to create your account and use Mattermost, you agree to our Terms of Service and Privacy Policy. If you do not agree, you cannot use Mattermost.

2. After you have created the user, you will want to create a team:

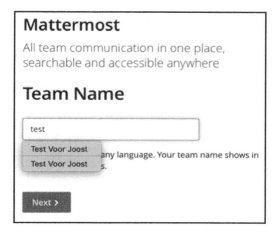

3. That team needs a URL as well:

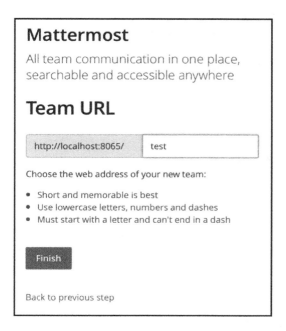

4. You can click the hamburger menu to reveal options for the team:

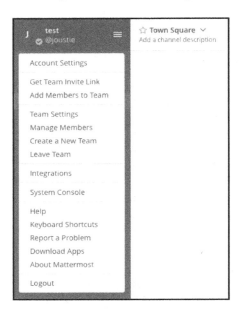

5. Go to the system console:

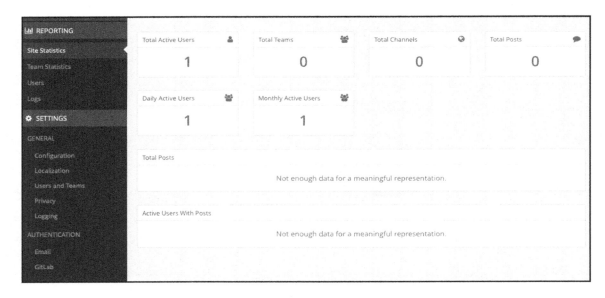

6. Look for **Custom Integrations** and check that slash commands are enabled. Save the settings:

Enable Custom Slash Commands: ● true ○ false

When true, custom slash commands will be allowed. See documentation to learn more.

Enable OAuth 2.0 Service Provider: ○ true ● false

7. After this, click the hamburger menu and click **Switch back to....** Clicking the hamburger menu in the team context, you can click **Integrations**. Here, you can click on **Slash Command**, where you will find a page where you can define a slash command that can be triggered by Mattermost:

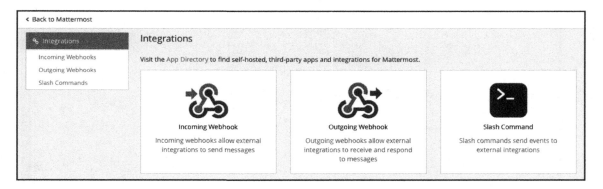

8. The information we need to fill in here can be got from GitLab:

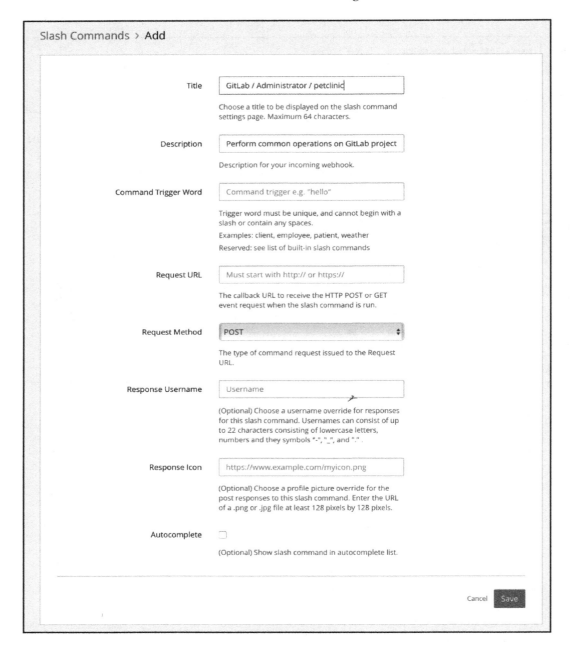

Slash Commands > **Add**

Title

GitLab / Administrator / petclinic

Choose a title to be displayed on the slash command settings page. Maximum 64 characters.

Description

Perform common operations on GitLab project

Description for your incoming webhook.

Command Trigger Word

Command trigger e.g. "hello"

Trigger word must be unique, and cannot begin with a slash or contain any spaces.

Examples: client, employee, patient, weather

Reserved: see list of built-in slash commands

Request URL

Must start with http:// or https://

The callback URL to receive the HTTP POST or GET event request when the slash command is run.

Request Method

POST

The type of command request issued to the Request URL.

Response Username

Username

(Optional) Choose a username override for responses for this slash command. Usernames can consist of up to 22 characters consisting of lowercase letters, numbers and they symbols "-", "_", and ".".

Response Icon

https://www.example.com/myicon.png

(Optional) Choose a profile picture override for the post responses to this slash command. Enter the URL of a .png or .jpg file at least 128 pixels by 128 pixels.

Autocomplete

☐

(Optional) Show slash command in autocomplete list.

Cancel   Save

9. Log in to GitLab and go to **Integrations** in the settings part of your repository. Then, click **Mattermost slash** command. Here is the information you need to fill in in Mattermost:

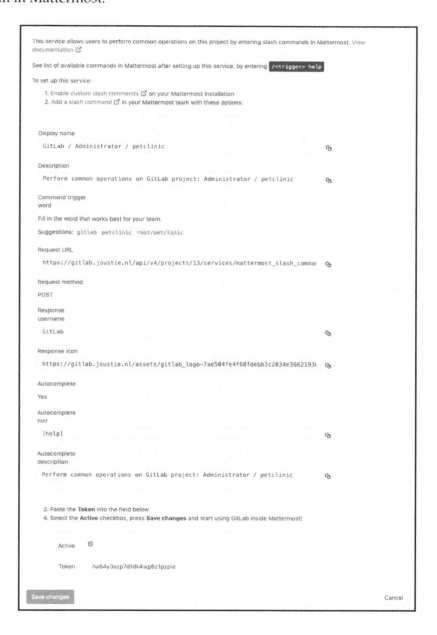

This service allows users to perform common operations on this project by entering slash commands in Mattermost. View documentation 🗗

See list of available commands in Mattermost after setting up this service, by entering `/<trigger> help`

To set up this service:

1. Enable custom slash commands 🗗 on your Mattermost installation
2. Add a slash command 🗗 in your Mattermost team with these options:

Display name

GitLab / Administrator / petclinic

Description

Perform common operations on GitLab project: Administrator / petclinic

Command trigger
word

Fill in the word that works best for your team.

Suggestions: gitlab petclinic root/petclinic

Request URL

https://gitlab.joustie.nl/api/v4/projects/13/services/mattermost_slash_commar

Request method

POST

Response
username

GitLab

Response icon

https://gitlab.joustie.nl/assets/gitlab_logo-7ae504fe4f68fdebb3c2034e3662193(

Autocomplete

Yes

Autocomplete
hint

[help]

Autocomplete
description

Perform common operations on GitLab project: Administrator / petclinic

3. Paste the **Token** into the field below
4. Select the **Active** checkbox, press **Save changes** and start using GitLab inside Mattermost!

Active ☑

Token   ha64y3ozp7d1dk4sqj6z1pzpie

Save changes   Cancel

10. In the following screenshot, you can see the settings as we copied them. Click **Save** or **Update** when you are done:

Slash Commands > Edit

Title	GitLab / Administrator / petclinic

Choose a title to be displayed on the slash command settings page. Maximum 64 characters.

Description	Perform common operations on GitLab project: Administr

Description for your incoming webhook.

Command Trigger Word	gitlab

Trigger word must be unique, and cannot begin with a slash or contain any spaces.
Examples: client, employee, patient, weather
Reserved: see list of built-in slash commands

Request URL	https://gitlab.joustie.nl/api/v4/projects/13/services/mattei

The callback URL to receive the HTTP POST or GET event request when the slash command is run.

Request Method	POST

The type of command request issued to the Request URL.

Response Username	gitlab

(Optional) Choose a username override for responses for this slash command. Usernames can consist of up to 22 characters consisting of lowercase letters, numbers and they symbols "-", "_", and ".".

Response Icon	https://gitlab.joustie.nl/assets/gitlab_logo-7ae504fe4f68fd

(Optional) Choose a profile picture override for the post responses to this slash command. Enter the URL of a .png or .jpg file at least 128 pixels by 128 pixels.

Autocomplete	☑

(Optional) Show slash command in autocomplete list

Autocomplete Hint	[help]

(Optional) Arguments associated with your slash command, displayed as help in the autocomplete list.

Autocomplete Description	Perform common operations on GitLab project: Administr

(Optional) Short description of slash command for the autocomplete list.

Cancel   Update

11. You will now be presented with a token to be used in GitLab. Copy the Mattermost token:

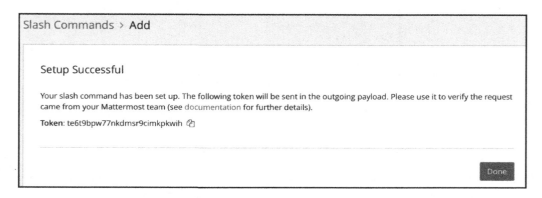

12. Paste it into the settings page for your Mattermost integration in GitLab, and save the changes:

13. Now, go to your team channel in Mattermost and press /. If you issue `/gitlab help`, Mattermost will ask you to connect your GitLab account:

14. You will be redirected to GitLab, where you will have to authorize the connection:

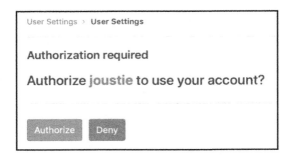

15. Now, by going back to Mattermost and issuing `/gitlab help` once more, you will be presented with the options for the command. There are several, and these can help your support people run ChatOps:

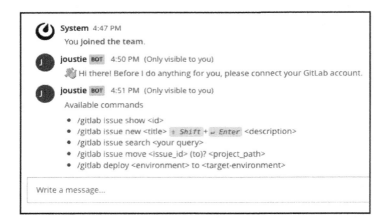

16. Let's create a new issue called `gitlab issue new test`:

17. If you go back to GitLab, you will find that a new issue has been created for the GitLab project:

The ultimate integration is to use CI command functions, as described here: `https://docs.gitlab.com/ee/ci/chatops/`.

Since GitLab 11.9, ChatOps is even part of GitLab Core, so its functionality isn't limited to the GitLab Enterprise Edition.

In this section, we have showed you how to integrate your GitLab repository issues with the Mattermost chat application. There are endless possibilities if you create your own slash commands. Now, let's take a look at using webhooks for events.

Using webhooks for events

Webhooks are used as a signal between applications. You can see it as a callback from a different context. This call is made with the HTTP protocol (possibly with SSL). An attempt is made to provide information as efficiently as possible and in real time, and JSON is usually used as a data format.

The strength lies in the fact that as few operations as possible are necessary in order to get feedback. Usually, the most work lies in the implementation of the *signal*.

For a proof of concept, consider the following. Let's assume that when we push new code to GitLab, we have to send a signal from GitLab to an application that we have built ourselves.

To implement this model, we've chose the lightweight Flask micro-framework for Python:

```python
from flask import Flask, request
import json
app = Flask(__name__)

def runsomething():
 print "This is triggered"

@app.route('/',methods=['POST'])
def trigger():
 data = json.loads(request.data)
 print "New commit by: {}".format(data['commits'][0]['author']['name'])
 print "New commit by: {}".format(data['commits'][0]['author']['email'])
 print "New commit by: {}".format(data['commits'][0]['message'])

 runsomething()
 return "OK"

if __name__ == '__main__':
 app.run()
```

Let's run through this code step by step. In the following code, the basic app has been initiated. The imports are purely the basic Flask framework and, in particular, the request object. The app is instantiated:

```python
from flask import Flask, request
import json
app = Flask(__name__)
```

The following function can be used to do the real work:

```python
def runsomething():
 print "This is triggered"
```

Then follows the method that is decorated with a route, and parses the request for certain information. There's no check here – just reading the information from the JSON webhook, running the real work function, and returning OK:

```python
@app.route('/',methods=['POST'])
```

```
def trigger():
data = json.loads(request.data)
print "New commit by: {}".format(data['commits'][0]['author']['name'])
print "New commit by: {}".format(data['commits'][0]['author']['email'])
print "New commit by: {}".format(data['commits'][0]['message'])

runsomething()
return "OK"
```

The following `main` part, combined with the first block, is part of the basic Flask implementation:

```
if __name__ == '__main__':
app.run()
```

When you run this code with `python server.py`, it will open port `5000` on the localhost:

```
Joosts-iMac:gitlab-webhook joostevertse$ python server.py
* Running on http://127.0.0.1:5000/
```

If we want something on the internet to connect to it, we can use the venerable ngrok to link the port:

```
Joosts-iMac:Downloads joostevertse$ ngrok http 5000
```

ngrok is now running, as shown in the following screenshot:

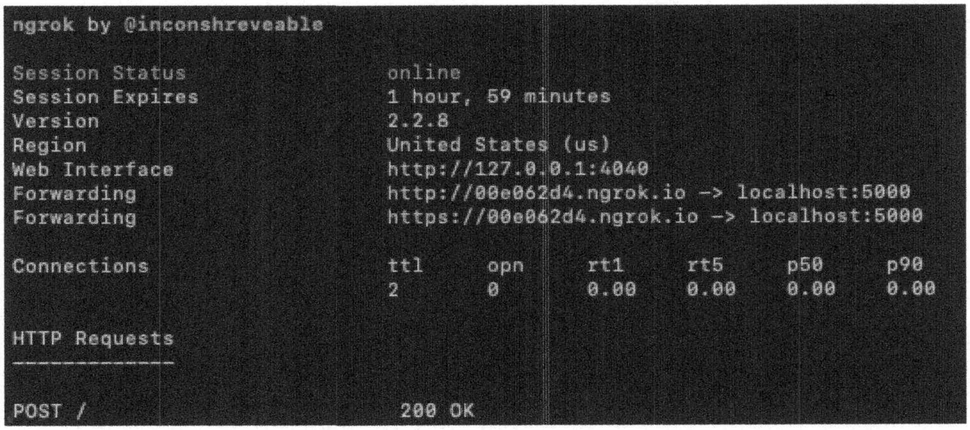

We can now define the webhook in GitLab. You can find it in the **Settings** | **Integrations** section of your GitLab project. After you have defined the hook, you can run a test to verify its operation:

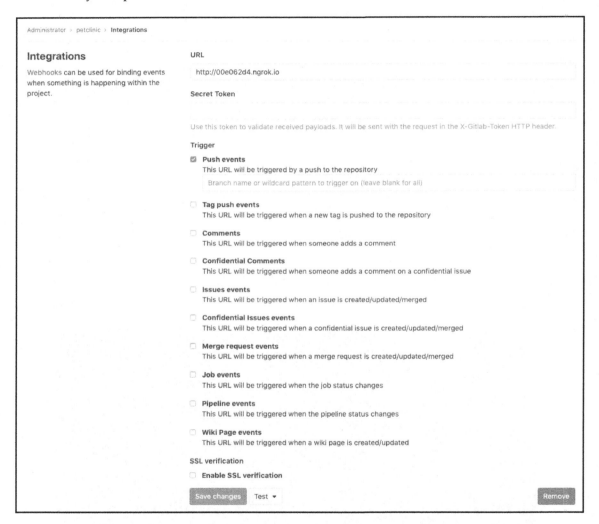

We get the following result when a call is triggered through GitLab. This is the connection going through the ngrok proxy:

In GitLab, if you click the **Edit** button, you will see the result of the webhook call. It will contain the body that was sent:

You will also see the response that was given by the other end. You can see the
OK response clearly:

```
Response headers:

Content-Type: text/html; charset=utf-8
Content-Length: 2
Server: Werkzeug/0.9.6 Python/2.7.10
Date: Sun, 03 Mar 2019 16:10:39 GMT

Response body:

OK
```

The result of this call was that our custom method was triggered and some specific
information such as author, email, and message was printed on stdout:

```
Joosts-iMac:gitlab-webhook joostevertse$ python server.py
* Running on http://127.0.0.1:5000/
New commit by: Joost
New commit by: joustie@gmail.com
New commit by: Added text
This is triggered
127.0.0.1 - - [03/Mar/2019 17:10:39] "POST / HTTP/1.1" 200 -
```

We have seen that it is also possible to use a generic event mechanism such as webhooks.
You can modify your own software or **commercial-off-the-shelf** (COTS) application to
receive events from GitLab.

Summary

In this chapter, we discussed the ways of integrating GitLab with other products. Every
integration has its own special instruction, but the basic idea is that you have to set up trust
relationships and map attributes. GitLab is already shipped with a lot of possible
integrations out of the box. These are called **project services**, and the documentation can be
found here: https://docs.gitlab.com/ee/user/project/integrations/project_
services.html. This chapter concludes the third section of this book, in which we've
discussed the GitLab workflow and the underlying rationale behind it.

In the next part of this book, we will discuss the most successful part of GitLab: GitLab CI
and runners. We will start by talking about how to set up a project for GitLab CI.

Questions

1. What is Jira used for?
2. Jira is from which company?
3. Which ID or IDs are needed to manipulate issues in Jira?
4. Which project is Jenkins forked from?
5. What mechanism does Jenkins use to extend functionality?
6. What is ChatOps?
7. How can you control things from a Mattermost channel?
8. In GitLab, where can you find the status of a webhook?

Further reading

- *Jira 8 Essentials - Fifth Edition,* by *Patrick Lee*: https://www.packtpub.com/in/application-development/jira-8-essentials-fifth-edition
- *Jenkins 2.x Continuous Integration Cookbook - Third Edition,* by *Mitesh Soni* and *Alan Mark Berg*: https://www.packtpub.com/in/networking-and-servers/jenkins-2x-continuous-integration-cookbook-third-edition
- *Jenkins Fundamentals,* by *Joseph Muli* and *Arnold Okoth*: https://www.packtpub.com/in/networking-and-servers/jenkins-fundamentals
- *GitLab ChatOps*: https://docs.gitlab.com/ee/ci/chatops/

Section 4: Utilize GitLab CI and CI Runners

After reading this section, you will be able to describe the GitLab CI components and create pipelines and jobs. You'll also be able to set up runners to be used in your project.

This section comprises the following chapters:

14
Setting Up Your Project for GitLab Continuous Integration

Continuous Integration (CI) is one of the most important pillars of **Extreme Programming (XP)**. Continuous Integration has been one of GitLab's most popular features since it was built in version 8. It is very popular with independent developers and open source projects and is currently gaining popularity in other market segments.

Getting started is easy. As we showed you earlier, in Chapter 10, *Create Your Product, Verify, and Package it* (in the *Release* and *Configure* sections), Auto DevOps is switched on by default, so that when adding code to a project, a deployment pipeline is automatically set up in which various jobs are running. These jobs will be run by a GitLab Runner, which you will have to set up. This is completely configurable to the wishes of the developer. The results of the jobs are collected and showed as passed or failed and are part of the logic in the pipeline. Based on the result, other automation in the pipeline can be triggered. The basis for this functionality is in the `.gitlab-ci.yml` file. If this file is present in a project, it will be parsed and different pipelines and jobs will start running.

In this chapter, we will be covering the following topics:

- Pipelines
- Jobs
- Creating `.gitlab-ci.yml`
- Configuring a Runner

Technical requirements

To follow along with the instructions in this chapter, please download the Git repository with the examples available at GitHub: `https://github.com/PacktPublishing/` `Mastering-GitLab-12/tree/master/Chapter14`.

GitLab CI must be enabled in your GitLab instance (see `Chapter 3`, *Configuring GitLab Using the Web UI*).

Pipelines

A pipeline in the software engineering world is understood as a chain of events (of processes, components, and so on) that automatically triggers and delivers input to the next element. It resembles the physical pipelines that exist in the real world.

In a CI context, a pipeline is a collection of sequential steps that integrate code from different developers. The chain of events is triggered by a commit or push to a source code repository such as GitLab. The build system (for example, Jenkins or GitLab CI) is notified of a new version, compile, and source code and runs unit testing.

Before we go any further, you should understand that without unit tests, or other automated tests, the effort of integrating pieces of code by different developers is very difficult. So, before you begin building pipelines, make sure that your developers have written test code. That way, you can make sure that the code is checked and at least adheres to certain quality checks.

If the unit tests succeed in your pipeline, the next step is to run integration tests. If they also succeed, the artefact that was built can be pushed or saved in a binary repository, or it can be directly deployed to a staging environment where the code will run.

Some pipelines can even be deployed to an acceptance or semi-production environment, where user validation of the solution built takes place. This is called **Continuous Deployment** (**CD**). Some call this Deployment to Production CD, but it depends on your definition of the concept.

Modern build software has the concept of building pipelines as part of their architecture. Products such as Jenkins have adopted it in their workflow, but cloud solutions, such as Azure DevOps (which is TFS in the cloud), have too.

You can find pipelines in GitLab for your project in the left-hand menu bar, under CI/CD, as shown in the following screenshot:

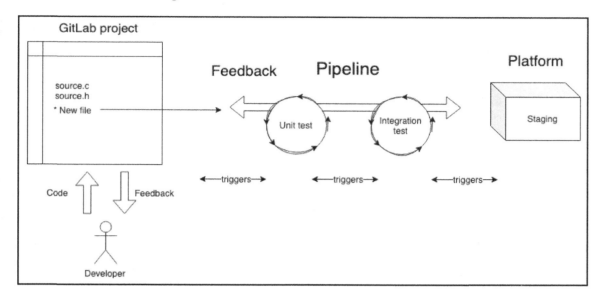

The first item in the menu is a link to an overview of your **Pipelines**. Here, you can see whether pipelines have passed or failed, retry pipelines, or download artifacts, as shown in the following screenshot:

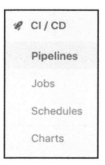

The second link in the menu takes you to the list of **Jobs** for a project (which we will cover shortly), as shown in the following screenshot:

The third link is a feature of GitLab CI called **Schedules**. As you can see in the following screenshot, we have created a schedule for a run of the pipeline to be executed for the Eventmanager project:

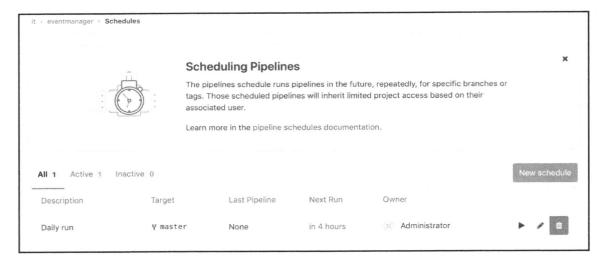

If you click an item in the schedule list, you will see that there are many configurable items in it. For example, you can specify which branch to run on, as shown in the following screenshot:

A nice way of discovering more about your build is the chart feature in GitLab CI, where insight into the metrics of your pipelines is provided, as shown in the following screenshot:

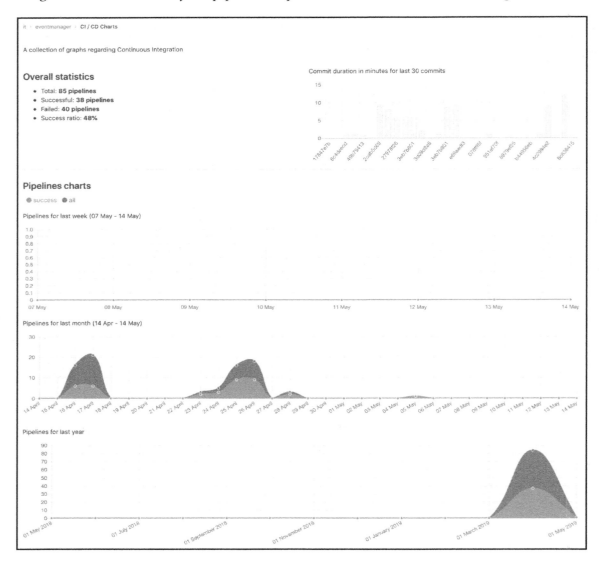

The following screenshot shows a high-level design of a pipeline that runs in GitLab:

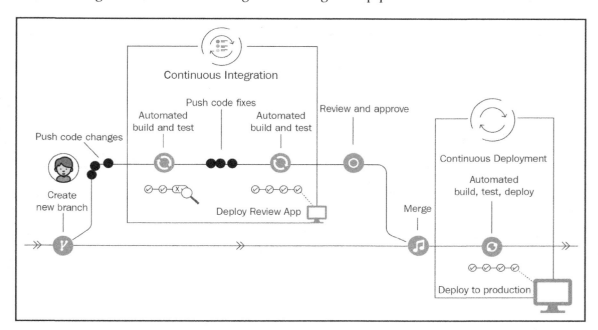

We have now demonstrated that GitLab CI incorporates the general concept of a build pipeline and also records several metrics about the successes or failures of the pipeline's steps. In the following section, we will take a look at these individual steps.

Jobs

Pipeline configuration begins with jobs:

- Jobs are the most fundamental element of a pipeline and are executed by GitLab Runners
- Jobs are created with constraints, which govern under what conditions they should be executed
- Jobs are top-level elements that can have an arbitrary name and must contain the script element as a minimum requirement
- There can be an unlimited number of jobs

In the pipeline overview, you'll find several jobs. They have a status, an ID, are part of a stage, and have a name, as shown in the following screenshot:

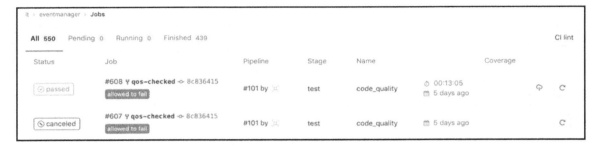

You can create jobs by adding them to a configuration file called `.gitlab-ci.yml`. We will discuss this file in more depth in the following section.

An example of a pipeline containing two jobs is as follows:

```
job1:
  script: "execute-this-script-for-job1"
job2:
  script: "execute-this-script-for-job2"
```

The preceding example is a basic CI/CD pipeline that consists of two named jobs (`job1` and `job2`), which execute a script section (in our example, this does nothing). In the script section, you can specify a command, script, or a chain of commands. For instance, to build a JavaScript, you can set `script` as `npm build` or run a shell unit test called `unit-test.sh`.

Jobs are not run on the GitLab application server, but are picked up by GitLab Runners. The runners execute the jobs in their own environment; for example, runner A can build `job1` and runner B can build `job2`. Note that the jobs are independent from each other. The results from these jobs are aggregated on the GitLab server.

Creating .gitlab-ci.yml

How GitLab CI interacts with your profile is largely controlled by the `.gitlab-ci.yml` file, which must be added to the root of your project. When you push code to your repository, GitLab will test whether it's there and start a pipeline with jobs for that specific commit.

The format of the file is **YAML Ain't Markup Language (YAML)**. YAML is currently a widely used format for configuration files and is best described as a data serialization language.

We have already given you an example of a `.gitlab-ci.yml` file with two jobs in an earlier section. In other chapters, we used a `.gitlab-ci.yml` file to describe a deployment. So, what are the available possibilities of this file?

A lot of combinations are possible, but the fundamental way of working is to first define stages in the file and then add script sections. The complete reference of this file can be found here: `https://docs.gitlab.com/ee/ci/yaml/README.html`.

When you are creating your YAML file, it is nice to know that, after saving, it will be checked by a linter to verify the syntax of the file, as shown in the following screenshot:

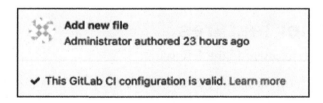

The possibilities for this file are endless, so the best way to figure out what works for you is to look at open source projects on the GitLab website for inspiration, available at: `https://docs.gitlab.com/ee/ci/examples/README.html`.

Configuring a runner

We briefly described the concept of GitLab Runners in `Chapter 1`, *Introducing the GitLab Architecture*. Runners are essentially build environments that run on a separate machine that connects to the GitLab application's server and asks jobs to execute. Runners help to automate product development and achieve DevOps integration.

We configure a runner on the GitLab side, and on the GitLab Runner client side. Remember that there is not a single type of runner.

There are different kind of runners, including:

- A Shell executor
- A Docker executor
- A Docker Machine and Docker Machine SSH (auto-scaling) executor

- A Parallels executor
- A VirtualBox executor
- A SSH executor
- A Kubernetes executor

For the GitLab CI interface, this does not matter. All runners look the same.

The GitLab Runner clients are available on multiple platforms, as it is a Go binary that runs on many platforms. The configuration file is called `config.toml` and is in the TOML format, which is less complex than the YAML format.

The specification of this format is publicly available and can be found at `https://github.com/toml-lang/toml`.

GitLab Runner features

Features of GitLab Runner include the following:

- The ability to run multiple jobs concurrently
- The use of multiple tokens with multiple servers (even per project)
- The ability to limit the number of concurrent jobs per token

The jobs GitLab Runner can execute can do the following:

- Run on a local computer without containers or virtualization
- Run inside Docker containers
- Run inside Docker containers and execute jobs over SSH
- Run using Docker containers with autoscaling on different clouds and virtualization hypervisors
- Run by connecting to a remote SSH server, where it can be executed

Additional features include the following:

- GitLab Runner supports Bash, Windows Batch, and Windows PowerShell
- The runner binary works on GNU/Linux, macOS, and Windows (all Docker-supported platforms)
- A runner allows the customization of a job-running environment
- A runner can have an automatic configuration reload without restart
- It is to easy set up, with support for Docker, Docker SSH, Parallels, or SSH-running environments

- Runners also support the caching of Docker containers
- The Runner package supports installation as a service for GNU/Linux, macOS, and Windows
- You can enable an embedded Prometheus metrics HTTP server in a runner

You can find an overview of the registered runners in GitLab by logging in as an admin and checking the **Runners** menu on the left, as shown in the following screenshot:

You should now see a list of runners that have registered on your GitLab instance, as shown in the following screenshot:

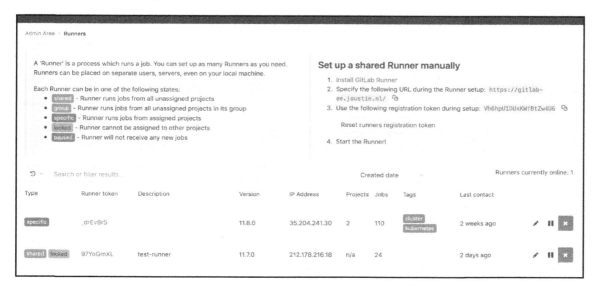

As shown in the following screenshot, if you click a runner, you will see that it is possible to do the following:

- Configure a paused runner not to accept new jobs
- Designate a runner as protected
- Set a runner to pick up jobs with or without tags
- Lock a runner to projects
- Set a maximum timeout for a job
- Tag runners

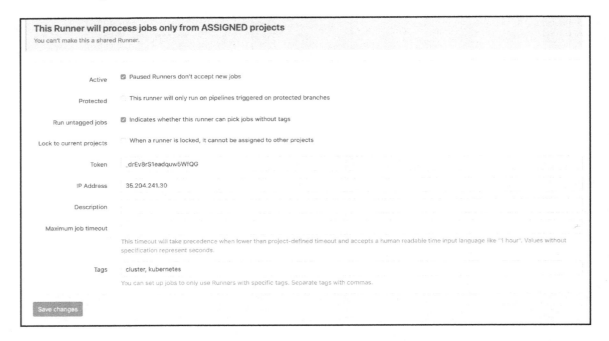

On the left, you will be able to see which jobs have been recently processed by a runner, as shown in the following screenshot:

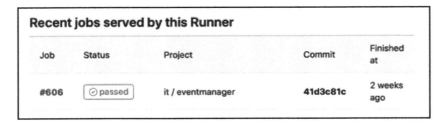

So far, you have seen how GitLab CI fits in with the GitLab product and also how GitLab Runners are registered with an instance. We have also looked at the basic features of GitLab Runners and showed you how to create a configuration file for jobs to be picked up and executed by a runner.

Summary

In this chapter, we discussed GitLab CI, the most critical feature of GitLab after offering version control. We explained how to trigger pipelines and how to design them using the `.gitlab-ci.yml` file. Then, we showed you the jobs that make up the pipelines. We finished with some information on how GitLab runners fit into this architecture. In the next chapter, we are going to show you more about the GitLab Runner client.

Questions

1. Name one of the pillars of Extreme Programming.
2. What file is used to describe jobs and pipelines?
3. How does a build system know when to build software in a pipeline?
4. What tests are necessary for reaching the integration phase?
5. Which tag is used in the `.gitlab-ci.yml` file to execute a job?
6. What is the name of the configuration file used by the runner?
7. How many concurrent sessions can a runner start?
8. How can you get metrics about the execution of a GitLab runner?

Further reading

- *gRPC [Golang] Master Class: Build Modern API and Microservices [Video]* by *Stephane Maarek*: `https://www.packtpub.com/web-development/grpc-golang-master-class-build-modern-api-and-microservices-video`.
- *Hands-On Auto DevOps with GitLab CI [Video]* by *Alan Hohn*: `https://www.packtpub.com/in/application-development/hands-auto-devops-gitlab-ci-video`.

15
Installing and Configuring GitLab Runners

In this chapter, we will take a look at the GitLab Runner client architecture. After studying this topic, you will understand the basic flow of control between GitLab CI and Runners. In the second part of this chapter, I will show you how to install Runner software on different operating systems. Since the Runner program is written in Golang, there are many platforms that are capable of running the client. Golang is known for its excellent multi-platform support.

In this chapter, we will cover the following topics:

- The Runner client architecture
- Creating a basic runner with the shell executor

Technical requirements

To follow along with the instructions in this chapter, please download the Git repository with the examples available from GitHub: https://github.com/PacktPublishing/Mastering-GitLab-12/tree/master/Chapter15.

The other requirements for this chapter are as follows:

- **GitLab Runner client – Linux 64-bit**: https://gitlab-runner-downloads.s3.amazonaws.com/latest/binaries/gitlab-runner-linux-amd64
- **Linux 32-bit**: https://gitlab-runner-downloads.s3.amazonaws.com/latest/binaries/gitlab-runner-linux-386
- **Linux ARM**: https://gitlab-runner-downloads.s3.amazonaws.com/latest/binaries/gitlab-runner-linux-arm

- **macOS 64-bit**: `https://gitlab-runner-downloads.s3.amazonaws.com/latest/binaries/gitlab-runner-darwin-amd64`
- **FreeBSD 64-bit**: `https://gitlab-runner-downloads.s3.amazonaws.com/latest/binaries/gitlab-runner-freebsd-amd64`
- **FreeBSD 32-bit**: `https://gitlab-runner-downloads.s3.amazonaws.com/latest/binaries/gitlab-runner-freebsd-386`
- **Windows 32-bit**: `https://gitlab-runner-downloads.s3.amazonaws.com/latest/binaries/gitlab-runner-windows-386.exe`
- **Windows 64-bit**: `https://gitlab-runner-downloads.s3.amazonaws.com/latest/binaries/gitlab-runner-windows-amd64.exe`
- **cURL**: `https://curl.haxx.se/download.html`

The Runner client architecture

We took a brief look at the GitLab architecture in Chapter 1, *Introducing the GitLab Architecture*. It was explained that a GitLab Runner registers with a GitLab instance and waits for a job to execute. Unlike the individual components that are a part of the GitLab frontend application server, the runner has a very straightforward architecture. The communication between a runner and its GitLab host is basically one-way.

Basic architecture

The main network communication is from the GitLab Runner to the GitLab CI, never the other way around. This is shown in the following diagram:

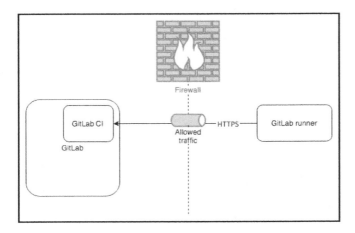

The behavior is best depicted by a sequence diagram like the following one:

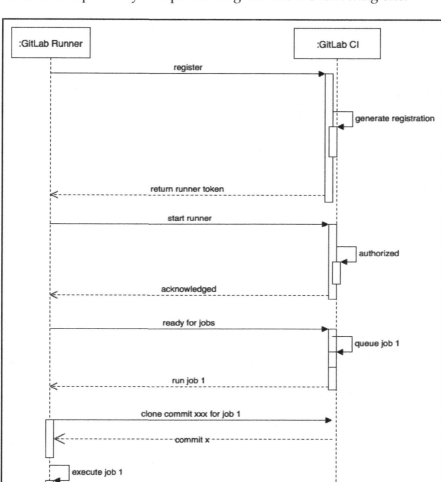

When the GitLab Runner starts, it tries to find its coordinator by contacting the GitLab URL. When it registers itself with the registration token, it gets a special token to connect to GitLab. After a restart, it connects and waits for a job from GitLab CI. It polls GitLab in intervals, and when there is nothing to do, it will check GitLab less often to prohibit too much network traffic.

When a job is queued in GitLab CI, it will try to find an available runner. After receiving the command, it will clone the project-specific commit that triggered the job and will execute the steps defined in the `.gitlab-ci.yml` file. After execution, the results are sent back to GitLab.

GitLab CI has two types of runners:

- **Specific Runners**: As a developer, you can create your own runners and register them to a project in GitLab. Only then is the project visible to the runner.
- **Shared Runners**: A GitLab administrator can also designate a runner to be shared. It can then pick up jobs from several projects. Because this is potentially classed as a security breach, be careful when you're promoting runners to be shared.

In the following screenshot, you can see the CI/CD configuration of a project in GitLab, where you can set which runner to use:

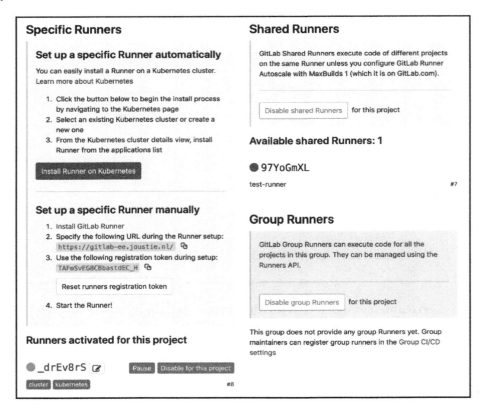

The GitLab Runner clones the repository and performs steps that are defined in the `.gitlab-ci.yml` file. It is possible to inject special variables that can be protected on the GitLab project level:

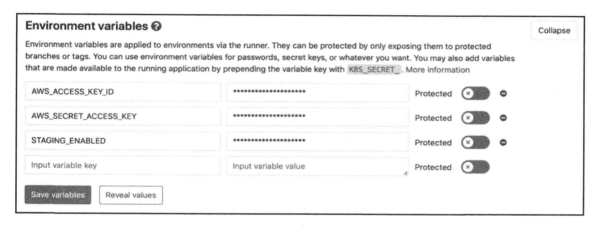

We've explained the basic architecture of the runner platform, so now we'll install the software on different operating systems.

The GitLab Runner software is available for the following operating systems:

- Linux
- FreeBSD
- macOS
- Windows

The installation procedure is largely identical on all systems, with subtle differences. In the next section, we will show you how to install the basic Runner on several types of operating systems.

Creating a basic Runner with the shell executor

On the machine where you install the GitLab Runner software, you can run the shell executor to locally build software. This shell type of executor can be run on all platforms where the runner software is installed. Therefore, you can run Bash or a Bourne shell on a Unix-like system, or CMD or PowerShell on the Windows platform.

It isn't a very safe way to build because it can access local resources on the system where the runner executes. More secure executors will be introduced in later chapters.

In the next section, we will demonstrate how to install the GitLab Runner software for your platform.

Installing Runner on Linux

If you run a Linux distribution with a package management system such as

`yum` or `apt`, you can install the GitLab Runner package using that method. Alternatively, you can install the software manually. First, we will cover the installation via a package manager.

Using a package manager

For yum-based systems, you can add the official GitLab package repository:

```
curl -o script.rpm.sh
https://packages.gitlab.com/install/repositories/runner/gitlab-runner/scrip
t.rpm.sh
 less script.rpm.sh #(check the contents, if you are fine with it make it
executable and run it)
 chmod +x script.rpm.sh
 ./script.rpm.sh
```

After that, you can install GitLab with this basic command (as root or with `sudo`):

```
yum install gitlab-runner
```

For apt-based systems, it's a bit more tricky to stay up to date with the latest and greatest. We can add a link to GitLab apt repositories, but unfortunately, Debian has named the package in the base repository the same as GitLab. This means that the base packages automatically take precedence. A solution to this is to `pin` the package to the right repository. This can be done by adding a file to `/etc/apt/preferences.d`:

```
cat <<EOF >> /etc/apt/preferences.d/pin-gitlab-runner.pref
 Explanation: Pin GitLab-runner package
 Package: gitlab-runner
 Pin: origin packages.gitlab.com
 Pin-Priority: 999
 EOF
```

After that, you can install the correct `apt` package repositories:

```
curl -o script.deb.sh
https://packages.gitlab.com/install/repositories/runner/gitlab-runner/scrip
t.deb.sh
 less script.deb.sh #(check the contents, if you are fine with it make it
executable and run it)
 chmod +x script.deb.sh
 ./script.deb.sh
```

The output from the preceding command is shown in the following code block. As you can see, it checks the `gpg` key and adds the package repository:

```
Detected operating system as debian/stretch.
 Checking for curl...
 Detected curl...
 Checking for gpg...
 Detected gpg...
 Running apt-get update... done.
 Installing debian-archive-keyring which is needed for installing
apt-transport-https on many Debian systems.
 Installing apt-transport-https... done.
 Installing /etc/apt/sources.list.d/runner_gitlab-runner.list...done.
 Importing packagecloud gpg key... done.
 Running apt-get update... done.

 The repository is setup! You can now install packages.
```

The next step is much simpler – you just install it via `apt-get`:

```
apt-get install gitlab-runner
```

In the output, you will find a message like the following, which means that you have now installed all the binaries. However, you have to register the GitLab Runner first before running it:

```
 ...
 gitlab-runner: Service is not running.
 ...
```

The process of registering the runner is explained in more detail in the *Registering a runner* section.

Updating the package is done just as updating all the other packages on the system is done: you can run the `apt-get update` or `yum update` command.

When installing with `apt-get` or `yum`, package management will give you a GitLab Runner install with the necessary configuration files and init scripts for your Linux distribution. You can also choose to just download the runner binary and run it in a generic way.

Using a manual installation

Simply download one of the binaries for your CPU architecture (x86-64, x86-32, or ARM):

- **x86-64 bit architecture**:

```
curl -o /usr/local/bin/gitlab-runner
https://gitlab-runner-downloads.s3.amazonaws.com/latest/binaries/gi
tlab-runner-linux-amd64
```

- **x86-32 bit architecture**:

```
curl -o  /usr/local/bin/gitlab-runner
https://gitlab-runner-downloads.s3.amazonaws.com/latest/binaries/gi
tlab-runner-linux-386
```

- **ARM architecture**: This is the binary for the ARM CPU architecture, in a list:

```
curl -o  /usr/local/bin/gitlab-runner
https://gitlab-runner-downloads.s3.amazonaws.com/latest/binaries/gi
tlab-runner-linux-arm
```

When you're getting binaries this way, you have to make them executable:

```
chmod +x /usr/local/bin/gitlab-runner
```

Then, you can create a GitLab Runner user as root:

```
useradd --create-home gitlab-runner
```

You then need to install it and run it as a service:

```
gitlab-runner install --user=gitlab-runner --working-
directory=/home/gitlab-runner
gitlab-runner start
```

Although the manual installation is a bit more work than via the package managers, it still isn't a complex process. One advantage is that, when using the manual installation, you can't install newer versions of the runner. The package manager maintainers will never install a development version, while you can. Updating the binary is not very hard either.

Updating a manually installed runner binary

The process we are following when updating is to replace the Golang binary that was downloaded previously. It does have to be stopped, so make sure it isn't running, otherwise the installation will fail.

Stop the service (you need root permissions, like before):

```
gitlab-runner stop
```

Then, download a new binary to replace the older one:

```
curl -o /usr/local/bin/gitlab-runner
https://gitlab-runner-downloads.s3.amazonaws.com/latest/binaries/gitlab-run
ner-linux-386
  curl -o /usr/local/bin/gitlab-runner
https://gitlab-runner-downloads.s3.amazonaws.com/latest/binaries/gitlab-run
ner-linux-amd64
```

Set the execute bit on the runner binary:

```
chmod +x /usr/local/bin/gitlab-runner
```

Start the runner again:

```
gitlab-runner start
```

The manual install is much easier, but you have to manage the updates yourself. In this era of automation, it makes more sense to let the package manager that's available for your distribution to manage it.

Installing on Mac

Just like on Linux, there are several ways to install the GitLab Runner software. Unlike on Linux, where package management is recommended by GitLab, for macOS, they recommend the manual install. The other way to install is by using the Homebrew installation method, which you saw earlier in the book (*Installing Redis* section of Chapter 1, *Introducing the GitLab Architecture*).

The manual way of installing a runner

First, get the binary for your system (with `sudo`):

```
sudo curl -o  /usr/local/bin/gitlab-runner
https://gitlab-runner-downloads.s3.amazonaws.com/latest/binaries/gitlab-run
ner-darwin-amd64
```

Then, just like we did previously, make the binary executable:

```
$ sudo chmod +x /usr/local/bin/gitlab-runner
```

Now that we have the binary in place, we can run the program as another user if we want:

```
$ cd ~
$ gitlab-runner install
$ gitlab-runner start
```

The runner will be installed and will be run after a system reboot.

Installing and using the Homebrew package manager

A unified package manager for macOS doesn't really exist, but the one that's used the most is Homebrew, which can be found at `https://brew.sh/`. It works with formulas that contain scripts and settings to install binaries.

A Homebrew formula exists to install GitLab Runner:

```
brew install gitlab-runner
```

The next step is to install the runner as a service (this will also start it):

```
brew services start gitlab-runner
```

There are some drawbacks to using macOS as a runner platform. Many developers use runners on macOS to build iOS-related software. Often, UI testing is also involved. It isn't possible to automate this. You would have to run in the background as a system service (LaunchDaemon), and then the UI isn't reachable anymore. You can only run the runner in user mode to get access to the UI, which is why you must always log in to run the GitLab Runner.

Updating the runner is done by issuing `brew upgrade gitlab-runner`. For a manual install, it's a bit more complicated.

Updating a manually installed runner binary

Just like we did for Linux, we are replacing the Golang binary that was downloaded previously. It also needs to be stopped, so make sure it isn't running, otherwise the installation will fail:

1. First, we need to stop the service:

```
gitlab-runner stop
```

2. Like we did previously, get the binary to replace the runner's executable:

```
curl -o /usr/local/bin/gitlab-runner
https://gitlab-runner-downloads.s3.amazonaws.com/latest/binaries/gi
tlab-runner-darwin-amd64
```

3. Make the downloaded binary executable:

```
chmod +x /usr/local/bin/gitlab-runner
```

4. Start the GitLab Runner service again:

```
gitlab-runner start
```

The steps to install the GitLab Runner software are roughly the same on the Linux and macOS platforms. The good part about using a package manager is that the software is easier to upgrade.

Installing on Windows

Unlike GitLab itself, which doesn't run on Windows, you can operate the GitLab Runner software on Windows machines.

There are two types of runner binaries, depending on your CPU architecture:

- 32-bit version (https://gitlab-runner-downloads.s3.amazonaws.com/latest/binaries/gitlab-runner-windows-386.exe)
- 64-bit version (https://gitlab-runner-downloads.s3.amazonaws.com/latest/binaries/gitlab-runner-windows-amd64.exe)

Download it and copy it to gitlab-runner.exe in a folder on your local drive; for example, C:-runner.

Now, you need an elevated command prompt to register and install the software:

```
c:\cd c:\gitlab-runner
c:\gitlab-runner\gitlab-runner.exe register
```

The registration steps will be shown in the next section as they are almost universal for all platforms.

When registration succeeds, you can start the GitLab Runner:

```
c:\gitlab-runner\gitlab-runner.exe install
c:\gitlab-runner\gitlab-runner.exe start
```

Now that we have installed the runner software, the next step is to register with GitLab.

Registering a runner

A GitLab Runner needs some basic information to start:

- The URL where it can find GitLab, which is called the coordinator URL.
- The special token that you can find in GitLab that's meant to register runner instances.
- A description that will later show up in the GitLab CI.
- Tags, which you can give to the runner to make it easier to find in GitLab CI.
- The type of executor (remember that there are many types, all of which were named in the *Runner client architecture* section).

This basic information can be provided to the runner in two ways: interactive and non-interactive. First, we will discuss the interactive way.

The interactive way of registering a runner

The web location of the GitLab server to connect is the following:

```
sudo gitlab-runner register
```

Please enter the gitlab-ci coordinator URL (for example, https://gitlab.com):

```
https://gitlab-ee.joustie.com
```

You also need to enter the runner registration token since it's needed to register with GitLab:

```
Please enter the gitlab-ci token for this runner
  xxx
```

The runner registration token can be found on the **Admin Area | Overview | Runners** page or under **Projects**.

You want a nice description so that you can find the runner later (the default is hostname):

```
Please enter the gitlab-ci description for this runner
  [hostname] my-runner
```

Enter the tags that should apply to this runner (for example, javarunner). This can be changed later in GitLab:

```
Please enter the gitlab-ci tags for this runner (comma separated):
  javarunner,another-javarunner
```

The most important part is determining the type of executor (for this chapter, I chose the shell executor):

```
Please enter the executor: ssh, docker+machine, docker-ssh+machine,
kubernetes, docker, parallels, virtualbox, docker-ssh, shell:
  shell
```

The non-interactive way of registering a runner

In larger environments, deployments are frequently scripted. So, for the runner, there is also a non-interactive install available to help in the effort of automating the infrastructure. You can specify subcommands to the GitLab register argument. To find out about these options, type the following on the command line:

```
gitlab-runner register -h
```

To register a runner, using the most common options, you would do the following:

```
sudo gitlab-runner register \
  --description "docker-runner" \
  --url "https://gitlab-ee.joustie.com/" \
  --registration-token "xxxx" \
  --executor "docker" \
  --docker-image alpine:latest \
  --non-interactive \
  --tag-list "docker,aws" \
```

```
--run-untagged="true" \
--locked="false" \
```

When the runner is registered, it will show up in GitLab in the Runner list:

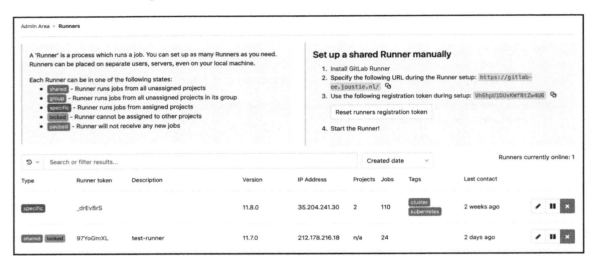

The registration process is basically the process of telling the runner where GitLab is situated, and initiating a key exchange to secure access to GitLab. Following a successful registration, the runner saves the configuration information in a TOML file, which looks as follows:

```
concurrent = 1
check_interval = 0

[[runners]]
  name = "runnerhost.joustie.nl"
  url = "https://gitlab-ee.joustie.nl"
  token = "801bd1f41a3bb7a42c0b6f43e9ffc8"
  executor = "shell"
  shell = "bash"
  [runners.cache]
```

The shell can also be set to sh for a simple Bourne shell or powershell on Windows. On Linux, this is usually placed in /etc/gitlab-runner/config.toml.

Running the nightly version

If you are feeling adventurous, you could also install the latest release, which isn't part of any release yet. Do this at your own risk. There could still be bugs in there:

- **Linux**:
    - https://s3.amazonaws.com/gitlab-runner-downloads/master/binaries/gitlab-runner-linux-386
    - https://s3.amazonaws.com/gitlab-runner-downloads/master/binaries/gitlab-runner-linux-amd64
    - https://s3.amazonaws.com/gitlab-runner-downloads/master/binaries/gitlab-runner-linux-arm
- **macOS**:
    - https://s3.amazonaws.com/gitlab-runner-downloads/master/binaries/gitlab-runner-darwin-386
    - https://s3.amazonaws.com/gitlab-runner-downloads/master/binaries/gitlab-runner-darwin-amd64
- **Windows**:
    - https://s3.amazonaws.com/gitlab-runner-downloads/master/binaries/gitlab-runner-windows-386.exe
    - https://s3.amazonaws.com/gitlab-runner-downloads/master/binaries/gitlab-runner-windows-amd64.exe
- **FreeBSD**:
    - https://s3.amazonaws.com/gitlab-runner-downloads/master/binaries/gitlab-runner-freebsd-386
    - https://s3.amazonaws.com/gitlab-runner-downloads/master/binaries/gitlab-runner-freebsd-amd64
    - https://s3.amazonaws.com/gitlab-runner-downloads/master/binaries/gitlab-runner-freebsd-arm

Now, we should have a runner installed and ready for use.

The easiest way to install a runner is by using a package manager running on the host operating system. Doing a manual install allows you to run development versions or patched versions easily because it has only one Golang binary.

Summary

In this chapter, we showed you the basic architecture of a GitLab Runner. Then, we showed you how to install it on several operating systems with a shell executor. On most systems, there is a more or less automated way to do this, which also manages updates and platform compatibility. There's also a manual way of installing the software on every system. Using the manual method allows you to run developer versions of the runner easily. The registration process of the runner can be done step by step or in one command.

In the next chapter, we will deploy GitLab Runner in a Docker container and also in a more managed way in a Kubernetes cluster.

Questions

1. What part of GitLab does a runner connect to?
2. What additional action has to be performed on Debian-based systems to install the right package?
3. In what language is the runner client written?
4. What is the default description that's given to a runner?
5. What command argument is used to communicate the registration token to the `gitlab register` command?

Further reading

- *Hands-On Full Stack Development with Go*, by *Mina Andrawos*: https://www. packtpub.com/web-development/hands-full-stack-development-go
- *Windows 10 for Enterprise Administrators*, by *Jeff Stokes, Manuel Singer*, and *Richard Diver*: https://www.packtpub.com/in/networking-and-servers/windows-10-enterprise-administrators
- *Hands-On Continuous Integration and Delivery*, by *Jean-Marcel Belmont*: https://www.packtpub.com/in/virtualization-and-cloud/hands-continuous-integration-and-delivery

16
Using GitLab Runners with Docker or Kubernetes

In the previous chapter, we installed a GitLab Runner with the shell executor. In this chapter, we will take a closer look at containerized GitLab Runners. You can run a GitLab Runner in a container in multiple ways:

- **With the Shell executor running in a custom-built Docker container**: This is not recommended because you are responsible for building and supporting this custom container afterward. On the other hand, if you want to tightly control the components inside the container and the behavior of them, then it might be a good way to containerize the Runner. Scaling this solution also requires more work from your side because the Runner itself only knows how to run jobs and connect to GitLab. You will collect state (files in /tmp or elsewhere) in your containers if they don't restart after a job, so be prepared to handle that as well.

- **With the Docker executor, which pulls and starts a Docker image for your job**: This is a much more scalable solution, with the added bonus of having no state. Each build gets a pristine clean environment and starts all over again. Another bonus is that you are able to create services for a job, which is another container or several that are started in parallel with a container for your job. For instance, you can start a MySQL database and it will be a linked service that is available under the service name.

- **With the Kubernetes executor so that you can use a Kubernetes cluster**: The Runner can communicate with the cluster management API and ask for resources to spin up containers. The Runners are completely stateless and when there is a decreasing number of jobs in the queue, the number of containers is scaled back automatically.

- **With the Docker executor and autoscaling enabled (Docker Machines creates new Runners)**: In this configuration, the GitLab Runner controls the Docker Machine binary. It can create new Runner containers on the fly and scale down again if there are less jobs in the queue.

In this chapter, we are going to take a look at the basic way of running a GitLab Runner, and how to orchestrate this using a management system such as Kubernetes. The autoscaling executors will be part of the next chapter. The reason for this is that the autoscaling Docker executor has a lot of options and requires more planning and system management features to maintain.

The following topics will be covered in this chapter:

- Runner client architecture
- Creating your own Dockerized GitLab Runner
- Using a prebuilt Docker container to deploy GitLab Runners
- Using a Kubernetes cluster to spawn GitLab Runners

Technical requirements

To follow along with the instructions in this chapter, please download this book's GitHub repository, along with the examples that are available, from GitHub at `https://github.com/PacktPublishing/Mastering-GitLab-12/tree/master/Chapter16`.

The other requirements for this chapter are as follows:

- Docker installed for your platform
- The `wget` command-line download tool (`https://www.gnu.org/software/wget/`)
- Access to the Alpine Docker image (`https://hub.docker.com/_/alpine`)
- Access to the Python Alpine Docker image (`https://hub.docker.com/r/lgatica/python-alpine`)
- Access to the GitLab Runner Docker image (`https://hub.docker.com/r/gitlab/gitlab-runner`)
- The `kubectl` utility on your system (you can find installation instructions at `https://kubernetes.io/docs/tasks/tools/install-kubectl/`)
- Helm or Tiller (a Kubernetes utility to help you to manage clusters: `https://helm.sh/docs/using_helm/`)

Runner client architecture

If you utilize a GitLab Runner with Docker, the resulting architecture differs from the one in the previous chapter in one way. The Runner binary is executed from inside a Docker container instead of directly on a host system. The following diagram shows this architecture:

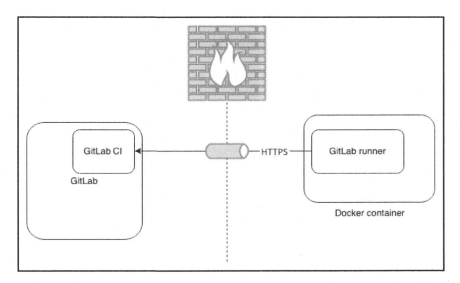

The image is the same whether you create a container yourself or you use an existing container from the internet.

If you are going to orchestrate your GitLab Runners using Kubernetes, the architecture is going to look a bit different. You can see that, inside the cluster, a **GitLab Runner** with the Kubernetes architecture can talk to the cluster's Kubernetes API to scale up the number of Runner instances:

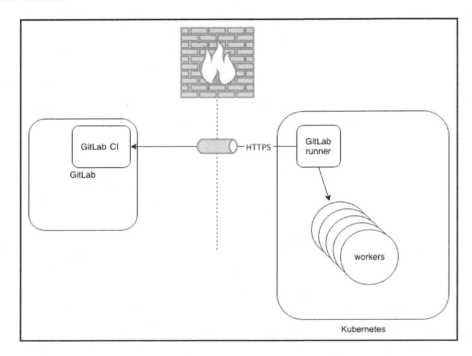

The two architectures both use Docker containers as the core unit of operation. The first needs more management in the field of scaling, upgrading the software, and setting up a network. Much of that has already been arranged with Kubernetes.

Now, we know about the difference between these architectures and that a Runner is deployed without a container, but what does this mean in practice? We will explore this in the following sections.

Creating your own Dockerized GitLab Runner

Most people will use prebuilt Docker containers, but there are reasons to build your own. Maybe you have special requirements when building your software that aren't installed in the default Docker images that are available or maybe it's just not possible because of security restrictions. A lot of default images have software included that contain vulnerabilities.

Let's create our own Dockerized GitLab Runner for the project from Chapter 10, *Create Your Product, Verify, and Package it*, that is, the event manager documentation, using a Dockerfile. You will find our first attempt in the next section.

 Let me stress that this Dockerfile is purely for demonstration purposes. We don't recommend building containers like this for production-like systems or even your own development systems. It's being used here to show you how easily you can wrap commands and services in containers.

The first line of the file is as follows:

```
FROM alpine:3.7
```

This is the base image we used for the container. It is from the Alpine Linux distribution, which contains only the bare minimum to run programs. It is only 4.41 MB and, when using container security scanners such as Clair (https://github.com/coreos/clair), it doesn't show vulnerabilities. You can also build containers from scratch (see https://ericchiang.github.io/post/containers-from-scratch/), but this is a very tedious task. The Alpine Linux image is safe enough and is ready to go immediately.

In the following lines, we install some basic packages:

```
RUN apk add --no-cache \
    ca-certificates \
    git \
    wget
```

We need CA certificates because we need the GitLab Runner client to connect to our HTTPS endpoint, where a TLS handshake will take place. The Git binary is also necessary to clone code from a project.

Finally, the last command that is set to run in the creation sequence of the container is used to download, execute, and register the GitLab Runner with our GitLab server:

```
RUN wget
https://s3.amazonaws.com/gitlab-runner-downloads/master/binaries/gitlab-run
ner-linux-386 && chmod +x gitlab-runner-linux-386 && \
  ./gitlab-runner-linux-386  register \
  --non-interactive \
  --url "https://gitlab-ee.joustie.nl/" \
  --registration-token "xxxxxxx" \
  --executor "shell" \
  --shell "sh" \
  --description "dockerized shell-runner" \
  --tag-list "docker" \
  --run-untagged="true" \
  --locked="false"
```

For this example's sake, we have hardcoded all of the arguments in the Dockerfile to show you how easy it is to Dockerize your command (don't do this normally):

- `non-interactive`: Without it, there would be a dialog that takes you through the configuration settings.
- `url`: This is the URL of our GitLab server.
- `registration-token`: This is the token of a Runner from the project, group, or GitLab instance's scope.
- `executor`: This specifies which kind of Runner to implement. We chose to use the shell executor.
- `shell`: This specifies which kind of shell to implement; this could be `bash`, `sh`, or `powershell` on Windows. We chose `sh` as it is the most basic one.
- `description`: This is what description you will see in GitLab.
- `tag-list`: We can put tags on Runners for easier management in GitLab. In this case, we have used `docker`.
- `run-untagged`: We set it to `true`, which means that any job with or without tags can be run on this Runner.
- `locked`: The Runner isn't tied to a project.

The next step is to build the Docker container with the `docker build` command (we specify -no-cache so that we can rebuild every time). The output is as follows, and we will go through it step by step. The first part is pulling the Alpine base image:

```
$ docker build --no-cache -t dockerrunner .
 Sending build context to Docker daemon    2.56kB
 Step 1/4 : FROM alpine:3.9
 3.9: Pulling from library/alpine
 Digest:
sha256:769fddc7cc2f0a1c35abb2f91432e8beecf83916c421420e6a6da9f8975464b6
 Status: Downloaded newer image for alpine:3.9
  ---> 055936d39205
```

The first Docker layer has been created. The second step is adding the necessary packages:

```
Step 2/4 : RUN apk add --no-cache ca-certificates git openssl      tzdata
wget
  ---> Running in 0ab19e2eef86
 fetch
http://dl-cdn.alpinelinux.org/alpine/v3.9/main/x86_64/APKINDEX.tar.gz
 fetch
http://dl-cdn.alpinelinux.org/alpine/v3.9/community/x86_64/APKINDEX.tar.gz
 (1/8) Installing ca-certificates (20190108-r0)
 (2/8) Installing nghttp2-libs (1.35.1-r0)
 (3/8) Installing libssh2 (1.8.2-r0)
 (4/8) Installing libcurl (7.64.0-r1)
 (5/8) Installing expat (2.2.6-r0)
 (6/8) Installing pcre2 (10.32-r1)
 (7/8) Installing git (2.20.1-r0)
 (8/8) Installing wget (1.20.3-r0)
 Executing busybox-1.29.3-r10.trigger
 Executing ca-certificates-20190108-r0.trigger
 OK: 21 MiB in 22 packages
 Removing intermediate container 0ab19e2eef86
  ---> 17ab7c7dd1b9
```

The previous code downloaded the packages we specified, as well as some dependencies. This is still a modest amount of packages. In the following build step, the GitLab Runner binary is downloaded:

```
Step 3/4 : RUN wget
https://s3.amazonaws.com/gitlab-runner-downloads/master/binaries/gitlab-run
ner-linux-386 && chmod +x gitlab-runner-linux-386 && ./gitlab-runner-
linux-386 register --non-interactive --url "https://gitlab-ee.joustie.nl/"
--registration-token "xxxx" --executor "shell" --shell "sh" --description
"dockerized shell-runner" --tag-list "docker" --run-untagged="true" --
locked="false"
  ---> Running in d90d35beaa37
```

```
--2019-05-22 21:05:18--
https://s3.amazonaws.com/gitlab-runner-downloads/master/binaries/gitlab-run
ner-linux-386
 Resolving s3.amazonaws.com... 52.216.18.115
 Connecting to s3.amazonaws.com|52.216.18.115|:443... connected.
 HTTP request sent, awaiting response... 200 OK
 ....
 2019-05-22 19:46:24 (2.22 MB/s) - 'gitlab-runner-linux-386' saved
[25824256/25824256]
```

The next step is the execution of the Runner:

```
Runtime platform    arch=386 os=linux pid=1 revision=5159dcdb
version=11.12.0~beta.1484.g5159dcdb
Running in system-mode.
```

Then, we need to register it:

```
Registering runner... succeeded runner=Vh6hpU1D
 Runner registered successfully. Feel free to start it, but if it's running
already the config should be automatically reloaded!
 Removing intermediate container b55a2ae6998a
 ---> be4317ad95b0
```

The binary was successfully downloaded, and the registration was successful; a specific Runner token was created and is now part of the Docker image. The final part of the build sets the entry point for the instantiation of a Docker instance with this image:

```
Step 4/4 : ENTRYPOINT ["./gitlab-runner-linux-386","run"]
 ---> Running in 8b54b77030bc
Removing intermediate container 8b54b77030bc
 ---> be206c4c268c
Successfully built be206c4c268c
Successfully tagged dockerrunner:latest
```

It automatically tagged the image with latest. The image is now available on the machine where its build was executed. You can view it by using the following command:

```
$ docker images
 ...
```

If you go to GitLab and open the Runner list in the administrative settings menu, a new Runner will appear there:

shared	znP-qQbv	dockerized shell-runner	11.12.0~beta.1...	82.161.132.207	n/a	1	docker

Now, it's time to start the Runner and try to build the eventmanager-documentation project. You can start the Runner in the foreground using the following command:

```
$ docker run -ti dockerrunner
```

The following output should appear after a brief pause:

```
Runtime platform arch=386 os=linux pid=1 revision=5159dcdb
version=11.12.0~beta.1484.g5159dcdb
 Starting multi-runner from /etc/gitlab-runner/config.toml ... builds=0
 Running in system-mode.

 Configuration loaded builds=0
 listen_address not defined, metrics & debug endpoints disabled builds=0
 [session_server].listen_address not defined, session endpoints disabled
builds=0
```

As you can see, it has successfully loaded a configuration that was saved in the container during the registration phase. It also mentions the fact that it didn't load a metrics and debug session server, so this Runner exposes no service of any kind to the outside world. It has connected to the GitLab server and is now waiting for commands.

When we try to run the eventmanager-documentation project pipeline for the master branch, it will spin off a build job to the new GitLab Runner:

```
Checking for jobs... received                         job=675
repo_url=https://gitlab-ee.joustie.nl/marketing/eventmanager-documentation.
git runner=LT7jz43c
 WARNING: Job failed: exit status 1                   duration=347.5203ms
job=675 project=10 runner=LT7jz43c
 ERROR: Failed to process runner                      builds=0 error=exit
status 1 executor=shell runner=LT7jz43c
```

Unfortunately, it's failed to build the project. If we look at the job log, we get the following output:

It's quite clear why the job failed. We created a basic GitLab Runner container without support for the Python language. That is why it complains about the **Python Package Manager (PIP)** not being found. We need Python to install the **Amazon Web Services Command-Line Interface (AWS CLI)** utility, which is defined in the `.gitlab-ci.yml` file for this project.

This is easy to fix. We can change the first line in the Dockerfile to the following:

```
FROM python:3.7-alpine
```

This will change the base image of the Docker container to a version of Linux with Python included. Now, you can rebuild the image using the exact same preceding command line and starting the container again.

If we run the pipeline for this project again, the job will succeed:

```
Running with gitlab-runner 11.12.0~beta.1484.g5159dcdb (5159dcdb)
  on dockerized shell-runner FhNfU__6
Using Shell executor...
Running on db5bc9e8cee5...
Initialized empty Git repository in /builds/FhNfU__6/0/marketing/eventmanager-documentation/.git/
Fetching changes...
Created fresh repository.
From https://gitlab-ee.joustie.nl/marketing/eventmanager-documentation
 * [new branch]      master     -> origin/master
Checking out 245d68fc as master...
Skipping Git submodules setup
$ pip install awscli
Collecting awscli
  Downloading https://files.pythonhosted.org/packages/65/c8/052a27efb2f19172fe7fc17d409e54b72eee805843cc7049e258f3eaa91c/awscli-1.16.164-py2.py3-none-any.whl (1.6MB)
Building wheels for collected packages: PyYAML
  Building wheel for PyYAML (setup.py): started
  Building wheel for PyYAML (setup.py): finished with status 'done'
  Stored in directory: /root/.cache/pip/wheels/ad/da/0c/74eb688767247273e2cf2723482cb9c924fe70af57c334513f
Successfully built PyYAML
Installing collected packages: jmespath, docutils, urllib3, six, python-dateutil, botocore, s3transfer, colorama, PyYAML, pyasn1, rsa, awscli
Successfully installed PyYAML-3.13 awscli-1.16.164 botocore-1.12.154 colorama-0.3.9 docutils-0.14 jmespath-0.9.4 pyasn1-0.4.5 python-dateutil-2.8.0 rsa-3.4.2 s3transfer-
0.2.0 six-1.12.0 urllib3-1.24.3
$ aws s3 cp public/*.html s3://$S3_BUCKET_NAME/
Completed 617 Bytes/617 Bytes (667 Bytes/s) with 1 file(s) remaining
upload: public/index.html to s3://joustie-1/index.html
Job succeeded
```

You can create much more elaborate container images, but this was a basic way to containerize a Runner.

In this section, we have created our own GitLab Runner container and registered it with a GitLab instance. In the next section, we will use a prebuilt image that GitLab provides from their site.

Using a prebuilt Docker container to deploy GitLab Runners

There are two basic flavors of prebuilt Docker containers available (Ubuntu-based and Alpine-based). The big difference between them is that the Alpine one is much smaller and has a better security track. You can find it here: `https://gitlab.com/gitlaborg/gitlabrunner/blob/master/dockerfiles/alpine/Dockerfile`.

You can run the container with arguments that will be passed through to the GitLab Runner binary that is started inside the container. This also enables easier runtime registration of the Runner with a GitLab instance. Remember from the *Creating your own Dockerized GitLab Runner* section that we baked the registration of the Runner inside the image. You can find the appropriate images on Docker Hub: `https://hub.docker.com/r/gitlab/gitlab-runner/tags`.

Just start a container using the following command. It will automatically download the right image:

```
$ mkdir /Users/shared/gitlab-runner && mkdir /Users/shared/gitlab-
runner/config
 $ docker run -d --name gitlab-runner -v /Users/shared/gitlab-
runner/config:/etc/gitlab-runner \
    -v /var/run/docker.sock:/var/run/docker.sock \
    gitlab/gitlab-runner:latest
```

You can check the logs of the running container with the following command:

```
$ dockers logs -f gitlab-runner
 ERROR: Failed to load config stat /etc/gitlab-runner/config.toml: no such
file or directory  builds=0
```

The preceding output means that the `gitlab-runner` software is running inside the container, but it isn't registered yet.

The next step is to register it and save the configuration file in the container (in the configuration volume you specified with -v):

```
docker run --rm -v /User/shared/gitlab-runner/config:/etc/gitlab-runner
gitlab/gitlab-runner register \
    --non-interactive \
    --executor "docker" \
    --docker-image python:3.7-alpine \
    --url "https://gitlab-ee.joustie.nl/" \
    --run-untagged="true" \
    --registration-token "xxx" \
    --description "docker-runner" \
    --tag-list "eventmanager" \
    --locked="false"
```

If you examine the container logs (maybe you left the window open) after this, a message should appear:

```
...
Configuration loaded                                        builds=0
```

This means that the Runner now has a valid configuration and is online with GitLab.

If we try to trigger the pipeline for the `eventmanager-documentation` project again, a job will be run:

```
Checking for jobs... received                        job=660
repo_url=https://gitlab-ee.joustie.nl/marketing/eventmanager-documentation.
git runner=8cX8wWCr
```

In GitLab, you will see this job running:

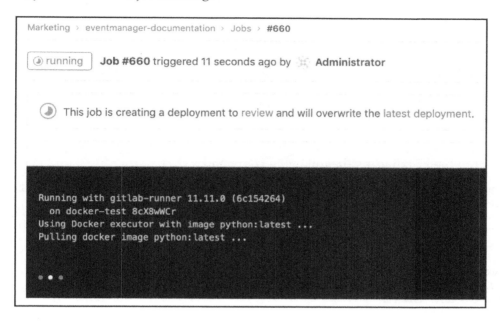

In the log file of the container, a message will appear if the job succeeds:

```
Job succeeded                                    duration=1m17.7055922s
job=660 project=10 runner=8cX8wWCr
```

This is also visible in the job log in GitLab:

```
$ aws s3 cp public/*.h
Completed 617 Bytes/61
upload: public/index.h
Job succeeded
```

This concludes the two ways of running Docker locally with relatively simple containers:

- Building your own container
- Using a prebuilt image

How can you manage this if you have massive amounts of build jobs? You can use an orchestration system such as Kubernetes, which is the subject of the next section.

Using a Kubernetes cluster to spawn GitLab Runners

The best method of deploying a GitLab Runner container into a Kubernetes cluster is by using the GitLab Runner Helm chart.

It contains all of the configuration information that's run using the GitLab Runner Kubernetes executor. For each new job it receives from GitLab CI/CD, it will provision a new pod within the specified namespace to run it.

You can run the install using the following command:

```
$ helm install --namespace gitlab --name gitlabrunner -f values.yaml
gitlab/gitlab-runner
```

This command can take some time to complete. After some time, you will receive the following output:

```
NAME: gitlabrunner
 LAST DEPLOYED: Tue May 21 21:11:15 2019
 NAMESPACE: gitlab
 STATUS: DEPLOYED

 RESOURCES:
 ==> v1/ConfigMap
 NAME DATA AGE
 gitlabrunner-gitlab-runner 5 0s

   . . .
```

This shows quite a bit of output, but the important part is that the status of the Helm chart is DEPLOYED.

The GitLab Runner should now be registered to the GitLab instance reachable at `https://gitlab-ee.joustie.nl/`.

We have run this deployment on my local Kubernetes cluster.

You can find out which Kubernetes pods are running by using the following command:

```
$ kubectl get pods -n gitlab
 NAME                                          READY   STATUS    RESTARTS
AGE
 gitlabrunner-gitlab-runner-787dddf5b5-58fzw   1/1     Running   0
2m
```

As you can see, the Runner was deployed in Kubernetes in the Runner list of the administrative section of GitLab:

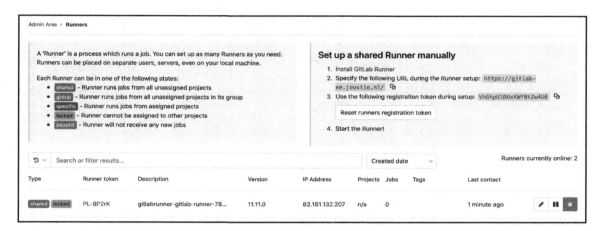

We can run the pipeline for the `eventmanager-documentation` project that was introduced in `Chapter 10`, *Create Your Product, Verifying it, and Packaging it,* to demonstrate the fact that multiple Runners are spawned on the Kubernetes cluster. Here is the pipeline view in GitLab showing multiple parallel jobs:

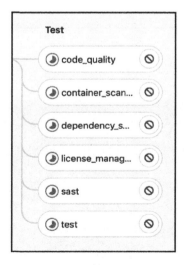

If you look into individual jobs, you will see that it takes some time to spin up the new Runner resources in the cluster. Until it is ready, the job is polled:

```
Running with gitlab-runner 11.11.0 (6c154264)
  on gitlabrunner-gitlab-runner-787dddf5b5-58fzw PL-8P2rK
Using Kubernetes namespace: gitlab
Using Kubernetes executor with image docker:stable ...
Waiting for pod gitlab/runner-pl-8p2rk-project-3-concurrent-0kk85s to be running, status is Pending
Waiting for pod gitlab/runner-pl-8p2rk-project-3-concurrent-0kk85s to be running, status is Pending
Waiting for pod gitlab/runner-pl-8p2rk-project-3-concurrent-0kk85s to be running, status is Pending
Waiting for pod gitlab/runner-pl-8p2rk-project-3-concurrent-0kk85s to be running, status is Pending
Waiting for pod gitlab/runner-pl-8p2rk-project-3-concurrent-0kk85s to be running, status is Pending
Waiting for pod gitlab/runner-pl-8p2rk-project-3-concurrent-0kk85s to be running, status is Pending
Waiting for pod gitlab/runner-pl-8p2rk-project-3-concurrent-0kk85s to be running, status is Pending
Waiting for pod gitlab/runner-pl-8p2rk-project-3-concurrent-0kk85s to be running, status is Pending
Waiting for pod gitlab/runner-pl-8p2rk-project-3-concurrent-0kk85s to be running, status is Pending
Waiting for pod gitlab/runner-pl-8p2rk-project-3-concurrent-0kk85s to be running, status is Pending
```

After some time, a Runner is spawned in the Kubernetes cluster and the jobs are dispatched to it:

```
Running with gitlab-runner 11.11.0 (6c154264)
  on gitlabrunner-gitlab-runner-787dddf5b5-58fzw PL-8P2rK
Using Kubernetes namespace: gitlab
Using Kubernetes executor with image docker:stable ...
Waiting for pod gitlab/runner-pl-8p2rk-project-3-concurrent-0pdxtv to be running, status is Pending
Running on runner-pl-8p2rk-project-3-concurrent-0pdxtv via gitlabrunner-gitlab-runner-787dddf5b5-58fzw...
Initialized empty Git repository in /builds/it/eventmanager/.git/
Fetching changes...
Created fresh repository.
From https://gitlab-ee.joustie.nl/it/eventmanager
 * [new branch]      cd          -> origin/cd
```

You can view a list of pods on the Kubernetes cluster and see that many pods were created:

```
CONTAINER ID     IMAGE           COMMAND                  CREATED         STATUS
a05460f9c464     bed64de70fa1    "dockerd-entrypoint.…"   6 minutes ago   Up 6 minutes
```

After some time, you will see that some parallel started jobs are finishing (in green):

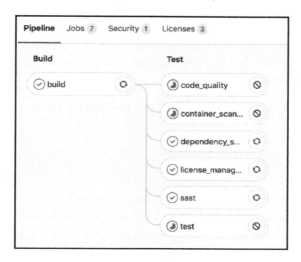

In the end, all of the jobs will succeed and the pipeline will be passed:

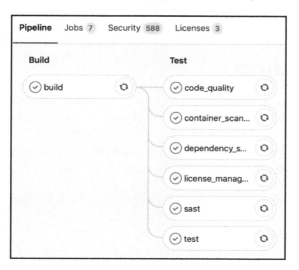

After this job, the number of GitLab Runners is reduced once more.

By doing this, we've shown you how to use Kubernetes to manage containers and how to handle scaling on the fly.

Summary

In this chapter, we showed you how to run GitLab Runners in containers. First, we looked at a quick way to containerize an existing Runner. Then, we showed you how to use existing Docker images that are provided by GitLab itself. Afterward, we talked about a way to manage a greater amount of containers and how you can handle this more economically with Kubernetes.

In the next chapter, we will discuss another way to scale Runners: with autoscaling.

Questions

1. What are the advantages of the Docker executor?
2. What is the basic build command for a Docker container?
3. Which file contains the building instructions for a container?
4. What is the name of a small Linux container distribution?
5. What tool is used to configure a Kubernetes cluster with much more ease?
6. How can you set the number of Runners to spawn by default in Kubernetes?

Further reading

- *Kubernetes Course from a DevOps Guru (Kubernetes and Docker)*, by *Tao W, James Lee, and Basit Mustafa*: https://www.packtpub.com/application-development/kubernetes-course-devops-guru-kubernetes-docker
- *Learn Docker – Fundamentals of Docker 18.x*, by *Gabriel N. Schenker*: https://www.packtpub.com/in/networking-and-servers/learn-docker-fundamentals-docker-18x
- *Hands-On Continuous Integration and Delivery*, by *Jean-Marcel Belmont*: https://www.packtpub.com/in/virtualization-and-cloud/hands-continuous-integration-and-delivery
- *Containers from Scratch*: https://ericchiang.github.io/post/containers-from-scratch/

Autoscaling GitLab CI Runners 17

In the previous chapter, we were able to scale GitLab Runners using the Kubernetes executor. Depending on your requirements of how many jobs should be able to run concurrently, the number of available Runners in a Kubernetes cluster can go up or down. Having a big number of runners available can be very costly. Even if they were to be turned off, they would still cost money. It's much better to have them created on demand and destroyed when they are no longer needed.

There is another GitLab Runner executor that can behave in this elastic way and dynamically add or remove Runner instances, and this is known as the Docker Machine executor. We will show you what this looks like from an architectural point of view, explain some of its settings, and provide you with some examples of running the Docker Machine executor with the VirtualBox driver and the Amazon EC2 driver.

In this chapter, we will cover the following topics:

- Runner client architecture
- Setting up the environment
- Configuring the GitLab Runner

Technical requirements

You can find the code file for this chapter in this book's GitHub repository at `https://github.com/PacktPublishing/Mastering-GitLab-12/tree/master/Chapter17`.

The other requirements for this chapter are as follows:

- Docker Machine is automatically installed with the Docker software distributions for macOS or Windows. If you don't have it, you can find it at the following link: `https://github.com/docker/machine/releases/`.
- You need a Linux bastion host with up-to-date patches.
- Access to the Docker registry image is required (`https://hub.docker.com/_/registry`).
- Access to the MinIO Docker images is required (`https://hub.docker.com/r/minio/minio`).
- You need VirtualBox installed on the bastion host (`http://www.virtualbox.org`).
- You need an AWS account, which will be used for scaling with the EC2 infrastructure.

Runner client architecture

First, we will describe the architecture of this solution. Expanding on the architecture that was put forward in previous chapters, we have a GitLab instance with a GitLab CI that receives a request from a GitLab Runner that's running a dedicated host. This can be either a local virtual machine or an instance in the cloud. The Runner is equipped with the Docker Machine program.

The Docker Machine executor type is basically a GitLab Runner that executes Docker Machine commands. With Docker Machine, you can create virtual hosts that run the Docker Engine. You can control these hosts with it and create new virtual machines with Docker Engine installed, which in turn can run GitLab Runner container instances. This is explained in the following diagram:

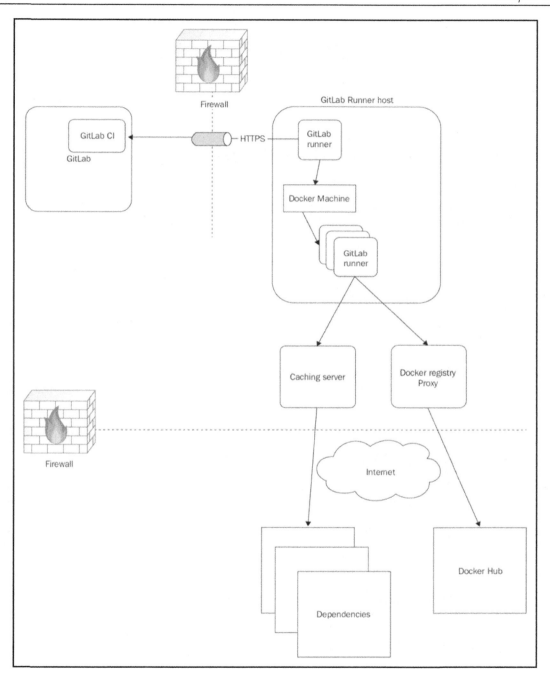

In the preceding diagram, you can see the **Docker Machine** component and that it can instantiate multiple runners. There are also two other components in the diagram called a **Caching server** (which can store dependencies for builds) and the **Docker registry proxy** (which can cache Docker images from places such as the Docker Hub). Both components will be explained in more detail in the *Configuring the Runner* section.

Setting up the environment

To enable a Docker Machine-based Runner, the following steps have to be performed:

1. Prepare a bastion host as the host where Docker will create new machines.
2. Deploy the GitLab Runner software on this machine.
3. Install Docker Machine.

Preparing a bastion host

For this example, we chose my macOS-based machine. This can be a Linux virtual machine or your laptop—any machine that can run a recent version of the GitLab Runner software. The only function this host will have is executing the GitLab Runner software with the Docker Machine executor. It should be tightly secured as a bastion to withstand attacks since it can control multiple Runner instances through the docker-machine commands, and that makes it a target.

Deploying the GitLab Runner software

On macOS, we use the Homebrew package manager. To install the Runner software, you can execute the following command:

```
brew install gitlab-runner
```

After that, you can register the Runner, as shown in Chapter 15, *Installing and Configuring GitLab Runners*:

```
gitlab-runner register
```

Choose the Docker Machine executor when you're asked for an executor in the registration process.

After the Runner has been registered, don't start it just yet—we need to edit the `config.toml` configuration file that's located in `~/.gitlab-runner/config.toml` on macOS. We will do that in the *Configuring the Runner* section.

First, though, we need to install the Docker Machine binary before we configure the Runner in order to start the Docker Machine executor.

Installing Docker Machine

If you've installed Docker on macOS or on Windows, you will already have the binary installed. You can test the installation by using the following command:

```
$ docker-machine -v
docker-machine version 0.16.1, build cce350d7
```

You can create new Docker hosts with this tool. They can be created on your local machine or network, but also in the cloud with the help of big providers such as Microsoft, Amazon, and Google. Docker Machine has plugins for many systems. The following is a list of them:

- All VMware products
- Virtualbox
- Microsoft Hyper-V
- DigitalOcean
- Amazon Web Services (EC2)
- Microsoft Azure
- Exoscale
- Google Computing Engine
- Scaleway
- IBM Softlayer
- Rackspace
- OpenStack
- Linode

If you are running Linux, you can download and install Docker Machine from `https://github.com/docker/machine/releases/`.

If you look at the Dockerfile of GitLab Runner on `https://hub.docker.com/r/gitlab/gitlab-runner/dockerfile`, which is used to build the default container, there is a line that says the following:

```
wget -q
https://github.com/docker/machine/releases/download/v0.7.0/docker-machine-Linux-x86_64 -O /usr/bin/docker-machine && \
    chmod +x /usr/bin/docker-machine
```

The Docker Machine binary is installed directly in this container image and is used by the GitLab Runner software. When you have verified that the Docker Machine binary is available, the next step is to configure the Runner.

Configuring the Runner

Now that you've installed the Runner software and Docker Machine, it's time to edit the Runner configuration file. On macOS, you can find the `config.toml` file in `~/.gitlab-runner/config.toml`. It is in your home directory because the Runner runs in the user space on macOS.

Now, we will take a look at some of the configuration options you can specify in the `config.toml` file that are specifically for the autoscaling Runner.

Off-peak time mode configuration

Most organizations don't have the need for 24/7 capacity since they don't need to use CI runners all of the time. The most work is done during work hours in a regular work week, and at the weekends, there's less of a need for software to be built. In this situation, it makes no sense to have machines sitting idle, waiting for jobs. By specifying a schedule with the `OffPeakPeriods` option, you can specify these times of lower productivity. During those times, the parameters to control the creation of the runner's capacity are different. You specify them by putting `OffPeak` in front of it. Therefore, `IdleCount` becomes `OffpeakIdleCount`, `IdleTime` becomes `OffPeakIdletime`, and so on. The functionality of the algorithm stays the same.

In the following schedule (which is common), you can see off-peak times on weekdays during the night, evening, and the entire weekend:

```
[runners.machine]
   OffPeakPeriods = [
      "* * 0-9,18-23 * * mon-fri *",
      "* * * * * sat,sun *"
   ]
```

Distributed runners caching

GitLab Runners have a built-in caching mechanism. It can be set on a global level, as well as for an individual project.

Setting the cache globally

You can set a path in your `config.toml` configuration file so that it will cache every job:

```
[runners.cache]
 Path = "/node_modules"
```

Setting the cache at the project level

You can set which path is to be cached in the `.gitlab-ci.yml` file for the project itself:

```
cache:
paths:
- node_modules/
```

The preceding settings apply to the context of just a single Runner host. If we use autoscaling, we need a way to have this cache shared by all of the runners to help gain speed. We can use external storage such as an S3 bucket to act as a cache. We just have to add the `[runners.cache.s3]` part to the `config.toml` file of the runners:

```
[runners.cache.s3]
   ServerAddress = "s3-website-us-east-1.amazonaws.com"
   BucketName = "joustie-gitlab-runner-cache"
   AccessKey = "xxx"
   SecretKey= "xxxx"
   Insecure = false
```

If this is your first time doing this, it will try to get the `cache.zip` file from the S3 storage bucket. However, if there is no file, it will complain and continue:

```
Checking cache for default...
 FATAL: file does not exist
```

After the build, which populates the `node_modules` directory with dependencies, the contents of that directory is zipped and sent to the S3 storage bucket:

```
Creating cache default...
 node_modules/: found 5728 matching files
 Uploading cache.zip to
https://joustie-gitlab-runner-cache.s3.amazonaws.com/project/14/default
 Created cache
 Job succeeded
```

If we retry the job, we will find that there's now a `cache.zip` file in S3, and it will be used instead of downloading all of those node dependencies again:

```
Checking cache for default...
 Downloading cache.zip from
https://joustie-gitlab-runner-cache.s3.amazonaws.com/project/14/default
 Successfully extracted cache
```

Distributed container registry mirroring

Another situation that can slow down building considerably is that the runners continuously download Docker containers from the internet. It is a much better idea to create a proxy for that. In `runners.machine`, you can specify which `engine-registry-mirror` should be used. If this is used on your local network, this saves a lot of traffic. Here, you see the section as I used it in our example project:

```
MachineOptions = [
"engine-registry-mirror=http://192.168.1.10:6000"
]
```

In the most basic way, the Docker Machine executor uses `docker-machine` to spawn new instances of the GitLab Runner container.

You can combine this with other features, such as shared caching and using a dedicate container registry to facilitate large amounts of instances.

If you enable these settings for your runner, you need to deploy a caching server and a registry mirroring service, which we will show you in the next section.

Installing and running a proxy container registry and a caching server

The two extra machines are necessary to help with performance when your plan is to deploy an entire elastic fleet of GitLab Runners. If you have more than five runners that can operate simultaneously, you will already gain an advantage when running a registry proxy and a caching server. An extra feature you get is that a bit of high availability is introduced in your architecture: you are able to do builds when your internet connection is flaky or offline.

For a proxy container registry, you need to have a proxy that implements the Docker Registry HTTP API V2, which we will install in the next section.

Proxy container registry

There is a convenient Docker container readily available to fulfill this role. You can start this Docker container immediately by using the following code:

```
docker run -d -p 6000:5000 -e
REGISTRY_PROXY_REMOTEURL=https://registry-1.docker.io  --name runner-
registry registry:2
```

If you create such a registry proxy and check the log file when the runners start a job, you will find that the proxy serves the Runner by fetching and caching images:

```
$ docker logs registry -f

172.17.0.1 - - [25/May/2019:14:28:40 +0000] "GET /v2/ HTTP/1.1" 200 2 ""
"docker/18.09.6 go/go1.10.8 git-commit/481bc77 kernel/4.14.116-boot2docker
os/linux arch/amd64 UpstreamClient(Go-http-client/1.1)"
...
```

 There isn't much to configure, but you can find more information here: https://hub.docker.com/_/registry.

Caching server

There are two options for creating a caching server. You can either get an S3 bucket in Amazon or another cloud provider or run an object storage service yourself such as MinIO, which can be found at `https://min.io`.

Creating an S3 bucket in Amazon Web Services

Log in to the Amazon Web Services console and find the S3 dashboard via **Services | S3**. Click on **Create bucket**:

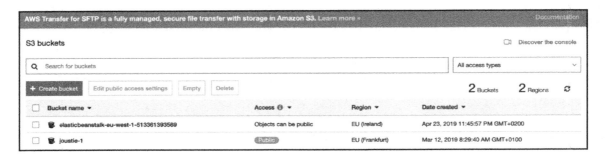

We have named it `joustie-gitlab-runner-cache` and left the rest as the default:

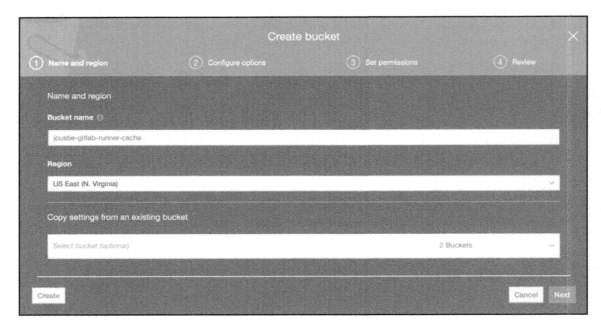

Creating your own MinIO server

This is also conveniently available as a Docker image. It is recommended to run this on a dedicated host because the storage that's involved can grow quite large, and you don't want this service to take down any other service that is running on that host.

Run the container with the following command:

```
docker run -it -p 9005:9000 -v ~/.minio:/root/.minio -v /s3:/export --name
caching-server minio/minio:latest server /export
```

Take note of the /s3 volume that is mounted in the container, which will serve as the directory that stores the cached objects.

The output of the preceding command will appear after some time:

```
latest: Pulling from minio/minio
 e7c96db7181b: Already exists
 94d4d681d0f2: Pull complete
 664c3f016f88: Pull complete
 b3235cce6961: Pull complete
Digest:sha256:244c711462a69303c0aa4f8d7943ba8b36dd55246e29da44c6653e39eaa42
e70
 Status: Downloaded newer image for minio/minio:latest
```

The container image will be downloaded.

After that, the MinIO container will start and report the location it uses, as well as AccesKey and SecretKey, which are to be used by the runners:

```
Endpoint:  http://172.17.0.4:9000  http://127.0.0.1:9000
 AccessKey: xxx
 SecretKey: xxx
```

We will demonstrate the usage of the cache by building a Node.js example project. It contains a node_modules directory, which we specify as a cached location in the .gitlab-ci.yml file.

When you build the Node.js project using a GitLab Runner, it will report its use of the cache in the Runner job log file:

```
node_modules/: found 5728 matching files
 Uploading cache.zip to
http://192.168.178.82:9005/joustie-gitlab-runner-cache/project/14/default
 Created cache
 Job succeeded
```

When we looked on the dedicated machine where the MinIO container was running, we found the following directory structure when we typed in the `tree` command in `/s3` (this is the directory that's used by the MinIO Docker container to store objects):

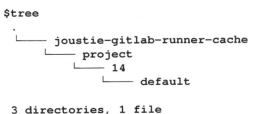

```
$tree
.
└── joustie-gitlab-runner-cache
    └── project
        └── 14
            └── default

3 directories, 1 file
```

We ran the GitLab Runner job again, which found `cache.zip` in the MinIO bucket.

This was an example of using a single runner. However, you may want to use these options to scale your Runner instances. Let's look at this in the next section.

Scaling your runners

In the previous section, we configured the software and prepared our environment so that we could scale up and down the number of runners while also providing some shared services like a registry proxy and a caching server. Now, let's look at two examples. We will run jobs on a Runner that's been configured to use VirtualBox and one that's been configured to use Amazon Web Services. VirtualBox is the open source virtualization solution from Oracle and can be found at `https://www.virtualbox.org/`.

Almost all of the Runner configuration files (the `config.toml` file) can be identical; we only change the machine driver part. Let's start with the VirtualBox option.

Using Docker Machines with a local VirtualBox instance

We start with the local `gitLab-runner` service with the `config` file for VirtualBox:

```
brew services start gitlab-runner
```

After a few seconds, we will see that VirtualBox spins up a number of virtual machines:

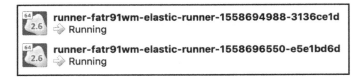

When we started a build of the event manager project in `Chapter 10`, *Create Your Product, Verify, and Package it*, we saw that it needs more runners (five parallel jobs) to run the pipeline. Therefore, we will start more machines:

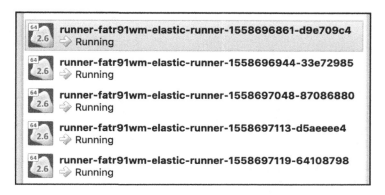

When the build has finished, after `IdleTime` has gone by, the number of machines will be reduced:

The VirtualBox driver is an excellent choice if you already have some servers with VirtualBox installed.

Using docker machines that have been created on Amazon Web Services (EC2)

If you change the machine driver from VirtualBox to Amazon EC2 and restart the runners, Docker Machine will spin up runners in Amazon if you have your credentials saved in your home directory or inserted in your shell environment. If not, then you will need to save them in the `config.toml` file.

After some time, the runners will appear in the EC2 web interface:

When those runners are started, you can change your Docker context to the one in Amazon so that you can run Docker commands and control those machines:

```
eval $(docker-machine env runner-fatr91wm-elastic-
runner-1558647049-87941946)
```

When you access the logs of the Runner on your bastion host, you will see that it will scale down the number of machines to `IdleCount`:

```
$docker logs  runner-fatr91wm
gitlab-runner[69056]:  WARNING: Removing machine : Too many idle machines
```

If we start the same job from earlier (event manager project), we will see that many jobs are queued following the start of the build pipeline:

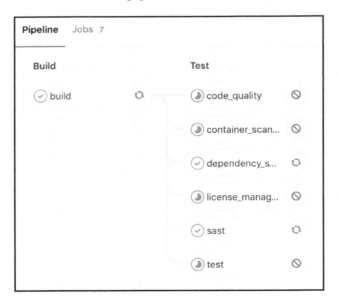

The `docker-machine ls` command will show us that many EC2 instances are started on AWS by the autoscaling GitLab Runner:

```
$ docker-machine ls
  NAME ACTIVE DRIVER STATE URL SWARM DOCKER ERRORS
  runner-fatr91wm-elastic-runner-1558702358-7e149fd0 * amazonec2 Running
tcp://3.86.53.66:2376 v18.09.6
  runner-fatr91wm-elastic-runner-1558702588-f8114aa8 - amazonec2 Running
tcp://34.207.177.20:2376
  runner-fatr91wm-elastic-runner-1558702591-6e1b6fd9 - amazonec2 Running
tcp://34.235.132.231:2376
  runner-fatr91wm-elastic-runner-1558702594-dd75b49b - amazonec2 Running
tcp://35.175.240.226:2376
```

You can also view new Runner instances in the AWS web console:

After successfully completing some of the jobs in the pipeline, the Runner will scale back down again:

runner-fatr91wm-elastic-runner-1558702588-f8114aa8	i-03d89362b42b403ff	t2.micro	us-east-1a		shutting-do...
runner-fatr91wm-elastic-runner-1558702594-dd75b49b	i-0476970633cbfc57d	t2.micro	us-east-1a		running
runner-fatr91wm-elastic-runner-1558702591-6e1b6fd9	i-05ff2e9ebc49fd7e3	t2.micro	us-east-1a		stopping
runner-fatr91wm-elastic-runner-1558702358-7e149fd0	i-0d6a15be17e45611f	t2.micro	us-east-1a		running

As you can see, it's quite simple to change the Docker Machine driver in the Runner configuration file and get the same behavior. The Runner scaled up virtual machines in VirtualBox are used to run Docker containers, as well as Amazon Web Services.

Summary

In this chapter, we explained the autoscaling feature of GitLab Runners. Like in Kubernetes, it gives you the option of creating Runner instances on demand and scaling back in times of less need. Under the hood, it uses Docker Machine to manage these replicas. There are several drivers available that instantly allow runners to be created on a big list of platforms.

In the next chapter, we will take a look at the options for monitoring all of these instances.

Questions

1. What Docker feature is used by the `docker-machine` executor?
2. What additional servers are recommended when you use autoscaling?
3. In what file is the runner's distributed cache saved?
4. What is the name of the object storage that was used in this chapter?
5. What is the name of the configuration file of a GitLab Runner?
6. What is the name of the Docker image that's used as a registry cache?

Further reading

- *Getting Started with Containerization*, by *Gabriel N. Schenker, Hideto Saito, Hui-Chuan Chloe Lee*, and *Ke-Jou Carol Hsu*: `https://www.packtpub.com/in/virtualization-and-cloud/getting-started-containerization`
- *Mastering Docker – Third Edition*, by *Russ McKendrick* and *Scott Gallagher*: `https://www.packtpub.com/in/virtualization-and-cloud/mastering-docker-third-edition`
- *Getting Started with Oracle VM VirtualBox*, by *Pradyumna Dash*: `https://www.packtpub.com/in/virtualization-and-cloud/getting-started-oracle-vm-virtualbox`
- *Hands-On AWS System Administration*, by *Glauber Gallego, Daniel Stori*, and *Satyajit Das*: `https://www.packtpub.com/in/virtualization-and-cloud/hands-aws-system-administration`

18
Monitoring CI Metrics

In this chapter, we will show you how to configure GitLab and its Runners to expose service metrics. These statistics are then collected by a system that specializes in data with a time dimension. GitLab uses Prometheus to do this and so will we.

Prometheus also provides the Alertmanager application, where you can define alert rules that trigger customizable actions, such as sending a mail or triggering a webhook, as described in Chapter 13, *Integrating GitLab with CI/CD Tools*. You can then either silence or deal with the alert. We will provide an example of how you can use this to enable an alert when some threshold you set is breached and the GitLab Runner is malfunctioning or not doing what you expect it to do.

In this chapter, we will cover the following topics:

- Enabling monitoring for Runners
- Enabling the GitLab Runner configuration file
- Runner business logic metrics
- General processing metrics

Technical requirements

For managing omnibus installation, there is one central configuration file, called `gitlab.rb`. You need to create it or copy an example. There is a template available at `https://gitlab.com/gitlab-org/omnibus-gitlab/blob/master/files/gitlab-config-template/gitlab.rb.template`. It is not updated after upgrades. In large parts of this chapter, we will quote and discuss parts of this file. Furthermore, we will use code examples from the GitHub repository that accompanies this book and you will need Prometheus and the Alertmanager software to run the samples:

- Code examples (`https://github.com/PacktPublishing/Mastering-GitLab-12`).
- Prometheus monitoring server (`https://prometheus.io`).
- Prometheus Alertmanager (`https://prometheus.io/docs/alerting/alertmanager/`).
- There are also containerized versions (find them with Docker by searching Prometheus):
  - **Alertmanager**: `https://hub.docker.com/r/prom/alertmanager/`
  - **Prometheus**: `https://hub.docker.com/r/prom/prometheus/`

You can find the code file for this chapter in this book's GitHub repository at `https://github.com/PacktPublishing/Mastering-GitLab-12/tree/master/Chapter18`.

Enabling monitoring for Runners

The GitLab omnibus installation package supports defining several monitoring components. At the time of writing, it does not have a built-in way to deploy GitLab Runners. You can deploy Runners with the Kubernetes GitLab Runner helm chart and monitor those, but for Runners that you created yourself, you are responsible for enabling the monitoring of them. What do you achieve when monitoring is enabled? Well, especially in an autoscaling environment, monitoring can keep you informed about how your fleet of Runners is doing. Monitoring can give you some insights into how your resources are used. The metrics are stored historically, so you can notice trends after some time.

The following is a high-level example of a monitoring setup for the architecture we created in the previous chapter. We have a GitLab instance with **continuous integration (CI)** enabled on the left-hand side:

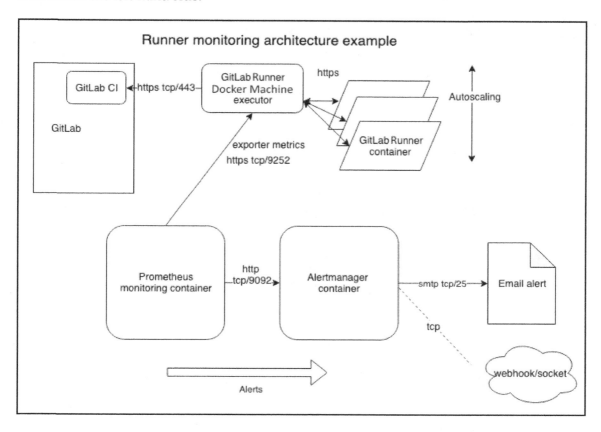

There is a GitLab Runner instance using a Docker Machine executor that can spawn GitLab Runner containers. The driver that is used can be of any type that Docker Machine supports. We used Amazon and VirtualBox to create a small-scale infrastructure that always has one idle Runner and scales up when there are more jobs in the queue. In this chapter, we'll talk about an example where we start up a separate Prometheus monitoring Docker container, and then make that monitoring application scrape the metrics that are generated by the GitLab Runner. The Prometheus monitoring system can also send alerts when certain thresholds are reached. There is a separate binary for this (the Alertmanager) and we'll choose to start it in a separated Docker container. It can also be manually installed on a dedicated server.

The preceding information is about the basic monitoring setup with alerting, which will give you more insight into the metrics of your GitLab Runners.

Editing the GitLab Runner configuration file

First, we have to configure the Runner to expose information, which is quite easy to do. The config.toml file, which resides at ~/.gitlab.runner on my system (macOS), has to be edited. We can enable the built-in server to serve information by adding a line with listen_address to this file, as shown in the following code block:

```
listen_address = ":9252"
```

After saving this file, we must restart our Runner with the following command (on macOS and a Homebrew installed Runner):

```
$ brew services  restart  gitlab-runner
```

On Linux or on a bare macOS installation, we can restart the Runner via the following command:

```
$ sudo killall -SIGHUP gitlab-runner
```

We can view the exposed information by opening the URL where it is running (in my case, http://192.168.178.82:9252), and then appending the metrics path (/metrics):

Now that we have exposed this information, we want to capture it in a database that checks the data every X seconds. We are going to start a Docker container with Prometheus to do this. We will start the container with the following configuration file:

```
global:
    scrape_interval: 15s
    scrape_timeout: 10s
    evaluation_interval: 15s
 alerting:
    alertmanagers:
    - static_configs:
      - targets: []
      scheme: http
      timeout: 10s
 scrape_configs:
 - job_name: prometheus
   honor_timestamps: true
   scrape_interval: 15s
   scrape_timeout: 10s
   metrics_path: /metrics
   scheme: http
   static_configs:
   - targets:
     - localhost:9090
   - targets:
     - 192.168.178.82:9252
```

The important part right now is as follows:

```
- targets:
    -  192.168.178.82:9252
```

As you can see, this is the exact URL of our Runner's metrics data. Now, we start the Prometheus container with the config file as an argument (it will download the container from Docker Hub if you do not have it locally):

```
$ docker run -p 9090:9090 -v
/Users/joostevertse/srv/prometheus:/etc/prometheus prom/prometheus
 level=info ts=2019-05-26T20:08:31.338Z caller=main.go:286 msg="no time or
size retention was set so using the default time retention" duration=15d
 level=info ts=2019-05-26T20:08:31.339Z caller=main.go:322 msg="Starting
Prometheus" version="(version=2.10.0, branch=HEAD,
revision=d20e84d0fb64aff2f62a977adc8cfb656da4e286)"
```

We can interrupt the container with *Ctrl+ C*, but we started it this way as an example. If we use the -d argument to the Docker run command, the container will run in the background.

In this example, the Prometheus container is running on port 9090, and the port is published via Docker -p 9090:9090.

If we visit the page (in my case, http://localhost:9090), we will be presented with a fresh Prometheus installation:

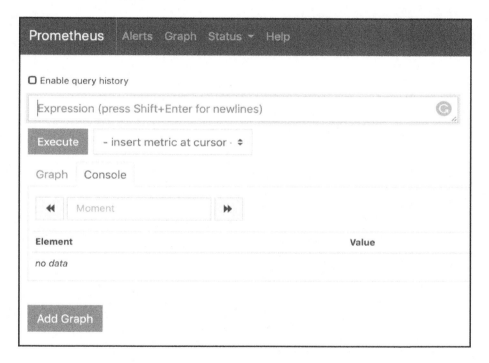

To find out whether it is actually getting information from the Runner, click on **-insert metric at cursor -**. We will see some Runner-related metrics, as follows:

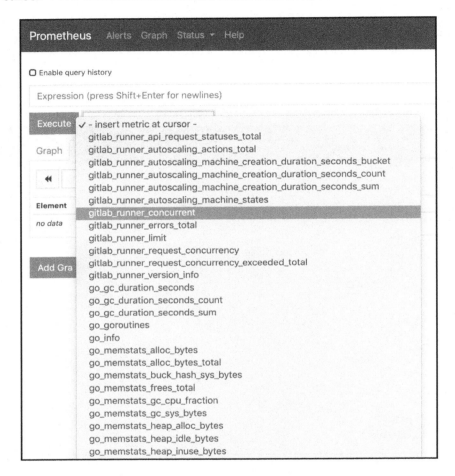

In the next section, we'll demonstrate some metrics that have value in determining the state of your builds.

Runner business logic metrics

Imagine that you have several developers working on a system and you have several integration tests that should pass before you can deploy to a production environment. If speed is important for your business, then you need to build your system quickly. To do this, there have to be GitLab Runners available and ready to run jobs. If they are unavailable or they perform badly, your development will slow down and so will your business. What follows are some business logic metrics that are viewable in Prometheus.

Key metrics to watch

There are a lot of metrics available, but let's look at some that have proven useful in the past:

- `gitlab_runner_jobs`: It is wise to monitor the number of pending jobs:

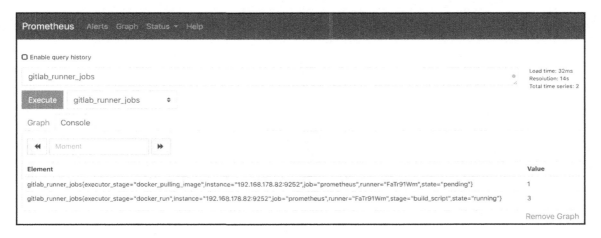

If this number gets too high, consider adding a higher limit for autoscalable Runners.

- `gitlab_autoscaling_options_total`: Another interesting metric is the type and number of scaling actions that are performed on the Runner:

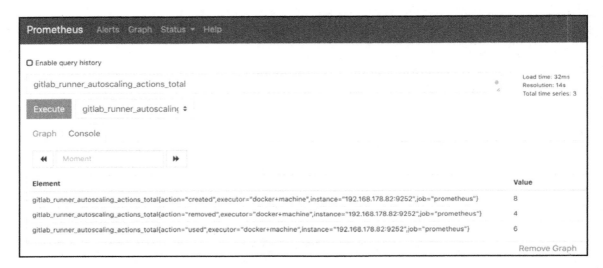

The actions created and removed should be about the same (too many created is expensive, and too many removed would signal a problem). When it is busy, you want a growing number of *used* instances, as this would indicate efficient resource use.

- `gitlab_runner_jobs_total`: The `gitlab_runner_jobs_total` information is nice to have during capacity planning:

If there is an ever-increasing number of jobs, scale the number of Runners up before you run out of capacity.

- `gitlab_runner_autoscaling_machine_creation_duration_seconds_count`: The Runners in this example are autoscaled on different platforms (Amazon and VirtualBox). The main GitLab Runner instance kept track of how many machines were created and how much time it took to spin up new machines:

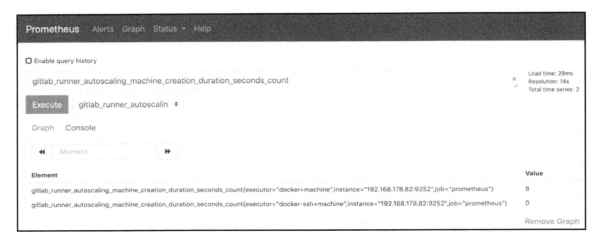

This can help you to determine whether you are running on the right platform.

- `gitlab_runner_limit`: If you are going to experiment with the limit of Runners that can be spawned by the **Docker Machine executor**, this metric is useful to record and you can use it in queries later on in order to compare data:

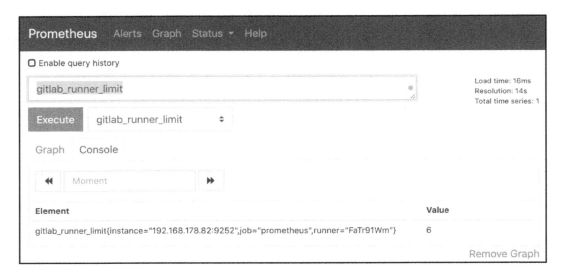

If you see the limit growing, it means your business is growing.

- `gitlab_runner_errors`: The next graph demonstrates the rate function, which can be used to query metrics and show how much the metric has increased or decreased for a chosen interval. The function is part of `PromQL`, which is the language for querying data in Prometheus:

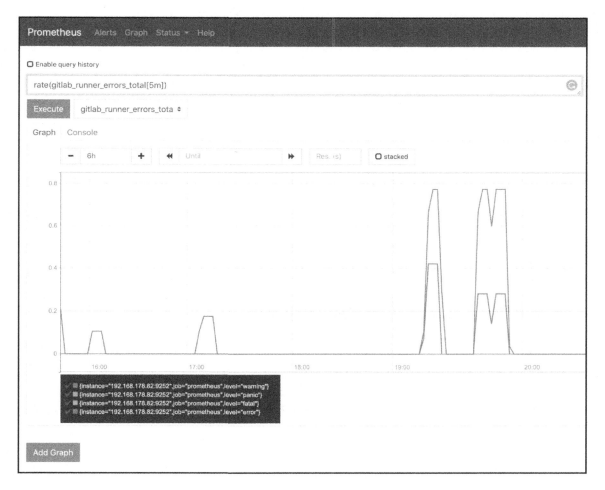

Here, we check the total number of errors that are generated by different Runners.

- `gitlab_runner_failed_jobs_total`: A potentially interesting metric is the rate of the number of failed jobs. In the following graph for our Runner, we can see that there is a sudden spike:

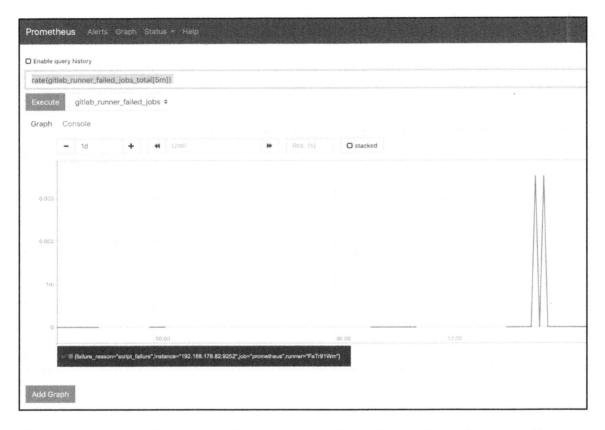

We should have no failed jobs at all, so this is a candidate for alerting, which we will discuss in the *Alert management* section of this chapter.

General process metrics

It is helpful to have metrics about the number of jobs processed, or the speed of the jobs. But, sometimes, we may also want to know whether the machine that is hosting the Runner is experiencing operational issues, such as low memory or CPU contention. The Prometheus exporter also records general process metrics such as these.

Key metrics to watch

The following metrics only cover the host in which the Docker Machine executor is running:

- `process_cpu_seconds_total`: If you have a small machine, it is useful to know whether the CPU is coping with the load. There is a count that records the total number of CPU seconds used by the Runner process:

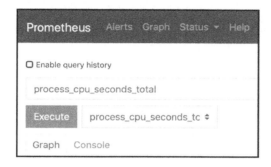

A big increase in a short period of time could indicate issues.

- `process_open_fds`: There is a maximum number of open file descriptors on a Unix system. If this number is reached, the system will generate errors and won't open files anymore:

If the maximum is reached, you can expect your jobs to fail.

- `process_resident_memory_bytes`: This is the amount of memory Prometheus is using from the kernel that is real memory and not virtual or swap memory. Big changes in this value can indicate issues:

As you can see, there are no problems on our demonstration server.

- `process_virtual_memory_bytes`: This metric represents all memory (including RAM and swap) that is managed by the Runner process:

Once again, there are no issues on our demonstration server.

- `process_start_time_seconds`: If there are issues, it is nice to know the time when the issues started and how they have developed:

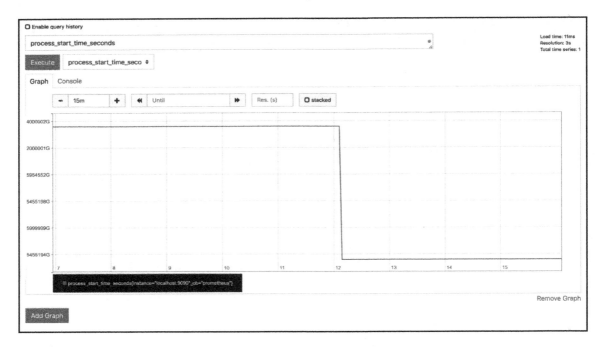

Recording the start time of the process can help debug issues.

- `scrape_duration_seconds`: The Prometheus server scrapes (downloads) the information that is exposed by the exporter. It also records how much time the scraping took:

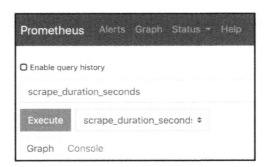

Long scraping times could indicate a network problem or a slow Runner.

- `go_gc_duration_seconds_count`: There are also metrics about the Golang runtime environment that the Runner is running in; for example; the amount of time it takes to do garbage collection:

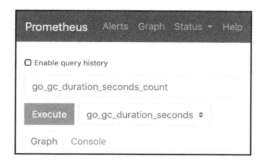

These metrics are very detailed, and are more interesting for developers of the GitLab Runner than for users.

All the general process metrics combined can give you an idea of how the Docker Machine Runner is behaving, and can be used to discover trends. Of course, it is also nice to be alerted to a value that has reached a certain threshold; that is the subject of the next section.

Alert management

Prometheus' Alertmanager (`https://prometheus.io/docs/alerting/alertmanager/`) is a tool that is especially designed for bigger infrastructures. Pager and alerting programs have been around for a long time, but this one and Prometheus itself are highly optimized for working in a scaling infrastructure. It is also available as a Docker container: `https://hub.docker.com/r/prom/alertmanager/`.

As we saw in the infrastructure diagram at the beginning of this chapter, we use a separate Prometheus and Alertmanager containers to demonstrate our Runner metrics collection.

The Alertmanager container has a configuration file (`srv/prometheus/alertmanager.yml`):

```
global:
   # The smarthost and SMTP sender used for mail notifications.
   smtp_smarthost: 'smtp.xs4all.nl:25'
   smtp_from: 'alertmanager@joustie.nl'

route:
   repeat_interval: 3h
```

```
    receiver: joustie

routes:
  - match_re:
      service: ^(.*)$
    receiver: joustie

receivers:
- name: 'joustie'
  email_configs:
  - to: 'joustie@somewhere.com'
```

The configuration has an email host defined, and it routes alerts via email to joustie@somewhere.com every 3 hours if it is not silenced.

The Alertmanager Docker container can be started with the following command:

```
docker run  -dp 9093:9093 --name=prom_alertmanager -v
/Users/joostevertse/srv/prometheus/alertmanager.yml:/alertmanager.yml
prom/alertmanager --config.file=/alertmanager.yml
```

We have already started a Prometheus container, but to make it connect to the Alertmanager container, we need to alter its configuration in two ways. We need an alerts file in which we determine what event should trigger an alert. In our example, we check the number of failed Runner metrics and make it turn red when there are more than two failed jobs. The alert.rules file for this is as follows:

```
groups:
  - name: joberror
    rules:
    - alert: HighErrorRate
      expr: gitlab_runner_failed_jobs_total > 2
      for: 1m
      labels:
        severity: email
      annotations:
        summary: High job errors
```

This configuration shows that joustie@somewhere.com will receive an email when there are more than two failed jobs.

The second change is to the main Prometheus configuration file (srv/prometheus/prometheus.yml). This new section is all about adding an alerting configuration (an Alertmanager is added that is running on 192.168.178.82 port 9093):

```
alerting:
  alertmanagers:
  - static_configs:
    - targets: ["192.168.178.82:9093"]
    scheme: http
    timeout: 10s
```

After changing the file, we have to activate the new configuration. We have to restart the container from scratch for this:

```
$ docker stop prom_server
ff55a556772
$ docker rm prom_server
ff55a556772
$ docker run  -dp 9090:9090 --name=prom_server -v
/Users/joostevertse/srv/prometheus/prometheus.yml:/etc/prometheus/prometheu
s.yml -v
/Users/joostevertse/srv/prometheus/alert.rules:/etc/prometheus/alert.rules
prom/prometheus  --config.file=/etc/prometheus/prometheus.yml
```

Notice that the container is recreated because we have to link the alert rules into the container.

After the containers have started, and we have kicked off some jobs and made them fail, there should be an alert triggered. You can find the alert in Prometheus in the web interface (in our case, http://localhost:9090/alerts):

We can also view this file in the Alertmanager instance. In our example, we go to `http://localhost:9093/#/alerts` to find the alert:

The Alertmanager was configured to send emails, so we received the following email:

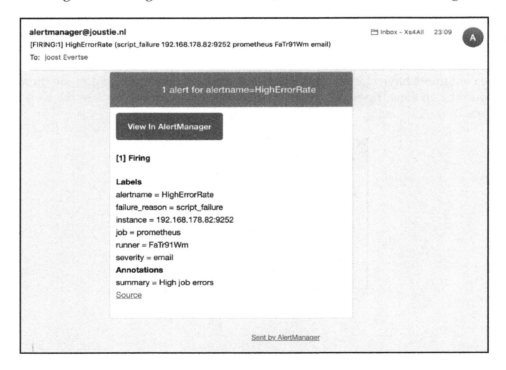

The Alertmanager has the concept of a Silence, which means you can suppress alerts from being sent depending on certain matches. If, for instance, we temporarily want to suppress alerts for **HighErrorRate**, we can set a duration of 2 hours, during which those alerts will be silenced:

With Alertmanager enabled and the alerts defined, it is much clearer how GitLab Runners perform, and if they are generating errors. You certainly need monitoring like this to learn from errors and create a faster and higher-quality CI/CD pipeline.

Summary

In this chapter, we continued with the Runner architecture from the previous chapter and showed you a way to monitor the autoscaling Runner, no matter which Docker Machine drivers are being used. The Prometheus monitoring solution offers a highly scalable time series database, and together with the Alertmanager, you can create sophisticated monitoring. In the example we used, Docker containers are used extensively as Prometheus is cloud-native software (https://prometheus.io/blog/2016/05/09/prometheus-to-join-the-cloud-native-computing-foundation/), but the software can also be run on dedicated hardware.

In the next chapter, we will learn about the options available to create a GitLab **highly available (HA)** infrastructure. In the first section of that chapter, we will discuss the basic setup for that.

Questions

1. What is the collection of metrics done by the Prometheus server called?
2. What is the Prometheus client program called?
3. In which section do you define a server to be monitored?
4. What is the default Prometheus port?
5. Name the first option to try when there are a lot of pending jobs.
6. Which PromQL function is used to query the average rate of increase for a dataset?

Further reading

- *Practical Site Reliability Engineering* by *Pethuru Raj Chelliah, Saravanan Pitchaimani,* and *Babu Jayaraj*: `https://www.packtpub.com/virtualization-and-cloud/practical-site-reliability-engineering`.
- *Cloud Native Programming with Golang,* by *Mina Andrawos* and *Martin Helmich*: `https://www.packtpub.com/application-development/cloud-native-programming-golang`.

5
Section 5: Scale the Server Infrastructure (High Availability Setup)

After reading this section, you will be able to choose which **high availability (HA)** setup fits your needs, monitor the results, and act on certain thresholds.

This section comprises the following chapters:

- Chapter 19, *Creating a Basic HA Architecture Using Horizontal Scaling*
- Chapter 20, *Managing a Hybrid HA Environment*
- Chapter 21, *Making Your Environment Fully Distributed*
- Chapter 22, *Using Geo to Create Distributed Read-Only Copies of GitLab*

19
Creating a Basic HA Architecture Using Horizontal Scaling

GitLab is an application that consists of many components. The GitLab omnibus package makes it easy to run all these components on one physical server; however, there comes a time when one server is no longer enough to run GitLab. On a typical 4-CPU core machine with 16 GB of RAM, you can support about 2,000 users. Once you run an application on virtual hardware, it scales better (it is cheaper to reproduce virtual hardware); however, using more than 32 cores is still quite expensive and there comes a time when it is more economical to split up the functionality and scale horizontally. In this chapter, we will try to achieve this using Terraform and Ansible DevOps tools to deploy infrastructure as code. We will be using the **Amazon Web Services (AWS)** cloud offering as a backend.

You can build entire virtual infrastructures with Terraform and configure them using Ansible. These infrastructures can leverage the scaling features that cloud providers such as Amazon provide.

In this chapter, we will cover the following topics:

- The underlying architecture of the high available and scalable GitLab setup
- Setting up the bastion hosts
- Configuring the database nodes
- The Redis configuration
- Connecting the shared filesystem
- Setting up the application servers

Technical requirements

For managing omnibus installations, there is one central configuration file called `gitlab.rb`. You need to create it or copy an example. There is a template available from `https://gitlab.com/gitlab-org/omnibus-gitlab/blob/master/files/gitlab-config-template/gitlab.rb.template`. Upgrades don't replace or edit this file. In large parts of this chapter, I quote and discuss parts of this file.

For creating our virtual infrastructure, we are going to use Terraform (≥ v0.11.12). You can download it from `https://www.terraform.io`. Terraform is a multiplatform binary.

Terraform providers use the following:

- `provider.ansible` v0.0.4: Get it from `https://github.com/nbering/terraform-inventory`.
- `provider.aws` v2.1.0: Automatically downloaded with the `terraform init` command (see later on in *Starting with the code* section).
- `provider.tls` v1.2.0: Automatically downloaded with the `terraform init` command (see later on in *Starting with the code* section).

For automating our deployments, we use Ansible (≥ version 2.7). You can download it from `https://github.com/ansible/ansible`, or use a package manager such as `brew` or `pip` to install it.

To follow along with the instructions in this chapter, please download the Git repository, which contains examples and is on GitHub: `https://github.com/PacktPublishing/` `Mastering-GitLab-12/tree/master/Chapter19https://github.com/PacktPublishing/` `Mastering-GitLab-12/tree/master/Chapter19`.

The underlying architecture of this solution

What is the first iteration of a horizontally scaled GitLab? We not only need to scale horizontally to enable efficient growth, but also to enhance availability of the solution. Availability is usually measured in uptime, that is the percentage of the day, month, or year that your system is operational. To get this to a higher level, you need to eliminate single points of failure and make the components redundant. Also, be sure that the components can take over from each other when needed and have a good system in place that monitors and detects failures. If your system is doing this, it is said to be a **high availability (HA)** system.

What does it mean to scale horizontally? It means that you will split workloads into different layers. A load balancer will be placed at the front of the infrastructure. This will get one IP address and this will be the new external URL from GitLab. The traffic that enters here is distributed on the basis of the round-robin principle. One traffic flow goes to one GitLab application server, and the other goes to a second one. Because the load balancer supports sticky cookies, each web session will always choose the same route and end up at the same application server.

Because you now have two application servers, you need to share certain things to make it all work. For instance, if one of the GitLab application servers goes down, you want the other to take over the current HTTP sessions; therefore, you need a Redis server that is reachable by both application servers. The Redis server is where certain session information is kept.

Another example is the repository data. We can't keep this confined on one GitLab server anymore, it needs to be shared! There are several options for this, but we will start with the simplest one: a **Network File System (NFS)**.

The database can serve many clients, but it will also run several standby servers as a failover precaution. We also need a cluster mechanism to determine which database is the master and who is online.

The following is a diagram of the AWS GitLab horizontal scaling example solution, which is the basic HA solution:

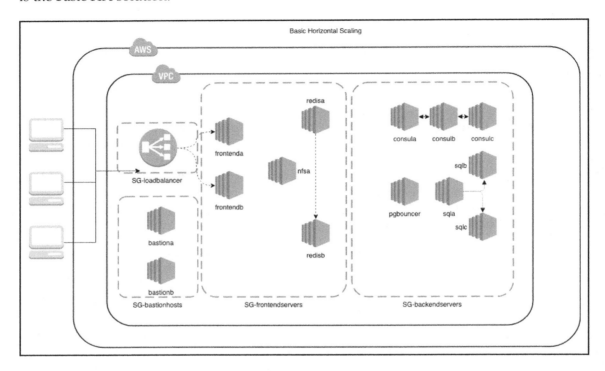

On the left-hand side, you can find the clients. On the right-hand side, you can see the Amazon infrastructure. Everything is contained in a **Virtual Private Cloud** (**VPC**). Inside this VPC, you can see several security groups, which are mapped onto subnets.

The clients enter the infrastructure through the **SG-loadbalancer** security group. The requests for GitLab are then routed to the frontend application servers. They are connected to a shared filesystem and are connected to a Redis cluster that is also in the **SG-frontendservers** security group. The frontend application servers also connect to a database in the **SG-backendservers** zone through a **pgbouncer** proxy. There are three database servers: one master and two slaves. The health of the database servers is monitored through a consul cluster.

The bastion servers that are in the SG-bastion hosts security group have two special functions:

- They are accessible with SSH from the outside as jump hosts to other instances.
- They have a squid proxy server installed for the installation of packages by nodes in the **SG-frontendservers** and **SG-backendservers** zones.

We will use a cloud provider (Amazon) in our examples to build a basic scalable platform. With a little refactoring, the Terraform configuration could be rewritten to the specification of another cloud provider.

First, we will discuss the basic building blocks of this architecture.

Amazon services

AWS was the first big cloud offering. It started out by selling overcapacity from the Amazon server farms. In the last 10 years, it has grown rapidly and diversified its services. You can use it to virtualize your entire IT stack or create new services from the ground up. For this example, we use AWS because it performs very well and a lot of people are familiar with the concepts.

AWS has different kinds of building blocks that you can use to create your infrastructure. The basic ones are as follows.

Elastic compute cloud (EC2)

Amazon EC2 is a popular product in AWS. It was one of the first cloud-scale virtual machine offerings on the market. You can rent virtual computers that can provide compute resources. You can run several kinds of operating systems in that virtual machine, and there are several ways to interact with this service. It is manageable through the AWS web console, and you can also use the extensive APIs to create and control EC2 instances. You can load custom applications into the virtual machines and use other Amazon services from them. It is effortless to scale up the number of machines, and security functions are available out of the box, as well as basic monitoring capabilities.

Classic load balancer

This is a public internet-facing interface with a **Fully Qualified Domain Name (FQDN)**, and it routes requests from internet hosts to EC2 instances that have been registered with it. It has some built-in monitoring capabilities and a health check mechanism. For instance, it checks the HTTP port of the EC2 instances that are registered by default; however, in our case, that leads to trouble because the main GitLab page on the first boot always redirects. When this happens, the health check reports out of service and closes the port. We can change this to let the load balancer do a basic **Transmission Control Protocol (TCP)** health check only.

Virtual private cloud and subnets

Amazon Virtual Private Cloud (Amazon VPC) is the highest abstraction of a group of resources within AWS. In a VPC, you can provision several AWS resources such as virtual networks and hosts. You are entirely in control of this space and can also create network route tables and gateways. There can be subnets that are accessible to the internet and ones that only communicate internally, inside your VPC. Network **Access Control Lists (ACLs)** and **Security Groups (SGs)** help defend your VPC from intruders. You have the option to use IPv4 and IPv6 as network protocol to enable communication over your networks.

SGs

SGs are a very important part of the security that you can use to control inbound and outbound network traffic. In traditional networks, you would usually place firewall appliances between networks or subnets to control network flows. In AWS, an SG takes on this role. Besides not being a physical device, the other difference is that SGs are not specified on the subnet level. In a VPC, you assign EC2 instances to these security groups, so the security rules are on an instance level. There can be a maximum of five security groups assigned. If you don't assign anything, an instance will get the default security group for the VPC.

Terraform

A useful tool for handling multicloud configurations is Terraform by HashiCorp – the folks that also gave us Vagrant and many other tools. It is a tool that can interact with a lot of APIs that are exposed by cloud providers. You tell Terraform what you want your infrastructure to look like in declarative files, and it takes care of the rest. Before it makes changes to existing infrastructure, it builds a graph of the resources that have already been deployed. It even has a dry run mode (`terraform plan`) where it calculates and reports the actions it will execute.

Tools such as Terraform enable the *Infrastructure as code* paradigm. It creates a reproducible infrastructure, and this greatly enhances the DevOps life cycle.

It is not only multi-cloud but also multiplatform, which means it can run on different operating systems, as we will see in the next section.

Installing Terraform

You can find a version of Terraform for your platform to download here: `https://www.terraform.io/downloads.html`. There are versions compiled for the following platforms:

- macOS
- FreeBSD
- Linux
- OpenBSD
- Solaris
- Windows

Inside the ZIP package is a single binary written in Golang that runs on your machine. After downloading and unpacking, you should put it somewhere in your path, for example, `/usr/local/bin/` on Linux. After that, check your version on the command line as follows:

```
$terraform -v
Terraform v0.11.12
 Make sure you have a version of at least v0.11.12. The binary is all you
need. We also want the Ansible plugin for Terraform, but let's first
install Ansible before this.
```

Ansible

Ansible is an agentless automation platform whose name is based on the hyperspace communication system, which features in science fiction literature. It is easy to set up, but powerful. It can play a role in configuration management, application deployment, and task automation. It is also suited for IT orchestration as a whole, where you have integrated security with the Ansible Tower backend and run tasks in sequence and create a chain of events that run on multiple different servers or devices. In our basic infrastructure example, for instance, it can run tasks for all web servers in the *web* group.

We are going to use Ansible to configure all the systems after they are provisioned with Terraform in the AWS infrastructure.

We mentioned that Ansible is *agentless* at the beginning of this section. Unlike Puppet or Chef, it doesn't run as an agent on the remote target. Ansible uses SSH instead, so that is a requirement for all the systems you want to manage. Another dependency is Python, which needs to be installed on the remote target because Ansible itself is written in that language. To run Ansible, you do not need a dedicated server machine; instead, you can initiate the tasks from your local workstation or any other system with the basic Python runtime and SSH clients. If you need more integrated security, you can use Ansible Tower, in order to have a central place that connects with your enterprise identity management. It is technically possible to use Puppet in standalone mode, but you still need to install it on the targets.

Ansible is a free and open source product that runs on Linux, macOS, BSD, and even Windows. RedHat bought the company behind it in 2015, and, since then, Ansible has gotten more integrated with the RedHat enterprise product.

The real power of Ansible lies in its *playbooks*. A playbook is like a recipe or an instructions manual that tells Ansible what to do when it connects to each machine. It knows which machines to configure by checking an inventory, and which can be read from a file or passed in through a command (this is then called a **dynamic inventory**).

Installing the Ansible Terraform provider

When Terraform generates the infrastructure, it keeps a local cache of the objects it has built. All information needed to generate a dynamic inventory is available from this file, but we need a plugin or provider to parse and transform the data so Ansible can understand it. We use the following Ansible provider to do that: `https://github.com/nbering/terraform-inventory`.

It's easy to install. You need to download the `terraform.py` file, place it in your patch, and mark it as executable, as shown in the following example:

```
$cd /usr/local/bin && sudo wget
https://raw.githubusercontent.com/nbering/terraform-inventory/master/terraf
orm.py && sudo chmod 755 terraform.py
```

Starting with the code

When you have cloned the code from https://github.com/PacktPublishing/Mastering-GitLab-12.git, change the current directory to the project:

```
cd Mastering-GitLab-12/CHP18/ha-configuration
```

We are going to use Terraform to create our infrastructure objects in AWS. The basic usage of Terraform is that you define the objects in files ending in `.tf`, and you can then start deploying them. If you have cloned the repository, the `.tf` files are already there, so you can then initialize Terraform (to retrieve the necessary plugins):

```
$ terraform init
Initializing provider plugins...
- Checking for available provider plugins on
https://releases.hashicorp.com...
- Downloading plugin for provider "tls" (2.0.1)...
- Downloading plugin for provider "aws" (2.9.0)...
...
* provider.ansible: version = "~> 0.0"
* provider.aws: version = "~> 2.9"
* provider.tls: version = "~> 2.0"
Terraform has been successfully initialized!
```

Now that Terraform is ready to go, you need to make sure the `.tf` definitions are valid. You can do that with a dry run where nothing will be installed, using the `plan` argument:

```
$ terraform plan
An execution plan has been generated and is shown below.
Resource actions are indicated with the following symbols:
  + create

Terraform will perform the following actions:
...
```

If there are no errors, you can then let Terraform create the objects for real by using the script in `scripts/deploy-with-ansible.sh`. To let Terraform deploy the objects manually, you can run `apply`, as follows:

```
$ terraform apply --auto-approve
tls_private_key.mykey: Creating...
 algorithm: "" => "RSA"
 ecdsa_curve: "" => "P224"
 private_key_pem: "" => "<computed>"
 public_key_fingerprint_md5: "" => "<computed>"
 public_key_openssh: "" => "<computed>"
 public_key_pem: "" => "<computed>"
 rsa_bits: "" => "4096"
aws_vpc.gitlabha: Creating...
```

In the next sections, we describe each `.tf` file and give an example of its use.

vpc.tf

In the *Virtual private cloud and subnets* section, we explained that a VPC is the beginning of an AWS infrastructure. In the `vpc.tf` file, we define this:

```
resource "aws_vpc" "gitlabha" {
    cidr_block = "10.0.0.0/16"
    enable_dns_hostnames = true
    enable_dns_support = true
    tags{
        Name = "VPC-${var.environment}"
    }
}
```

We assign the VPC a private network address that, again, can be divided into subnets:

```
cidr_block = "10.0.0.0/16"
```

We want to enable DNS hostnames for this VPC:

```
enable_dns_hostnames = true
enable_dns_support = true
```

We can use tags to give the VPC a name that fits with the environment we define:

```
tags{
 Name = "VPC-${var.environment}"
}
```

Now that we have a basic VPC, we can divide it into further networks and create more objects.

subnet.tf

In this file, the subnets that we can use to create networks are defined. We like to split frontend and backend networks, and then apply rules from SGs to them in order to allow or disallow traffic. The following example is of an entry in that file:

```
resource "aws_subnet" "public-frontend_az-a" {
  availability_zone = "eu-central-1a"
  cidr_block = "10.0.11.0/24"
  map_public_ip_on_launch = true
  vpc_id = "${aws_vpc.gitlabha.id}"
  tags {
      Name = "Subnet-eu-central-1a-Frontend"
  }
}
```

We can see that the availability zone is defined (which can be found at `https://docs.aws. amazon.com/AWSEC2/latest/UserGuide/using-regions-availability-zones. html#concepts-available-regions`):

```
availability_zone = "eu-central-1a"
```

The specific IP range for this subnet is defined as follows:

```
cidr_block = "10.0.11.0/24"
```

It's also possible to let Amazon create a public IP that maps onto the hosts created in this subnet. It does not mean it is reachable; that is determined by our security rules:

```
map_public_ip_on_launch = true
```

The next setting is the VPC that this subnet belongs to:

```
vpc_id = "${aws_vpc.gitlabha.id}"
```

The last setting is the tag that is given to this object, which makes it easier to search:

```
tags {
    Name = "Subnet-eu-central-1a-Frontend"
}
```

When all the subnets have been created, the frontend and backend components can communicate with each other.

instance.tf

In this file, we declare the Amazon EC2 instances. We have several instances, but we will start with the first frontend application server defined in this file:

```
resource "aws_instance" "FRONTEND_A" {
    ami = "${lookup(var.aws_ubuntu_amis,var.region)}"
    subnet_id = "${aws_subnet.public-frontend_az-a.id}"
    key_name = "${aws_key_pair.keypair.key_name}"
    vpc_security_group_ids = ["${aws_security_group.SG-
frontendservers.id}"]
    instance_type = "t2.medium"
    tags {
        Name = "${var.environment}-FRONTEND001"
        Environment = "${var.environment}"
        sshUser = "ubuntu"
    }
}
```

The declaration that this block starts with constitutes an Amazon resource of `aws_instance` type and is called `FRONTEND_A`:

```
resource "aws_instance" "FRONTEND_A" {
```

Next, the first line of the block defines the **Amazon Machine Image (AMI)** that is used as the base for this instance. In our case, we run an Ubuntu image in our region. It is defined as a variable in `variable.tf`:

```
ami = "${lookup(var.aws_ubuntu_awis,var.region)}"
```

This machine will be part of a network. The following line describes which subnet the machine is connected to:

```
subnet_id = "${aws_subnet.public-frontend_az-a.id}"
```

We need a way to connect to the machine to configure them. For this, we need an SSH connection that, in turn, needs an SSH key pair from which the public key is registered:

```
key_name = "${aws_key_pair.keypair.key_name}"
```

We need to assign a security group to the machine, in order to make sure the network ACLs are applied:

```
vpc_security_group_ids = ["${aws_security_group.SG-frontendservers.id}"]
```

Next is the type of instance: t2.medium. A list of these can be found at https://aws.
amazon.com/ec2/instance-types/:

```
instance_type = "t2.medium"
```

The next section of this block sets tags that will be associated with this machine:

```
Name = "${var.environment}-FRONTEND001"
Environment = "${var.environment}"
sshUser = "ubuntu"
```

You can see here that the name is based on the environment variables and a string.

This information is all that is needed to create a virtual machine in the Amazon EC2 cloud.
We also need a way to control it afterward with Ansible, which is done in the next section.

ansible_host.tf

We are going to use the Terraform Ansible provider to translate a Terraform state file into a
dynamic Ansible inventory. We are going to create resources of the
ansible_host type, which are taken care of by the Ansible provider. As an example, the
host that defines our frontend application server is as follows:

```
resource "ansible_host" "FRONTEND001" {
  inventory_hostname = "${aws_instance.FRONTEND_A.private_dns}"
  groups = ["frontend"]
  vars
  {
    ansible_user = "ubuntu"
    role = "master"
    ansible_ssh_private_key_file="/tmp/mykey.pem"
    ansible_python_interpreter="/usr/bin/python3"
    ansible_ssh_common_args= " -o ProxyCommand=\"ssh -o
StrictHostKeyChecking=no -i /tmp/mykey.pem -W %h:%p -q
ubuntu@${aws_instance.BASTIONHOST_A.public_dns}\""
    proxy = "${aws_instance.BASTIONHOST_A.private_ip}"
    subnet = "${aws_subnet.public-frontend_az-a.cidr_block}"
  }
}
```

Let's connect an EC2 instance to this resource, which will then feature as a host in the
Ansible inventory:

```
inventory_hostname = "${aws_instance.FRONTEND_A.private_dns}"
```

We also define an Ansible host group, which, in this case, is `frontend`:

```
groups = ["frontend"]
```

The last part of this Ansible resource is dealing with `vars`, which will become Ansible facts. The SSH user that is used for executing playbooks will be `"ubuntu"`, and a `sudo` mechanism will be used afterward:

```
ansible_user = "ubuntu"
```

During the deployment of software on the hosts, we need to know which role the hosts will play in the HA infrastructure:

```
role = "master"
```

For the SSH connection to succeed with certificate-based authentication, we need the created private key:

```
ansible_ssh_private_key_file="/tmp/mykey.pem"
```

Ansible uses Python as its interpreter, so we must specify the version:

```
ansible_python_interpreter="/usr/bin/python3"
```

We are not going to connect directly to the different EC2 hosts; we have to go through our bastion hosts. We need to instruct Ansible to connect through them:

```
ansible_ssh_common_args= " -o ProxyCommand=\"ssh -o
StrictHostKeyChecking=no -i /tmp/mykey.pem -W %h:%p -q
ubuntu@${aws_instance.BASTIONHOST_A.public_dns}\""
```

To install the software and updates, we need a proxy server, because, by default, the machines in the backend cannot connect to the internet:

```
proxy = "${aws_instance.BASTIONHOST_A.private_ip}"
```

Because we are going to configure some software on the machines, we need the subnets of the instances. They are already defined in Terraform, so we can just pass them through as Ansible facts, in order to use them in our templates and playbooks. What follows is the defined subnet in which the frontend application server resides:

```
subnet = "${aws_subnet.public-frontend_az-a.cidr_block}"
```

Here, all the different nodes that are created in `instance.tf` are coupled to an Ansible host, which will be exposed via the dynamic inventory script when called.

route_table.tf

Now that we have hosts and networks, we have to find a way to make them communicate with each other. When they live in the same subnet, that is fine, but we need to route some traffic because we have multiple networks. Here is an example of such an AWS resource, which is called a `aws_route_table` resource:

```
resource "aws_route_table" "default" {
  vpc_id = "${aws_vpc.gitlabha.id}"

  route {
      cidr_block = "0.0.0.0/0"
      gateway_id = "${aws_internet_gateway.internet_gateway.id}"
  }

  tags {
      Name = "Default route table"
  }
}
```

The first property is the VPC it belongs to:

```
vpc_id = "${aws_vpc.gitlabha.id}"
```

Then, a route is defined. In this example, it is the default route, 0.0.0.0/0:

```
cidr_block = "0.0.0.0/0"
```

The gateway in this block is the internet gateway for this VPC:

```
gateway_id = "${aws_internet_gateway.internet_gateway.id}"
```

There are several other routes defined for enabling traffic between the subnets that were created.

security_group.tf

In this file, we define the security groups that are in use for this VPC. A security group consists of `ingress` (incoming) and `eggress` (outgoing) traffic definitions:

```
resource "aws_security_group" "SG-frontendservers"
{
    name = "SG-frontendservers"
    vpc_id = "${aws_vpc.gitlabha.id}"
    description = "Security group for frontendservers"
    ingress {
```

```
                from_port = 22
                to_port = 22
                protocol = "TCP"
                security_groups = ["${aws_security_group.SG-bastionhosts.id}"]
                description = "Allow incoming SSH traffic from bastion hosts"
        }
```

The first two attributes define the name for the group, as well as the ID of the VPC to which this group belongs:

```
        name = "SG-frontendservers"
        vpc_id = "${aws_vpc.gitlabha.id}"
        description = "Security group for frontendservers"
```

The last attribute is a description of this group. Then, the first `ingress` traffic definition follows:

```
        from_port = 22
        to_port = 22
        protocol = "TCP"
```

It states the source, the destination port, and the protocol (in this case, it is `TCP`).

The last parts of the `ingress` definition mention the security group IDs and the description of this `ingress` rule:

```
        security_groups = ["${aws_security_group.SG-bastionhosts.id}"]
        description = "Allow incoming SSH traffic from bastion hosts"
```

Several other rules are defined as well, but they follow the same specification.

variable.tf

We have used a special file to declare some high-level variables – in this case, the region where the infrastructure will be run:

```
        variable "region"
        {
          default = "eu-central-1"
        }
```

If the variables are not declared, the scripts will either fail or ask for an input.

keypair.tf

During the Terraform deployment, a custom SSH key pair will be created; in this file, we define some properties for it:

```
resource "tls_private_key" "mykey"
{
    algorithm = "RSA"
    rsa_bits = 4096
}

resource "aws_key_pair" "keypair"
{
    key_name = "${var.key_name}"
    public_key = "${tls_private_key.mykey.public_key_openssh}"
}

output "mykey" {
  value = "${tls_private_key.mykey.private_key_pem}}"
  sensitive = true
}
```

The resource type we first define is an SSH private key:

```
resource "tls_private_key" "privkey"
{
  algorithm = "RSA"
  rsa_bits = 4096
}
```

We determine what kind of algorithm will be used and the key size in bits.

The next resource is the key pair as a bundle:

```
resource "aws_key_pair" "keypair"
{
  key_name = "${var.key_name}"
  public_key = "${tls_private_key.privkey.public_key_openssh}"
}
```

Here, we define the name of the key and the public key accompanying it.

The last part of the file is to make sure we can dump the contents of the private key to a file, so we can use it to connect from our Ansible host:

```
output "mykey" {
  value = "${tls_private_key.mykey.private_key_pem}}"
  sensitive = true
}
```

After being generated, the key can be extracted with the `terraform output` command.

lb.tf

This file holds the declaration of the load balancer we use in front of the GitLab application hosts, in order to distribute network traffic:

```
resource "aws_elb" "lb" {
    name_prefix = "${var.environment}-"
    subnets = ["${aws_subnet.public-frontend_az-a.id}",
"${aws_subnet.public-frontend_az-b.id}"]
    health_check {
        healthy_threshold = 2
        unhealthy_threshold = 2
        timeout = 3
        target = "TCP:80"
        interval = 30
    }
    listener {
        instance_port = 80
        instance_protocol = "http"
        lb_port = 80
        lb_protocol = "http"
    }
    cross_zone_load_balancing = true
    instances = ["${aws_instance.FRONTEND_A.id}",
"${aws_instance.FRONTEND_B.id}"]
    security_groups = ["${aws_security_group.SG-loadbalancer.id}"]
}

  resource "aws_lb_cookie_stickiness_policy" "gitlab" {
  name                     = "gitlab-policy"
  load_balancer            = "${aws_elb.lb.id}"
  lb_port                  = 80
  cookie_expiration_period = 600
}
```

The first part of the resource block contains a name prefix (such as dev-) and the subnets that this load balancer is connected to:

```
name_prefix = "${var.environment}-"
subnets = ["${aws_subnet.public-frontend_az-a.id}", "${aws_subnet.public-frontend_az-b.id}"]
```

Then, there is a definition of the health check the load balancer performs, in order to determine whether an upstream destination is still running:

```
health_check {
  healthy_threshold = 2
  unhealthy_threshold = 2
  timeout = 3
  target = "TCP:80"
  interval = 30
}
```

As mentioned before, we are changing this from the default HTTP check to a TCP check because of the redirect mechanism of GitLab's default page. After two consecutive failures to check whether TCP port 80 is open, the load balancer will set an upstream target to OutOfService and stop using it. With an interval of 30 seconds and a timeout of 3, the upstream target will take about 2 minutes to go in to service or out of service.

You also have to define a listener block, where you register which ports the load balancer should open at the front, and to which ports on the backend instances it should connect:

```
listener {
  instance_port = 80
  instance_protocol = "http"
  lb_port = 80
  lb_protocol = "http"
}
```

Finally, the last part of the lb block is used to check whether it is possible to load balance across zones, and whether there are instances defined that will be used by the load balancer:

```
cross_zone_load_balancing = true
instances = ["${aws_instance.FRONTEND_A.id}",
"${aws_instance.FRONTEND_B.id}"]
security_groups = ["${aws_security_group.SG-loadbalancer.id}"]
```

The preceding final attribute is the specific security group this load balancer is part of.

providers.tf

We keep a `providers.tf` file to define some basic variables for the AWS provider. We already defined `region` as a variable, so we are going to reuse it (`${var/region}`):

```
provider "aws" {
region = "${var.region}"
}
```

To summarize, we have a number of `.tf` files in the directory here that all describe Amazon resources. They are named after the functions that can be recognized in them. Here is the list of files containing Terraform definitions:

- `ansible.tf`: Where we define our Ansible hosts to be
- `instances.tf`: Which defines the EC2 instances (in our case, 14)
- `keys.tf`: Where we define generated SSH key properties
- `lb.tf`: Where we define our classic load balancer (such as stickiness and health checks)
- `networking.tf`: Where we define the VPC and subnets
- `providers.tf`: Where we put provider-specific information
- `routes.tf`: Where we put our routing between subnets
- `security.tf`: Where we define the security groups
- `variables.tf`: Where we define global variables

Now that we have our infrastructure definitions, it's time to test our declarations, and, after that, deploy the code.

Preparing to run Terraform to deploy the virtual hardware

Before Terraform executes the API calls to AWS that create or delete resources, it first parses your `.tf` files and generates a graph of the resources it is going to change. It then checks what is already in Amazon and compares the two. It will then ask for confirmation. It is always a good plan to do a dry run first, which can be done with the `plan` feature:

```
$ terraform plan
Refreshing Terraform state in-memory prior to plan...
The refreshed state will be used to calculate this plan, but will not be
persisted to local or remote state storage.
tls_private_key.privkey:
```

```
Refreshing state... (ID: 874768c0573f85ee35688f91b96793940376786c)
...
```

After building graphs and doing a comparison, Terraform will report how much it will change when executed for real:

```
Plan: 51 to add, 0 to change, 0 to destroy.
---
```

As you can see, we don't have anything in there yet, and we will proceed in running the provisioning.

Running the deployment

You can run the deployment with the following command:

```
terraform apply
```

You can also add the `--auto-approve` argument; then, it will not ask for confirmation.

Running the `apply` command will start and produce a lot of output, as follows:

```
tls_private_key.privkey: Refreshing state... (ID:
874768c0573f85ee35688f91b96793940376786c)
 aws_key_pair.keypair: Refreshing state... (ID: ec2key)
 aws_vpc.gitlabha: Refreshing state... (ID: vpc-0d623120e0d5401f9)
 aws_subnet.pub-web-az-b: Refreshing state... (ID:
subnet-03908026eb72659e1)
 aws_subnet.priv-db-az-a: Refreshing state... (ID:
subnet-0e65b8cb35e8ef116)
```

In the end, if all goes well, you should receive a message to say that the application is complete:

```
Apply complete! Resources: 51 added, 0 changed, 0 destroyed.
Outputs:
private_key = <sensitive>
```

It also tells you whether it has outputs, which means there is a variable saved in the Terraform state. This is actually the private key we defined in the `keys.tf` file. After deployment, we should now save this in a file somewhere so we can configure Ansible, in order to use it to set up SSH connections to AWS hosts.

You can do this as follows:

```
terraform output -json|jq .private_key.value -r >/tmp/privkey.pem && chmod
600 /tmp/privkey.pem
```

If you log in to the AWS web console, you can view your created resources. Here is a list of created EC2 instances:

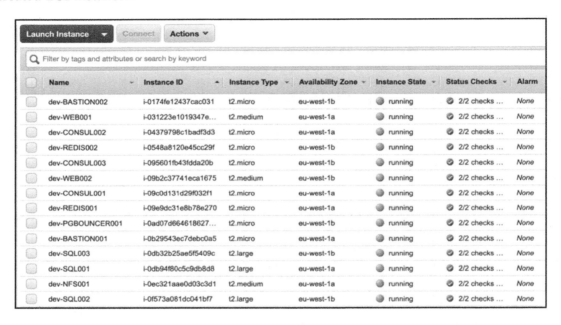

Before we start using Ansible to deploy to the machines, let's walk through the files that Ansible uses. We keep our playbooks in the main Git project directory: https://github.com/PacktPublishing/Mastering-GitLab-12/tree/master/Chapter18/ha-configuration:

```
├── files
│   └── .ansible.cfg
├── install-consul.yml
├── install-gitlab.yml
├── install-nfs.yml
├── install-pgbouncer.yml
├── install-postgres-core.yml
├── install-postgres-slaves.yml
├── install-redis.yml
├── install-bastion-hosts.yml
└── templates
    ├── databases.ini.j2
    ├── gitlab.rb.consul.j2
```

```
├──── gitlab.rb.j2
├──── gitlab.rb.pgbouncer.j2
├──── gitlab.rb.postgres.j2
├──── gitlab.rb.redis.j2
├──── nfs_exports.j2
└──── pgpass.j2
```

First, you see playbooks with the `.yml` extension. Then, there is a `files` directory, which is intended to accommodate files that must be copied without modification. We also have a `templates` directory, which holds Jinja2 (Python templating engine) templates that are copied and modified in some playbooks.

An important thing to remember is that this example uses fairly simple playbooks. Every playbook does what the name implies, and we don't use Ansible roles or error handling. This makes the code easier to understand, but it also makes it a bit less robust.

Before you run the `ansible-playbook` commands, have a look at the playbooks in order to understand what they do. Further on, we will discuss the Jinja2 templates that are used. Most of the nodes are configured with the GitLab omnibus installer, which relies heavily on a `gitlab.rb` file as a parameter file, and runs all kinds of configuration actions based on the file.

Setting up the bastion hosts

The bastion hosts are the first two machines in the VPC and are used as jumphosts to connect to other instances in your VPN. That is why they are installed first. They will be provided with a squid cache and function as a proxy for the other hosts to install packages and such:

- **Script**: `install.yml`
- **Jinja template**: None
- **Run command**: `ansible-playbook -i /usr/local/bin/terraform.py deploy/install.yml`

After installation, you can connect using the following script:

`connect_ssh.sh bastion0`

Or, if you want to connect to the second bastion host, use the following script:

`connect_ssh.sh bastion1`

The hosts will be used by the Ansible scripts as jumphosts for deployments.

Configuring the database nodes

The installation of the database nodes is done through two Ansible scripts. The master database is installed through `install-postgres-core.yml` and the slave databases through `install-postgres-slave.yml`. They both share the same Jinja template (`gitlab.rb.postgres.j2`); however, inside the template, there are some conditionals where values are replaced based on whether a host is a database master or slave:

- **Script**: `install-postgres-core.yml` and `install-postgres-slaves.yml`
- **Jinja template**: `gitlab.rb.postgres.j2`
- **Run the following commands**:
    - **For master databases**: `ansible-playbook -i /usr/local/bin/terraform.py deploy/install-postgres-core.yml`
    - **For slave databases:** `ansible-playbook -i /usr/local/bin/terraform.py deploy/install-postgres-slaves.yml`

Contents of the gitlab.rb.postgres.j2 template

The first declaration in the `gitlab.rb.postgres.j2` template is which role the instance will play in our infrastructure:

```
# Disable all components except PostgreSQL
roles ['postgres_role']
```

The next setting is to determine whether a database should be initialized as a master database, which should only be performed on the master node:

```
# Only the master database should become master
{% if hostvars[inventory_hostname].role == "slave" %}
repmgr['master_on_initialization'] = false
{% endif %}
```

The general database properties are the same for the master and the slaves. The database should listen on all interfaces and be prepared to sync their data:

```
# Database properties
postgresql['listen_address'] = '0.0.0.0'
postgresql['hot_standby'] = 'on'
postgresql['wal_level'] = 'replica'
postgresql['shared_preload_libraries'] = 'repmgr_funcs'
```

We are going to use PgBouncer to create sessions to the database. For this, it needs an account password, which is configured here:

```
# Replace pgbouncer_user_password with a generated md5 value :packtpub
# gitlab-ctl pg-password-md5 pgbouncer packtpub
postgresql['pgbouncer_user_password'] = '5da810d253b27c0a30ce8a19c4361659'
```

The default `postgres` password is configured next. We need to get the hash value of the password. You can generate it by running `gitlab-ctl pg-password` in a Docker container:

```
$ docker run -ti  gitlab/gitlab-ee:latest --name gitlab-ee
$ docker exec -ti   gitlab-ee  gitlab-ctl pg-password-md5 gitlab
Enter password:
Confirm password:
319e2283a175820cc15a0c7ed742f336
```

In the template, replace POSTGRESQL_PASSWORD_HASH with the generated md5 value (for example, you entered `packtpub`):

```
postgresql['sql_user_password'] = '319e2283a175820cc15a0c7ed742f336'
```

None of the database installations should run Rails migrations, which means no data is loaded into the database. That job is left to the backend application servers:

```
# Disable automatic database migrations
gitlab_rails['auto_migrate'] = false
```

The database saves changes to the logs before writing them into the database files. This is called **Write-Ahead Logging (WAL)**. An important part of the database's HA mechanism is that the master database sends these database logs to the slaves and lets them replay these logs against their databases. This setting determines how many WAL sender processes are allowed (to make sure there are not too many connections, which would slow things down):

```
#Set the number of wal senders to how many postgresql servers +1
postgresql['max_wal_senders'] = 4
```

By default, connections to the database are not allowed. We specify a whitelist of allowed networks and hosts for different services. The variables that begin with `hostvars` are Ansible-specific and refer to the dynamic inventory that is created by `terraform-ansible.py`.

The master and slave databases are allowed to connect for replication purposes without a password:

```
postgresql['trust_auth_cidr_addresses'] = %w({{
hostvars[groups['db'][0]]['subnet'] }} {{
hostvars[groups['db'][1]]['subnet'] }} {{
hostvars[groups['db'][2]]['subnet'] }})
```

The application servers are allowed to connect with a password:

```
postgresql['md5_auth_cidr_addresses'] = %w({{
hostvars[groups['web'][0]]['inventory_hostname'] }} {{
hostvars[groups['web'][1]]['inventory_hostname'] }})
```

The `repmgr` service is also allowed to connect without a password, in order to manage replication:

```
repmgr['trust_auth_cidr_addresses'] = %w({{
hostvars[groups['db'][0]]['subnet'] }} {{
hostvars[groups['db'][1]]['subnet'] }} {{
hostvars[groups['db'][2]]['subnet'] }})
```

The databases should all have the `consul` agent installed, which is used to signal whether the database is available:

```
# Configure the consul agent
consul['services'] = %w(postgresql)
```

The `consul` agent has to know where to connect to, in order to report about cluster health, which is done where the `consul` nodes are inserted:

```
Consul nodes
consul['configuration'] = {
retry_join: %w({{ hostvars[groups['consul'][0]]['inventory_hostname'] }}
{{ hostvars[groups['consul'][1]]['inventory_hostname'] }} {{
hostvars[groups['consul'][2]]['inventory_hostname'] }})
}
```

When the Ansible jobs for the database master and slaves have run, you should have an operations PostgreSQL database cluster with failover capabilities.

Configuring the consul nodes

The deployment of `consul` is necessary to keep track of the database service. When `consul` detects that one of the agents in the database is reporting a failure or not answering, it will let PGBouncer know and make sure the application servers will use the working database. If the master database is offline, it failover to a standby node:

- **Script**: `install-consul.yml`
- **Jinja template**: `gitlab.rb.consul.j2`
- **Run command**: `ansible-playbook -i /usr/local/bin/terraform.py deploy/install-consul.yml`

Contents of gitlab.rb.consul.j2

The first declaration in this file is which role the instance will play in our infrastructure:

```
# Disable all components except Consul
roles ['consul_role']
```

The second set of declarations disables *all* other functions for this host. GitLab omnibus will only configure services for running `consul`:

```
## Disable all other services
sidekiq['enable'] = false
gitlab_workhorse['enable'] = false
unicorn['enable'] = false
postgresql['enable'] = false
nginx['enable'] = false
prometheus['enable'] = false
alertmanager['enable'] = false
pgbouncer_exporter['enable'] = false
gitlab_monitor['enable'] = false
gitaly['enable'] = false
```

In the next section, the nodes that will be part of the `consul` cluster are defined:

```
# Consul nodes
consul['configuration'] = {
server: true,
retry_join: %w( {{ hostvars[groups['consul'][0]]['inventory_hostname'] }}
{{ hostvars[groups['consul'][1]]['inventory_hostname'] }} {{
hostvars[groups['consul'][2]]['inventory_hostname'] }})
  }
```

As with disabling the other functions, we must also prohibit omnibus from trying to run Rails database migration actions:

```
# Disable db auto migrations
 gitlab_rails['auto_migrate'] = false
```

After running the deployment script, you will have a running `consul` cluster that can communicate between nodes. The `consul` agents are installed via other roles in `gitlab.rb`.

Configuring the PgBouncer node

The PgBouncer component is used to multiplex database connections and switch between active and passive database nodes:

- **Script**: `install-pgbouncer.yml`
- **Jinja template**: `gitlab.rb.pgbouncer.j2, databases.ini.j2, pgpass.j2`
- **Run command**: `ansible-playbook -i /usr/local/bin/terraform.py deploy/install-pgbouncer.yml`

Contents of gitlab.rb.pgbouncer.j2

The first declaration in this file is which role the instance will play in our infrastructure:

```
# Disable all components except Pgbouncer and Consul agent
roles ['pgbouncer_role']
```

Again, we want omnibus to disable all other functions for this host:

```
# Disable all other services
sidekiq['enable'] = false
gitlab_workhorse['enable'] = false
unicorn['enable'] = false
postgresql['enable'] = false
nginx['enable'] = false
prometheus['enable'] = false
alertmanager['enable'] = false
gitlab_monitor['enable'] = false
gitaly['enable'] = false
```

We must set the usernames that will be used through PgBouncer:

```
# Configure Pgbouncer
pgbouncer['admin_users'] = %w(pgbouncer gitlab-consul)
```

The `consul` agent that runs on this machine must keep an eye on the PostgreSQL service:

```
# Configure Consul agent
consul['watchers'] = %w(postgresql)
```

We need to set the application password for the `gitlab-consul` and PgBouncer users:

```
# Setup application passwords
pgbouncer['users'] = {
'gitlab-consul': {
password: '46ae9788c600a7d8483796466f64033a'
},
'pgbouncer': {
password: '5da810d253b27c0a30ce8a19c4361659'
}
}
```

The `consul` agent has to know which `consul` nodes are around:

```
# Consul nodes
consul['configuration'] = {
retry_join: %w({{ hostvars[groups['consul'][0]]['inventory_hostname'] }}
{{ hostvars[groups['consul'][1]]['inventory_hostname'] }} {{
hostvars[groups['consul'][2]]['inventory_hostname'] }})
}
```

There are two more Jinja templates that are used in this Ansible script:

- `databases.ini.j2`: In this file, the connection string for the initial database connection is set:

  ```
  [databases]
  gitlabhq_production = host={{
  hostvars[groups['db'][2]]['inventory_hostname'] }}
  auth_user=pgbouncer
  ```

- `pgpass.j2`: This contains the plaintext password for PgBouncer:

  ```
  127.0.0.1:*:pgbouncer:pgbouncer:packtpub
  ```

On completion of running the `install-pgbouncer.yml` script, there should be a single PgBouncer node connected to the databases and `consul`.

The Redis configuration

One of the most important components of GitLab Redis is installed as a master/slave cluster in this setup:

- **Script**: `install-redis.yml`
- **Jinja template**: `gitlab.rb.redis.j2`
- **Run command**: `ansible-playbook -i /usr/local/bin/terraform.py deploy/install-redis.yml`

Contents of gitlab.rb.redis.j2

The first declaration in this file is which role the instance will play in our infrastructure:

```
# Enable Redis
redis['enable'] = true
```

Again, all other functions are disabled:

```
# Disable all other services
sidekiq['enable'] = false
gitlab_workhorse['enable'] = false
unicorn['enable'] = false
postgresql['enable'] = false
nginx['enable'] = false
prometheus['enable'] = false
alertmanager['enable'] = false
pgbouncer_exporter['enable'] = false
gitlab_monitor['enable'] = false
gitaly['enable'] = false
```

In this part, we also check the role of the Redis node, which is passed through by Terraform to Ansible via the dynamic inventory:

```
# Check the role of the redis server
{% if hostvars[inventory_hostname].role == "master" %}
roles ['redis_master_role']
{% else %}
roles ['redis_slave_role']
redis['master_ip'] = '{{
hostvars[groups['redis'][1]]['ansible_eth0']['ipv4']['address'] }}'
{% endif %}
```

We specify that Redis should listen on all network interfaces:

```
redis['bind'] = '0.0.0.0'
```

Then, we specify which TCP port it will listen on:

```
# Define a port so Redis can listen for TCP requests which will allow
other
# machines to connect to it.
redis['port'] = 6379
```

For this example, we use a very simple password in order for the slave Redis instance to connect:

```
# Set up password authentication for Redis (use the same password in all
nodes).
redis['password'] = 'packtpub'
```

Like some other machines, we don't want this one to run Rails database migrations, so we specify this:

```
#Don't run database migrations
gitlab_rails['auto_migrate'] = false
```

After running `install-redis.yml`, there should be two extra nodes that have a master and a slave Redis node, respectively.

Connecting the shared filesystem

The creation of a shared filesystem in this basic architecture is done without the GitLab omnibus package. We just configure a basic Linux node with NFS functionality:

- **Script**: `install-nfs.yml`
- **Jinja template**: `nfs_exports.j2`
- **Run command**: `ansible-playbook -i /usr/local/bin/terraform.py deploy/install-nfs.yml`

The NFS server is a server that is not configured through omnibus, so there is no `gitlab.rb` template file. Most of the installation is through the `install-nfs.yml` file and the only template is the NFS exports file, which is placed in `/etc` and transformed.

Contents of nfs_exports.j2

The NFS exports file is used read by the NFS server at startup to determine which folders should be shared on the network and to which addresses this export is allowed. In the case of our example we want the root folder /nfs to be shared to our GitLab application servers in the 'frontend' Ansible hostgroup. In the Jinja template a for loop is used to iterate through the hostnames of the 'frontend' hostgroup:

```
/nfs {% for host in groups['frontend'] %} {{
hostvars[host]['inventory_hostname']
}}(rw,sync,no_root_squash,no_subtree_check) {% endfor %}
```

After processing, the resulting NFS shared filesystem can only be mounted by the application servers.

Setting up the application servers

The most important pieces of this infrastructure are the application servers themselves. They are also installed with Ansible, but they have slightly bigger template files than the other components because a lot has to be configured:

- **Script**: install-gitlab.yml
- **Template**: gitlab.rb.j2
- **Run command**: ansible-playbook -i /usr/local/bin/terraform.py deploy/install-gitlab.yml

Contents of gitlab.rb.j2

The first declaration in this file is which role the instance will play in our infrastructure:

```
# Disable components that will not be on the GitLab application server
roles ['application_role']
nginx['enable'] = true
```

Along with the role, another function (nginx) is activated, which acts as an auxiliary function to the application role. NGINX is the reverse proxy in front of the Unicorn web server.

An important setting is the external URL that is going to be used to reach GitLab via HTTP. For our example, we use HTTP, but you can also use HTTPS. The URL is pulled again from the dynamic inventory:

```
# The URL GitLab is available on
external_url 'http://{{ hostvars[groups['lb'][0]]['inventory_hostname']
}}'
```

We are going to use NFS as a shared filesystem, so we need to indicate that we use a high-availability mount point. The application check in the filesystem is mounted; otherwise, it won't start its services:

```
# Indicate that nfs mountpoint is used
high_availability['mountpoint'] = '/var/opt/gitlab/git-data'
```

We specify the PgBouncer node as the database for GitLab, and the node will talk to the active master database. The hostname is pulled from the dynamic inventory again:

```
# PostgreSQL connection attributes
gitlab_rails['db_adapter'] = 'postgresql'
gitlab_rails['db_encoding'] = 'unicode'
gitlab_rails['db_password'] = 'packtpub'
gitlab_rails['db_host'] = '{{
hostvars[groups['pgbouncer'][0]]['inventory_hostname'] }}'
# IP/hostname of database server
gitlab_rails['db_port'] = 6432
```

We specify the Redis host we find in the dynamic inventory:

```
# Redis connection details
gitlab_rails['redis_port'] = '6379'
gitlab_rails['redis_host'] = '{{
hostvars[groups['redis'][1]]['inventory_hostname'] }}'
# IP/hostname of Redis server
gitlab_rails['redis_password'] = 'packtpub'
```

Because we are using a shared filesystem, it makes sense to keep the UIDs and GIDs the same:

```
# Ensure UIDs and GIDs match between servers for permissions via NFS
user['uid'] = 9000
user['gid'] = 9000
web_server['uid'] = 9001
web_server['gid'] = 9001
registry['uid'] = 9002
registry['gid'] = 9002
```

Next, we use a control flow to test whether the server is a master or a slave to make sure that only one GitLab application server executes Rails database migrations:

```
# Make sure only 1 GitLab server executes migrations
{% if hostvars[inventory_hostname].role == "slave" %}
gitlab_rails['auto_migrate'] = false
{% endif %}
```

Again, the information attribute that determines this is pulled from the dynamic inventory. In this example, we don't use HTTPS, so we disable the autogeneration of certificates:

```
#disable letsencrypt for demo purposes
letsencrypt['enable'] = false
```

Now that we have looked at all the files, let's try to run them.

Running all the Ansible playbooks

I have created a shell script that runs all steps sequentially, and when one fails, it will stop processing. It is called `deploy-with-ansible.sh`. You can run it like this in the HA configuration directory of your project:

```
../deploy-with-ansible.sh
tls_private_key.privkey: Refreshing state... (ID:
874768c0573f85ee35688f91b96793940376786c)
aws_key_pair.keypair: Refreshing state... (ID: ec2key)
aws_vpc.gitlabha: Refreshing state... (ID: vpc-0d623120e0d5401f9)
aws_subnet.pub-web-az-b: Refreshing state... (ID: subnet-03908026eb72659e1)
aws_subnet.priv-db-az-a: Refreshing state... (ID: subnet-0e65b8cb35e8ef116)
aws_security_group.bastionhostSG: Refreshing state... (ID:
sg-0c9043cd8f71becab)
aws_internet_gateway.inetgw: Refreshing state... (ID:
igw-05a45a3163391b294)
aws_subnet.priv-db-az-b: Refreshing state... (ID: subnet-023c4157ba90f1805)
```

You can also run the individual playbooks manually. But before you run any playbooks, the following environment variable will prohibit SSH connection errors:

```
export ANSIBLE_HOST_KEY_CHECKING=false
```

When you run the playbooks, please perform these steps in the following order:

1. Install the bastion hosts as follows:

   ```
   ansible-playbook -i /usr/local/bin/terraform.py deploy/install.yml
   ```

2. Install the master PostgreSQL database as follows:

   ```
   ansible-playbook -i /usr/local/bin/terraform.py deploy/install-
   postgres-core.yml
   ```

3. Install the slave PostgreSQL databases as follows:

   ```
   ansible-playbook -i /usr/local/bin/terraform.py deploy/install-
   postgres-slaves.yml
   ```

4. Install the `consul` nodes as follows:

   ```
   ansible-playbook -i /usr/local/bin/terraform.py deploy/install-
   consul.yml
   ```

5. Install the PgBouncer nodes as follows:

   ```
   ansible-playbook -i /usr/local/bin/terraform.py deploy/install-
   pgbouncer.yml
   ```

6. Install the Redis nodes as follows:

   ```
   ansible-playbook -i /usr/local/bin/terraform.py deploy/install-
   redis.yml
   ```

7. Install the NFS server as follows:

   ```
   ansible-playbook -i /usr/local/bin/terraform.py deploy/install-
   nfs.yml
   ```

8. Install the GitLab application servers as follows:

   ```
   ansible-playbook -i /usr/local/bin/terraform.py deploy/install-
   gitlab.yml
   ```

After all the operations are executed successfully, you will end up with a working GitLab cluster. You can verify whether it works by looking at the properties of your classic load balancer and looking for the DNS name, as shown in the following screenshot:

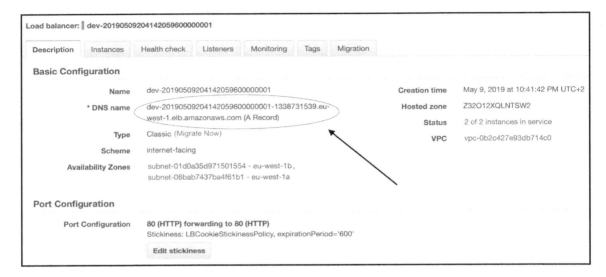

If you copy and paste this URL into your browser, a clean GitLab instance that asks for a password is installed, as shown in the following screenshot:

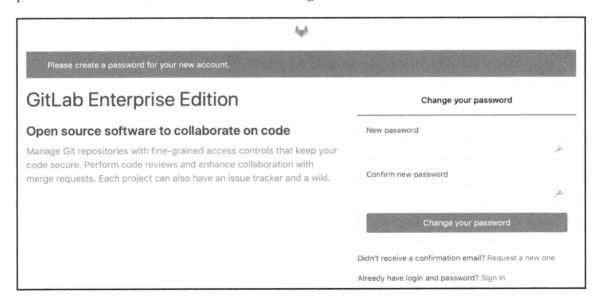

If this isn't working, then check whether the instance is set to **InService** in the **Instances** tab of your load balancer, as follows:

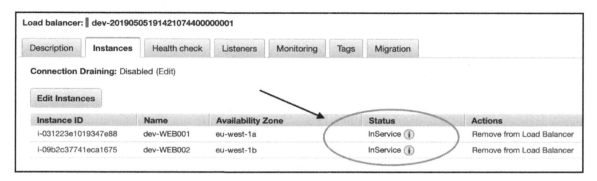

If the status entry says **Outofservice**, then you need to check whether all instances are green.

You can log in to all your services with my special `connect_ssh.sh` script. First, check whether the hosts are available:

```
$ ./connect_ssh.sh show_host_codes
hostcode: pg0 -- hostname: "ip-10-0-2-18.eu-west-1.compute.internal"
hostcode: db1 -- hostname: "ip-10-0-2-125.eu-west-1.compute.internal"
hostcode: db0 -- hostname: "ip-10-0-2-83.eu-west-1.compute.internal"
hostcode: db2 -- hostname: "ip-10-0-1-217.eu-west-1.compute.internal"
hostcode: red0 -- hostname: "ip-10-0-12-18.eu-west-1.compute.internal"
hostcode: red1 -- hostname: "ip-10-0-11-224.eu-west-1.compute.internal"
hostcode: frontend1 -- hostname: "ip-10-0-12-25.eu-
west-1.compute.internal"
hostcode: frontend0 -- hostname: "ip-10-0-11-43.eu-
west-1.compute.internal"
hostcode: nfs0 -- hostname: "ip-10-0-11-69.eu-west-1.compute.internal"
hostcode: cs1 -- hostname: "ip-10-0-2-165.eu-west-1.compute.internal"
hostcode: cs0 -- hostname: "ip-10-0-1-145.eu-west-1.compute.internal"
hostcode: cs2 -- hostname: "ip-10-0-1-99.eu-west-1.compute.internal"
hostcode: bastion0 -- hostname: "ec2-34-245-42-209.eu-
west-1.compute.amazonaws.com"
hostcode: bastion1 -- hostname: "ec2-54-229-146-28.eu-
west-1.compute.amazonaws.com"
```

You can then connect to the first database server like so:

```
$ ./connect_ssh.sh db0
```

Once connected, you can switch to root with the `sudo -i` command, check all log files, and inspect things on the virtual machines.

Hopefully, there were no errors and you have a running GitLab instance, and, if not, you are able to debug the problem.

Summary

In this chapter, we first looked at what a basic HA architecture of GitLab should look like, and we determined the minimum amount of infrastructure that should be built. We then explained how we could do this through AWS. With Terraform, Ansible, and some scripting, we showed how you can create an HA environment with 14 hosts.

In the next chapter, we will further split the nodes and functionalities to eliminate even more single points of failure. This will grow your HA capability. Secondly, you prepare your GitLab system for serving more users because you can scale your system much more easily to accommodate the higher load.

Questions

1. What does HA stand for?
2. What language is Terraform written in?
3. What does EC2 stand for?
4. How many `consul` nodes are defined in our example?
5. What templating engine is used in Ansible?
6. What script can run all deployment actions at once?
7. If all is OK in the health check, what does the load balancer say?
8. What script can you use to connect to the Amazon hosts with SSH?

Further reading

- *Mastering Ansible – Third Edition* by *James Freeman* and *Jesse Keating*: `https://www.packtpub.com/in/virtualization-and-cloud/mastering-ansible-third-edition`
- *Getting Started with Terraform – Second Edition* by *Kirill Shirinkin*: `https://www.packtpub.com/in/networking-and-servers/getting-started-terraform-second-edition`
- *AWS Certified Developer – Associate Guide – Second Edition* by *Vipul Tankariya* and *Bhavin Parmar*: `https://www.packtpub.com/in/virtualization-and-cloud/aws-certified-developer-associate-guide-second-edition`
- *Learn Linux Shell Scripting – Fundamentals of Bash 4.4* by *Sebastiaan Tammer*: `https://www.packtpub.com/in/networking-and-servers/learn-linux-shell-scripting-fundamentals-bash-44`

20
Managing a Hybrid HA Environment

In the previous chapter, we created a basic scalable GitLab architecture using Terraform and Ansible. In this chapter, we will continue with the same structure, but we will change some things and create even more resiliency. One of the weak points of the architecture we first designed was that the frontend servers had more than one GitLab component installed, which could prove to be a problem if one component breaks down. We will run the Sidekiq component on another server to mitigate this risk. Another weakness was the shared filesystem. **Network File System (NFS)** is known to have some performance and file-locking problems; GitLab has developed Gitaly as a replacement, and we will install it in this chapter. Another issue is that there was no monitoring available in the basic scalable architecture. We will install that in this chapter as well.

In this chapter, we will cover the following topics:

- The basic architecture of this solution
- A renewed Terraform configuration
- Splitting application components into frontend and middleware tiers
- Connecting the shared filesystem
- Changes in Ansible files
- Script enhancements

Technical requirements

For managing omnibus installs, there is one central configuration file called `gitlab.rb`. You need to create it or copy an example. A template is available from `https://gitlab.com/gitlab-org/omnibus-gitlab/blob/master/files/gitlab-config-template/gitlab.rb.template`. Upgrades don't replace or edit this file. In large parts of this chapter, I quote and discuss parts of this file.

To create our virtual infrastructure, we are using Terraform (≥ v0.11.12). You can download it at `https://www.terraform.io`. Terraform is a multiplatform binary.

Terraform providers use the following:

- **provider.ansible v0.0.4**: Get it from `https://github.com/nbering/terraform-inventory`.
- **provider.aws v2.1.0**: This is automatically downloaded with the `terraform init` command (see *Starting with the code* section of previous chapter).
- **provider.tls v1.2.0**: This is automatically downloaded with the `terraform init` command (see *Starting with the code* section of previous chapter).

For automating our deployments, we are using Ansible (≥ version 2.7). You can download it from `https://github.com/ansible/ansible`, or use a package manager such as `brew` or `pip` to install it.

To follow along with the instructions in this chapter, please download the Git repository with examples available on GitHub, at: `https://github.com/PacktPublishing/Mastering-GitLab-12/tree/master/Chapter20`.

The basic architecture of this solution

What will be included in the second iteration of a horizontally scaled GitLab? We have chosen to split components even more and change the shared filesystem type. We will introduce two monitoring components.

The following diagram is of the second iteration of the **High Availability (HA)** solution for GitLab:

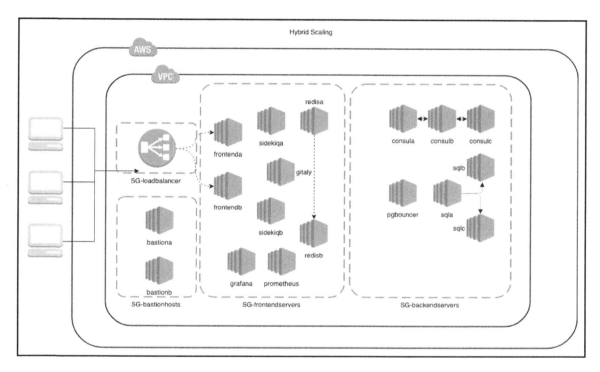

The frontend servers in the basic HA design run the Unicorn/NGINX Rails application, as well as the background jobs, via the Sidekiq component. These are all installed as part of the GitLab omnibus package. In the second iteration, you can see that the NFS server in the diagram has been replaced with a Gitaly server. Gitaly is an **Remote Procedure Call (RPC)** server that is specifically designed to handle Git traffic and has the ability to scale better than NFS servers, while using less bandwidth.

In the basic HA solution, the shared filesystem was a basic Linux NFS Version 4 server that was mounted on both frontend application servers. In the second iteration, we replaced this with a dedicated Gitaly server, which you can find in the previous diagram.

The monitoring components are a combination of a Prometheus server (to accumulate time series data) and a Grafana dashboard (to display metrics from the Prometheus database). Both components can be installed using the GitLab omnibus package.

A renewed Terraform configuration

In this new version of the solution, there are some changes in the Terraform part, mainly in the amount of instances. Let's look at the file that contains the AWS EC2 instances. With Terraform, you can create very elaborate structures, but for this example, we only add instances to make it more understandable.

instance.tf

The first machine to add is the Sidekiq node. It will be placed in the frontend servers' security group (SG-frontendservers). As you can see from the following code, the node uses an **Amazon Machine Image** (**AMI**), which is defined in the variable.tf file. The instance type is t2.medium; you can find a list of instances types at https://aws. amazon.com/ec2/instance-types/. The instance description mentions the subnet, the public key pair, and the security group to be used:

```
resource "aws_instance" "SIDEKIQ_A" {
    ami = "${lookup(var.aws_ubuntu_amis,var.region)}"
    instance_type = "t2.medium"
    tags {
        Name = "${var.environment}-SIDEKIQ001"
        Environment = "${var.environment}"
        sshUser = "ubuntu"
    }
    subnet_id = "${aws_subnet.public-frontend_az-a.id}"
    key_name = "${aws_key_pair.keypair.key_name}"
    vpc_security_group_ids = ["${aws_security_group.SG-
frontendservers.id}"]
  }
```

The key pair that is generated at install time is also inserted into this machine, and the subnet where it is created is the public frontend one.

Using only one machine would not be very sufficient for our example, so we create an identical one with the new name of SIDEKIQ_B. It is placed in another availability zone.

The following is the description of this second Sidekiq instance, which is almost similar to the first, but for the name and availability zone:

```
resource "aws_instance" "SIDEKIQ_B" {
    ami = "${lookup(var.aws_ubuntu_amis,var.region)}"
    instance_type = "t2.medium"
    tags {
        Name = "${var.environment}-SIDEKIQ002"
```

```
        Environment = "${var.environment}"
        sshUser = "ubuntu"
    }
    subnet_id = "${aws_subnet.public-frontend_az-b.id}"
    key_name = "${aws_key_pair.keypair.key_name}"
    vpc_security_group_ids = ["${aws_security_group.SG-
frontendservers.id}"]
  }
```

We create an instance for our monitoring dashboard:

```
resource "aws_instance" "GRAFANA_A" {
    ami = "${lookup(var.aws_ubuntu_amis,var.region)}"
    instance_type = "t2.medium"
    tags {
        Name = "${var.environment}-GRAFANA001"
        Environment = "${var.environment}"
        sshUser = "ubuntu"
    }
    subnet_id = "${aws_subnet.public-frontend_az-b.id}"
    key_name = "${aws_key_pair.keypair.key_name}"
    vpc_security_group_ids = ["${aws_security_group.SG-
frontendservers.id}"]
  }
```

Notice that the Grafana server is also placed in the frontend servers' subnet and security group. In this example, we are not creating redundant Grafana dashboards. This is possible, but most companies run this on one machine, which we are also doing for this example.

Like the Grafana instance, the Prometheus server is again placed in the frontend servers subnet and security group:

```
resource "aws_instance" "PROMETHEUS_A" {
    ami = "${lookup(var.aws_ubuntu_amis,var.region)}"
    instance_type = "t2.medium"
    tags {
        Name = "${var.environment}-PROMETHEUS001"
        Environment = "${var.environment}"
        sshUser = "ubuntu"
    }
    subnet_id = "${aws_subnet.public-frontend_az-b.id}"
    key_name = "${aws_key_pair.keypair.key_name}"
    vpc_security_group_ids = ["${aws_security_group.SG-
frontendservers.id}"]
  }
```

The other main configuration change is in the Ansible host definition.

ansible_host.tf

We create another Ansible host called SIDEKIQ001, which is coupled to SIDEKIQ_A in AWS. The extra attribute we give is the group, which we call middleware. This attribute is used in Ansible scripts to determine which hosts should be processed in a playbook. A custom attribute we create is role. In a clustered situation, we always designate the server to be either a slave or a master:

```
resource "ansible_host" "SIDEKIQ001" {
    inventory_hostname = "${aws_instance.SIDEKIQ_A.private_dns}"
    groups = ["middleware"]
    vars
    {
        ansible_user = "ubuntu"
        role = "slave"
        ansible_ssh_private_key_file="/tmp/mykey.pem"
        ansible_python_interpreter="/usr/bin/python3"
        ansible_ssh_common_args= " -o ProxyCommand=\"ssh -o
StrictHostKeyChecking=no -i /tmp/mykey.pem -W %h:%p -q
ubuntu@${aws_instance.BASTIONHOST_A.public_dns}\""
        proxy = "${aws_instance.BASTIONHOST_A.private_ip}"
        subnet = "${aws_subnet.public-frontend_az-a.cidr_block}"
    }
}
```

We also create a second host here, which has the role of master:

```
resource "ansible_host" "SIDEKIQ002" {
    inventory_hostname = "${aws_instance.SIDEKIQ_B.private_dns}"
    groups = ["middleware"]
    vars
    {
        ansible_user = "ubuntu"
        role = "master"
        ansible_ssh_private_key_file="/tmp/mykey.pem"
        ansible_python_interpreter="/usr/bin/python3"
        ansible_ssh_common_args= " -o ProxyCommand=\"ssh -o
StrictHostKeyChecking=no -i /tmp/mykey.pem -W %h:%p -q
ubuntu@${aws_instance.BASTIONHOST_B.public_dns}\""
        proxy = "${aws_instance.BASTIONHOST_B.private_ip}"
        subnet = "${aws_subnet.public-frontend_az-b.cidr_block}"
    }
}
```

The monitoring components are also created as Ansible hosts. For Grafana, we create an Ansible group called `monitoring-dashboard`:

```
resource "ansible_host" "GRAFANA001" {
    inventory_hostname = "${aws_instance.GRAFANA_A.private_dns}"
    groups = ["monitoring-dashboard"]
    vars
    {
        ansible_user = "ubuntu"
        ansible_ssh_private_key_file="/tmp/mykey.pem"
        ansible_python_interpreter="/usr/bin/python3"
        ansible_ssh_common_args= " -o ProxyCommand=\"ssh -o
StrictHostKeyChecking=no -i /tmp/mykey.pem -W %h:%p -q
ubuntu@${aws_instance.BASTIONHOST_A.public_dns}\""
        proxy = "${aws_instance.BASTIONHOST_A.private_ip}"
        subnet = "${aws_subnet.public-frontend_az-a.cidr_block}"
    }
}
```

For the Prometheus server, we create a group called `monitoring-server`:

```
resource "ansible_host" "PROMETHEUS001" {
    inventory_hostname = "${aws_instance.PROMETHEUS_A.private_dns}"
    groups = ["monitoring-server"]
    vars
    {
        ansible_user = "ubuntu"
        ansible_ssh_private_key_file="/tmp/mykey.pem"
        ansible_python_interpreter="/usr/bin/python3"
        ansible_ssh_common_args= " -o ProxyCommand=\"ssh -o
StrictHostKeyChecking=no -i /tmp/mykey.pem -W %h:%p -q
ubuntu@${aws_instance.BASTIONHOST_A.public_dns}\""
        proxy = "${aws_instance.BASTIONHOST_A.private_ip}"
        subnet = "${aws_subnet.public-frontend_az-a.cidr_block}"
    }
}
```

These are all the changes needed for Terraform to create the Amazon EC2 instances. You can deploy them using the following command:

```
terraform apply
```

After successful creation of the AWS instances, you should find all instances in the AWS web console:

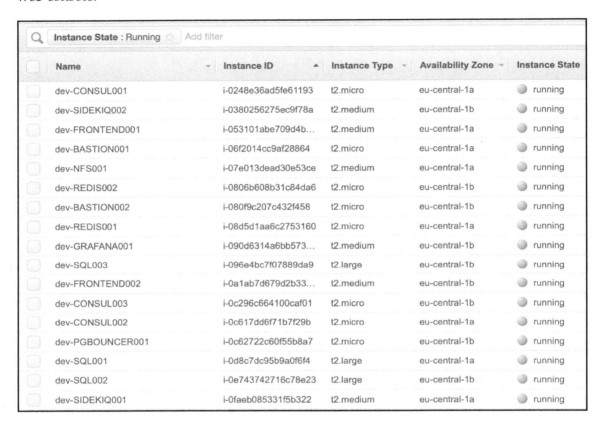

Name	Instance ID	Instance Type	Availability Zone	Instance State
dev-CONSUL001	i-0248e36ad5fe61193	t2.micro	eu-central-1a	running
dev-SIDEKIQ002	i-0380256275ec9f78a	t2.medium	eu-central-1b	running
dev-FRONTEND001	i-053101abe709d4b...	t2.medium	eu-central-1a	running
dev-BASTION001	i-06f2014cc9af28864	t2.micro	eu-central-1a	running
dev-NFS001	i-07e013dead30e53ce	t2.medium	eu-central-1a	running
dev-REDIS002	i-0806b608b31c84da6	t2.micro	eu-central-1b	running
dev-BASTION002	i-080f9c207c432f458	t2.micro	eu-central-1b	running
dev-REDIS001	i-08d5d1aa6c2753160	t2.micro	eu-central-1a	running
dev-GRAFANA001	i-090d6314a6bb573...	t2.medium	eu-central-1b	running
dev-SQL003	i-096e4bc7f07889da9	t2.large	eu-central-1b	running
dev-FRONTEND002	i-0a1ab7d679d2b33...	t2.medium	eu-central-1b	running
dev-CONSUL003	i-0c296c664100caf01	t2.micro	eu-central-1b	running
dev-CONSUL002	i-0c617dd6f71b7f29b	t2.micro	eu-central-1a	running
dev-PGBOUNCER001	i-0c62722c60f55b8a7	t2.micro	eu-central-1b	running
dev-SQL001	i-0d8c7dc95b9a0f6f4	t2.large	eu-central-1a	running
dev-SQL002	i-0e743742716c78e23	t2.large	eu-central-1b	running
dev-SIDEKIQ001	i-0faeb085331f5b322	t2.medium	eu-central-1a	running

We have shown you the new parts of the Terraform configuration, and you have applied them to your Amazon AWS configuration. Now you can execute Ansible deployment scripts.

Splitting application components into frontend and middleware tiers

The split has already been prepared on the Terraform infrastructure level by creating extra EC2 instances in the correct subnets. Now it is time to configure those virtual machines. With the creation of extra instances, we basically defined a split in functionality, which means we have a frontend tier, a backend tier, and now also a middleware tier. Now we have to run the Ansible scripts to make the application use that infrastructure. We describe the function and the name of the script. We mention the Jinja template that is used in the deployment, and the run command to use is the `ansible-playbook` command.

Splitting Sidekiq from the frontend

In the former chapter all application services were running on the frontend. In this chapter we create a new middleware layer by splitting the frontend into more layers.
Our current middleware is Sidekiq background processing, let's put that functionality on separate nodes. The deployment is contained in the following playbook and template and you can apply the playbook using the Run command:

- **Script**: `install-middleware-services.yml`
- **Jinja template**: `gitlab.rb.middleware.j2`
- **Run command**: `ansible-playbook -i /usr/local/bin/terraform.py deploy/install-middleware-services.yml`

Contents of gitlab.rb.middleware.j2

The GitLab URL or endpoint will be the address of the load balancer. The value of this address can be extracted from our dynamic Ansible inventory command, `/usr/local/bin/terraform.py`. In the Ansible scripts, we can refer to a specific host variable:

```
external_url 'http://{{ hostvars[groups['lb'][0]]['inventory_hostname'] }}'
```

Sidekiq uses GitLab Shell, which needs to authenticate to the frontend servers as follows:

```
gitlab_rails['internal_api_url'] = "http://{{
hostvars[groups['frontend'][0]]['inventory_hostname'] }}:8080"
```

This server should have the application role:

```
roles ['application_role']
```

We specifically want to enable Sidekiq on this machine:

```
# Enable sidekiq
sidekiq['enable'] = true
```

Disable components that will not be on the GitLab application server:

```
gitaly['enable'] = false
gitlab_workhorse['enable'] = false
unicorn['enable'] = false
postgresql['enable'] = false
nginx['enable'] = false
prometheus['enable'] = false
alertmanager['enable'] = false
pgbouncer_exporter['enable'] = false
gitlab_monitor['enable'] = false
```

We specify that this will use the central Gitaly server:

```
# Gitaly
 git_data_dirs({
   'default' => { 'path' => '/var/opt/gitlab/git-data','gitaly_address' =>
'tcp://{{ hostvars[groups['gitaly'][0]]['inventory_hostname'] }}:8075' }
 })
 gitlab_rails['gitaly_token'] = 'abc123secret'
 gitaly['enable'] = false
```

We also have to specify a database connection to `pgbouncer`:

```
gitlab_rails['db_adapter'] = 'postgresql'
gitlab_rails['db_encoding'] = 'unicode'
gitlab_rails['db_password'] = 'packtpub'
gitlab_rails['db_host'] =  '{{
hostvars[groups['pgbouncer'][0]]['inventory_hostname'] }}'
gitlab_rails['db_port'] = 6432
```

Sidekiq also connects to Redis, so we need the relevant connection details:

```
gitlab_rails['redis_port'] = '6379'
gitlab_rails['redis_host'] = '{{
hostvars[groups['redis'][1]]['inventory_hostname'] }}'
gitlab_rails['redis_password'] = 'packtpub'
```

We only want a master server to execute migrations:

```
{% if hostvars[inventory_hostname].role == "slave"  %}
gitlab_rails['initial_root_password'] = "packtpub"

# Make sure only 1 GitLab server executes migrations
gitlab_rails['auto_migrate'] = false

{% endif %}
```

We definitely want to disable `letsencrypt` on this server:

```
#disable letsencrypt for demo purposes
letsencrypt['enable'] = false
```

After successfully running this script, the middleware tier should exist and we should have succeeded in transferring Sidekiq from the frontend servers to the middleware servers.

Creating a monitoring instance

In the basic setup, there was no active monitoring installed. For an HA cluster, this is not something we want. In `Chapter 12`, *Monitoring with Prometheus*, we discussed the ways we can use Prometheus to monitor GitLab instances. We can install it as well using Ansible in our infrastructure. In the following Ansible playbook script, we install in the cluster:

- **Script**: `install-prometheus.yml`
- **Jinja template**: `gitlab.rb.prometheus.j2`
- **Run command**: `ansible-playbook -i /usr/local/bin/terraform.py deploy/install-prometheus.yml`

Contents of gitlab.rb.prometheus.j2

To create a Prometheus server, enable it in the omnibus configuration file:

```
prometheus_monitoring['enable'] = true
```

The server should listen on every interface, as follows:

```
prometheus['listen_address'] = '0.0.0.0:9090'
```

Disable all other services:

```
gitlab_workhorse['enable'] = false
unicorn['enable'] = false
postgresql['enable'] = false
nginx['enable'] = false
prometheus['enable'] = false
alertmanager['enable'] = false
pgbouncer_exporter['enable'] = false
gitlab_monitor['enable'] = false
```

After running this playbook, we have a Prometheus instance running in our cluster.

Creating a monitoring dashboard with Grafana

The Prometheus server provides the datastore to save metrics. There is a simple admin-interface which can produce graphs, but for decent monitoring you need a product which can create better ones. Grafana allows you to create fancy monitoring dashboards with data from Prometheus. The following Ansible playbook installs and configures this:

- **Script**: `install-grafana-dashboard.yml`
- **Jinja template**: `gitlab.rb.grafana.j2`
- **Run command**: `ansible-playbook -i /usr/local/bin/terraform.py deploy/install-grafana-dashboard.yml`

Contents of gitlab.rb.grafana.j2

The URL of our GitLab instance is as follows:

```
external_url 'http://{{ hostvars[groups['lb'][0]]['inventory_hostname'] }}'
```

Set the following to `true` to enable Grafana:

```
grafana['enable'] = true
```

The default admin password is `admin`; change it here:

```
grafana['admin_password'] = 'admin'
```

After running this playbook, the Grafana dashboard is available under the following URL, at `/grafafa`.

Connecting the shared filesystem

In the former chapter we used NFS as the location to store git repositories inside of GitLab. In this chapter we switch to Gitaly, the new application layer that eliminates the need for NFS. The Ansible playbook for installing Gitaly is new, and is basically a GitLab omnibus install that only activates the Gitaly service. The playbook, the accompanying template and the command to run it are:

- **Script**: `install-gitaly.yml`
- **Jinja template**: `gitlab.rb.gitaly.j2`
- **Run command**: `ansible-playbook -i /usr/local/bin/terraform.py deploy/install-gitaly.yml`

Contents of the gitlab.rb.gitaly.j2 file

Avoid running unnecessary services on the Gitaly server:

```
postgresql['enable'] = false
redis['enable'] = false
nginx['enable'] = false
prometheus['enable'] = false
unicorn['enable'] = false
sidekiq['enable'] = false
gitlab_workhorse['enable'] = false
```

Prevent database connections during `gitlab-ctl reconfigure` and disable migrations as follows:

```
gitlab_rails['rake_cache_clear'] = false
gitlab_rails['auto_migrate'] = false
```

Configure the `gitlab-shell` API callback URL:

```
gitlab_rails['internal_api_url'] = "http://{{
hostvars[groups['frontend'][0]]['inventory_hostname'] }}:8080"
```

Make Gitaly accept connections on all network interfaces:

```
gitaly['listen_addr'] = "0.0.0.0:8075"
gitaly['auth_token'] = 'abc123secret'
```

Define the storage locations to use:

```
gitaly['storage'] = [
    { 'name' => 'default', 'path' => '/mnt/gitlab/default/repositories' },
    { 'name' => 'storage1', 'path' => '/mnt/gitlab/storage1/repositories' },
]
```

After running this Ansible playbook, you should have a working Gitaly server that can be used to store GitLab items.

Changes in Ansible files

Of course, there have not only been changes in the Jinja templates, but playbooks have aslo been added. You can see the new list here:

```
├── files
├── install-bastion-hosts.yml
├── install-consul.yml
├── install-frontend-services.yml
├── install-gitaly.yml
├── install-grafana-dashboard.yml
├── install-middleware-services.yml
├── install-pgbouncer.yml
├── install-postgres-core.yml
├── install-postgres-slaves.yml
├── install-prometheus.yml
├── install-redis.yml
└── templates
    ├── databases.ini.j2
    ├── gitlab.rb.consul.j2
    ├── gitlab.rb.frontend.j2
    ├── gitlab.rb.gitaly.j2
    ├── gitlab.rb.grafana.j2
    ├── gitlab.rb.middleware.j2
    ├── gitlab.rb.pgbouncer.j2
    ├── gitlab.rb.postgres.j2
    ├── gitlab.rb.prometheus.j2
    ├── gitlab.rb.redis.j2
    └── pgpass.j2
```

The newly added playbooks can be executed in the following fashion:

1. Install the Gitaly server as follows:

    ```
    ansible-playbook -i /usr/local/bin/terraform.py deploy/install-
    gitaly.yml
    ```

2. Install the GitLab middleware servers as follows:

    ```
    ansible-playbook -i /usr/local/bin/terraform.py deploy/install-
    middleware-services.yml
    ```

3. Install the Prometheus monitoring server as follows:

    ```
    ansible-playbook -i /usr/local/bin/terraform.py deploy/install-
    prometheus.yml
    ```

4. Install the Grafana monitoring dashboard server as follows:

    ```
    ansible-playbook -i /usr/local/bin/terraform.py deploy/install-
    grafana-dashboard.yml
    ```

Now that we have shown you all the changes in the Terraform code and Ansible playbooks, you should have a new, more HA-capable infrastructure. These changes also impact the scripts that are part of the Git repository.

Script enhancements

The directory in the repository (https://github.com/PacktPublishing/Mastering-GitLab-12/tree/master/Chapter20) contains a script to connect to the instances that you first create with Terraform.

The connect_ssh.sh script is changed for the situation in this chapter, so you can connect to the new instances after they are created. You can execute the script with show_host_codes to check which hosts you can connect to:

```
$scripts/connect_ssh.sh show_host_codes
  hostcode: pg0 -- hostname: "ip-10-0-2-195.eu-central-1.compute.internal"
  hostcode: gitaly0 -- hostname: "ip-10-0-11-29.eu-
central-1.compute.internal"
  hostcode: middleware1 -- hostname: "ip-10-0-11-160.eu-
central-1.compute.internal"
  hostcode: middleware0 -- hostname: "ip-10-0-12-252.eu-
central-1.compute.internal"
  hostcode: frontend1 -- hostname: "ip-10-0-11-76.eu-
```

```
central-1.compute.internal"
  hostcode: frontend0 -- hostname: "ip-10-0-12-164.eu-
central-1.compute.internal"
  . . .
```

The new servers for Gitaly are visible in the previous output, and the rest of the output is truncated for better readability.

Remember, once you are connected, you can switch to root with the `sudo -i` command, check all log files, and debug the machine.

Summary

In this chapter, we created a second iteration of an HA architecture of GitLab. The frontend tier was split into frontend and backend, and a middleware tier containing Sidekiq nodes was created. The shared filesystem was changed from NFS to Gitaly, and we created nodes for a monitoring server (Prometheus) and a dashboard (Grafana) to connect to it. We changed the Terraform files, the Ansible playbooks and templates, and the shell scripts.

In the next chapter, we will go even further into splitting up nodes, and introduce a new middleware tier, which runs several background nodes that handle different kinds of traffic.

Questions

1. Why is NFS not always a good choice to use in the cloud?
2. What component is split from the frontend servers in the enhanced architecture laid out in this chapter ?
3. What file describes Ansible hosts?
4. How many Grafana dashboards are in this architecture?
5. What is the name of the Ansible group used for Sidekiq?

Further reading

- *Mastering Ansible – Third Edition* **by** *James Freeman* **and** *Jesse Keating*: https://www.packtpub.com/in/virtualization-and-cloud/mastering-ansible-third-edition

- *Getting Started with Terraform – Second Edition* **by** *Kirill Shirinkin*: https://www.packtpub.com/in/networking-and-servers/getting-started-terraform-second-edition

- *AWS Certified Developer – Associate Guide – Second Edition* **by** *Vipul Tankariya* **and** *Bhavin Parmar*: https://www.packtpub.com/in/virtualization-and-cloud/aws-certified-developer-associate-guide-second-edition

- *Learn Linux Shell Scripting – Fundamentals of Bash 4.4* **by** *Sebastiaan Tammer*: https://www.packtpub.com/in/networking-and-servers/learn-linux-shell-scripting-fundamentals-bash-44

Making Your Environment Fully Distributed

21

In Chapter 18, *Monitoring CI Metrics*, and Chapter 19, *Creating a Basic HA Architecture Using Horizontal Scaling*, we created a basic scalable GitLab architecture using Terraform and Ansible. In this chapter, we will create even more nodes and, by doing so, strengthen the **High Availability (HA)** capabilities of GitLab. One of the weak points of the architecture we first designed was that the frontend servers had more than one GitLab component installed, which could prove to be a problem if one component breaks down. We will run the Sidekiq component on another server to mitigate this risk. Another weakness was the shared filesystem.

In this chapter, we will cover the following topics:

- The basic architecture of this solution
- The changes to the Terraform configuration
- Splitting more application components
- The clustered Redis/Sentinel configuration
- Changes in Ansible files
- Script enhancements

Technical requirements

To manage omnibus installs, there is one central configuration file called `gitlab.rb`. You need to create it or copy an example. There is a template available and you can find it here: `https://gitlab.com/gitlab-org/omnibus-gitlab/blob/master/files/gitlab-config-template/gitlab.rb.template`. It is not updated after upgrades. In large parts of this chapter, I will quote and discuss parts of this file.

To create our virtual infrastructure, we are going to use Terraform (≥ v0.11.12). You can download it at `https://www.terraform.io`. Terraform is a multiplatform binary.

The following Terraform providers will be used:

- **provider.ansible v0.0.4**: Get it from `https://github.com/nbering/terraform-inventory`.
- **provider.aws v2.1.0**: This is automatically downloaded with the `terraform init` command (see `Chapter 19`, *Creating a Basic HA Architecture Using Horizontal Scaling*, particularly the *Preparing to run Terraform to deploy the virtual hardware* section).
- **provider.tls v1.2.0**: This is automatically downloaded with the `terraform init` command (see `Chapter 19`, *Creating a Basic HA Architecture Using Horizontal Scaling*, particularly the *Preparing to run Terraform to deploy the virtual hardware* section). To automate our deployments, we'll use Ansible (≥ version 2.7). You can download it from `https://github.com/ansible/ansible` or use a package manager such as `brew` or `pip` to install it.

To follow along with the instructions in this chapter, please download the Git repository with examples, which is available on GitHub: `https://github.com/PacktPublishing/Mastering-GitLab-12/tree/master/Chapter21`.

The basic architecture of this solution

We already created a more scalable combination of GitLab components in the previous chapter. But, of course, there are even more options. If you wanted go for a 100% breakdown into smaller, more cloud-native components, you would have to stop using the `omnibus-gitlab` package. If you did that, an elastic, fault-tolerant database service such as Aurora could be used from Amazon itself and other Amazon-specific services such as ElastiCache. It would mean much more management overhead, but it could be the way to go if you have the time and money to build big production sites. It would be harder to switch to another cloud vendor, though.

Because we like to use an example that can be deployed on another cloud and because the omnibus package is used throughout this book, we will use that again.

In the following diagram, you will find the third iteration of the HA solution for GitLab:

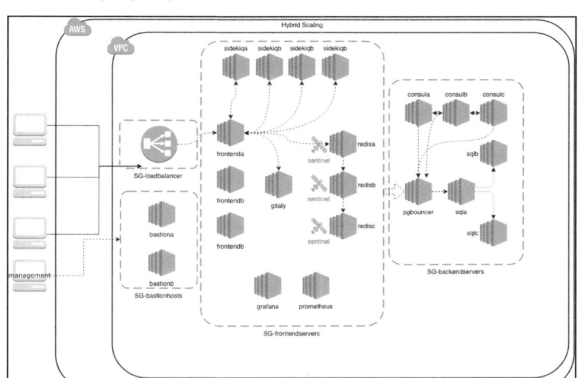

There is no change in the bastion hosts part (SG-bastionhosts) or the backend part (SG-backendservers). That is still equipped with one master database (sqla) and two read-only replicas (sqlb and sqlc). The cluster of consul agents and the nodes keep an eye on the database and notifies the pgbouncer node to switch to the active database node. This pgbouncer node also multiplexes PostgreSQL client connections. On the frontend side (SG-frontendservers), there are more changes. The Sidekiq component was installed alongside other components on the frontend servers in earlier chapters but is now split into a new layer: a middleware layer (sidekiqa-d). There are four dedicated nodes for Sidekiq and they have different functions. The first one handles near real-time background jobs such as merge requests. The second one handles jobs that cannot wait too long (such as commits and deployments). The third node is responsible for the queues handling CI pipeline jobs, and the last node handles the other background jobs from the Ruby on Rails GitLab web application.

The two Redis nodes that existed in a master-slave configuration in the earlier chapters have now increased to three (another slave has been added). The Sentinel HA component of Redis is also installed. It can detect failures in your Redis cluster and can handle automatic failover. It runs next to Redis on the same node.

The shared storage in use is still Gitaly in this architecture but can be swapped for NFS as well. Unfortunately, there are no simple solutions to make the shared storage HA-capable. There are several options, but they are not created out of the box and require tuning.

Some examples include the following:

- **Amazon Elastic Filesystem (EFS)**—it sounds OK, but has been tried by several people and is not performing well enough to handle the load in GitLab (`https://docs.gitlab.com/ee/administration/high_availability/nfs.html#avoid-using-awss-elastic-file-system-efs`).
- An NFS cluster with replication software (such as **Distributed Replicated Block Device (DRBD)**) and heartbeat software is quite complex to set up.
- Gitaly in an HA configuration—this is not ready yet (`https://docs.gitlab.com/ee/administration/high_availability/gitaly.html`).

The monitoring components are still present in this architecture and can provide valuable information about your components.

Performing changes to the Terraform configuration

Adding more nodes to the infrastructure, as proposed in the basic architecture of this solution, means we have to change some Terraform files. The first one we will change is the one where the EC2 instances are defined.

instance.tf

The functional composition of the frontend servers is going to change a lot in this version of the infrastructure. The first instance will serve regular web UI traffic, the second will serve only API traffic, and a third instance will be created to handle Git-SSH traffic:

```
resource "aws_instance" "FRONTEND_C" {
    ami = "${lookup(var.aws_ubuntu_amis,var.region)}"
    subnet_id = "${aws_subnet.public-frontend_az-b.id}"
    key_name = "${aws_key_pair.keypair.key_name}"
```

```
        vpc_security_group_ids = ["${aws_security_group.SG-
    frontendservers.id}"]
        instance_type = "t2.medium"
        tags {
            Name = "${var.environment}-FRONTEND003"
            Environment = "${var.environment}"
            sshUser = "ubuntu"
        }
    }
```

On the middleware side of things, the amount of Sidekiq nodes is growing. The third node, which is going to be responsible for CI pipeline jobs, has to be instantiated:

```
resource "aws_instance" "SIDEKIQ_C" {
        ami = "${lookup(var.aws_ubuntu_amis,var.region)}"
        instance_type = "t2.micro"
        tags {
            Name = "${var.environment}-SIDEKIQ003"
            Environment = "${var.environment}"
            sshUser = "ubuntu"
        }
        subnet_id = "${aws_subnet.public-frontend_az-b.id}"
        key_name = "${aws_key_pair.keypair.key_name}"
        vpc_security_group_ids = ["${aws_security_group.SG-
    frontendservers.id}"]
    }
```

A fourth Sidekiq node is created to handle real-time jobs that cannot wait:

```
resource "aws_instance" "SIDEKIQ_D" {
        ami = "${lookup(var.aws_ubuntu_amis,var.region)}"
        instance_type = "t2.micro"
        tags {
            Name = "${var.environment}-SIDEKIQ004"
            Environment = "${var.environment}"
            sshUser = "ubuntu"
        }
        subnet_id = "${aws_subnet.public-frontend_az-b.id}"
        key_name = "${aws_key_pair.keypair.key_name}"
        vpc_security_group_ids = ["${aws_security_group.SG-
    frontendservers.id}"]
    }
```

We will need a third Redis node, as the new situation will require a Redis cluster with one master and two slave nodes, which will be watched by a sentinel cluster:

```
resource "aws_instance" "REDISC" {
    subnet_id = "${aws_subnet.public-frontend_az-b.id}"
    key_name = "${aws_key_pair.keypair.key_name}"
    vpc_security_group_ids = ["${aws_security_group.SG-
frontendservers.id}"]
    ami = "${lookup(var.aws_ubuntu_amis,var.region)}"
    instance_type = "t2.micro"
    tags {
        Name = "${var.environment}-REDIS003"
        Environment = "${var.environment}"
        sshUser = "ubuntu"
    }
}
```

Now that we have created our AWS instance, we will also define our Ansible host definitions, which use AWS instances.

ansible_host.tf

The first new Sidekiq host is the pipeline background job handler, which will get the `ci_pipeline` role in the Ansible definition:

```
resource "ansible_host" "SIDEKIQ003" {
    inventory_hostname = "${aws_instance.SIDEKIQ_C.private_dns}"
    groups = ["middleware_pipeline"]
    vars
    {
        ansible_user = "ubuntu"
        role = "ci_pipeline"
        ansible_ssh_private_key_file="/tmp/mykey.pem"
        ansible_python_interpreter="/usr/bin/python3"
        ansible_ssh_common_args= " -o ProxyCommand=\"ssh -o
StrictHostKeyChecking=no -i /tmp/mykey.pem -W %h:%p -q
ubuntu@${aws_instance.BASTIONHOST_B.public_dns}\""
        proxy = "${aws_instance.BASTIONHOST_B.private_ip}"
        subnet = "${aws_subnet.public-frontend_az-b.cidr_block}"
    }
}
```

The second new Sidekiq host is the real-time background job handler, which will get the `realtime` role in the Ansible definition:

```
resource "ansible_host" "SIDEKIQ004" {
    inventory_hostname = "${aws_instance.SIDEKIQ_D.private_dns}"
    groups = ["middleware_realtime"]
    vars
    {
        ansible_user = "ubuntu"
        role = "realtime"
        ansible_ssh_private_key_file="/tmp/mykey.pem"
        ansible_python_interpreter="/usr/bin/python3"
        ansible_ssh_common_args= " -o ProxyCommand=\"ssh -o
StrictHostKeyChecking=no -i /tmp/mykey.pem -W %h:%p -q
ubuntu@${aws_instance.BASTIONHOST_B.public_dns}\""
        proxy = "${aws_instance.BASTIONHOST_B.private_ip}"
        subnet = "${aws_subnet.public-frontend_az-b.cidr_block}"
    }
}
```

As you can see in the following, we also define the added Redis server with the `slave` role:

```
resource "ansible_host" "REDIS003" {
    inventory_hostname = "${aws_instance.REDIS_C.private_dns}"
    groups = ["redis"]
    vars
    {
        ansible_user = "ubuntu"
        role = "slave"
        ansible_ssh_common_args= " -o ProxyCommand=\"ssh -o
StrictHostKeyChecking=no -i /tmp/mykey.pem -W %h:%p -q
ubuntu@${aws_instance.BASTIONHOST_B.public_dns}\""
        ansible_ssh_private_key_file="/tmp/mykey.pem"
        ansible_python_interpreter="/usr/bin/python3"
        proxy = "${aws_instance.BASTIONHOST_B.private_ip}"
    }
}
```

These are all of the changes needed for Terraform to create the Amazon EC2 instances. You can deploy them using this:

terraform apply

After successful creation, you should find all instances in the AWS web console:

There are now three extra nodes in the infrastructure. In the next section, we will execute the Ansible deployment scripts to configure them.

Splitting more application components

The first node we will configure is the frontend server, which is added especially to handle Git-SSH traffic. First, we mention the Ansible script name. The second item is the Jinja template that is used to configure the `omnibus-gitlab` package on that host. The last item is the command to execute the Ansible script.

The third application server for Git SSH

The Ansible playbook that is used to configure the node consists of different parts. It consists of the following:

- **Script**: `frontend-services-ssh.yml`
- **Template**: `gitlab.rb.frontend_ssh.j2`
- **Run command**: `ansible-playbook -i /usr/local/bin/terraform.py deploy/frontend-services.yml`

This part of the deployment is the installation of the Git SSH frontend application servers.

Contents of gitlab.rb.frontend_ssh.j2

We will have to define an internal URL, which is used to authenticate users:

```
gitlab_rails['internal_api_url'] = "http://{{
hostvars[groups['frontend'][0]]['inventory_hostname'] }}:8080"
```

We disable all other services on this node:

```
# Disable components that will not be on the GitLab application server
roles ['application_role']
nginx['enable'] = false
sidekiq['enable'] = false
unicorn['enable'] = false
```

The repositories should be reachable for Git SSH:

```
# Gitaly
gitlab_rails['gitaly_token'] = 'abc123secret'
git_data_dirs({
  'default' => { 'path' => '/var/opt/gitlab/git-data','gitaly_address' =>
'tcp://{{ hostvars[groups['gitaly'][0]]['inventory_hostname'] }}:8075' }
})
gitlab_rails['gitaly_token'] = 'abc123secret'
gitaly['enable'] = false
```

Let's keep the user IDs the same everywhere:

```
# Ensure UIDs and GIDs match between servers for permissions via shared
filesystem
 user['uid'] = 9000
 user['gid'] = 9000
 web_server['uid'] = 9001
 web_server['gid'] = 9001
 registry['uid'] = 9002
 registry['gid'] = 9002
```

Also, here, don't run migrations, because only one node should do this:

```
gitlab_rails['auto_migrate'] = false
```

We don't want this node to generate SSL certificates:

```
#disable letsencrypt for demo purposes
letsencrypt['enable'] = false
```

The middleware layer – Sidekiq

As explained in the *The basic architecture of this solution* section of this chapter, we created four separate Sidekiq nodes. They were created using Terraform. Now, we have to configure them with four different Ansible scripts.

The ASAP Sidekiq instance

The Ansible playbook that is used to configure the node consists of different parts. It consists of the following:

- **Script**: `install-sidekiq-asap.yml`
- **Template**: `gitlab.rb.sidekiq_asap.j2`
- **Run command**: `ansible-playbook -i /usr/local/bin/terraform.py deploy/install-sidekiq-asap.yml`

This part of the deployment is the installation of the Sidekiq node for background jobs that need to run as soon as possible.

Contents of gitlab.rb.sidekiq_asap.j2

We set up specific queues for this `sidekiq-cluster`, the realtime instance:

```
sidekiq_cluster['enable'] = false
 sidekiq_cluster['ha'] = true
 sidekiq_cluster['max_concurrency'] = 15 # The maximum number of threads
each Sidekiq process should run
 sidekiq_cluster['queue_groups'] = [
    "update_merge_requests,auto_merge",
    "process_commit",
    "deployment"
  ]
```

Disable other services that start by default on an `omnibus-gitlab` installation:

```
## Disable all other services
 gitlab_workhorse['enable'] = false
 unicorn['enable'] = false
 postgresql['enable'] = false
 nginx['enable'] = false
 prometheus['enable'] = false
 alertmanager['enable'] = false
 pgbouncer_exporter['enable'] = false
 gitlab_monitor['enable'] = false
 sidekiq['enable'] = false
 gitaly['enable'] = false
```

This Sidekiq instance now only handles background jobs for commits and deployments.

The real-time Sidekiq instance

The Ansible playbook that is used to configure the node consists of different parts. It consists of the following:

- **Script**: `install-sidekiq-realtime.yml`
- **Template**: `gitlab.rb.sidekiq_realtime.j2`
- **Run command**: `ansible-playbook -i /usr/local/bin/terraform.py deploy/install-sidekiq-realtime.yml`

This part of the deployment is the installation of the Sidekiq node that handles real-time communications.

Contents of gitlab.sidekiq.realtime.j2

The first settings enable the cluster and define HA settings:

```
sidekiq_cluster['enable'] = false
 sidekiq_cluster['ha'] = true
 sidekiq_cluster['max_concurrency'] = 20 # The maximum number of threads
each Sidekiq process should run
```

We set up specific queues for this `sidekiq-cluster`, the realtime instance:

```
sidekiq_cluster['queue_groups'] = [
    "merge",
    "pipeline_processing"
  ]
```

Disable other services:

```
## Disable all other services
 gitlab_workhorse['enable'] = false
 unicorn['enable'] = false
 postgresql['enable'] = false
 nginx['enable'] = false
 prometheus['enable'] = false
 alertmanager['enable'] = false
 pgbouncer_exporter['enable'] = false
 gitlab_monitor['enable'] = false
 sidekiq['enable'] = false
 gitaly['enable'] = false
```

This Sidekiq instance only handles background jobs that need to happen in real time; otherwise, users have a hanging web interface. The queues that are processed contain jobs that perform merges and pipeline processing tasks.

The pipeline Sidekiq instance

The Ansible playbook that is used to configure the node consists of different parts. It consists of the following:

- **Script**: `install-sidekiq-pipeline.yml`
- **Template**: `gitlab.rb.sidekiq_pipeline.j2`
- **Run command**: `ansible-playbook -i /usr/local/bin/terraform.py deploy/install-sidekiq-pipeline.yml`

This part of the deployment is the installation of the Sidekiq node that handles jobs in CI pipelines.

Contents of gitlab.sidekiq.pipeline.j2

The first settings enable the cluster and define HA settings:

```
sidekiq_cluster['enable'] = false
sidekiq_cluster['ha'] = true
sidekiq_cluster['max_concurrency'] = 10 #
```

Again, we set up specific queues for this `sidekiq-cluster`, the pipeline instance:

```
sidekiq_cluster['queue_groups'] = [
"pipeline_processing",
"pipeline_creation",
"pipeline_default,pipeline_cache,pipeline_hooks,pipeline_background"
]
```

This Sidekiq node is dedicated to run tasks that have to do with the CI pipeline functionality in GitLab. The reason to create a specific one is that it guarantees that a very busy build pipeline does not slow your whole GitLab application down.

The normal Sidekiq instance

You probably expect the fourth Sidekiq node to also have a special function. It doesn't. It's just the same Sidekiq node as in the previous architecture, and it runs all other jobs.

The clustered Redis/Sentinel configuration

The Ansible playbook that is used to configure the node consists of different parts. It consists of the following:

- **Script**: `install-redis-cluster.yml`
- **Template**: `gitlab.rb.redis-cluster.j2`
- **Run command**: `ansible-playbook -i /usr/local/bin/terraform.py deploy/install-redis-cluster.yml`

This part of the deployment is the installation of the extra Redis slave and Sentinel node.

Contents of gitlab.rb.redis-cluster.j2

We have to enable Redis:

```
## Enable Redis
redis['enable'] = true
```

Disable all other services because `omnibus-gitlab` defaults to starting them all:

```
sidekiq['enable'] = false
gitlab_workhorse['enable'] = false
unicorn['enable'] = false
postgresql['enable'] = false
nginx['enable'] = false
prometheus['enable'] = false
alertmanager['enable'] = false
pgbouncer_exporter['enable'] = false
gitlab_monitor['enable'] = false
gitaly['enable'] = false
```

Check the role of the Redis server:

```
{% if hostvars[inventory_hostname].role == "master"    %}
roles ['redis_sentinel_role', 'redis_master_role']
{% else %}
roles ['redis_sentinel_role', 'redis_slave_role']
redis['master_ip'] = '{{
hostvars[groups['redis'][1]]['ansible_eth0']['ipv4']['address'] }}'
{% endif %}
```

Make sure Redis listens on all interfaces:

```
redis['bind'] = '0.0.0.0'
```

Make sure sentinel listens on all interfaces:

```
# General sentinel settings
sentinel['bind'] = '0.0.0.0'
sentinel['quorum'] = 2
```

Define a port so Redis can listen for TCP requests, which will allow other machines to connect to it:

```
redis['port'] = 6379
```

Set up password authentication for Redis (use the same password in all nodes):

```
redis['password'] = 'packtpub'
```

Don't run database migrations:

```
gitlab_rails['auto_migrate'] = false
```

The four-node Sidekiq configuration should be running and makes sure every background job receives the right priority.

Changes in Ansible files

Of course, there have not only been changes in the Jinja; templates playbooks has also been added. You can see the added files in a list here:

```
.
├── install-frontend-services-ssh.yml
├── install-sidekiq-asap.yml
├── install-sidekiq-pipeline.yml
├── install-sidekiq-realtime.yml
├── install-redis-cluster.yml
└── templates
    ├── gitlab.rb.frontend_ssh.j2
    ├── gitlab.rb.redis-cluster.j2
    ├── gitlab.rb.sidekiq_asap.j2
    ├── gitlab.rb.sidekiq_pipeline.j2
    ├── gitlab.rb.sidekiq_realtime.1.j2
```

The newly added or changed playbooks can be executed in the following fashion.

Installing the frontend services (web) server can be done as follows:

```
ansible-playbook -i /usr/local/bin/terraform.py deploy/install-frontend-
services.yml
```

Installing the frontend services (SSH) server can be done as follows:

```
ansible-playbook -i /usr/local/bin/terraform.py deploy/install-frontend-
services-ssh.yml
```

Installing the GitLab sidekiq-asap servers can be done as follows:

```
ansible-playbook -i /usr/local/bin/terraform.py deploy/install-sidekiq-
asap.yml
```

Installing the GitLab `sidekiq-pipeline` servers can be done as follows:

```
ansible-playbook -i /usr/local/bin/terraform.py deploy/install-sidekiq-
pipeline.yml
```

Installing the GitLab `sidekiq-realtime` servers is done as follows:

```
ansible-playbook -i /usr/local/bin/terraform.py deploy/install-sidekiq-
realtime.yml
```

Installing the Redis cluster can be done as follows:

```
ansible-playbook -i /usr/local/bin/terraform.py deploy/install-redis-
cluster.yml
```

The templates and scripts could also have been designed by creating Ansible roles and by introducing a more modular approach, but handling changes in Ansible scripts makes the example easier to read, especially in combination with the Terraform files.

Script enhancements

The `connect_ssh.sh` script is changed as well (following added hosts can be seen as an example), so you can connect to the new instances after they are created:

```
$scripts/connect_ssh.sh show_host_codes
 hostcode: middleware1 -- hostname: "ip-10-0-11-160.eu-
central-1.compute.internal"
 hostcode: middleware2 -- hostname: "ip-10-0-11-160.eu-
central-1.compute.internal"
 hostcode: middleware3 -- hostname: "ip-10-0-12-252.eu-
central-1.compute.internal"
```

The new server for the Git SSH connections is as follows:

```
hostcode: frontend2 -- hostname: "ip-10-0-12-164.eu-
central-1.compute.internal"
```

The Redis cluster is as follows:

```
    hostcode: red0 -- hostname: "ip-10-0-12-240.eu-central-1.compute.internal"
    hostcode: red1 -- hostname: "ip-10-0-11-54.eu-central-1.compute.internal"
    hostcode: red2 -- hostname: "ip-10-0-11-54.eu-central-1.compute.internal"
```

The new servers for the frontend (Git SSH), and middleware (extra Sidekiq nodes), and Redis are listed in the preceding code.

Summary

In this chapter, we created a third iteration of an HA architecture of GitLab. The frontend tier was increased with one server and, in the middleware tier, extra Sidekiq nodes were created. Also, we created an extra Redis node. We changed the Terraform files, the Ansible playbooks and templates, and the shell scripts. In the next chapter, we are going to test Geo, for replication across data centers.

Questions

1. What three frontend services were split in this chapter?
2. How many Sidekiq nodes are created?
3. How many Redis nodes are created?
4. What is watching Redis and signals downtime?
5. How can you reach Grafana after installing this infrastructure?

Further reading

- *Mastering Ansible – Third Edition* by *James Freeman* and *Jesse Keating*: https://www.packtpub.com/in/virtualization-and-cloud/mastering-ansible-third-edition
- *Getting Started with Terraform – Second Edition* by *Kirill Shirinkin*: https://www.packtpub.com/in/networking-and-servers/getting-started-terraform-second-edition
- *AWS Certified Developer – Associate Guide – Second Edition* by *Vipul Tankariya* and *Bhavin Parmar*: https://www.packtpub.com/in/virtualization-and-cloud/aws-certified-developer-associate-guide-second-edition
- *Learn Linux Shell Scripting – Fundamentals of Bash 4.4* by *Sebastiaan Tammer*: https://www.packtpub.com/in/networking-and-servers/learn-linux-shell-scripting-fundamentals-bash-44
- *Advanced Solutions in Go - Testing and Distributed Systems [Video]* by *Aaron Torres*: https://www.packtpub.com/in/application-development/advanced-solutions-go-testing-and-distributed-systems-video

22
Using Geo to Create Distributed Read-Only Copies of GitLab

In the previous chapters, we created a basic scalable GitLab architecture using Terraform and Ansible. In this chapter, we will continue with this technique, but we scale down the number of nodes that we'll use so that we don't over complicate matters. To create globally synchronized read-only copies of GitLab instances, we will need to create Geo-enabled GitLab instances that can replicate data. The Geo feature is part of the GitLab enterprise license, so you'll need this license or a trial version to activate it.

You could try and sync copies of databases and files yourself with standard tools such as rsync, but Geo is much more fine-grained than they are. It offers synchronization that's based on events and doesn't continually scan for change delta's such as rsync. Another of Geo's features is that it can do HA failover from your primary GitLab instance to a secondary one. We will demonstrate how to set up a two-node Geo installation in this chapter.

In this chapter, we will cover the following topics:

- The basic architecture of this solution
- Preparing the infrastructure
- Setting up Geo

Technical requirements

To successfully run the code sample you need a trail license from GitLab which you can generate here: `https://about.gitlab.com/free-trial/`. The license that you receive via email should be saved in the local copy of the code example repository in `Chapter22/geo-setup/deploy/files` directory in `Gitlab.gitlab-license` file.

To manage omnibus installations, you need to use a central configuration file called `gitlab.rb`. You'll need to create it yourself or copy an example of one. A template of this configuration file is available at `https://gitlab.com/gitlab-org/omnibus-gitlab/blob/master/files/gitlab-config-template/gitlab.rb.template`. Please note that it isn't updated after upgrades. In some sections of this chapter, I will quote and discuss parts of this file.

In order to create our virtual infrastructure, we are going to use Terraform (v0.11.12 or later). You can download it from `https://www.terraform.io`. Terraform is a multiplatform binary. This means it can run on Linux, macOS, and Windows. This makes it easy to install.

Terraform providers need the following:

- **provider.ansible v0.0.4**: You can get it from `https://github.com/nbering/terraform-inventory`
- **provider.aws v2.1.0**: Automatically downloaded with the `terraform init` command (see Starting with the code of `Chapter 19`, *Creating a Basic HA Architecture Using Horizontal Scaling*)
- **provider.tls v1.2.0**: Automatically downloaded with the `terraform init` command(see Starting with the code of `Chapter 19`, *Creating a Basic HA Architecture Using Horizontal Scaling*)

To automate our deployments, we will use Ansible (version 2.7 or later). You can download it from `https://github.com/ansible/ansible`, or use a package manager such as brew or pip to install it.

To follow along with the instructions in this chapter, please download this book's GitHub repository, along with its examples, which are available at `https://github.com/PacktPublishing/Mastering-GitLab-12/tree/master/Chapter22`.

The basic architecture of this solution

The following diagram shows the architecture for this solution. The main feature of this setup is that you have a master GitLab installation on site *A (called gitlab-eu)* and have it completely replicated to site *B(called gitlab-us)*. This way, you can create read-only mirrors of a GitLab instance all over the world. Remote users can then fetch files and projects from that server and push them to the primary GitLab instance. To create instances in different AWS regions, we will need to create two Virtual Private Clouds(VPC) and copy the infrastructure. We need to make sure that the sites can reach each other:

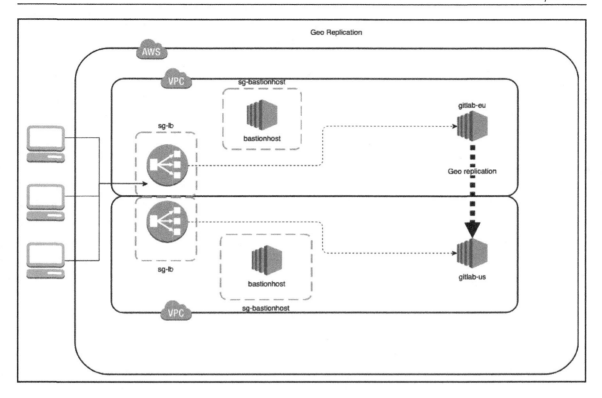

What this boils down to is that we have to set up database replication and application replication, which is exactly what Geo does. It takes care of the management side of things. For this example, we chose site *A* to be Amazon's Europe-Central-1 region and site *B* to be the US-West-1 region.

Preparing the infrastructure

If we want to automate the installation of the GitLab Geo-enabled instances, we have to change our Terraform setup a bit. Because we want to use two different regions, we are going to use Terraform modules. In the previous chapters, we only used the context of the root module, but now we are going to expand on the module concept.

The Terraform AWS provider always operates in a certain region's context, and we can use these modules to create a GitLab instance template that will be installed as service modules for site *A* and site *B*.

The example project has the following file structure:

```
.
├── connect.sh
├── deploy
│   ├── configure_replication.yml
│   ├── files
│   │   └── Gitlab.gitlab-license
│   ├── install_bastionhost.yml
│   ├── install_gitlab.yml
│   └── templates
│   ├── gitlab.rb.j2
│   ├── gitlab.rb.primary.j2
│   └── gitlab.rb.secondary.j2
├── main.tf
├── modules
│   └── services
│   ├── gitlab
│   │   ├── main.tf
│   │   ├── outputs.tf
│   │   └── vars.tf
│   └── keypair
│   ├── main.tf
│   ├── outputs.tf
│   └── vars.tf
├── readme.md
└── vars.tf
```

In the main directory, we have the following files:

- `connect.sh`: A script so that we can SSH to the machines that are created
- `main.tf`: The top-level Terraform declarations
- `readme.md`: Provides an explanation about the files
- `vars.tf`: Provides a definition of some of the variables that are used in other files

Now, let's go through the files in this directory.

The root module explained – main.tf

At the top of the file, you will see the different sites that are defined, all of which call the GitLab module in the `modules/services/` directory.

The first site is the main site that's located in the EU. The GitLab module takes several arguments that allow us to specify different settings for each site:

```
module "gitlab_eu" {
  source = "modules/services/gitlab/"
  region = "eu-central-1"
  instance_type = "t2.medium"
  vpc_cidr_block = "10.0.0.0/16"
  subnet_frontend_cidr_block = "10.0.1.0/24"
}
```

The secondary Geo site is going to be in the US, on the West Coast. We also chose a different internal subnet to make it different from the EU one:

```
module "gitlab_us" {
  source = "modules/services/gitlab/"
  region = "us-west-2"
  instance_type = "t2.medium"
  vpc_cidr_block = "172.16.0.0/16"
  subnet_frontend_cidr_block = "172.16.1.0/24"
}
```

The following entries in this file are the `ansible_host` definitions. We need them to be on this level because Ansible is going to execute transactions in all the regions. Because the declarations are on the top level, we can reference output variables in child modules. Another approach would be to run Ansible scripts separately for each location, but that would lead to a lot of duplication:

```
resource "ansible_host" "GITLABHOST001" {
  inventory_hostname = "${module.gitlab_eu.gitlabhost_fqdn}"
  groups = ["gitlab"]
  vars
  {
    role = "primary"
    geo_primary_address = "${module.gitlab_eu.lb_address}"
    geo_secondary_address = "${module.gitlab_us.lb_address}"
    ansible_user = "${var.sshuser}"
    ansible_ssh_private_key_file = "${var.ssh_private_key_primary}"
    ansible_python_interpreter = "${var.python_interpreter}"
    ansible_ssh_common_args = " -o ProxyCommand=\"ssh -o
StrictHostKeyChecking=no -i /tmp/mykey1.pem -W %h:%p -q
```

```
ubuntu@${module.gitlab_eu.bastionhost_fqdn}\""
  proxy = "${module.gitlab_eu.bastionhost_private_ip}"
  subnet = "10.0.1.0/24"
 }
}
```

The `ansible_host` declaration in the preceding code isn't very different from what was shown in the previous chapters, but there are some differences. The first obvious one is that we define `geo_primary_address` and `geo_secondary_address`. These are the external addresses of the load balancers. We need these variables because Ansible will insert the values in the configuration files that are installed on each site. Another general difference is that you will see that more variables have been defined. This is happening because we have more sites now, and so some values have to be more generic.

Utilizing the keypair module – modules/services/keypair/main.tf

This module is responsible for creating a public/private keypair that is used to connect to the instances with SSH. It was available in the previous chapters, but it was in the root module. Now, it is a standalone module that's called from the GitLab module with certain arguments:

```
provider "aws" {
  region = "${var.region}"
}

resource "tls_private_key" "mykey"
{
    algorithm = "RSA"
    rsa_bits = 4096
}
resource "aws_key_pair" "keypair"
{
    public_key = "${tls_private_key.mykey.public_key_openssh}"
}
```

At the top of the preceding code, you can see the region that's been defined. This is an argument on the top level that's passed through to the child module.

Variables for the keypair module – modules/services/keypair/vars.tf

The `vars.tf` file determines which variables are expected to be defined for this module:

```
variable region{}
```

As you can see, it should be called with the region argument.

Outputs from the keypair module – modules/services/keypair/output.tf

The only function of this module is to create keys, so the output variable that's defined is the value of this key:

```
output "mykey" {
    value = "${aws_key_pair.keypair.key_name}"
    sensitive = true
}
```

Usually, a generated key is sensitive information, and you can suppress the output of the value to the Terminal with `sensitive=true`. It's `false` by default.

Explaining the GitLab module

This module can be used as a template for GitLab installations. Compared to the structure of the `.tf` files in previous chapters, there are more variables being defined and less have been hardcoded. This is because using modules forces you to refactor quite a bit.

The main module file – modules/services/gitlab/main.tf

This is the main file of the GitLab module. It's quite big, but we kept it this way to focus on the overall architecture. With Terraform, we could refactor this into a well-formed module structure, but we'll keep it simple for this demonstration.

At the top of the file, we define the region so that we can use this variable in other modules:

```
provider "aws" {
  region = "${var.region}"
}
```

The next module that we call is the keypair module, which will provider SSH key pairs to the instances. As you can see, the only arguments are the location of the module file and the region:

```
module "keypair" {
    source = "../keypair"
    region = "${var.region}"
}
```

Then, we define the actual EC2 instances. We use the output variable from the keypair module by referring to `module.keypair.key_name`. So, in order to call variables that exist in the child modules, you need to prepend `module`:

```
resource "aws_instance" "gitlab_host" {
    ami = "${lookup(var.aws_ubuntu_amis,var.region)}"
    subnet_id = "${aws_subnet.subnet_public_frontend.id}"
    key_name = "${module.keypair.key_name}"
    vpc_security_group_ids = ["${aws_security_group.sg_gitlab.id}"]
    instance_type = "${var.instance_type}"
}
```

We also need to create a bastion host, which we will use to execute Ansible commands:

```
resource "aws_instance" "bastion_host" {
    ami = "${lookup(var.aws_ubuntu_amis,var.region)}"
    subnet_id = "${aws_subnet.subnet_public_frontend.id}"
    key_name = "${module.keypair.key_name}"
    vpc_security_group_ids = ["${aws_security_group.sg_bastionhost.id}"]
    instance_type = "t2.micro"
}
```

Then, there is the very important load balancer node, which is the frontend component facing the internet:

```
resource "aws_elb" "lb" {
    subnets = ["${aws_subnet.subnet_public_frontend.id}"]
    health_check {
        healthy_threshold = 2
        unhealthy_threshold = 2
        timeout = 3
        target = "TCP:80"
        interval = 30
    }
    listener {
        instance_port = 80
        instance_protocol = "http"
        lb_port = 80
        lb_protocol = "http"
```

```
    }
    listener {
    instance_port = 5432
    instance_protocol = "tcp"
    lb_port = 5432
    lb_protocol = "tcp"
    }
```

As you can see, an additional port has been defined for PostgreSQL (5432), which is closed by default. We will add the firewall rule to allow traffic between the sites later. The rest of the objects that are defined in this file are the same as in the previous chapters.

The variable file – modules/services/gitlab/vars.tf

In this file, a lot of the variables are defined for the GitLab module. All of them can be overridden, but have a default value set. The first variable is expected as an argument and it defines the region. This makes this module usable in multiple AWS regions:

```
variable "region" {
  description = "Which Amazon region this instance will run"
  }
```

Another input for this module is the type of Amazon instance we are using:

```
variable "instance_type" {
  description = "Which type of Amazon EC2 instance to use"
  }
```

For each region, we define the base image to be used:

```
variable "aws_ubuntu_amis"
  {
  description = "List of default AMI images per region"
  default = {
  "eu-central-1" = "ami-0f041b9708f60ca57"
  "us-west-2" = "ami-0ddba1929e996e2dc"
  }
```

We then define the management IPs (mgmt_ips) of hosts that can connect to the bastion hosts:

```
  }
  variable "mgmt_ips" {
  default = ["0.0.0.0/0"]
  }
```

The private range to be used in the VPC is also taken as input:

```
variable "vpc_cidr_block" {
description = "Which network range to use"
}
```

Just like the range, we need to use the frontend private network:

```
variable "subnet_frontend_cidr_block" {
description = "Which network range to use"
}
```

All of the variables in this file are used, and the ones without a default value should be given as input.

The outputs for the module – modules/services/gitlab/outputs.tf

The GitLab module itself also has outputs that are defined. These are used in the `ansible_host` declarations in the top-level `main.tf` file.

The load balancer Fully Qualified Domain Name (FQDN)is as follows:

```
output "lb_address"{
value ="${aws_elb.lb.dns_name}"
}
```

The bastion FQDN is as follows:

```
output "bastionhost_fqdn" {
value= "${aws_instance.bastion_host.public_dns}"
}
```

The private IP of the bastion host is as follows:

```
output "bastionhost_private_ip" {
value= "${aws_instance.bastion_host.private_ip}"
}
```

The private IP of the GitLab instance is as follows:

```
output "gitlab" {
value= "${aws_instance.bastion_host.private_ip}"
}
```

The FQDN of the GitLab instance is as follows:

```
output "gitlabhost_fqdn" {
  value = "${aws_instance.gitlab_host.public_dns}"
  }
```

The three files (`main.tf`, `vars.tf`, and `outputs.tf`), when put together, form the GitLab module that's called for each site.

Setting up Geo

GitLab Geo is a feature of GitLab that is part of the premium Enterprise version and higher. It is used to create a replica of a whole GitLab instance in another geographical location. Items such as user accounts, issues, events, and other objects are synced—not only items from the database, but also files from the filesystem.

There are several steps involved in installing Geo for your environment:

1. Install the GitLab software and license on both nodes, but don't activate them.
2. Prepare the database replicas.
3. Change the SSH key lookup method to the database.
4. Add the secondary node via the web UI.

The first two steps in our example project can be executed by the Ansible scripts that are part of the repository for this book. Steps 3 and step 4 have to be done manually. Let's deep dive into these steps.

Installing the GitLab software and license

The Ansible playbook that is used to configure the node consists of different parts. It consists of the following:

- **Script**: `install_gitlab_primary.yml`
- **Template**: `gitlab.rb.j2`
- **Run command**: `ansible-playbook -i /usr/local/bin/terraform.py deploy/install_gitlab_primary.yml`

This Ansible script will configure and start the database replication between the primary and secondary Geo nodes.

Contents of gitlab.rb.j2

The only entry in the `gitlab.rb` file is `geo_primary_role`. Assigning this role will install every component on the server:

```
roles ['geo_primary_role']
```

We do this in order to install the license automatically as well. It should be placed in the `files` directory of this repository before running the Ansible script. It will copy the file to `/etc/gitlab`.

The following part of the Ansible script is responsible for doing this:

```
- name: Install license file to enable geo functionality
copy:
src: "Gitlab.gitlab-license"
dest: /etc/gitlab
mode: 0755
```

It will only work on the initial installation of GitLab. Afterward, changes to the license have to be done via the web UI. Also, if you don't have this license file in place, the installation will fail. Comment out or remove the task if you want to install the license later or via the web UI.

When GitLab is installed, we can run the scripts so that we can start replicating the databases.

Preparing the database replicas

The Ansible playbook that is used to configure the node consists of different parts. It consists of the following:

- **Script**: `configure_replication.yml`
- **Template**: `gitlab.rb.primary.j2`, `gitlab.rb.secondary.j2`
- **Run command**: `ansible-playbook -i /usr/local/bin/terraform.py deploy/configure_replication.yml`

This Ansible script will configure and start the database replication between the primary and secondary Geo nodes.

Contents of gitlab.rb.primary.j2

We have to define the main URL for the GitLab instance:

```
external_url 'http://{{
hostvars[groups['gitlab'][0]]['geo_primary_address'] }}'
```

For this demonstration, we will disable SSL:

```
letsencrypt['enable'] = false
```

The role remains the same:

```
roles ['geo_primary_role']
```

In the Ansible script, we are going to generate a database password that we will use on our secondary node as well:

```
postgresql['sql_user_password'] = "{{ generated_db_pass }}"
```

We will explicitly make the PostgreSQL database listen on the eth0 interface:

```
postgresql['listen_address'] = "{{
hostvars[groups['gitlab'][0]]['ansible_eth0']['ipv4']['address'] }}"
```

Here, we will define the IP addresses that will be allowed to connect to the database. We have put the primary and secondary hostnames in here by using variables from the Ansible inventory:

```
postgresql['md5_auth_cidr_addresses'] = %w({{
hostvars[groups['gitlab'][0]]['geo_primary_address'] }} {{
hostvars[groups['gitlab'][0]]['geo_secondary_address'] }})
```

The following setting determines that there is only one other node that is being replicated. If we are going to add more Geo nodes, we have to increase this number:

```
postgresql['max_replication_slots'] = 1
```

In the Ansible script, we create a special replication user that is used to synchronize the databases:

```
postgresql['sql_replication_user'] = "gitlab_replication"
```

For the first installation of this synchronization, we don't want migrations to run, nor change the database structures:

```
gitlab_rails['auto_migrate'] = false
```

After running the first part of the Ansible script, you should see a PostgreSQL database ready for synchronization and a TLS (Transport Layer Security) certificate ready for distribution in the project directory (it is copied by the script).

Contents of gitlab.rb.primary.j2

The secondary database node is also configured in this script. The gitlab.rb file is a bit different, but we can see the role that's defined at the top:

```
roles ['geo_secondary_role']
```

Here's listen_address for PostgreSQL that's defined:

```
postgresql['listen_address'] = ""{{
hostvars[groups['gitlab'][1]]['ansible_eth0']['ipv4']['address'] }}""
```

We can also see the two addresses of the database servers in the array of allowed hosts:

```
postgresql['md5_auth_cidr_addresses'] = ["{{
hostvars[groups['gitlab'][1]]['ansible_eth0']['ipv4']['address'] }}"]
```

The database password hash that was generated on the primary node is inserted here, as well as the clear text password:

```
postgresql['sql_user_password'] = "{{ generated_db_pass }}"
gitlab_rails['db_password'] = 'packtpub'
```

The Geo tracking database is also installed on the secondary node. This can help speed up synchronization:

```
geo_secondary['db_fdw'] = true
```

After running this Ansible script, the databases should be syncing. The next step is to prepare GitLab itself.

Changing the SSH key lookup method to the database

The Ansible script that's used to install GitLab already copies the host keys and settings in order to enable fast SSH key lookup. The only thing that's left to do to enable this feature (which is necessary for Geo) is to disable writes to the `authorized_keys` file by using GitLab. The following screenshot shows how to adjust performance optimization:

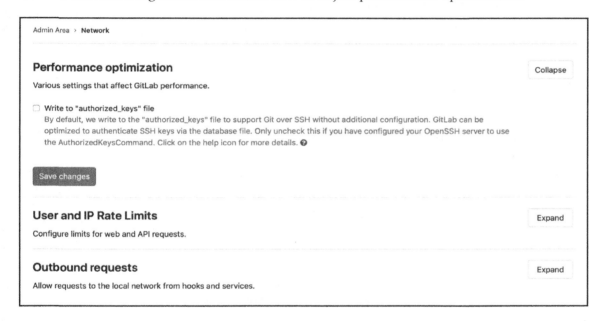

This is done by unchecking the **Write to "authorized_keys" file** option in **Admin Area** | **Settings** | **Network** | **Performance optimization** in the web UI.

Adding the secondary node via the web UI

Visit the admin page for Geo by going to **Admin Area** | **Geo (/admin/geo/nodes)**. Then, you have to do the following:

1. Add the secondary Geo by specifying the HTTP(s) URL.
2. Make sure that **This is a primary node** isn't checked.
3. If you want, you can pick which groups should be copied by the secondary node.

4. Don't fill in anything to replicate.
5. Click the **Add** button.
6. On your secondary server, restart the service:

```
gitlab-ctl restart
```

7. You can run a check to see whether everything is in order:

```
gitlab-rake gitlab:geo:check
```

8. Go to the primary server and execute the check:

```
gitlab-rake gitlab:geo:check
```

If everything is OK, the initial synchronization will start in the background.

Activating hashed storage

Since GitLab 12.0, hashed storage has become mandatory for using Geo. It was introduced in GitLab 10.0 and is much faster then the legacy storage option. The biggest use case for using hashed storage is that it eliminates the synchronization of URL and disk location(foldername). Before hashed storage, when a project was moved to another group, it was effectively relocated to another top-level folder. If, for any reason, a backup has to be restored, you had to hope that the name wasn't already taken. With hashed storage, every project uses a unique ID.

For Geo, this means that a move to another top-level folder will not trigger mass synchronizations. It only has to change a reference. This makes using hashed storage with Geo a lot faster as well.

You can enable this by going to the **Repository** page in the **Admin Area** | **Settings** | **Repository** settings and checking the **Use hashed storage paths for newly created and renamed projects** checkbox:

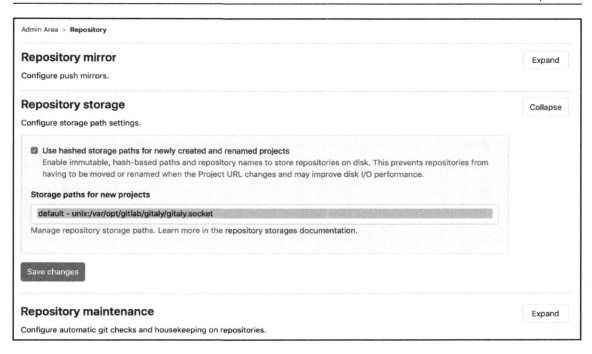

Now, let's create a new project and check the file structure of the disk of one of the nodes in the `/var/opt/gitlab/git-data/repositories` path:

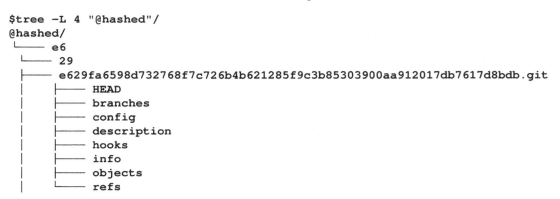

You should see that there are no project names anymore, just hash values.

Checking the status of the secondary node

At this point, the secondary Geo should be set up. We can check the status of the node by browsing to **Admin Area | Geo**. You should see an enabled Geo secondary node and some information about the state of the synchronization. When the first synchronization starts, the initial sync called 'backfill' runs:

If you encounter errors in this dashboard, then note that they are mainly caused by the database replication not working properly or because something is blocking communication between the nodes. Firewalls could be blocking traffic, or network links may be down. It is also possible that your custom SSL certificates aren't properly installed or are not valid.

Currently, this is what is synced:

- Git repositories
- Wikis
- **Large File storage (LFS)**objects
- Issues, merge requests, snippets, and comment attachments
- Users, groups, and project avatars

In this section, we have covered setting up Geo with some Ansible scripts that did a lot of the manual work in the Terminal. We finished by setting up some options in the web UI.

Summary

In this chapter, we created a final HA architecture of GitLab. If you want to globally sync GitLab to different locations, you can use the Geo feature, which is part of the Enterprise Edition of GitLab. You can set up two VPCs in Amazon and create two separate hosts that will synchronize.

Questions

1. How many load balancers are there in this chapter's scenario?
2. Which Terraform feature is used in this chapter?
3. Where can you upload a license to install on the command line?
4. What is necessary to run Geo and make it work?
5. How is the initial synchronization called?

Further reading

- *Mastering Ansible – Third Edition* by *James Freeman* and *Jesse Keating*: https://www.packtpub.com/in/virtualization-and-cloud/mastering-ansible-third-edition
- *Getting Started with Terraform – Second Edition* by *Kirill Shirinkin*: https://www.packtpub.com/in/networking-and-servers/getting-started-terraform-second-edition
- *AWS Certified Developer – Associate Guide – Second Edition* by *Vipul Tankariya* and *Bhavin Parmar*: https://www.packtpub.com/in/virtualization-and-cloud/aws-certified-developer-associate-guide-second-edition
- *Learn Linux Shell Scripting – Fundamentals of Bash 4.4* by *Sebastiaan Tammer*: https://www.packtpub.com/in/networking-and-servers/learn-linux-shell-scripting-fundamentals-bash-44

Assessments

Chapter 1: Introducing the GitLab Architecture

1. It was developed by Dimitri Zaporozhets with the help of Valery Sizov in 2011.
2. The company is funded by venture capital.
3. It is mainly developed in Ruby, with some components in Golang, and JavaScript is used in the frontend.
4. GitLab Community Edition carries the open source MIT License; GitLab Enterprise edition uses a proprietary one.
5. Open source is one of GitLab's core values. The core product (GitLab CE) is exactly that, and the Enterprise Edition is based on the CE core, but has extra functionality, the development of which is paid for by the proprietary license.
6. Unicorn, Sidekiq, NGINX, Gitaly, database, Redis and GitLab Workhorse.
7. One.
8. Key-value pairs, which have five different datatypes.
9. A shared NFS filesystem.
10. GCP.

Chapter 2: Installing GitLab

1. Using the Omnibus-GitLab installer
2. TCP port `22`, `80` and `443`
3. Ubuntu, Debian, CentOS/Red Hat, openSuse and Raspbian
4. `gitlab-ctl`
5. 2.9.5
6. The `pg_trgm` extension

7. gitlab/gitlab-ce
8. /srv
9. Python
10. Using Helm charts

Chapter 3: Configuring GitLab Using the Web UI

1. The tool icon
2. Users, projects, and groups
3. 1 MB
4. InfluxDB and Prometheus
5. CodeSandbox
6. PlantUML
7. Circuit breaker
8. Git housekeeping
9. AutoDevOps
10. Zero

Chapter 4: Configuring GitLab from the Terminal

1. Postgresql, repmgr, and consul services
2. /home/git/gitlab/config
3. IMAP
4. Large File Storage
5. Mattermost
6. An Enterprise license
7. Rack Attack
8. kubectl

Chapter 5: Importing Your Project from GitHub to GitLab

1. Merge request
2. GitHub importer, GitHub token, Gitlab-rake import
3. A GitLab account that uses OAuth-based login in using the GitHub icon, or a GitLab account with an email address that is the same as the public email address of the GitHub account
4. OAuth
5. Personal token
6. Repository
7. `github_importer` and `github_importer_advance_stage`
8. Via new project dialog
9. `import:github`
10. Yes

Chapter 6: Migrating From CVS

1. CVS is centralized, Git is decentralized
2. pserver
3. False, CVS uses filesets.
4. It records a unique SHA for an object.
5. Correct the type and `--amend` the last commit.
6. No
7. `cvs init <location>`
8. `git init`
9. Eric S. Raymond
10. `git remote add gitlab url-to-gitlab-repo && git push gitlab master`

Chapter 7: Switching from SVN

1. `https://subversion.apache.org/`
2. SVN follows a centralized architecture, while Git uses a distributed network.
3. `svnserver` server plain, svn server through SSH and Apache module `dav_svn`
4. On the SVN server
5. Revisions
6. Two-way merge
7. >= 1.8.2
8. As a local directory, a network share, or via object-storage.
9. One pass migration and mirroring
10. Pushing the new Git repository to GitLab

Chapter 8: Moving Repositories from TFS

1. Collaboration and communication
2. TFVC uses a centralized architecture.
3. ALM (Application Lifecycle Management)
4. Just change the remote and push it to a GitLab project.
5. They are path scoped.
6. On the server
7. Git-svn
8. Chocolatey

Chapter 9: GitLab Vision: The Whole Toolchain in One Application

1. Software Development Life Cycle
2. 17
3. 1970
4. The Chrysler Comprehensive Compensation System (C3) project
5. Must have, Should have, Could have, Would have (the o's mean nothing)

6. Gent, 2009
7. The development side of a project using Agile methodologies
8. Puppet and Chef

Chapter 10: Create Your Product, Verify, and Package it

1. Manage
2. An issue
3. To evolve an idea
4. `/estimate 4d`
5. Using protected branches
6. `Privileged=true`
7. Add the URL to the environment
8. Enable container registry in GitLab

Chapter 11: The Release and Configure Phase

1. `.gitlab-ci.yml`
2. A deploy utility
3. To run the whole DevOps cycle from one tool: GitLab
4. In the GitLab registry
5. Clair
6. Auto-deploy
7. Two
8. `sitespeed.io`

Chapter 12: Monitoring with Prometheus

1. Borgmon
2. Exporters
3. `/~/metrics`

4. Ruby
5. `Set prometheus['enable'] = true in gitlab.rb`
6. Static Application Security Testing
7. Dynamic Application Security Testing
8. `.gitlab-ci.yml`

Chapter 13: Integrating GitLab with CI/CD Tools

1. Project management
2. Atlassian
3. Transition-id
4. Hudson
5. Plugins
6. Controlling your support environment from a chat channel
7. With a slash command
8. In **Settings | Integrations** of your project

Chapter 14: Setting Up Your Project for GitLab Continuous Integration

1. **Continuous Integration (CI)**
2. `.gitlab-ci.yml`
3. Via a notification by the source code management system.
4. Unit tests
5. Script tag
6. `config.toml`
7. No limit; you can specify this in the runner configuration file
8. Enable the built-in Prometheus exporter

Chapter 15: Installing and Configuring GitLab Runners

1. GitLab CI
2. Pinning the package
3. Golang
4. Hostname
5. Nine
6. `--registration-token`

Chapter 16: Using GitLab Runners with Docker or Kubernetes

1. It is more secure and provides a clean build environment
2. `docker build -t container:v1`
3. A Dockerfile
4. Alpine Linux
5. Gitlab Runner Helm chart
6. Change the values in the Helm chart

Chapter 17: Autoscaling GitLab CI Runners

1. Docker Machine
2. Registry proxy and a caching server
3. `cache.zip`
4. S3
5. `.gitlab-ci.yml`
6. Registry

Chapter 18: Monitoring CI Metrics

1. Scraping
2. A Prometheus exporter
3. `- targets:`
4. `9090`
5. Running with a higher limit
6. `rate`

Chapter 19: Creating a Basic HA Architecture by Using Horizontal Scaling

1. High availability
2. Go
3. Elastic Computing Cloud
4. Three
5. Jinja
6. `deploy-with-ansible.sh`
7. **InService**
8. `connect_ssh.sh`

Chapter 20: Managing a Hybrid HA Environment

1. Sometimes, there are issues with locking and it scales badly.
2. Sidekiq
3. `ansible.tf`
4. One
5. Middleware

Chapter 21: Making Your Environment Fully Distributed

1. Web, API, and Git SSH
2. Four
3. Three
4. Sentinel
5. `/-/grafana`

Chapter 22: Using Geo to Create Distributed Read-Only Copies of GitLab

1. Two
2. Modules
3. `/etc/gitlab`
4. Hashed storage
5. By using a backfill

Other Books You May Enjoy

If you enjoyed this book, you may be interested in these other books by Packt:

Hands-On Infrastructure Monitoring with Prometheus
Pedro Araújo, Joel Bastos

ISBN: 978-1-78961-234-9

- Grasp monitoring fundamentals and implement them using Prometheus
- Discover how to extract metrics from common infrastructure services
- Find out how to take full advantage of PromQL
- Design a highly available, resilient, and scalable Prometheus stack
- Explore the power of Kubernetes Prometheus Operator
- Understand concepts such as federation and cross-shard aggregation
- Unlock seamless global views and long-term retention in cloud-native apps with Thanos

DevOps with Kubernetes - Second Edition
Hideto Saito, Hui-Chuan Chloe Lee, Cheng-Yang Wu

ISBN: 978-1-78953-399-6

- Learn fundamental and advanced DevOps skills and tools
- Get a comprehensive understanding of containers
- Dockerize an application
- Administrate and manage Kubernetes cluster
- Extend the cluster functionality with custom resources
- Understand Kubernetes network and service mesh
- Implement Kubernetes logging and monitoring
- Manage Kubernetes services in Amazon Web Services, Google Cloud Platform, and Microsoft Azure

Leave a review - let other readers know what you think

Please share your thoughts on this book with others by leaving a review on the site that you bought it from. If you purchased the book from Amazon, please leave us an honest review on this book's Amazon page. This is vital so that other potential readers can see and use your unbiased opinion to make purchasing decisions, we can understand what our customers think about our products, and our authors can see your feedback on the title that they have worked with Packt to create. It will only take a few minutes of your time, but is valuable to other potential customers, our authors, and Packt. Thank you!

Index

Made in the USA
Coppell, TX
03 November 2021

65139471R00334